Remember, A.S.K.
your way to riches
in all areas of
your life.
Best Wishes.

How to Build Riches

by
BRUCE S. DAVIS

The Macquarie Dictionary defines:

Build: *to form or construct a plan*

Riches: *abundant and valuable possessions; wealth*

This book is designed to assist you to construct your own personal plan to build abundant wealth in your life beginning right now.

First published in 1998 by
Signature Books Pty Ltd
P.O. Box 620
Newtown NSW 2042
Australia

Reprinted in 1999
Reprinted in 2000
Reprinted in 2001

Copyright 1998, Bruce S. Davis of Signature Books Pty Ltd
ACN 058 292 792
Printed in Australia by Griffin Press Pty Limited (ACN 051 748 139)
National Library of Australia
Cataloguing-in-Publication data:

Davis, Bruce S., 1958-
How to Build Riches

ISBN 1876 501 01 4

1. Finance/personal–Australia. 2. Investments–Australia. I. Title

All rights reserved. No part of this publication may be reproduced, stored in a retrieval system or transmitted in any form or by any means, electronic, mechanical, photocopying, recording or otherwise, without prior written permission of the copyright holders.

Author's Note

I have every desire to make this book as relevant as possible for my readers. So, if you have any financial matters that you would like included in future editions, please write to me, Bruce Davis at *Building Riches*, P.O. Box 620, Newtown, NSW 2042, Australia

Dedication

In loving memory of my father, grandmother and grandfather who passed away during the last two years. I miss you and will carry with me always, your love and wisdom.

To my mother and my two living grandparents, I love you dearly and appreciate your patience and guidance that has brought me to where I am.

Dedicated also to all those people whose love and actions will build a richer Australia for the future.

Disclaimer:
The purpose of this book is to educate, and this book is designed to provide knowledge, in regard to the subject matter covered. Every care has been taken to ensure the accuracy of the material contained herein at the time of publication. However, the laws relating to taxation, social security and the investment and handling of money are constantly changing. No responsibility or liability can be accepted by the author, the distributor, or the printer, for any action taken by any persons, organisations or entities, with respect to any perceived loss or damage caused directly, or indirectly, by the information contained in this book. It is recommended that you seek independent financial advice before proceeding with any action.

About the Author

A self-made millionaire, Bruce Davis is an entrepreneur and proud Australian. He is the founder of numerous companies, several trusts, and two charities. His companies produce millions of dollars of annual profit that remains in Australia, and he employs many Australians.

Bruce contributes part of the profits from all of his business initiatives to charity. He will be using part of the proceeds from the sale of this book to assist underprivileged Australian youth to build riches themselves.

Bruce is happily married with a teenage son. As well as being an author, philanthropist, Black Belt Karate instructor and husband, he is a successful businessman and consultant.

Bruce is personally involved in inspiring people from all starting places, to maximise their potential for excellence and riches, and also to build a stronger Australia.

Acknowledgements

To my gorgeous wife, Tanya, and our son, Scott, your love and support enrich my life and inspire me to greater accomplishments daily. Thank you for your love, and patience during the enormity of the research and effort that has gone into this book.

Many people were instrumental in the team effort that produced this book. Without the tireless dedication of my wife, Tanya and our business associates, this book would not have been as elaborate and as refined as it is. Thank you. Also, my mother Margaret, provided her expertise and assistance. It is as a result of the work ethic that she and her mother Sally have blessed me with, that I have become as rich as I have in all areas of my life.

To the many hard working people who have been actively involved in this book, I salute you. They include: Penny Woolcott, and Josephine Calman. It is a pleasure to work with committed professionals who all strive for excellence.

I wish to also thank Garry Allen, Mary Mathieson and the professional team at Gary Allen Pty Ltd whose efforts have made the distribution of this book such a success.

Several other people provided exceptional skill and commitment to this project including Simon Whitfield and Paul Woodbury.

Many, many others have provided assistance and guidance to me over the decades. Special thanks to one particular mentor and friend who requests anonymity, who has enriched my life in many ways. Thank you all for providing me with the skills and wisdom needed to fulfil my mission of inspiring others to realise their excellence and riches.

Contents

INTRODUCTION   **1**

- Key principles   5
- Building riches only requires three steps   7
- ASK your way to riches   10

SECTION 1   **WHY BUILD RICHES?**   **17**

Chapter 1   <u>What Makes Building Riches Important?</u>   19
- Longevity   24
- The Baby Boomer Crisis   29
- The Information Age   41

SECTION 2   **WHAT KNOWLEDGE DO YOU NEED TO BUILD RICHES?**   **47**

Chapter 2   <u>How Do You Assess Your Current Financial Position and Start Building Riches?</u>   51
- Where does your money currently go?   52
- Superannuation   52
- Income tax   53

Chapter 3   <u>What Is a Personal Spending Plan?</u>   57
- How do you create a spending plan?   58

Chapter 4   <u>What Are Your Current Financial Riches?</u>   61
- How do you use consumer loans wisely?   66
- How do security loans effect you?   68

Chapter 5   <u>How Can You Pay Off Your Home Loan in Half the Time?</u>   71
- Principle & Interest Home Loan   72

	• Line of Credit Home Loan	74
	• Paying off a mortgage faster	78
Chapter 6	How Do Loans and Taxes Affect Your Business?	81
	• What New CGT Relief is Now Available to Business Owners?	81
Chapter 7	How Do You Compare Investments That Can Make You Rich?	87
	• The awesome power of compound interest	88
	• The Rule of 72	90
	• Investing using borrowed money	95
Chapter 8	What Is the Real Return on Cash and Fixed Interest Investments?	97
	• The safest investment	97
	• What effect do taxes and inflation have on fixed interest investments?	99
Chapter 9	What Affect Will the Economic Cycle Have on Your Investments?	103
	• The economic cycle	104
	• What happens in a boom?	105
	• What happens in the gloom?	106
Chapter 10	How Do You Build Income by Investing in the Sharemarket?	109
	• What is dividend imputation?	111
	• What costs are associated with investing in the sharemarket?	114
Chapter 11	How Do You Make Decisions about Investing in the Sharemarket?	117
	• What are the financial ratios to assist you to invest in shares?	119
	• What are the differences between traders and investors?	123
	• How will compulsory superannuation change the sharemarket for decades?	124

CONTENTS

Chapter 12	How Do You Build Capital Riches by Investing in the Sharemarket?	127
	• $1,000 invested from 1978–1998	130
	• What effect will reinvesting your dividends have on your investment?	132
Chapter 13	How Does Borrowing Money to Buy Shares Accelerate Your Capital Profit (or Loss)?	135
	• What are margin loans?	135
	• What are protected equity loans?	139
Chapter 14	Why Build Riches in the Sharemarket?	141
	• What are the advantages of investing in the sharemarket?	141
	• What are the disadvantages?	142
	• Should you plan your affairs to minimise tax?	144
Chapter 15	How Do You Profit From Investing in Real Estate?	145
	• Should you buy a home or an investment property first?	147
	• What type of real estate should you buy, and where?	148
	• How do you buy real estate with confidence and ease?	157
Chapter 16	How Do You Build Income by Investing in Real Estate?	161
	• Are there any benefits to owning real estate using no borrowed funds?	162
	• What are the non cash tax deductions you can claim?	165
Chapter 17	How Do Savers Make Investors Rich?	169
	• How much does it cost to buy an investment property?	172
	• Why is an interest only loan better for most people?	176
Chapter 18	How Can You Get Rich and Help the Economy?	179
	• What affect will the G.S.T. have on real estate prices?	180
	• How does borrowing money increase your profit?	186
	• What is positive leverage?	189

Chapter 19	How Does Knowledge Destroy Fear?	195
	• Why do most people remain poor?	197
Chapter 20	What Are Managed Funds?	201
	• Can you transfer your money between different types of funds?	204
Chapter 21	How Do You Build Super Riches?	207
	• Why would you want to run your own super fund?	210
	• How much can you contribute to build super riches?	211

SECTION 3 WHAT STRATEGIES DO YOU NEED TO BUILD RICHES? 213

Chapter 22	How Will Your Strategy Make You Rich?	215
	• What are the 7 steps to a richer life?	217
Chapter 23	What Are You Going to Invest In?	219
	• How have different types of investment performed over the last twenty years?	223
	• Are shares or property more risky over time?	226
Chapter 24	How Does the New Capital Gains Tax Affect Your Riches?	229
	• Will the New CGT Suit Everybody?	232
Chapter 25	How Can You Get Rich on an Average Salary?	235
	• What do you want to achieve?	236
	• Positive leverage on real estate and shares	245
Chapter 26	How Can You Make More Money Using Superannuation Fund Managers?	251
	• How do you choose a fund manager?	255
	• What if your situation is different?	259
Chapter 27	How Can You Get Super Rich?	261
	• How can you make even more money by managing your own funds?	267

CONTENTS

Chapter 28   How Can You Keep Getting Richer After You Stop Working?   271
- How do you make your retirement income grow?   273
- How do you continue to create wealth after your death?   279

SECTION 4   HOW CAN YOU BEST TAKE ACTION TO BUILD RICHES AND RETAIN THEM?   283

Chapter 29   What Attention and Intention Will Make You Rich?   285
- How can you BAT your way to riches?   286
- How can you get richer by paying better attention?   288
- How can you get richer by using your intention?   294

Chapter 30   How Do You Motivate Yourself to Take Action and Keep Doing It?   301
- How can you turn adversity into something of value?   305
- What is the Riches Spiral?   308
- How can you develop your Action muscles?   311

Chapter 31   When Your Riches Are Building, How Do You Keep Them?   323
- How do you protect your assets?   324
- How do you create the time to build riches?   326

Chapter 32   Are There More Secrets to Building Riches?   335
- What other secrets do you need to apply before you take action?   337
- What are other considerations you need to look at?   342

SECTION 5   CONCLUSION   345

Chapter 33   What Happens When You Do Build Riches and Use Them Wisely?   347

- Who will you become when you are rich? 347
- What is your mission? 349
- How can you make an impact and change the world? 352

APPENDICES 355

Appendix 1 Statement of Income and Expenditure 356

Appendix 2 Cash Flow of Wise Family's First Investment Property 358

Appendix 3 Consumer Price Index Figures 359

Appendix 4 How to Calculate Net Capital Gains Tax Payable (Using the Old CGT Indexing System) 360

Appendix 5 Comparison of the New Capital Gains Tax System with the Indexing System 361

Appendix 6 Calculating the Net Capital Gains Tax Payable by a Taxpayer using the New CGT System 362

About the Bruce Davis Companies 363

Keep Building Riches 365

Book Order Form 367

Building Riches Audio Program Order Form 369

PERSONAL RICHES JOURNAL 371

Index 381

Introduction

INTRODUCTION

'Riches are not an end of life, but an instrument of life.'
~ **Henry Ward Beecher.**

We all want to be rich ... Every man, woman and child has imagined, and wants to believe, that they will become rich in many areas of their lives, albeit in different ways. Generally, we all want to be healthy, to have a beautiful home, wear quality clothing, drive a reliable car, have money to enjoy entertainment; and also have the funds to comfortably provide for the future needs of our loved ones and ourselves. We all want to be rich in health, love and happiness.

Deep down, I believe, we all have dreams of realising that we are important, that we have a special talent that we can use to help make the world a better place and to help others enjoy the rich experiences of life to the full. All of us have imagined that our dreams will come true at some time in the future. However, for far too many of us, our dreams of riches are lost in the day-to-day routine of making a living, or even surviving. Many people have lost sight of their earlier images and dreams of riches.

My life's mission is to inspire others by example, to achieve challenging goals whilst living in accordance with those things that deeply, truly matter most to me.

Today, I have learned how to turn images and dreams into reality. I take great pride in knowing that my companies make millions of dollars of profit per annum for my investors and myself and, through this process, I employ many people and provide a means for their families to realise their dreams. Yet it hasn't always been that way. I remember, only fifteen years ago, I was struggling to find and keep a job. Back then, I was fifteen kilograms overweight, living in a single rented room, with no job satisfaction, driving an unreliable old car, with a large credit card debt and no assets.

I certainly could imagine, back then, what I wanted, but I had no plan to realise my dreams and I felt alone, frustrated and fearful of how I was even going to continue to survive. Now I have learned that all of those negative experiences and emotions not only gave me the desire to make my life change, but also provided me with the impetus to learn how to do that ~ to transform adversity into a platform for the success which I have now achieved and continue to enjoy.

Over the years, I have been asked to explain how I have achieved the success I have, in so many areas of my life in such a short period of time, and why I give so much of my time and money to assist others who are not currently able to enjoy the benefits of the riches that I do today. These questions are not easily answered but will unfold as you read this book.

Some of the Successes I Regard as Highlights of this Period in my Life Include:

In Business: Consistently earning millions of dollars of net profit per year, for myself and those who invest with my companies; creating hundreds of jobs for my fellow Australians; building and owning companies while living in Sydney, Melbourne, Perth and California; and doing business throughout Asia.

Mentally: Being awarded a degree in Commerce at the University of NSW and working as an accountant; being awarded a Security Dealer's Licence (a prerequisite for a Stock Broking Licence) and advising others on how to use their money wisely; being awarded a Real Estate Licence and completing all of the necessary academic and practical experience in several States of Australia; studying Neuro Linguistic Programming (NLP) at Practitioner, Master Practitioner and Trainer levels and working with the best in the world in this art and science; attending and learning from dozens of personal development courses on several continents; reading hundreds of books and listening to over one thousand audio tapes.

Physically: Gaining my Black Belt and competing internationally in Chito Ryu Karate (the same style in which Elvis Presley received his Black Belt while doing his military service); playing first grade Rugby Union, representing NSW for several years and travelling overseas to

INTRODUCTION

represent Australia; and enjoying scuba diving and snow skiing.

In the Community: Establishing a charity with Nick Farr-Jones, of rugby union fame, to provide attitudinal, motivational and technical skills for underprivileged Australian youth; giving financial and strategic support to other caring organisations; personally working in schools and on the streets with young people who are crying out for the assistance they often don't get at home and in the education system; using NLP and my other skills which assist people to overcome social problems like drug addiction, physical and mental abuse, and personal issues concerning their weight and self-esteem.

And, important to me also, *in my family:* Throughout it all, finding and marrying my loving wife, Tanya, and being the proud father of our teenage son, Scott; assisting my mother, Margaret, to pay out her mortgage; and taking the time to enjoy my family, with all my grandparents, brothers and other family and extended family members.

I outline these items not to impress you, but rather to impress upon you, that, whatever your current circumstances, you and you alone hold the key to the door to your future successes.

The methods by which I have achieved my success are detailed throughout this book ~ I share them with you to support you, too, in achieving the success and riches you deserve. However, I'd also like to give you, in this introduction, an overview of some of the principles I see as being critical to success.

Key Principles:

One major reason for my success has been **my ability to use what I have learned** and to concentrate single-mindedly on whatever was the most important part of my success plan at any time.

Another major reason for my success has been **my determination to hold myself responsible and accountable in terms of my honesty and integrity in all of my interactions with others.** Yes, I have been lied to, robbed, conned and tricked, but as I became better able to spot the sharks and con-people (an intuitive skill I think women utilise much more often than men!), I learned how best to keep my money and integrity intact.

Another critical element is **to have long-term goals.** I encourage people to set goals for more than just personal purposes. Goals compel you to succeed and find solutions to any challenge or opposition you may meet on your quest to build riches, for yourself and your loved ones.

HOW TO BUILD RICHES

I have mentioned my own mixed associations with money and some highlights on my way to understanding *How to Build Riches*. I have learned to train my brain to find ways to make money and build riches in a way where I can share some of this money with others. This has allowed me to gain enormous pleasure and joy in the process of building riches. It became so addictive that it has driven me to continue to ask myself:

'How can I achieve all of my goals in a way where I can influence others to passionately enjoy life enough to make changes for the better, in their own lives?'

The answer to this question has driven me to spend the past twenty years applying the material detailed in this book.

You see, I have yet to meet one person who could not achieve all that I have done and more. The question for them ~ and for you, if you like ~ is:

'Will you help yourself to build riches if you are given the methodology and the framework in which to succeed?'

The part of your brain and body which you use to imagine your future success, or read this book now, or write down your goals and values and the reasons why you desire riches and success, is no different from the same neurology in myself, or anyone else. The difference lies only in how we use what we have to get more of what we want, desire and deserve.

Did you know that surveys in Australia, North America and the United Kingdom continually show that considerably less than 10% of the population can support themselves for the last decades of their life, in retirement? In fact, the figure is much closer to 5%.

Recently, I went to visit one of my two living grandfathers on his ninety-sixth birthday, in the nursing home where he then resided. He owned a waterfront home that was vacant and not earning anything for him, while he lived in average circumstances. He did everything he was supposed to do in life, but his money ran out before he did. He was living in the dementia ward of a modest nursing home. There were some very caring and dedicated people amongst the staff but, there is a limit to what they can do for any individual under the circumstances. Fortunately many of our family (some of whom are doctors) visited him often.

INTRODUCTION

When he arrived, he was only old ~ in a matter of weeks he was indistinguishable from many of the other people suffering from dementia.

I didn't have the legal right to sell his house and let him use the money from it to provide a greater quality of life in his remaining years. His pride and desire to leave his house to his family prevented him from selling, as is the case for many older people who own a valuable home yet live frugally. For him, sadly, it is too late. But this situation inspires me to build the riches to make sure that this will never happen to my mother and my immediate family. Like many, my grandfather's life's choices didn't focus on building riches or organising his affairs in a way where what he worked for could accumulate to allow him to enjoy a good quality of life, and still support him when he needed it most, in his retirement. He worked for the same large company for fifty-five years and rose through the ranks from office boy to General Manager, yet his success, undirected, was not enough.

His wife, my grandmother, who died recently, at the age of ninety, spoke with me often about her excitement for what I teach people, and her wish that she had taken a few more calculated risks with money, so she could have enjoyed the excitement and rewards of building more riches in her life. Regrettably, when she was in a position to do this, I wasn't alive or skilled enough to share that knowledge or those skills with her.

If 100% of people want to be rich, but only about 5% of the population do it, then you may well ask: *'What do the 5% who get rich do?'*

Action precedes every accomplishment. Action itself is not enough. Our gaols and cemeteries are full of people who took action before they had a strategy! Strategy produces results. In order to develop winning strategies you will require specific knowledge of what you want and what is available. Knowledge is a base upon which you will build your riches.

Building Riches Only Requires Three Steps:

Step One: *Know what your long-term goals are, and what knowledge you need to achieve them.*

You need to know what you want before you start. Knowledge of the goals you really commit to is the first step to any accomplishment. Throughout this book I will italicise the word **Knowledge** because without it there is no foundation upon which you can build your riches.

HOW TO BUILD RICHES

We all have many dreams in life. The difference between a dream and a goal is the fact that a goal is something you decide to believe you can achieve, and then set out to accomplish. To turn a dream into a goal, first decide that it is worth achieving, then develop a *Knowledge* and certainty in yourself that you can achieve it. Set a time limit on its completion, and write it down. Once you have the *Knowledge* of exactly what you want and you commit to it, your mind begins to identify ways to achieve your objective. If the goal is truly important to you, you'll find out what *Knowledge* you need to acquire in order to achieve your goal and succeed. As you will discover, <u>if you have enough reasons why</u> it matters to you to succeed, how to do it <u>will become apparent.</u>

Step Two: *Write out a Strategic plan for achieving and protecting your riches.*

It has been claimed that the reason for most mistakes in life is the tendency for people to act on a goal without a plan, or strategy, and I agree. You will discover in Section Three ~ *What STRATEGIES Do You Need To Build Riches?* ~ how one couple can earn in excess of $3,000,000 (after inflation) more than another couple earning the same income, by having a different strategy and then applying it.

Throughout this book I will italicise the word *Strategy* because it provides you with the direction and certainty to continue to take action towards what really matters to you in life. It is the second critical element in your success formula.

Every one of us is unique and our Creator has endowed us all with the ability to excel at something. The trick is to find what you love to do and do it with love. Then you will always be employed, happy and capable of building riches. The key to actually succeeding is to develop an appropriate *Strategy*, whatever your starting point.

Step Three: *Take massive Action towards your goals and be flexible enough to change your plan.*

Action makes up for many shortcomings and provides you with valuable lessons to refine your plans. Flexibility offers you the ability to take advantage of new opportunities and offers faster, easier ways

INTRODUCTION

of achieving your goals. If you are given an opportunity that will save you time and effort and help to build your riches even faster, be prepared to change direction.

Throughout this book I will also italicise the word **Action** because it provides you with the results and the certainty to continue to do what really matters to you in life. It is the third critical element in your success formula.

Without *Action* you are an observer, and not a participant, in the game of life. Flexibility allows you to play the game better and to continue to improve. As you grow in experience and self-confidence, you will be better equipped to take future *Action*, make even more sound plans and continue to set bigger and better goals.

I encourage you to read this whole book before taking *Action* on long-range financial objectives, in order that you are properly equipped. There are plenty of sharks out there ready to take advantage of you if you do not have the *Knowledge* and *Strategies* to avoid being taken by them. As you develop and build your specialist *Knowledge* and *Strategies*, con persons and sharks will be less able to trick you by appealing to either your greed or fear.

The three critical elements required for your success in building riches in any area of your life are: *Action, Strategies* and *Knowledge*. The first letter of these three words spells ASK. Throughout this book I will italicise the word *ASK* because it not only summarises the three elements of your success detailed above: it is also what you do whenever you ask a question to gain information in order to acquire *Knowledge* to plan your future *Actions* and *Strategies*.

On the following page I have inserted a diagram of how you can *ASK* your way to riches. As you acquire more specific *Knowledge* about your goals and the investment choices available to you, you will find yourself designing better *Strategies*, which will in turn give you the confidence to take *Action* to achieve your goals. This gives you more *Knowledge* on how to motivate yourself to take future *Action* and so the interaction of these three elements continues in an ever empowering cycle.

It is my hope that, through sharing with you the key elements I've learned along the way, I can significantly support you in knowing what you need to succeed.

ASK Your Way to Riches

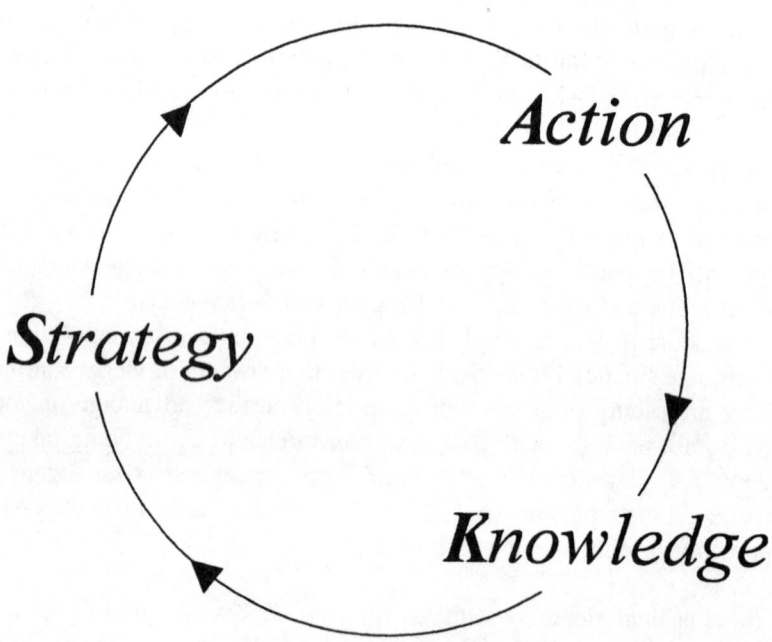

If building riches is as simple as outlined in the three steps above, you may well *ASK*:
'If all it takes to build riches is to set goals and plans in writing and then continue to take flexible Action until I reach my goals or replace them with others, why isn't everybody rich?'

The Major Reasons Why People Don't Set Goals and then Keep Taking Action to Achieve Them are:-

1) *They were never taught how to set goals.*
   One of the biggest shortfalls in most education systems, in the English-speaking world, is that you can go right to the top in academic achievement and become a professor yet not have studied one hour of goal-setting. To become a professor you have to complete twelve years of high school, three or more

INTRODUCTION

years of university to attain your initial degree, and a minimum of one year writing your paper for admission for the doctorate of your chosen vocation. At least sixteen years of formal education and no goal-setting! Survey after survey shows that less than 10% of the population have goals and less than 5% have written goals with reasons for their accomplishment and a plan for their attainment. By the time you have finished reading this book ~ if you use what it contains ~ you will have joined the 5% and be ready to enter the Goal Achievers' Club!

If enough people were willing even to begin such a simple process, it mightn't take long before this percentage increased. As far as I'm concerned, the more people who are enabled to truly take charge of their own financial well-being and future prosperity, the happier and more harmonious the world is likely to be.

2) ***FEAR stops many.***
Fear is shown for what it commonly is, in the acronym that spells:

> **F** alse
> **E** vidence / (Expectations)
> **A** ppearing
> **R** eal

If people were to list all the fears they had, over a year, and then count the number which eventuated, most would probably find that only about 1% to 5%, of the things they create a fear for, actually happen. Once you realise how powerful your mind is at achieving your objectives, you will want to fill your mind only with positive images of your desired goals. We will deal with how to turn fear to your advantage later in this book. But, for now, realise that most fears never happen. Another cause of fear are well meaning friends and family members who give advice to others about getting rich (who are not rich themselves). Fear can be fanned by people who are not rich themselves and, based on their track record, are not the types of people you want to be taking advice from in the first place.

3) *A faulty Belief System:*
Many people believe they have to earn a huge salary before they can build riches ~ an extension of that old aphorism 'it takes money to make money'. This myth will be dispelled when I show you that, on an average wage, a couple can become multi-millionaires, as well as provide a good education and financial assistance for their children, and enjoy a good quality of life, at the same time.

4) *Resistance to, or resentment of, change:*
Change is the one constant. Trying to hold back change is as futile as trying to count the grains of sand on a beach. We have come to the end of the Age that began with the Industrial Revolution (in the Western world, at least), and already have entered what is being called the Information Age, yet little in our education or thinking has prepared us for that change. Rather, most people are still trying to handle the challenges that have come with that change. They were taught to do and expect certain things in order to succeed. That world no longer exists.

Firstly, we need to recognise that the world is no longer the way we grew up believing it would be ~ enormous change, already, has taken place, and there is no going back.

Secondly, we are going to have to develop a willingness to learn, or be left behind.

Many people resent that the expectations they had throughout their lives ~ of working hard and paying taxes, with an agreement that the government would look after them in their twilight years ~ are not being met. To realise this problem you need only to speak with aged pensioners, to find out how deeply they feel that governments are cutting their quality of life back, by not indexing pensions fully and by eroding and eliminating benefits. If you add to this, that, in about twenty years time, there will be twice the percentage of aged people wanting welfare, you may begin to *realise that a crisis is looming*. And this crisis will not only affect those who expect something that governments are increasingly incapable of delivering, but also, those who will be paying the taxes to fund whatever attempts governments may make to meet those old, now increasingly unrealistic, expectations.

INTRODUCTION

Many in middle management and unskilled workers have become victims of the transition into the 21st Century. With 40% of the world's population earning significantly less than they did in 1980, in real terms, these people are susceptible to the lure of various 'fast money' schemes. Unemployment will rise as a direct result of cheap foreign goods replacing those goods that otherwise would be produced in our country using the Australian workforce. What was once 'tried and true' financial advice for people in the workforce can no longer produce the expected results. *Who will take care of the future for them, if they don't?*

Even more at risk are those who put short-term savings and immediate gratification, in one form or another, ahead of provision for their futures and the futures of their children. These people have some vague belief, or hope, that the future will take care of itself.

We probably all have our own attitudes and judgements about what other people do and the choices they make. But, what seems to me to be most obvious, is that people can't make the best choices for themselves if they don't have the information they need to base those choices on.

In our formal education, this information is mostly missing. Certainly, socially, it is evident that most people simply don't know what they need to know to ensure the quality of life they really want for themselves and their families. What is needed is *Knowledge* that, when applied, will provide the riches that allow for security and certainty for the future.

We will explore this subject more in following chapters.

5) *Ignorance and no desire to learn.*
This is similar to a resistance to change, but relates more to the fact that most people stop reading and learning, when they leave school, and many stop looking for work, when they find a job! In the USA, surveys reveal that the average person reads less than one book per annum, and that nearly 58% of the population never finish reading a non-fiction book after they leave high school! Probably 80%, or maybe even 90%, of all books are sold to 20% of the population (this being the richest 20% of the population).

HOW TO BUILD RICHES

You can take pride and credit in the fact that, right now, you are reading this book, which may forever change your life and your destiny, depending on your desire to build riches and the *Actions* you take as a consequence of your learning.

The Chinese have a saying that *'a journey of one thousand miles starts with the first step'*. I believe that you and I are both on a journey and that our spirits may well meet in the pages of this book. You see, it was your desire that made you acquire this book, and my desire that compelled me to write it. No matter how well you have succeeded in your life to date, or how big the challenges that face you in your immediate life, I'm sure that you, and I, believe you can go beyond where you are today. You are destined for greatness, whether that be as a loving parent, as a business person or professional, a salesperson, a labourer or manager, or something else.

By picking up and reading this book you have taken the greatest step, in that you not only believe that you can achieve more, you've taken *Action* towards being more. You will have already surpassed 80% of the population when you have read this book. Surveys show, tragically, that only 10% of people who buy books read past the first chapter ~ what a waste. Certainly, whatever the desire or concern was that led you to begin reading this book, it is highly likely that what is most important to you in addressing that concern, or fulfilling that desire, is what will have you follow through and read this book. <u>You aren't about to cheat yourself out of the secrets that lie within this book.</u> I do believe there is information here that you can use to make a significant difference on your own road to building riches. **I challenge you, not just to read this book, but to finish it, do the processes suggested, and make the best use of it you can.**

If you look back over the history of many hundreds of successful men and women, you will see that those who have built enormous riches, or have had an enormous impact on their societies and on millions of other people, frequently have had to face enormous challenges themselves. The secret is to learn how to grow and become stronger with each new challenge, to take responsibility for those challenges and learn creative solutions to build greater riches. One fundamental characteristic that distinguishes men and women who achieve greatness, is that they have

INTRODUCTION

learned the habit of expecting more of themselves than anyone else could ever have expected from them.

I have no way of knowing how many riches you have been able to build to date. The concepts and principles, outlined in this book, can inspire and support you only to the extent that you approach them with an open mind. Embrace them with enthusiasm and make them your own and, most importantly, put them into *Action*. Knowing *How to Build Riches* is not enough. It takes *Action*, and the ability to build this into a habit which eventually leads to your destiny.

When I learned the martial art of Karate, first I became a student and, over time, developed skills, achieved different coloured belts and finally became a Black Belt. Later, I opened several Karate schools and taught many new students the skills and techniques of this style of Karate. As well as teaching my students the skills associated with the art of Karate, it was important to me to also teach them the intangible skills and principles ~ those of respect, discipline, patience, peace of mind ~ and the many other important lessons one must learn to become a master of that art.

Competing against other martial artists, in Australia and overseas, I have had the opportunity to be invited to train students of other martial arts, and also have been a student of many other instructors, world-wide.

Mastery in building riches is like mastery in any other area. We all learn from others first, before we become leaders and teachers ourselves. In education, we all had teachers; in sport, we all had coaches; and in business, we all had employers, mentors and associates.

With your permission, I would like to be your personal trainer, throughout this book, supporting and coaching you in learning the skills and embodying the principles behind building riches; so that you grow in all areas of your life, and continue to share and build greater riches for yourself, your family, your community and your world.

You see, we all need coaching, no matter what level of skill we currently have or what level of riches we have achieved to date. The greatest athletes and business people in the world have specific coaching to help them in the game of life, be they Cathy Freeman, in athletics; Lachlan Murdoch, in the business of News Corporation, or James Packer of Consolidated Press; or Susie Moroney, in swimming.

So, how is it that personal trainers actually assist others to develop expertise and their full potential in any given area? Instructors, or masters, develop expertise in any field, through many years of diligent study and commitment. They have also learned many lessons and realised how to communicate these easily and with the maximum amount of benefit to the student. Importantly, the instructor cares about the student's development and growth. An instructor can have a number of students who may be at various levels of development, yet a true master instructor will be able to share ideas, concepts and distinctions that can help students at any level.

Certainly, I have developed expertise in the field of building riches over many years, and I have learned to impart the principles and skills of that *Knowledge* to people at many levels. It is my hope to share with you the ideas, concepts and distinctions that can help you to develop and build greater riches, in whatever area of life to which you choose to apply these skills. I know, through the thousands of people I've worked with, in groups and in one-on-one consultations, that frequently, it is through the sharing of **one idea at the right time**, (it may even be something that person already knows), that remarkable results can be created. Many of my clients have a net worth in millions of dollars and some have several tens of millions of dollars more in assets than I have at present, yet, they still invest in business opportunities with my companies and myself, and I continue to share concepts and ideas that build greater riches in, and for, myself and all of those with whom I am involved.

If you are willing and enthusiastic about learning and applying the skills and principles of building riches that I am about to share with you, then I know you will gain maximum benefit from reading this book and achieve your own, remarkable results. You'll learn how two individuals build more financial wealth than others on the same incomes, and experience greater happiness and peace of mind during the process. You'll also learn principles, *Strategies* and skills that have taken billionaires and other highly successful people, decades to learn, to find and articulate.

Once you apply all of these lessons, you will be at the level of mastery in your life where you can bring about and build the riches you have always dreamed of. It all begins to work for you when you learn ...

1

Why Build Riches?

Chapter 1

WHAT MAKES BUILDING RICHES IMPORTANT?

*'You cannot strengthen the weak by weakening the strong,
You cannot help the small ... by tearing down the big,
You cannot help the poor by destroying the rich,
You cannot lift the wage earner by pulling down the wage payer,
You cannot keep out of trouble by spending more than your income,
You cannot further the brotherhood of man by inciting class hatreds,
You cannot build character and courage
by taking away initiative and independence,
You cannot help people permanently by doing for them
what they could, and should, do for themselves.'*
~ **Abraham Lincoln.**

Australia has been called the lucky country. It is a land of great beauty, with abundant natural resources and a relatively temperate climate. In my opinion, it is the richest country on Earth. There may be people who love Australia more than I, but, so far in my life, I've never met one.

A comprehensive study conducted by the World Bank, in 1995, put Australia as the richest country in the world. This study comprised income produced by every country, combined with the natural resources of each country, and divided it by the population, to come up with the amount of riches that each person in the country owned, on a pro-rata basis. It included all of the resources that most Australians take for granted, such as our freeways, schools, forests and beaches, and all the other ingredients that are important to measure wealth. Every Australian I know, who has travelled extensively overseas, upon return, always agrees that Australia is the best place in the world.

Australian history has only been accurately recorded for just over two hundred years. Many other nations can trace their histories back over many thousands of years. The Chinese can trace theirs back for more than ten thousand years. In the Middle East, the ancient trading city of Babylon has been traced back over six thousand years.

One hundred years ago, before the year 1900, Australia had developed from an English penal colony to become one of the richest trade nations on Earth. At the end of the 19th Century, Australia became rich from its export of rural products, particularly wool ~ hence the saying that Australia 'rode on the sheep's back'. Raw materials were, and still are, Australia's major exports.

Effects of the Industrial Revolution, especially in the late 19th Century, changed forever the way people lived. The invention of the internal combustion engine, factories, radio, television, computers and other agents of social change, have occurred in the past hundred years.

We are now moving beyond that 'Industrial Age' to what is now being called the 'Information Age'. So let's look at the Australian environment as we enter the 21st Century and at what that environment holds in store for every Australian.

Australia Today

The United Nations published a detailed *Human Development Report* in 1999 (some of the figures used in the report reflect development over a number of years, so figures quoted in this chapter may range across those years, with some being dated 1995, due to the delay in compiling data from all countries in the world). This report, published by Oxford University Press, New York, compares every country, by certain key criteria, in order to develop what it calls the Human Development Index ('HDI'). This index ranks all countries in the world on the basis of:

1) Life expectancy
2) Educational attainment
3) Income.

Australia was ranked seventh by the United Nations in the 1999 HDI (up from fifteenth in 1998 and fourteenth, in 1997).

WHAT MAKES BUILDING RICHES IMPORTANT?

In 1999, the top three countries in the world were Canada, in first place; Norway in second; the USA third, and Japan in fourth place. European countries held six of the top ten positions.

In fact, of the top twenty countries, fifteen were European. Throughout this chapter, I will refer back to this detailed HDI, in order to make meaningful comparisons between the riches we experience in Australia and those of other countries, rated as some of the top twenty richest in the world.

Let us now look at certain important criteria that make up the framework of the Australian economy, and the impact that the Information Age already is having on the environment in which you and I seek to build riches for our families and ourselves.

Income

The Australian Bureau of Statistics compiles data about income, based on the situation of people of various ages and including those who are working, retired, unemployed, unable or unwilling to work. Accordingly, the average income of all people will be lower than that for those who are working. The distribution of income for all Australians, shown by those statistics, for 1997-98 is detailed in the graph on the following page.

If we look at the position of employed people, as at August, 2001, the average weekly earnings of all employees in Australia (including part-time workers) was $673.30 per week (being over $35,000 per annum). The Average Weekly Ordinary Times Earnings (AWOTE) for full-time adult employees was $837.60 per week (or, just over $43,500 per annum). This relates to the average gross weekly wage paid to a full-time employee.

Your aim in building riches should be to earn as much as you can while still maintaining your quality of life. By the time you have finished reading this book, you will know that **it is possible to become a millionaire on an average income.**

When you become highly motivated about ethically building riches, and apply the *Knowledge* learned from this book, you will find it is easy to begin to increase your current effectiveness. Interestingly, that is also likely to result in an increase in your income. If your current employer is not prepared to pay you more money, then quite probably another employer will value your talents more and pay you more, accordingly.

HOW TO BUILD RICHES

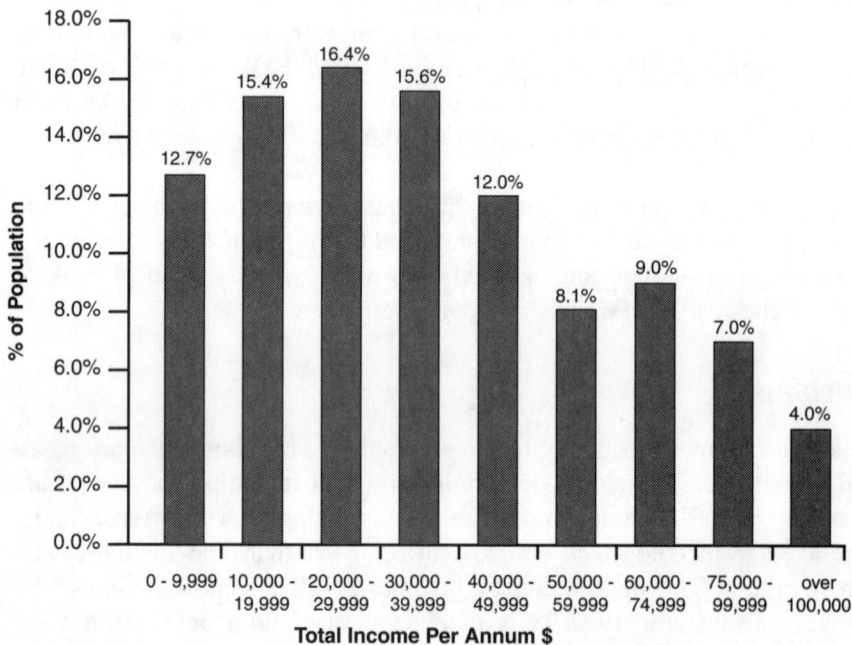

Source: Australian Bureau of Statistics

One method of comparing income between countries, is that adopted by the United Nations in its HDI ranking, which is, to divide the gross domestic product (GDP) by the total people in each country. The GDP is a measure of the total production of goods and services in the economy. In 1998, Australia was ranked twenty-one in the world with an income per person of US$19,632, (down from eighteenth in 1997).

Of the twenty countries that produced more per person than Australia, eleven were located in Europe, with Canada (US$21,916), the USA (US$26,977) and Japan (US$21,930) being some of the remaining nine. New Zealand produced (US$17,267).

A comparison of the ratio of the highest 20% of the country's income earners and the lowest 20%, for several of the world's richest countries, is shown in the graph below:

WHAT MAKES BUILDING RICHES IMPORTANT?

RATIO OF HIGHEST 20% TO THE LOWEST 20% OF INCOME EARNERS IN DIFFERENT COUNTRIES (1980-94)

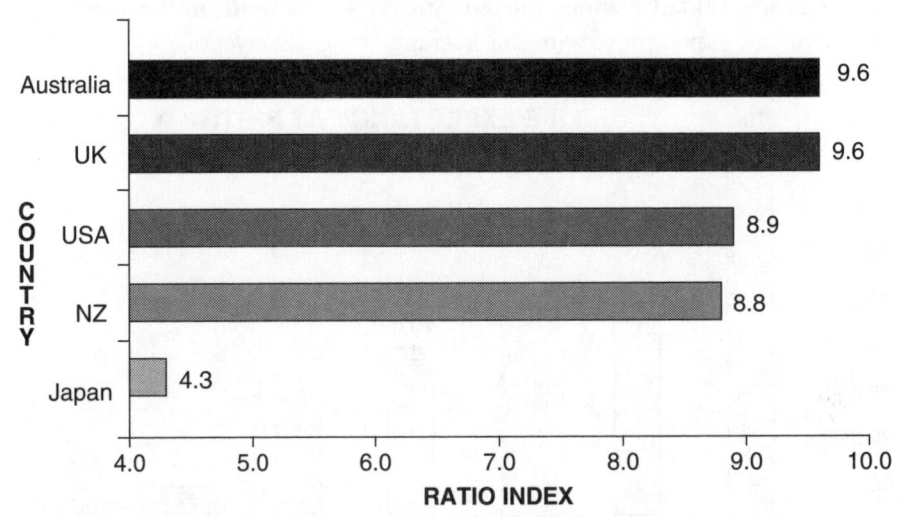

Country	Ratio Index
Australia	9.6
UK	9.6
USA	8.9
NZ	8.8
Japan	4.3

Source: United Nations 'Human Development Report 1999'

The above graph shows that Australia shares with the UK the dubious honour of having the highest ratio of difference between the incomes of the richest 20% and the poorest 20% of their populations of all of the developed countries that were detailed! Figures published by the Australian Bureau of Statistics for the year 1996-97 confirms the above report's findings. The top 20% earned an average of $1,485 per week (being 47.5% of all income) whereas the lowest 20% earned an average of $121 per week (being only 3.8% of all income).

The rich *are* getting richer, while the poor *are* getting poorer.

In later chapters, we will begin to identify what the difference is between those who become rich and those who remain poor, and how you can join the rich by becoming more flexible in your behaviour. Before we do, it is critical to further explore how our society is changing and how we can use that information to compel us toward the building of riches.

Longevity

In 1995, the United Nations ranked Australia as seventh in the world in terms of life expectancy, with the average being 78.2 years.

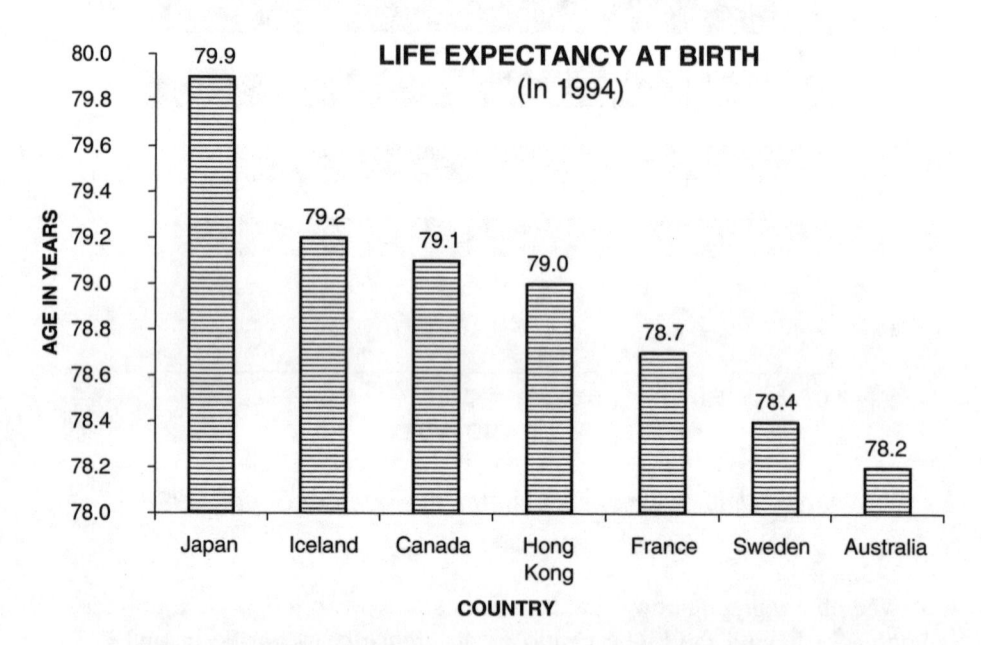

LIFE EXPECTANCY AT BIRTH (In 1994)

Country	Age in Years
Japan	79.9
Iceland	79.2
Canada	79.1
Hong Kong	79.0
France	78.7
Sweden	78.4
Australia	78.2

Source: United Nations 'Human Development Report 1997'

The top country in the world was Japan, with its average being 79.9 years, with less than two years greater life expectancy than ours. The ranking of the top seven countries in the world, in terms of life expectancy, is graphed above.

There is a clear difference between the life expectancy of men and women. Although the average life expectancy in Australia, in 1995, was predicted at 78.2 years, the average life expectancy for men was less than seventy-six years, and for women it was over eighty.

Life expectancy is continuing to rise in all Western countries, particularly Australia. In the early 1970's, a twenty-year-old male was expected to live to an average age of sixty-eight years. In comparison, a twenty-year-old male, in the late 1990's, is expected to live to seventy-six and, by the year 2020, a twenty-year-old will expect to reach an average age of over eighty. (*Source: Australian Life Tables*).

WHAT MAKES BUILDING RICHES IMPORTANT?

My own family provides an example ~ at the time of writing, I have two grandparents alive and my paternal grandmother, was ninety at the time of her death. My paternal grandfather was nearly ninety-seven when he recently passed away. My maternal grandparents are aged in their early eighties. Attending my maternal grandfather's eightieth birthday (five years ago), I was surprised to learn that, prior to himself, the longest any male member of his family had ever lived was to the age of fifty-eight.

Life expectancy figures take into account all causes of death. The biggest killer in Australia is heart disease, which accounts for almost 50% of deaths. The next biggest killer is cancer, which accounts for almost a third of Australian deaths. The combined death toll from heart disease and cancer exceeds 80% yet, today, despite this, average life expectancy is still approaching eighty years. In the vast majority of cases, heart disease and cancer are preventable causes of death. The easiest way to prolong your life, is to avoid the above diseases.

It has been predicted that within twenty years, for those people who eat well, do not smoke, and engage in regular exercise, life expectancy is likely to rise to approach a hundred years. This is partially due to the medical breakthroughs and, also, to state-of-the-art information available to people today, supporting them in developing their minds and bodies to live full and rewarding lives.

There is also evidence that those of us who join the rich are also more likely to live longer than those who remain, or become, poor.

Home Ownership

Australia has traditionally had a very high proportion of home ownership. In fact you have probably heard it said that the *Great Australian Dream* is to own your own home, with no mortgage. In the twenty years from 1978 to 1998, the proportion of homeowners dropped from 73.4% to about 60.9% of the population. Over the same period, the number of people renting homes increased by the same 12%, made up of an approximate 8% increase in private renters and a 4% increase in government assisted renters. This trend indicates that many Australians may be losing sight of the benefits of acquiring equity in their own homes.

The Australian Federal Government is unable to continue such an increase in public housing over the long-term. In the 1997 Federal Budget, the Federal Government stopped reimbursing State governments for public housing. This system was replaced with an allocation. This is a clear attempt to put more of the responsibility for public housing onto the States and away from the Federal Government. Every year there is a continuing and increasing tension between the State Premiers and the Federal Government when it comes to distribution of Federal money to the State governments. It is only a matter of time until the State governments start to put more of that pressure back onto the people on the public housing waiting lists. This will result in it becoming harder for the needy to qualify for government housing assistance.

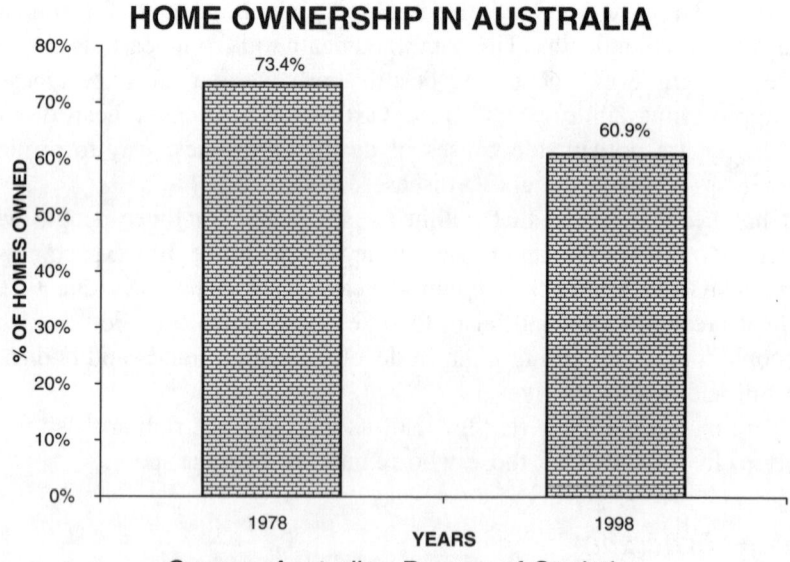

HOME OWNERSHIP IN AUSTRALIA

Year	% of Homes Owned
1978	73.4%
1998	60.9%

Source: Australian Bureau of Statistics

One thing is certain. The current tendency, for many people, to place great importance on lifestyle and therefore spend more than they earn can only exacerbate this problem. The short-term benefit is to have a good time, with the long-term cost being not only a lack of riches but, perhaps, a lack of basic housing and even poverty. The rich realise that home ownership creates a solid platform for building future wealth.

Later, you will discover how it is possible to repay your home loan in up to half the time it has taken traditionally, and why most banks don't encourage you to know this information. Careful selection of both the right location and type of home, together with the best type of financing for your home purchase, can result in a much faster journey towards your

WHAT MAKES BUILDING RICHES IMPORTANT?

future riches. Selection of the right type of investment real estate, for others to rent, also is one of the fastest ways to secure riches.

Overseas Debt

The amount of money that Australians collectively owe overseas has increased dramatically, but fortunately has slowed. In 1983-84, the total gross overseas debt was $44.1 billion. By 1993-94, it had increased to $204.1 billion. In June 1999 Australia owes others $228.1 billion.

AUSTRALIAN TOTAL FOREIGN DEBT in $BILLIONS

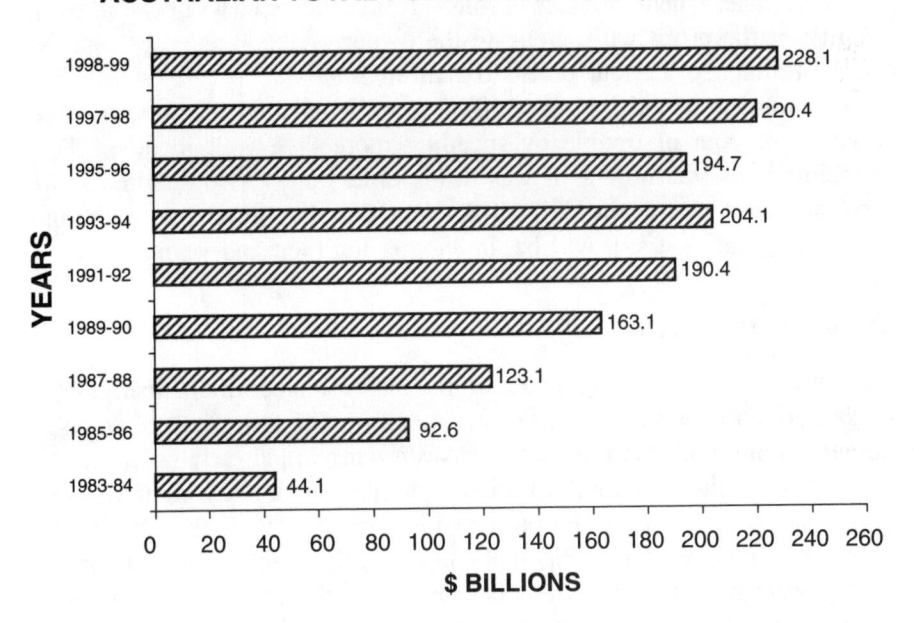

Years	$ Billions
1998-99	228.1
1997-98	220.4
1995-96	194.7
1993-94	204.1
1991-92	190.4
1989-90	163.1
1987-88	123.1
1985-86	92.6
1983-84	44.1

Source: Australian Bureau of Statistics

A legacy has been created by both governments and individuals spending more than they earn, which is going to be a burden on our children's generation and beyond, unless this pattern is reversed, dramatically. The previous graph shows that the amount of money Australians owe overseas increased by almost seven times in a thirteen-year period. It is not wise to blame governments, as we only get the governments we vote into power! Governments do, however, have a responsibility to pass legislation to create an environment for continuing economic viability, including profitability, for Australian citizens, companies, and employment. The greater the amount of money Australia owes overseas, the greater the financial pressures that Australia, as a whole, faces. Clearly, Australia has spent more than it has earned over that period. It has begun to be reversed. But there is a risk that future governments will overspend again if voters don't stop them.

A certain recipe for failure is to spend more than you earn, whether you are an individual, a company, a government, or an institution. If Australia is going to continue to be owned by Australians, there is a need for us to learn to borrow money *only* for investments, which can be repaid at a later date, when the asset is sold. Ideally, the asset will be sold for a profit and the profit will belong to the owner of the asset ~ preferably, an Australian, so that our profits remain in Australia.

As quoted at the beginning of this chapter, Abraham Lincoln said: 'You cannot keep out of trouble by spending more than your income.' This principle is as true now as it was in his time, almost two hundred years ago, and as it was in the days of Ancient Babylon, almost six thousand years ago, and as it still will be, in another ten thousand years.

Retirement in Australia

The prospect of retiring in Australia has changed dramatically. The increased cost to the government, of people in retirement, has risen greatly, along with the longevity of Australians. As already noted, in the early 1970's, the average Australian male lived until sixty-eight years of age, that is, of an age to be eligible for a pension for only three years. Now, the average Australian male lives until seventy-five, with many living well into their nineties. This means that the average male now retires at sixty-five and expects to live for at least another ten years ~ therefore being eligible for a pension for more than three times as long as previously expected. When we include the tendency for women to live longer than men, this hugely increased social cost is far greater. The pension for women begins currently at age sixty-two and a half (increasing to sixty-five over the next few years). With women now expected to live, on average, until eighty years of age, that is, almost twenty years of retirement.

As people continue to live longer, this puts an even greater strain on the public funding of retirement costs for our elderly. Next, let's look at the influence of *Baby Boomers* on future retirement benefits, which provides even more reason for concern and preventative *Action*.

The Baby Boomer Crisis

Have you ever heard of the term **Baby Boomers**? You probably know that this term relates to people born after World War II, from 1946 to 1964. Demographically, the group known as the Baby Boomers represents the largest segment of total population, not only in Australia and Europe but, also, in the rest of the Western world.

This has long been known to marketers and advertising agencies, who pitch their approach to align with whatever is the current age and, thus, probable desires and spending patterns of this large group. Baby Boomers make up the biggest market, but they also make up the largest percentage of population likely to require government support.

Given that government support, of any kind, is provided out of revenue derived from taxation, the amount of revenue available, for social services and other distribution, is obviously at its greatest while the Baby Boomers are at an age to earn money and pay tax. When, however, this great segment of our population arrives at retirement age, a smaller percentage of population, paying tax, will not be able to provide enough, even to sustain current rates of retirement benefits.

To assess the social consequences of the Baby Boomers, we need to look at the proportions of the Australian population in differing age groups. The graph on the following page does just that.

Generally speaking, the majority of people between birth and nineteen years of age are not actively involved in full-time work, particularly with the current trend of more people completing secondary education. Likewise, figures from the Australian Bureau of Statistics show that only about 5% of the population are still involved in full-time work after the age of sixty-five. The proportion of people working after the age of seventy drops to less than 2%. We can assume, therefore, that the majority of the working population in Australia is aged between twenty and sixty-four.

In 1961, more than 41% of the Australian population were younger than twenty. By 1996, this group represented only about 28% of the population and, by about 2030, it is predicted to drop to 23.4%. The actual number of people in this age group has remained reasonably constant, at somewhere between four and a half and five and a half million. However, at the same time, the Australian population, as a whole, has grown from about eleven million, in 1961, to over eighteen million, in 1996, and is expected to be almost twenty-five million by 2030.

PROJECTED & ACTUAL POPULATION IN AUSTRALIA

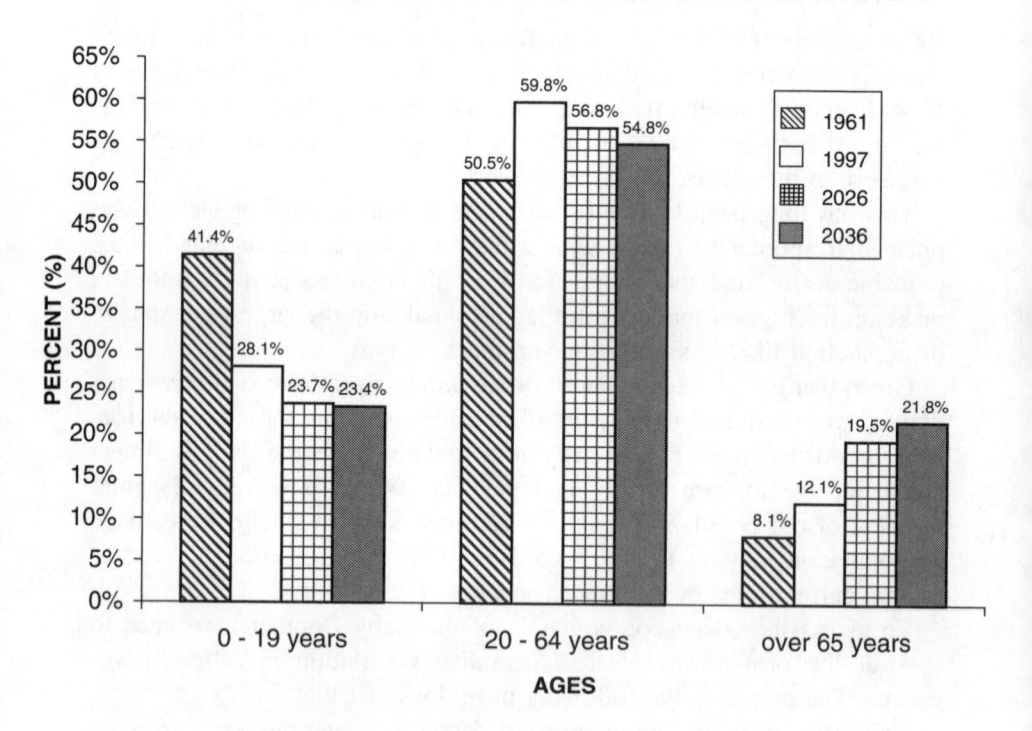

Source: Australian Bureau of Statistics

More dramatic is the change in the percentage of people aged over sixty-five, from 8.1%, in 1961, to 12.1%, in 1997, and expected to increase to about 21% by the year 2030. That means that the percentage of population, made up of people aged over sixty-five, is expected to double within about the next thirty-five years.

In the same period, the percentage of people working (those aged from twenty to sixty-four) is expected to drop by over 5%. This means in relative terms, less people working and more on the pension.

If the government has trouble handling welfare payments now, how will it be able to cope, when there could be twice as many old people

WHAT MAKES BUILDING RICHES IMPORTANT?

requiring financial assistance, not just for living expenses but, also, for services like accommodation and healthcare?

What do People Currently Experience in Retirement?

At the time of writing, the current aged pension is $205.25 per week, for single pensioners (about $10,670 per annum). For a couple it is $342.60 that is, $171.30 for each person per week (about $8,000 each per annum).

Let's assume you retire and your retirement income is more than double the aged pension at an amount of $400 per week before-tax. What affect will this have on your lifestyle?

While, at first glance, it might seem that an amount of about $400 per week, before tax, could provide a reasonable quality of living, a closer look shows that it barely covers basic needs, even for those who own their own home and have no rent to pay. Little money is available for any extras, as can be seen in the first column of the budget on page 33.

Those lucky enough to live a full life, like my grandfather, who recently died at age ninety-six, are perhaps not so lucky, if they are dependent, in retirement, on a government pension. They face the prospect of surviving for thirty years, on less than an amount needed to provide a reasonable quality of living.

It is important to realise the difference in lifestyle between pensioners and others aged over sixty-five who have financial independence. The budgeted weekly expenditure, detailed on page 33, depicts how difficult it is for most people over sixty-five to enjoy a reasonable standard of living.

The second column gives a budget for weekly expenditure for each individual on the pension who is married or who is paid at the rate for couples (1999-2000 weekly pension figures from the Department of Social Security). I have guessed how people aged over sixty-five, retiring on the pension, may spend about $171 per week each. The situation may be worse for a single person on the pension, as a single person does not get to share the expenses of maintaining a home.

What happens if the refrigerator, or microwave, or car needs replacing? The budget could be shot for months. My grandfather once confided in me that things were so tight for him, the most he could budget to save was $5 per week. This is not going to go far towards Christmas and birthday presents and cards for his three children, eight grandchildren and ever-increasing number of great-grandchildren. And what if he requires a medical specialist or hospitalisation? No matter how great you are at budgeting, it is a tough way to live for twenty or thirty years.

Imagine for a minute that you became a pensioner. Do you think that you could survive well on $154 per week, or even $186 if you're single? Do you think you could eat and drink well for $4 per day? Do you enjoy a bottle of wine occasionally? How many bottles of wine and packets of cigarettes could you get for $6 per week? What sort of clothing could you buy for $7 per week? What sort of medical treatment do you think you would receive on $10 per week if you were sick, of what quality would your recreation be on $3 per day?

Or, if you had only $20 left per week after surviving, how would you allocate that to cover emergencies and amongst all your grandchildren and family, for presents, travel and holidays, or anything else you may like to spend money on?

What if the government cannot afford to pay pensions in the future? The graph on page 31 shows that our population is ageing dramatically. If the government is having problems meeting welfare needs now, how will they cope when there is about twice the proportion of pensioners (when the baby boomers retire)?

A crisis is looming!

The third column represents that greater quality of life available to a self-supporting, retired person, enjoying the income of about $700 per week after-tax in retirement (which is about $1,000 a week before-tax). In case you think that is an unreasonable amount to expect to be able to earn, let me assure you that, before you have finished reading this book, you will have the *Knowledge* and *Strategies* you need to plan for and achieve this type of goal, or whatever amount is more appropriate to meet your own choices.

The fourth column provides a space for you to create your desired budget of expenditure in retirement. *How much will you want and how will you split it differently?*

How Much Income do People in Australia, Aged Over 65, Receive Today?

The majority of people aged over sixty-five receive less than $200 per week, which allows only a modest lifestyle. This is based on figures from the Australian Bureau of Statistics (ABS) census which include all people, aged over sixty-five, whether they are retired, working or have their own businesses. The ABS does a detailed census of every Australian household once every five years (with these figures being released to the public over

WHAT MAKES BUILDING RICHES IMPORTANT?

BUDGETED WEEKLY EXPENDITURE PER INDIVIDUAL RETIRED PERSON AGED OVER 65 YEARS (1998-99 DOLLARS)

Expenditure Group:	$400 per week before-tax $	Pensioners in a Couple $	RICH $	Your Desire $
BASIC NEEDS				
Housing Costs (Rates & Taxes, etc)	25	15	25	
Household furnishings & equipment	20	10	20	
Household Repairs & Maintenance	25	13	25	
Fuel & Power	20	6	20	
Food & non-alcoholic beverages	70	29	70	
Alcoholic beverages	20	4	20	
Tobacco	20	2	20	
Clothing & footwear	20	7	20	
Medical care and health expenses	20	10	20	
Transport & Motor Vehicle	50	20	50	
Recreation	45	20	45	
Personal Care	10	15	10	
Other commodities and services	10	20	10	
Add: WANTS & EXTRA'S				
Gifts for family			20	
Gifts for friends			20	
Donations to church & charities			20	
Assistance to family			20	
Motor Vehicle upgrade			30	
Private Health Assistance			30	
Masseur/Physio./Coaches			30	
Restaurants (family sometimes)			30	
Theatre/Movies (family sometimes)			30	
Travel/Holidays			60	
Beauty Care			20	
Fun Money			30	
After-tax weekly income	**$345**	**$171**	**$695**	
Pre-tax weekly income	**$400**	**$171**	**$1,000**	

How do these figures compare with what people are currently receiving?

the
next few years). Census figures are more accurate than other published figures because they represent the whole of Australia and not some small sample of people. The following graph shows 1996 census figures (which comprises data on almost two million people Australians aged over 65):

GROSS WEEKLY INCOME for all people aged over 65 in Australia (1995-1996)

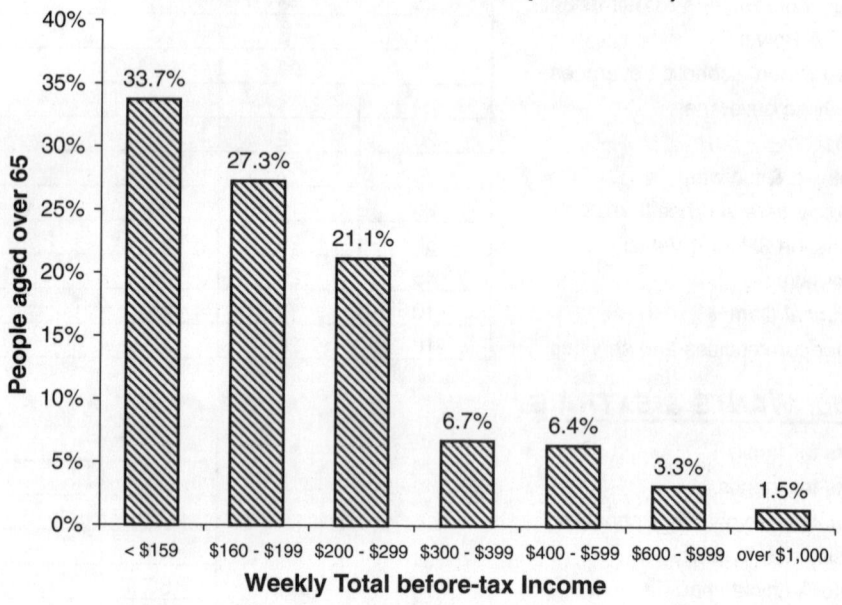

Weekly Total before-tax Income	People aged over 65
< $159	33.7%
$160 - $199	27.3%
$200 - $299	21.1%
$300 - $399	6.7%
$400 - $599	6.4%
$600 - $999	3.3%
over $1,000	1.5%

Source: Australian Bureau of Statistics (1996 Census)

The graph above shows that:

♦ Less than 5% of Australians aged over sixty-five earn in excess of the average weekly wage;
♦ Only 6.4% of people aged over 65 are shown to earn between $400 and $599 per week (refer to page 33 for what this might buy);
♦ Three in two hundred people retire rich on $1,000 or more per week before-tax (about $695 per week after tax).

WHAT MAKES BUILDING RICHES IMPORTANT?

Even though we Australians live in one of the richest countries on Earth, more than 82% of single people aged over sixty-five have to survive on under $299 per week and over 60% on less than $199 per week.

These figures are even more startling when we discover that they also include those people who are still in full-time and part-time work. Of people aged over sixty-five, 3.5% who are single, and 6.9% who are married, work in full-time employment, or in their own business. How many retired people aged over sixty-five actually have a pre-tax retirement income in excess of $400 per week? The number may be as low as 6% of this group of the population, after it is reduced for the people who are still working (most of which because they have to in order to achieve a decent standard of living for when they can afford to retire).

You have probably heard of a survey conducted with one hundred young men aged twenty-five, whose financial positions were re-assessed when they were sixty-five. While often quoted, that survey is about twenty years old, and originated in the USA (by the U.S. Health, Education and Welfare Department). Yet several Australian authors, as recently as last year, quoted these statistics in their books as current. Due to changing life expectations, for both men and women, it important to update this, for current Australian conditions. The result is shown on the next page.

The graph on the previous page reveals the sad truth. After we adjust for people that are working and we live in the richest country on Earth (in my totally unbiased opinion!), **about six in a hundred people**, after working hard for forty years, or more, **can support themselves with a reasonable standard of living**, using their own investments and savings.

Remember this graph's message well and vow that you will take the time and effort to read this book, and apply the principles and techniques it gives you, to build riches for yourself and the people you love. Once you learn the *Knowledge* outlined in this book, you will be able to use your awareness of the above desperate position to devise *Strategies* and to compel you to *Action* so that you can be the one person in two hundred who becomes rich. Riches provide not only financial freedom and security, but also, the ability to build a better world for those generations of Australians, who are to follow you. And who knows, you and I may even change these statistics!

HOW TO BUILD RICHES

INCOME POSITION of 100 men and women upon reaching 65 years of age in Australia (1995-1996) (before-tax)

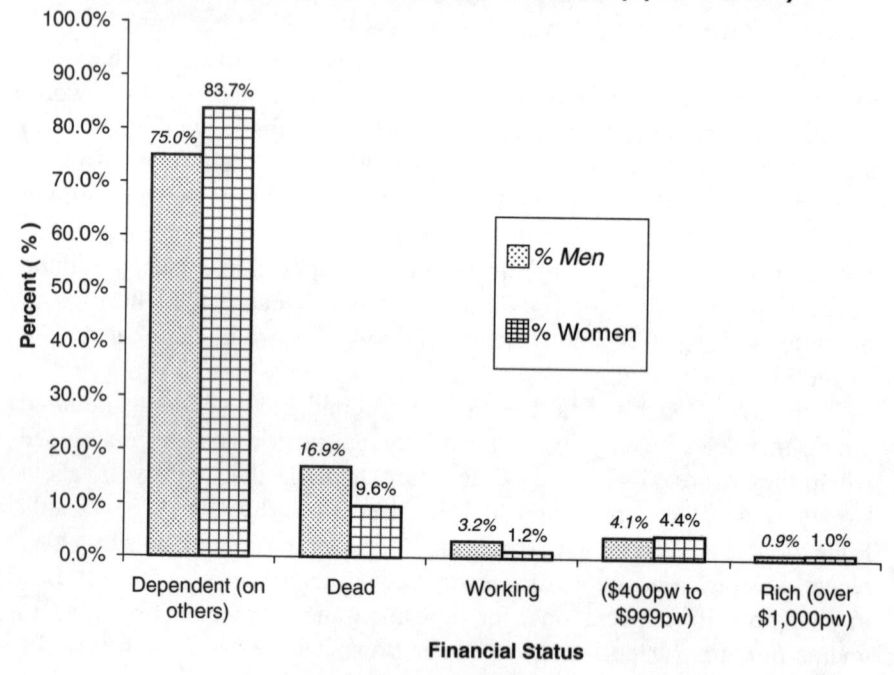

Financial Status	% Men	% Women
Dependent (on others)	75.0%	83.7%
Dead	16.9%	9.6%
Working	3.2%	1.2%
($400pw to $999pw)	4.1%	4.4%
Rich (over $1,000pw)	0.9%	1.0%

Source: Australian Bureau of Statistics

This graph may be the most important that you will ever see in your life.

As this dilemma is so pronounced (and likely to get worse, unless individual Australians do something about it) it is worthy of closer analysis. The key figures that underlie this graph are:

1) Only one in a hundred people over sixty-five earn more than $1,000 per week before-tax (ie. less than $700 a week after tax);

2) Women are far more likely to reach sixty-five years of age. They also are much more likely to live at least five years longer than men. Women are, on average, expected to live twenty years or more in

WHAT MAKES BUILDING RICHES IMPORTANT?

retirement (and this is increasing. Some will live for forty more years);

3) It is even more critical than ever before, that women take a much more active role in their family's financial planning;

4) Of those people working past the age of sixty-five, 73.9% are men and 26.1% are women (*Source: Australian Bureau of Statistics, 1995-96*). Again this makes it even more critical for women to start their financial plans as early as possible;

5) Five people in one hundred, of retirement age, can support themselves without needing to work (based on the assumption that $400 per week is a minimum required for a reasonable standard of living);

6) A staggering 75% of men and 84% of women, who make it to sixty-five, are dependent on others, or are forced to live a very modest life (up to $399 per week before-tax) for up to one third or more of their adult lives.

How Much Money will You Need to Be Able to Support Yourself in Retirement?

What would you do in the event that the government is unwilling, or unable, to pay the pension, or you wanted to support yourself?

If you were to **calculate a lump-sum, large enough to give you an income to meet your needs in retirement**, you would first need to know the return you would be likely to get on your investments. When most people retire, they will probably want to invest their accumulated riches conservatively and in a variety of ways. Such investments might include real estate (with little or no mortgages), shares, or fixed interest investments. I often allocate a return on such types of investment at 5%.

At that rate, a simple formula you can easily apply, to calculate how much money you require in retirement, is to multiply the annual required income (before-tax) by the number twenty. First decide what your retirement income will be!

For example, if you needed $20,000 per annum before-tax, (which would provide $385 before-tax per week), then the lump-sum you would need to have invested would be: $20,000 × 20 = $400,000. In other words, if you had investments of $400,000 returning 5%, that would produce an income of $20,000 per annum before-tax.

To replace the aged pension (of just under $10,000 per annum, excluding healthcare costs), if that should become necessary, would take an investment of about $200,000.

If you wanted a better standard of living, with, say, a before-tax income of about $600 per week, then you would need a lump-sum of approximately $600,000 (i.e. $30,000 per annum before-tax × 20).

To earn $1,000 per week before-tax (say $50,000 per annum) will require a lump sum of $1,000,000 (i.e. $50,000 × 20). To calculate how much you will need now! Multiply your desired retirement income by 20.

Perhaps what is most important is to realise that it can be done. Even on an average wage, it is possible to build riches, provided you know how to do it. This book supplies that *Knowledge*.

What Do You Need to Be Aware of, when Building Riches in a Changing World?

In order to build riches, it is not enough merely to understand what has happened and what is happening in the Australian environment. We must also look at the pressures and issues Australia will face in the near future, in order that we may combat these problems, overcome them, and build riches in spite of them.

Already, we have looked at projected population figures, life expectancy ~ including the likely impact of Baby Boomers reaching retirement age ~ and income for employed and retired people.

Other factors particularly important to note relate to unemployment and education.

Unemployment

Unemployment rates change in economies, as a result of the normal cycles within which businesses operate. With major companies now operating globally, rather than just nationally, there is greater employment instability in individual countries, especially as companies move their operations to countries where labour is cheap. This increases unemployment in countries where the cost of labour is high, like Australia and those of the European Union (the major countries of Europe).

WHAT MAKES BUILDING RICHES IMPORTANT?

Australia's unemployment rate increased from 4%, in the 1970's, to an average of 9%, during the 1990's. The fact that Australia's rate of unemployment has more than doubled over this period is tragic. When we compare Australia's performance to that of the European Union (EU), we see that the EU has also had a similar poor performance, with unemployment rates increasing from 5%, in the 1970's, to an average of 9.7%, in the 1990's, and escalating to 10% in 2001 (over 11% in 1998).

In the USA, the trend is different. While their unemployment rate was 6.5%, in the 1970's (higher than both Australia and the EU), and increased to 7.5% in the 1980's, in the 1990's it dropped, to 4.4% in 1999, and rose to 5.5% after the terrorist attack. Whether or not the criteria used for measurement of unemployment is similar to ours, the trend is towards a significant reduction in the number of people unemployed.

Japan's unemployment rate was rising slowly from 2%, in the 1970's, to 2.7% in the 1990's. Since the Asian melt-down in mid 1998 it has risen dramatically to 5.5% in 2001. This is 80% of the Australian rate, and only about a half as high as the rate of unemployment in the EU.

Obviously, whatever the Japanese and the USA are doing (albeit very differently) is working better than what we are doing in Australia and Europe. The graph on the next page identifies this alarming trend:

I hear people *ASK: 'Why doesn't the government do something about our high unemployment?'* It does, but not necessarily what is most effective. If we look at unemployment benefits, as a percentage of total government expenditure, in 1991, the USA spent 1.5%, Japan paid out 0.7%, in the UK it was 1.7% and, in Australia, it was a staggering 4% (*Source: United Nations Human Development Report 1997*).

These figures show that the Australian Government pays almost three times as much to the unemployed, as a percentage of government expenditure, as do the USA or the UK, or more than four times as much as is spent by the Japanese Government. Obviously, the Australian Government is doing something, but that something is not working.

Australia's expenditure on labour market programs is also three times that of the USA and in excess of what it is in the UK (*Source: United Nations Human Development Report 1997*). Clearly these programs, also, are not working to produce the desired results.

Unemployment is a very emotional issue, particularly for those who are unemployed, or who have family or friends who are unemployed. Tragically, this includes far too many Australians. Many politicians, who still don't do much about it, use unemployment as a political football for a

UNEMPLOYMENT RATES SINCE THE 1970s

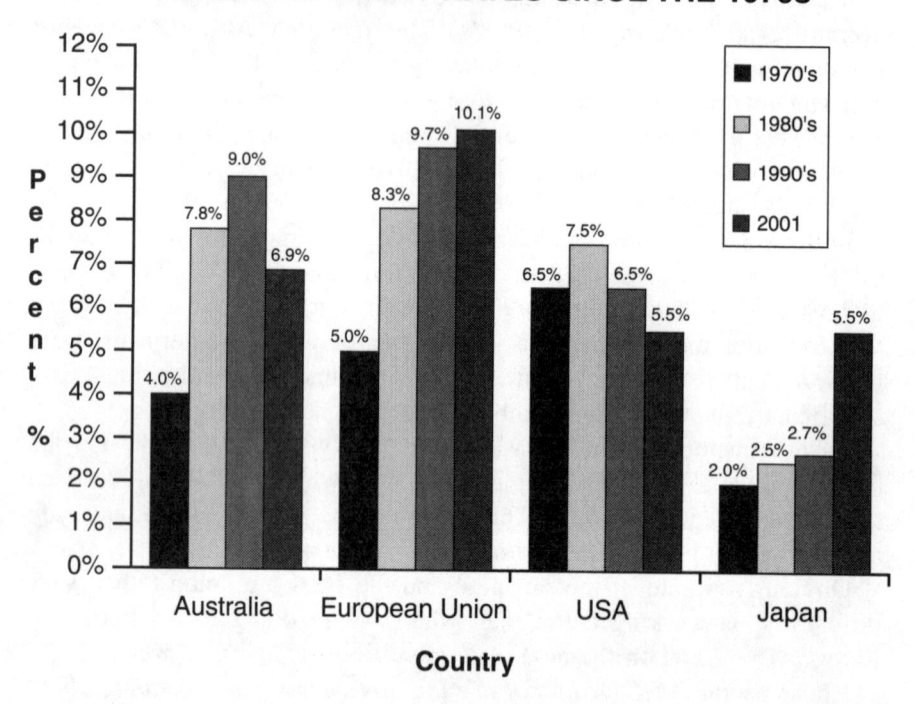

Country	1970's	1980's	1990's	2001
Australia	4.0%	7.8%	9.0%	6.9%
European Union	5.0%	8.3%	9.7%	10.1%
USA	6.5%	7.5%	6.5%	5.5%
Japan	2.0%	2.5%	2.7%	5.5%

Sources: United Nations 'Human Development Report 1999', ABS annual average unemployment figure for 1998–99

lot of rhetoric. Many of the world's top economists have looked at the reasons for the failure of the European Labour System and reasons why the USA's system appears to be working far more effectively. An excellent article on this topic, titled *The Politics of Unemployment*, was published in *The Economist Magazine, April 5, 1997* (English publication).

According to this article: 'if Europeans (and Australians) want to create more jobs, they will have to change the laws and habits that make it expensive to employ people.' The article goes on to say that, 'back in the days of full employment, the elements of the "caring" European system ~ minimum wages, job protection, generous sickness and unemployment benefits ~ were designed to help the working poor. Today, such policies just help the working. The poor are out of a job.'

World-wide, the trend looks even bleaker. Although birth rates are decreasing in Western countries (0.8 per Australian family), they are increasing alarmingly in poorer and developing countries (about four children per family). The United Nations International Labour Organisation (ILO) figures showed that 820 million people were either unemployed, or under employed, in 1993-1994. The ILO said this was the worst result since the Great Depression of the 1930's, then predicted that almost one billion people, or one in three workers throughout the world, would be unemployed, or under-employed, just one year later, in 1995. Commenting on high European unemployment figures, the ILO noted that, tragically, approximately a third of these people were less than twenty-five years of age. These are the same people who will need to be taxed heavily in coming years to support the Baby Boomers in their retirement.

The world's population is increasing at an alarming rate. Twenty-seven people are born every 10 seconds. Our population is set to increase from six billion to over eleven billion by 2050, as reported in issue 4 of the Time Magazine in October 1998.

Education:

Between 1992 and 1995, 7.6% of Australian Government expenditure was on education. Australia compared only reasonably with most other countries for the same period. Our performance was being outclassed by more than a dozen other countries. New Zealand spent twice as much. Israel, Ireland and Iceland came close to doubling Australia's expenditure on education, with Nordic countries spending about 50% more than we did as a percentage of GDP (*Source: United nations Human Development Report 1998*).

Most people are aware that, in recent years, government spending on education has been even further reduced in Australia. Many including myself find such cutbacks very short sighted with almost one in four young Australians (in many areas) unemployed, we need to force Australian governments to better educate our young and equip them with skills for the future. However, I believe we need, also, to take into account another factor:

The Information Age

The world is now often referred to as a *Global Village*. A major reason for this is that information can be transferred throughout the world faster than the speed of sound, not only by telephone lines, computers and facsimile machines but, also, through fibre optics and satellites. Add to this the invention of mobile telephones, personal computers (PCs) and the Internet. A person can be on holiday in Fiji, or floating down the Amazon River, and still be able to access information from their office, any major news studio in the world, the stock exchange or, via the Internet, tens of thousands of other information sources.

This **proliferation of information**, and its efficient distribution, has led to a doubling of information, on the planet every three to four years.

One of the by-products of this Information Age is the ability of major corporations in the Western world to diversify their manufacturing into overseas countries that have low wage structures. The media has been particularly critical of large companies who do this, establishing themselves as multinationals, operating from whichever country is the most cost effective. In Australia, for example, BHP, an Australian-based company, has come under sharp criticism from the Australian media, particularly the Australian Broadcasting Commission (ABC), for a number of its foreign and domestic investment decisions. In particular, BHP has received criticism for its overseas investments in the Ok Tedi Mine (one of the largest tin mines in the world) in Papua New Guinea, and the disposal of its waste. Implied in that criticism is that no company would have been allowed, in this country, to dispose of waste in that way. BHP has also been criticised for opening many factories and plants for the production of steel-related products in China and other Third World countries (in order to take advantage of cheap labour), while, in Australia, it is going to close the Newcastle Steel Works.

Throughout the world, large companies (listed on the share market) make similar investment decisions daily. One company that has come under scrutiny recently in the USA, is Nike. Nike has opened factories, using cheap labour, for the production of a large proportion of its shoes, and soccer balls. These products are being made in countries such as China and India, where the company pays its workers about $5 per day. Some workers sleep on the factory floors, while Nike makes over a hundred million dollars of profit a year.

Now, the poorest 40% of the world's population is likely to continue to be used as cheap labour, to supply consumer goods for the Western countries. Should our major companies educate the people in the Third World countries where they are currently using this cheap labour? Maybe then, the social cost in those countries may not be as great. The focus of

WHAT MAKES BUILDING RICHES IMPORTANT?

large companies on their *bottom line* and the justification that they cannot spend any extra dollars on educating these people, because they have to make profits for their shareholders, will probably mean that this does not occur. Shareholders can change company policies by investing more with companies who do care about employment and education as well as profits. Although such companies are in a minority, they do exist.

Like it or not, this is part of the change that is already happening, and it is unlikely to stop. In fact, change, and the production of goods in countries that have a cheap labour market, is definitely on the increase. Amongst other things, this means that, as long as Australians continue to buy products from overseas, other Australians will not be employed to make these products.

Such change has many consequences. These include high unemployment in Australia, exploitation of people in Third World countries (over one third of the world's population), rapid deterioration of the planet as a result of pollution from cars, factories and nuclear waste, and the potential eradication of rain forests. Also, there is increasingly an uneven distribution of riches into the hands of a small minority of people. We should be alarmed about future prospects, particularly in Australia.

Change is inevitable.

What matters, I think, is to know how to handle change. You need to be aware of what is happening and to respond in a way that is productive and generative. Rather than being a victim of change, you have to learn how to be the master of change.

As far as unemployment is concerned, you will always be employed if you perform in the top 20% of your trade or profession. In business, the principles are similar ~ to succeed in today's world, and maintain that success into the future, you need to be amongst the best at whatever you do, to be adding value to your employer and to continue to invest in your own skills.

For this, you need education. This is one critical area where, I believe, our elected governments can, and should, change their priorities, to provide significantly more education, particularly for our young Australians. Not so long ago, perhaps in the days of our parents, people could expect to take on a job and stay in it, or at least embark on a career, for life. Times have already changed. These days, it is taken for granted that people will probably need to be retrained at least three times throughout their working lives. Everyone needs to continue to get better or risk being left behind.

In that environment, education is a critical factor. If the government doesn't provide it, you need to make sure you can provide it for yourself. All of us are going to need to learn things that aren't even known yet, if we are to succeed in the 21st Century.

The world faces many problems, as we move into the Information Age.

The fact that you have invested the money to buy this book, and the time to read it, indicates that you are in the top percentage of our population who invest in their continuing excellence. I encourage you to continue your investment in yourself and your continuing education, by learning and applying the ideas in books like this one to build your riches.

Australia appears to be under siege, from many problems, including those just discussed. Despite relatively high incomes in Australia (while people are working full-time), our rate of home-ownership is decreasing, our relative educational excellence is decreasing, and our efforts to decrease the rate of unemployment (particularly for the long-term unemployed and the young) are failing, in comparison to America and Japan. Even worse, 95% of Australians are incapable of supporting themselves in the last twenty to thirty years of their lives. Many could be discouraged by the above facts. Indeed, if you read the newspapers and watch television, you will face a continual bombardment of negative facts, figures and stories.

Despite all of the negativity and problems that Australia faces, however, I still believe that Australia is the greatest country on Earth, and now is the easiest time that we will face to build riches for our families and ourselves.

In summary, these are some of the challenges that Western countries need to confront:

1) People and governments spend more than they earn. This creates a major debt to be repaid later by future generations and governments. The money has to come from somewhere. Generally, governments slowly reduce expenditure in the areas they can influence most easily, these being health, education, welfare and pensions for the elderly;

2) Increasing life expectancy, combined with the Baby Boomer crisis, means a huge problem for those who are going to retire in the first

WHAT MAKES BUILDING RICHES IMPORTANT?

forty years of the 21st Century. The day of reckoning, and the erosion, or elimination, of the old age pension, is imminent;

3) As more than 90% of people aged over sixty-five cannot support themselves now, the problem is likely to reach a crisis point;

4) The cost to society, in terms of unemployment, loss of health, increasing violence and other social problems, leaves a legacy for future generations ~ the young people of today (our children) ~ those generations that will follow those of us who are the Baby Boomers;

5) An increasing, older population, with no money, but plenty of time, creates a problem for the last ten to forty years of life, for all but a relatively small percentage of people, who will become rich.

Fortunately, there has never been an easier time to build riches.

The impact that people who answer the challenge to become rich, can make, for themselves and on others, will be tremendous. Ideally, this chapter has provided you with a factual understanding that it is critical to concentrate and make wise decisions, if you are to build riches and become one of the small percentage of people who will not be a burden on society.

Increasing numbers of people are learning *How to Build Riches*. For those who apply the information given here, the future is exciting. For those who answer the challenge to build riches, there are more opportunities for health preservation and quality of life, than ever before.

The Goods and Services Tax ('GST') and corresponding drop in taxation rates, provides great opportunities. The reduction in Capital Gains Tax ('CGT') also provides tremendous incentive for people like you and I to ethically build a fortune.

Currently, only about 1% of people finish their working lives rich, and less than 5% of the remainder can support themselves well, after age sixty-five. What does this 6% of the population do differently?

You may *ASK: 'If I do what the rich do, and follow through on it, will I also become rich?'* Now is the time to find out . . .

2

What KNOWLEDGE Do You Need to Build Riches?

WHAT KNOWLEDGE DO YOU NEED TO BUILD RICHES?

'Knowledge itself is power.'
~ **Francis Bacon.**

Congratulations. *If you are reading this book right now*, then you are one of the few people in our population who seek out specialist *Knowledge* on how to make their lives even better and then follow through on it. Many people want to become rich. Most want their lives to get better. Very few of them follow through on their dreams.

Like you, I've invested my time and money in gaining specialist *Knowledge* and the experience of **How to Build Riches**. I'm committed to giving you the *Knowledge* and principles that will assist you to build riches for yourself.

As discussed in the first section of this book, we live in one of the richest countries in the world. Despite this, only about 4% of our population are able to support themselves with a satisfying lifestyle when they stop working. With the *Baby Boomer Crisis* looming, this situation is expected to get even worse. It has become imperative that we find out what we need to know to provide security and financial freedom for ourselves and those we love.

The *Knowledge* contained in the coming chapters is critical to your ability to build greater riches in your life. **I strongly urge you to read all of this book before you take major *Action* towards achieving your financial goals.**

The reason I make this statement is that on many occasions I have seen people get tremendously motivated based on only some of the information that is contained in this book. They have raced off in a hugely excited state and committed to an investment (often being taken advantage of by a fast-talking salesman), only to learn later that they could have built greater riches had they applied the rest of the material covered in this book.

HOW TO BUILD RICHES

On dozens of occasions, I have seen this happen to people who could have made hundreds of thousands of dollars more money, if they had calmed down and taken more considered Action.

Provided in this book is the *Knowledge* that you can use to make yourself rich. Once you have acquired the *Knowledge*, the next step is to learn how to apply that *Knowledge* to a *Strategy* that you tailor-make for your circumstances and goals. This approach may save you many thousands of dollars in taxes and consultancy fees, as well as provide better protection for your assets, for yourself and your family, in the coming years.

Temper your enthusiasm for the *Knowledge* that will make you rich, with the wisdom of developing a specific *Strategy* to achieve your goals. Take *Action* on this *Strategy*, once you have learned about the other material covered in this book, and you will dramatically increase the riches in your life.

The three main sections of *Knowledge* that will make you rich are:

1) Assessing your current financial position and knowing how to start building riches;

2) Comparing alternative investments;

3) Investing prudently.

The first step towards riches is to know ...

Chapter 2

HOW DO YOU ASSESS YOUR CURRENT FINANCIAL POSITION AND START BUILDING RICHES?

'If money is your hope for independence you will never have it. The only real security that a man can have in this world is a reserve of knowledge, experience and ability.'
~ **Henry Ford.**

The first step towards building riches is to get an accurate understanding of where you are currently spending your income (your current Spending Plan) and what your current **Statement of Assets** and **Liabilities** (debts) is.

Many people have started from a position of having no money to build their fortunes. Some of Australia's richest families, including the Smorgan family (assumed to be worth over $1 billion), Harry Triguboff (also assumed to be worth over $1 billion), Kerry Stokes (assumed to be worth about $700 million), all started with virtually no assets. Bill Gates and Warren Buffet, the two richest people in the USA (with Bill Gates over $150 billion and Warren Buffet over $60 billion Australian dollars), both started with no financial assistance from their families and have amassed their fortunes in their lifetimes. A little over ten years ago, I had more debts than I had assets. Using the information contained in this book, I have been able to accumulate many millions of dollars of profit for my investors and myself and employ, directly and indirectly, hundreds of other people, while I became rich myself. No matter what your financial position is now, if you combine it with ambition, desire and the principles covered in this book, and you continue to follow through on your plan, you will build riches in your lifetime.

Where Does Your Money Currently Go?

Let us first look at how taxation and compulsory superannuation effect money paid to us as individuals. Did you know?;

1) Most people pay about one third of their lifetime earnings in taxation;

2) Including superannuation, about one half of many people's wages are not used to build as many riches as they could;

3) Our laws give us the legal right to arrange our affairs in a way that minimises the taxes we pay;

4) The **superannuation guarantee charge (SGC)** will raise more money in coming years than our stock exchange has raised throughout this whole century.

Superannuation

Compulsory superannuation ~ the SGC ~ has been in place since 1992 and employers are responsible for paying a minimum percentage, above each person's wage, into a superannuation fund that complies with government requirements. That percentage based on your salary is as follows:

Taxation Year dated	**% Salary paid over and above salary, into Superannuation**
1 July 1999 – 30 June 2000	7%
1 July 2000 – 30 June 2001	8%
1 July 2001 – 30 June 2002	8%
After 1 July 2002	9%

From 1992 to 1999, the SGC rate was between 3% and 7% of your salary.

In later chapters, you will learn how to make this money work harder to make you richer.

HOW DO YOU ASSESS YOUR CURRENT FINANCIAL POSITION AND START BUILDING RICHES?

Income Tax

Wage-earning taxpayers pay most of the tax in this country. Tax on wage earners raises about two-thirds of all tax revenue. Tax on companies, and all other revenue-raising initiatives by the government, raises only half as much money as the taxes paid by ordinary Australians. Taxation is needed to provide for education, health, police, defence and a range of other services most people take for granted. We all need to pay some tax in order to enjoy the standard of living we have in this country.

With the lowering of tax rates on companies and the introduction of the consumption based **Goods and Services Tax (GST)**, ordinary taxpayers will continue to pay most of the taxes in Australia. The GST will be received by State Governments. Individuals will have greater chances to build riches after the GST, but only if they invest wisely.

Is it patriotic to pay too much tax?

Enshrined in the legal system and court rulings throughout the English-speaking world is the legal right that says: **Taxpayers can arrange their affairs in a manner that reduces the taxation they pay**.

I believe that governments, generally, want the best for our people and that government employees, generally, want to assist our country. Unfortunately, for a variety of reasons (that would fill several books, and that I will not elaborate on here), governments are *much* more inefficient than individuals working for themselves. It follows that you can use your income (and particularly some of the income you are currently losing in tax) in a way that can stimulate the economy, and assist society, much more efficiently than the government can. Our society will become strongest, in my opinion, when more Australians take responsibility for ethically directing all of their income in ways that stimulate the economy and provide employment, housing, education and hope for those in our society who can, and want to, do more with their lives.

Income tax on individuals is charged on what is termed **marginal taxation rates**. The more money you earn, the more you are taxed. On top of the tax you pay, you also pay another 1.5% of your taxable salary as a **Medicare levy**. The Medicare levy goes to the government to pay for contributions towards health costs (whether you use them or not). Taxpayers who have a taxable income of over $50,000 per year, and do not have private health insurance, are charged an additional 1.0% Medicare levy (totalling 2.5%) whether they need this insurance or not.

HOW TO BUILD RICHES

The taxation rates in Australia for individuals and partnerships are set to change significantly from 1st July, 2000.

The **Goods and Services Tax ('GST')** (often called a 'Consumption Tax') has been a cause of concern for many people despite the fact that most of the countries with whom we trade already have it (including the USA, Germany, the United Kingdom, New Zealand, etc.). The Howard Liberal government was re-elected in 2001 after they introduced a Consumption Tax. The personal taxation rates after the introduction of the GST (proposed at 10%) from 1 July 2000 are:

TAXATION RATES AFTER THE GST

Taxable income (column 1)	Tax on column 1	% on Excess (marginal rates)
$ 6,000	Nil	17%
$20,000	$ 2,380	30%
$50,000	$11,380	42%
$60,000	$15,580	47%

The Medicare levy (of 1.5%) must be added to this tax as detailed above.

Although we will all pay a GST when we buy goods and services, there will be a reduction in a range of taxes that we currently pay (that most people are unaware of) i.e. wholesale sales taxes and other taxes.

The net effect of the new personal taxation rates will be that there will be an incentive for people to increase their taxable income due to the fact that the marginal tax rates are lower.

Let us create, as an example, a husband and wife. One of them earns $36,000 and the other earns $20,400 (including all overtime and annual bonuses and after all allowable tax deductions) in the year starting on 1st July, 2001 (i.e. after the GST). Their taxation and superannuation contributions are calculated on the following page.

Please complete your own personal figures in the last column of the graph above. Your last year's taxation return should give you enough information to figure this out for yourself, at least approximately.

First take your gross income figure. Then estimate the gross amount of SGC that is paid by your employer (7%, 8% or 9% as shown in the table on page 52). This is the amount, over and above your salary, that must

HOW DO YOU ASSESS YOUR CURRENT FINANCIAL POSITION AND START BUILDING RICHES?

TAX & SUPER RATES AFTER GST IN JULY 2000

	Spouse 1	Spouse 2	Your Figures
SGC paid by Employer *over and above* Gross Salary at 8% (in 2000–01)	$1,632.00	$2,880.00	
Pre-Tax Income (after allowable deductions)	$20,400.00	$36,000.00	
Less: Tax Payable			
Tax on First $6,000	$0.00	$0.00	
Tax on $6,000 to $20,400	($2,500.00)		
Tax on $6,000 to $20,000		($2,380.00)	
Tax on $20,000 to $36,000		($4,800.00)	
Tax above $36,000			
Sub Total	($2,500.00)	($7,180.00)	
Less: Medicare Levy on $20,400	($306.00)		
Less: Medicare Levy on $36,000		($540.00)	
TAX PAYABLE	($2,806.00)	($7,720.00)	
AFTER-TAX INCOME (NET)	**$17,594.00**	**$28,280.00**	

be paid each year into a superannuation fund on your behalf. Your SGC contributions do have tax taken out (currently at a rate of 15%), but, most important for you to know, is that **this is your money and it is part of the total income you have available to invest to build riches**, now.

Next, start with the gross figure again and, this time, work out the tax payable and, thus, your net income. (For this you can insert your figures in the spaces provided in the table on the next page).

If your employer pays you a net wage, then, the amount of tax deducted (weekly/monthly) is likely to be greater than is required over a full year. In that case, you will get the difference back as a tax refund at the end of the year.

What is the effect of the GST on this couple? The one who earned $20,000 per annum was taxed at about 34% marginal tax rate before the GST but will only be taxed at 30% after a Consumption tax. The other spouse on $36,000 before the GST was about to enter the 47% marginal tax rate but will only be taxed at 30% after the GST. This person could ambitiously increase his or her income to $50,000 and still pay the same marginal tax as is paid now. This will provide incentive for all Australians earning less than $60,000 per annum to ambitiously increase their taxable income. If all Australians do this, our production and riches as a country will be dramatically improved.

For now, what is useful is for you to have at least an approximate idea of your personal figures for your:

SCG   contribution p.a.
Gross salary p.a.
Tax   payable p.a.
Net   salary

In following chapters, we'll explore how you can use this money wisely to build your riches.

Chapter 3

WHAT IS A PERSONAL SPENDING PLAN?

'He is rich whose income is more than his expenses; and he is poor whose expenses exceed his income.'
~ **Jean de La Bruyere.**

Accountants call them budgets. Banks call them **Statements of Income and Expenditure**. What it takes to start and continue your riches building is to earn more than you spend. You can do this by earning more, or spending less, or a combination of the two approaches. All successful companies, governments and rich people use budgeting to stay in business. Your spending plan will determine your ultimate success.

Tragically, most people take better care when spending their employer's or their business's money than they do when spending their own hard-earned cash. Most people only ever consider their net take-home pay, and not their gross salary, before taxes, or their superannuation payments. In this, and the next chapter, you will learn how to use all of your income to maximum effect for building your riches.

If you have ever borrowed money, or applied for a credit card, you will have filled out a bank application, which will have detailed some of the information you need in order to understand how to start your riches growing. It may, initially, take the investment of some of your time to organise your spending plan over the coming months. However, I can assure you the long-term riches and benefits will be there for you, once you do it. If you can make yourself a millionaire by controlling your expenditure (and redirecting it to investments that will make you rich), will you do it? Of course you will, or you probably wouldn't be reading this book right now. Read this section to get an understanding of how it works, and start controlling your spending as soon as possible. Then you will have money available to invest wisely, once you have completed reading this book.

How Do You Create a Spending Plan?

The process of freeing up money to make you rich is often easier than it seems. A simple way to monitor and accumulate your monthly expenditure and income into categories, is to buy a ruled **Cash Payments Journal** from a newsagent, or stationer. It will come with vertical lines, or you can draw them in yourself. An example of how to set it out follows on the next page. Each item of expenditure is written in with a corresponding column for the amount and you also write the amount again, on the right, in the Total column. At the end of each month you simply add up each column and the sum of all those columns, added together, should equal the sum of the Total column on the right. This gives you your Monthly Total. Appendix 1 has an annual spending plan for your use. You can copy Appendix 1 or create your own form. It will be easier if you enlarge it to A3 size. You can start this process at the beginning of next month.

If your figures do not balance, you need to check that each figure is recorded correctly and then add it up again until it works, or have someone else check it! Like anything else, the more you do it the better you will become at doing it.

Once people have an accurate record of their spending, most people realise that they are spending a lot more in a few categories than they expected. For example, someone might actually be spending $150 a month on entertainment, when they thought they only spent $100 a month. Later in this book you will discover that this extra $50 after-tax per month, wisely invested, has the potential to make you a millionaire, once you have enough assets and income to invest this extra $50 per month for maximum growth.

Do you know exactly where you are spending all your money now? If you are like most people, then you probably don't know where your money is going. An estimate of your current spending pattern is a good place to begin. Over time, you will become more aware of where you spend your money and make the adjustments to achieve your riches plan.

WHAT IS A PERSONAL SPENDING PLAN?

MONTHLY SPENDING PLAN

Date Month Year

Sep	XX	Details	Mortgage/Rent	Food	Children's Expenses	Car(s)	Entertainment	Insurance	etc.	Balance
1	Sept	XX	Shopping		$85.23						$85.23
2	Sept	XX	Children's pocket money			$40.00					$40.00
6	Sept	XX	Petrol				$20.00				$20.00
9	Sept	XX	Dinner & Wine					$62.00			$62.00
14	Sept	XX	Car Insurance						$190.20		
"	"	"									
"	"	"	etc....							etc....	
"	"	"									
"	"	"									
30	Sept	"	Mortgage payment	$1,000.00							$1,000.00
Total	Sept	XX		A	B	C	D	E	F	...	Monthly total

59

HOW TO BUILD RICHES

Appendix 1 has a summary Statement of Income and Expenditure report for you to use if you wish. You can copy these two pages (in their entirety) and use them for your own personal use later. If you use the one in the Appendix, fill it in with pencil, then you can change any figures when you have a more accurate record of your spending patterns. You also may wish to redesign this form to suit your circumstances. A great place to keep this financial information is in a bound journal so you can come back to it at a later date and check your progress.

Your aim is to end up with a monthly surplus. To build riches you need to generate more monthly income than monthly expenditure, so you generate an *available monthly surplus*. How you invest this monthly surplus will depend upon your existing Assets and Liabilities (debts) and how you change those, in order to build riches faster, to achieve your financial goals.

Begin now! A simple way to commence building riches is to take 10% of your after-tax salary and treat it as investment capital. Then, invest this money and handle your expenses out of what is left. Later, I will explore with you different types of investment alternatives to which you might apply this 10% of your income, to generate maximum riches. The very first step, however, requires that you adjust your spending plan to allow you to spend no more than 90% of your net income. The remaining 10% is used to build your riches. The next step is to understand ...

Chapter 4

WHAT ARE YOUR CURRENT FINANCIAL RICHES?

'Economy is in itself a source of great revenue.'
~ **Seneca.**

Do you have an accurate Knowledge of your Assets and Liabilities? Getting rich faster, means wisely using what you currently have.

A Statement of Assets and Liabilities follows on the next page. You can complete this now, or at a later date. In order to chart your financial and personal accomplishments on your path to riches, I encourage you to buy a bound journal from a newsagent. Call this your **Riches Journal**. Use it to record any thoughts or insights, as well as your financial position along the way. This will allow you to easily see your progress. Many of the most successful people who ever lived, kept journals. Because this is so critical, I have allocated pages 371–380 of this book for your *'PERSONAL RICHES JOURNAL'*. Please begin the process of using a journal for yourself while you read this book. As you become more aware of your goals, *Strategies* and *Action* plans, write them down in the space provided. Later, you may transfer your insights into your own special purpose Riches Journal.

The table on the next page has certain sub-headings for both liabilities (in the form of loans) and assets.

Assets

Your assets are divided into four categories, these being consumer assets, security assets, business assets and investment assets. So what do these types of assets really mean to you in your desire to build riches?

HOW TO BUILD RICHES

STATEMENT OF ASSETS & LIABILITIES

Date / /

LIABILITIES OWING $		PRESENT VALUE $	
Consumer Loans		**Consumer Assets**	
Personal Loans		Furniture/Effects	
Credit Cards Limit $		Motor Vehicles	
Tax Outstanding		Boats, Jet Skis, Toys, etc.	
Other Consumer Loans		Other Consumer Assets	
Total Consumer Loans (1)		Total Consumer Assets (3)	
Security Loans		**Security Assets**	
Home Mortgage		Family Home	
Other Home Mortgages		Bank Accounts	
Other Security Loans		Other Bank Deposits	
Business Loans		**Business Assets**	
Overdraft		Equipment	
Secured Lines of Credit		Stock	
All Other Business Loans		Goodwill	
		All Other Assets (cars, etc.)	
Investment Loans		**Investment Assets**	
Investment Property Loans		Investment Properties	
Other Investment Loans		Shares	
Share Loans		Superannuation	
		Other Investment Assets	
Total Other Loans (2)		Total Other Assets (4)	
Total Loans (1) + (2)		Total Assets (3) + (4)	
		Less: Total Loans (1) + (2)	
		Net Assets	

WHAT ARE YOUR CURRENT FINANCIAL RICHES?

What are Consumer Assets?
Consumer assets are, basically, assets that take money out of your pocket. Broadly speaking, these are items like furniture, boats and motor bikes, that cost you money to buy and maintain. Motor vehicles for personal use cost money that is not tax deductible, to purchase and maintain. You may use your motor vehicle primarily for business purposes, in which case you may choose to put it, or a percentage of its value, under the category of business assets. Many people drive expensive motor vehicles and their justification for doing so is to impress their clients. I know several self-made millionaires, who drive older model vehicles yet are still able to impress their clients, without needing to have a luxury car. If you are a real estate agent or a salesman who escorts people in your motor vehicle, you may well need a reliable, recent model car. Later in this chapter you will discover, in an example I use, that one couple who bought a brand new vehicle, really lost out. They lost over $100,000 worth of potential interest savings by driving a new car, (which meant spending a fixed amount per month), instead of concentrating on reducing their security loan on their home.

What are Security Assets?
Security assets are those assets that provide you with the security on which to build future riches. In this category I put bank accounts and cash management accounts, because the cash in these accounts can be used to build riches when properly invested. An asset like the family home costs money until the mortgage is paid out, and then saves you rent from that date. A home also gives security for your family as well as being an asset you can use as security to build substantial riches. It has often been said that owning your own home free and clear is the '**Great Australian Dream**'. Owning your own home, free and clear, is a great investment and can be an excellent place from which to start building riches.

What are Business Assets?
Business assets are those assets that provide you with a means of earning wages and profits. Ideally, your business assets should put money into your pocket in the form of these wages and profits.

What are Investment Assets?
Investment assets put money into your pocket, by providing income and capital growth (i.e. the investment asset should increase in value).

Investment assets are those assets that you should concentrate on to build your riches. Once your investment assets are substantial enough to provide you with an income stream, in the form of rents, dividends and other income that is sufficient to fund your lifestyle, you no longer have to work for anyone else. As well as providing income, the growth of the capital value (what you can sell your investment assets for) allows you to sell some of these investment assets at a later date to derive a profit. This can be spent or reinvested as your needs and wants arise.

Liabilities

Liabilities have also been divided into four categories, these being consumer loans, security loans, business loans and investment loans. Let us look at each of these categories.

What are Consumer Loans?

Consumer loans take money out of your pocket. Worse than costing you money is the fact that consumer loans are not tax-deductible, and therefore cost you much more money than just the interest you pay on them. Many people borrow to buy themselves consumer assets as a reward for something they have recently done, or as a means of gaining some pleasure in the future. Consumer loans can give you short-term pleasure at a huge long-term cost! You will discover the real cost of consumer debt in the next chapter, in an example that shows how expensive consumer loans really can be. Consumer loans often take the form of personal loans and credit cards, etc.

What are Security Loans?

Security loans are loans that allow us to buy security assets. The most common is a home mortgage. The family home is a tremendous asset that provides not only security, but also stability and peace of mind for families and individuals alike.

For many Australians, buying the family home is the biggest initial financial decision that they will make. Few people really consider all of the important areas related to this purchase with as much merit as they deserve. When buying a family home, there is the tendency, for many, to borrow as much money as the bank will lend them. A choice that will lead to amassing riches, is to buy a home that is less expensive than you can afford and pay off this home mortgage sooner. Few people give enough attention to the specific type of home loan they should choose.

WHAT ARE YOUR CURRENT FINANCIAL RICHES?

We will look at an example of the difference this critical decision can make in the next chapter.

What are Business Loans?
Business loans are loans that allow business owners to buy or expand a business. Business loans can be useful, and good, because they allow the business to generate both wages and a profit for the owner. This profit can be invested to generate Investment Assets and riches.

What are Investment Loans?
Borrowing in order to invest can be one of the smartest ways to expand your riches. **Investment loans** are often referred to as '**good debt**', whereas consumer loans are usually referred to as '**bad debt**'. This means that investment loans can make you rich. They have the ability to allow you to buy more investments that will supply income, (in the form of rents and dividends), as well as future capital growth. In comparison, consumer loans are bad as they cost you after-tax money. They usually do not bring you an income and the consumer asset often goes down in value. A major benefit of investment loans is that they are tax deductible. We will explore the exciting world of using other people's savings to make you rich, in coming chapters.

Your aim in building riches is to increase the value and amount of your business and investment assets. The income and capital growth generated by these assets produces an income stream that supports your lifestyle, and frees you to work only on things that interest and inspire you.

Throughout this chapter and the next I will illustrate some of what is possible with consumer assets and security and investment assets. To do this I have created two imaginary couples, whom I will call Peter and Anne Wise and David and Shirley Battler. Both of these couples are exactly the same age and earn exactly the same income in exactly the same professions. Peter and David are both electricians and Anne and Shirley are both hairdressers. These two couples work for different companies and both of these couples were married when Peter and David were aged 25 and Anne and Shirley were aged 20. Both couples bought houses of the same value, in different suburbs, and borrowed the same amount of money to buy their houses. The specific details are covered in Chapter 25.

Peter and Anne Wise purchased a copy of my *Building Riches* audio tape. In these 18 hours of audio tapes, Peter and Anne were exposed to various concepts that reinforced and added to those outlined in this book. They decided to minimise the use of their consumer loans and to eliminate their home mortgage as quickly as possible. They decided to invest in books and audio tapes because they wanted to know the best way to do that and what else was available to them. David and Shirley Battler were encouraged by a friend to buy *Building Riches* and the audio tapes but decided to have a weekend away instead. Besides, they thought they knew all they needed to know in order to look after their own financial affairs.

Let us look at these two couples and the impact certain decisions they made had in the area of consumer, security and investment loans. In coming chapters we will see that the choices the Wise family made, resulted in them becoming rich, while the Battler family remained poor.

How Do You Use Consumer Loans Wisely?

Peter and Anne Wise realised that consumer loans would stop them from building riches as quickly as they wanted. They decided to pay out their credit cards every month by the due date and to only buy consumer assets that they could afford with cash. David and Shirley Battler, on the other hand, made generous use of their credit cards and occasionally didn't pay out the balance for many months. They then only paid the minimum monthly balance (of 5% per month). The Battlers also borrowed to buy other personal use assets, such as motor vehicles and loans for overseas holidays. Both couples had $10,000 on hand, to spend.

Peter and Anne Wise decided to buy two cars between them and bought two late model reliable, second-hand vehicles for $10,000 cash. David and Shirley Battler spent their $10,000 on buying only one second-hand car for Shirley and then having a good time with the balance.

David Battler wanted a new car and he and Shirley decided to buy a brand new van with all the extras! Having spent all of their available cash, David decided to put the whole cost of the new car on a consumer loan in the form of a lease. David leased the car from a dealer (with all on road costs and inclusions) for $28,750. The leasing interest rate was 7.65% for five years with a 30% residual value. What this means is that David drove away in the new car without having to outlay any money, but he had an obligation to pay $460 per month for the next five years (sixty months). At the end of that time, he has to repay $8,625 (30% of the purchase price of $28,750).

Peter Wise bought an older model van (as detailed above), that he kept

WHAT ARE YOUR CURRENT FINANCIAL RICHES?

in good condition. He and Anne decided to use the $460 per month, that a lease on a new vehicle would have cost them, towards their mortgage repayment.

What is the real cost to David and Shirley Battler of deciding to buy and finance this new car? If you look at the after-tax cost, it is very easy to calculate. The after-tax cost is $460 a month for twelve months a year, which equals $5,520 per annum for the next five years. In order to work out the before-tax cost for David's car, we first need to know David's income and his marginal taxation rate. Let us assume that both David and Peter earn $36,000 per annum as a gross salary (before-taxation and compulsory superannuation payments). On page 55, I showed you the superannuation and taxation payments made by a person earning a salary of $36,000. David and Peter's taxation rate for every dollar earned over $20,000 is 31.5% (30% tax and 1.5% Medicare levy as detailed on page 54). The before-tax cost of David's new car is as follows:

$$\text{Before-tax cost per annum on consumer debt (David's new car)} = \frac{\text{Annual after-tax payments}}{(1 - \text{Marginal Tax Rate})}$$

$$\text{Annual before-tax cost} = \frac{\$460 \times 12}{(1 - 31.5\%)}$$

$$= \frac{\$5,520}{0.685} = \$8,058$$

Most people only ever concentrate on what their consumer debt (and other debt for that matter) costs them in after-tax dollars (i.e. the money that comes out of their pockets). I encourage you to start to look at the cost of debt in terms of what it costs you in before-tax dollars. In the example above, David has an obligation to pay $5,520 for the next five years, on his new motor vehicle, in after-tax dollars. In before-tax dollars the real cost of this vehicle is over $8,000 per year.

Throughout this chapter and this book, I will show you how to recognise the importance of eliminating consumer and security loans, combined with increasing investment debt. These habits can make a difference of literally millions of dollars over the course of your working lifetime.

How Do Security Loans Effect You?

Another area of debt that the majority of Australians experience is that of security loans, in the form of a home mortgage. In this example we will assume that Anne Wise and Shirley Battler both earn $20,400 per annum as gross income (before-tax). This salary of $20,400 was also used in an earlier example to calculate the superannuation and taxation that someone on this wage would pay.

In this example we will assume that both couples buy homes that cost $175,000 and both have had to borrow $140,000 from the bank as a home mortgage. This means that each of these couples had $35,000 deposit. They also had additional money, to pay for the loan costs needed to establish the mortgage, and to cover the government and legal costs of purchasing their new real estate. Not all young couples aged twenty-five and twenty have saved enough money to cover a deposit for a home and the associated costs. However, we will assume that both of these couples have just been married and that they have accumulated this amount through their own savings, investments, inheritance and some financial assistance from their respective families. If the parents of the Wises and the Battlers had applied the principles taught in this book, then they would have easily been able to provide financial assistance for their children to buy their first homes.

Many people buying their first house are caught in a dilemma that is called a **deposit gap**. A deposit gap occurs when people, saving money to buy a home, find that by the time they have saved the amount of money (including the fees) to pay the deposit to buy the house that they wanted, house prices may have increased by $10,000 or more. This means that, if the purchasers of the house wanted to put down a 20% deposit, then they would need to have on hand another $2,000 (plus additional costs).

This deposit gap is dramatic in cities like Sydney and Melbourne where the house prices in the better areas are already very expensive (often over $300,000). It is not easy to come up with the deposit for your home if your parents haven't learned and applied the skills of how to build riches for themselves and are, therefore, unable to provide financial assistance to you. (This applies to most people, including myself). To save a home deposit yourself, you will need to apply the principle of your Spending Plan I shared with you in the last chapter. You will also need to continue to put aside 10% of your salary in savings and investments until you have accumulated enough equity to use as a deposit and to pay the costs on a home.

WHAT ARE YOUR CURRENT FINANCIAL RICHES?

If you currently have more loans than you do assets (as was my situation in the past), then it is important not only to save and invest 10% of your current salary, but also to immediately allocate an additional 10% or 20% of your salary towards reducing your other loans. This will more rapidly accumulate your deposit. This will also result in your overall assets increasing and liabilities (loans) decreasing. This then allows your statement of assets and liabilities (that I went through earlier), to grow strong enough to enable you to acquire a bank loan to purchase a home. Discounts on stamp duty and other costs are also of assistance for first home buyers. This is worth checking with your relevant State Government Taxation Office. A $7,000 rebate is offered to first home buyers after 1st July 2000 to assist in offsetting the costs of the GST.

Most people spend a tremendous amount of time deciding which house or apartment they would like for their home. Few, however, spend anywhere near this amount of time choosing the right home loan for purchasing their new home. Over recent months, I have published a series of twenty articles that were shown on Telstra's Big Pond internet home page. These articles are accessible via our own web site '*buildingriches.com.au*'. It is my intention to write another book that complements this one in helping people like you to safely build riches faster. Please register your interest in this book at our web site or by mail.

Australia has been exposed to immense amounts of competition in recent years in the area of home loans. The choice of the right home loan and the discipline of sticking to a spending plan in order to reduce your home loan as quickly as possible, is probably one of the most important financial decisions that you will ever make. In making this decision, most Australians go to their bank manager, or loans officer, and find out how much the lending institution will lend them to buy their house. Once they know how much they can borrow, they will then go and look for a house that they can afford. In the next chapter I will demonstrate what a huge difference it can make to the time taken to repay a home loan, if the home owners choose the right mortgage and have the discipline and the desire to pay out this home mortgage quickly. Before I do that, I would like to point out that the type of home loan detailed in the next chapter will not suit all purchasers, and **I suggest that people seek financial advice from a qualified professional or an independent representative, before selecting or changing their current home mortgage**. In dealing with our many clients, I have been unimpressed by the overly high interest rates they have been charged for inferior loans. The main thing to realise is that there are professionals you can talk to. There are many independent loan brokers who do not charge the borrower for their services. The largest is an organisation called Mortgage Choice, although you will see others in any major phone book or via an internet search.

For many people, paying off their home loan quickly is a major priority. In order to do this faster you will probably want to know ...

Chapter 5

HOW CAN YOU PAY OFF YOUR HOME LOAN IN HALF THE TIME?

*'A single idea, if it is right,
saves us the labour of an infinity of experience.'*
~ **Jacques Maritian.**

You can pay off your home loan in half the time by having the right home loan and the discipline to follow a Spending Plan. The following comparison of the Battler and Wise home loans demonstrates this. David and Shirley Battler went to see their local bank manager and borrowed the $140,000 to buy their family home on a twenty-five year principle and interest home loan. This is the traditional type of home loan and most people (the vast majority of whom don't get rich) use such a home loan to pay off their home mortgage. There is nothing wrong with this type of loan, although there are better types of home loans for certain purchases, if you qualify for them.

David and Shirley Battler decided to arrange their home loan like most Australians. Their income, after the payment of taxation and superannuation, was paid into a bank savings account. This savings account had a chequebook linked to it and, from this savings account, they made payments on a credit card facility that they both had. David and Shirley had arranged with their bank that the monthly mortgage repayment towards their home loan would be deducted automatically from their bank savings account at the end of each month. I have assumed that the average interest rate on the loan that David and Shirley took out was

7.25% over twenty-five years. This means that on a $140,000 loan, the Battlers would make mortgage repayments of $1,007 every month for the next twenty-five years.

The amount of after-tax income left each month, after the bank has taken its monthly mortgage payment out, is then used for living expenses. These include paying David Battler's van lease payment of $460 (mentioned earlier), luxuries and emergency expenses. Following is a diagram that shows how this type of home loan operates.

THE BATTLER FAMILY'S 25 YEAR PRINCIPAL & INTEREST HOME LOAN:

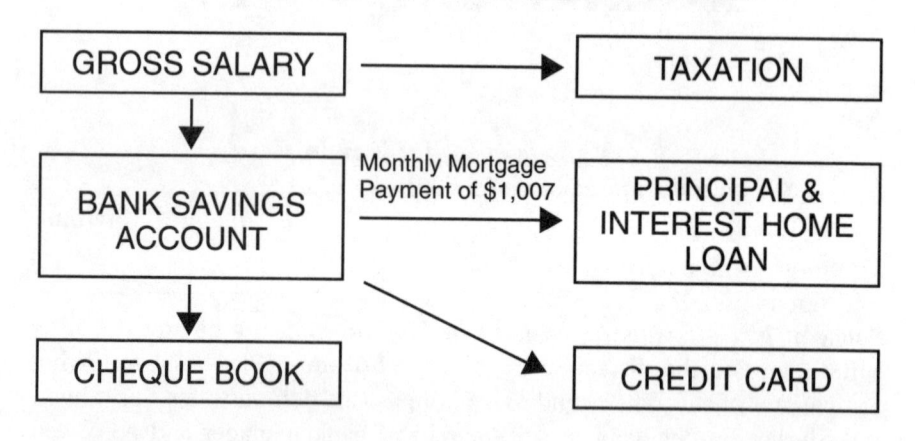

```
GROSS SALARY  ────────────▶  TAXATION
     │
     ▼
                  Monthly Mortgage
BANK SAVINGS      Payment of $1,007    PRINCIPAL &
  ACCOUNT      ────────────▶           INTEREST HOME
     │          ╲                           LOAN
     ▼            ╲
CHEQUE BOOK        ▶  CREDIT CARD
```

There are several problems with the Battler's approach that hamper their likelihood of ever getting rich. One is that when the Battlers have additional amounts of money left over, after paying their mortgage and car payments, it remains sitting in a bank savings account that only earns a small amount of interest, somewhere in the order of 0% to 3.5%. This interest is, in turn, taxed at the Battler's marginal taxation rate.

Another problem, for most people, is that when the bank savings account finally does accumulate to a reasonable amount (if they spend less than they earn), then they tend to spend this money on other consumer assets and luxuries, such as holidays, furniture, clothes, or rewards. The long-term effect of this is that most people with a twenty-five year home loan end up taking the full twenty-five years to repay it. Many of them fail to put their surplus money into investment assets. The resulting consequence is that they have little more than a home and a few consumer assets, after twenty-five years or more of hard work.

HOW CAN YOU PAY OFF YOUR HOME LOAN IN HALF THE TIME?

Peter and Anne Wise, after doing their research, discovered that they had other options and decided that paying off their home loan was a major priority. As they were not spending money on a monthly basis on a car lease, they put all of this saving into their home mortgage payment. Peter and Anne also followed up on information they learned from this book and found that there was a more efficient way to pay off their home loan. They used a consultant to put this home loan in place for them, at no cost to themselves (such consultants are often paid by the banks for bringing home loans to them). This is a smart move on the banks' part because it frequently takes more money in overheads, for banks to advertise and run suburban bank branches, than it does to simply pay a fee to a broker for bringing a new loan application to the bank. Because these brokers do not spend huge amounts on advertising and generally have low overheads, they can pass the savings on to their clients in the form of a lower interest rate on their property loans. Peter and Anne Wise took out a $140,000 home loan in what is called a **line of credit**. So let's see what happens with this type of home loan (mortgage).

This product is offered by many banks and goes under different names including home equity loans and revolving lines of credit. Other lending institutions give this type of home loan their own names, i.e. 'Mortgage Power', or 'Equity Loan', etc.. With this type of home loan, all of Peter and Anne's income was paid directly into their home loan line of credit. This meant that the Wise's home loan reduced by the full amount of their salary, the same day that their salary entered their line of credit account. This **reduced the amount of interest they paid every day that the money remained in the account**. It was only when they drew their living expenses out of the line of credit that they again, increased the amount on which they were paying interest. It is this effect, of saving a little interest every day, that allows this home loan to be repaid so quickly. As a part of this line of credit, there is a facility whereby Peter and Anne Wise can transfer money into their chequebook, to pay monthly living expenses and also to completely pay off their credit card at the end of each month (before any interest is charged). A diagram showing how this operates follows on the next page.

The key to Peter and Anne Wise paying off their home mortgage (line of credit) is the use of their spending plan (as mentioned earlier), in conjunction with the savings on interest on their home loan on a daily basis. Assuming that Peter and Anne stick to their target, and pay all their money into this home loan line of credit, they effectively make a monthly payment of $1,467 off their home loan. They will be able to pay out their home loan sometime during the twelfth year. In comparison David and Shirley Battler have a monthly home loan payment of $1,007 (plus an extra $460 per month car loan). Their home loan will not be paid out until the end of the twenty-fifth year.

THE WISE FAMILY'S
LINE OF CREDIT HOME LOAN:

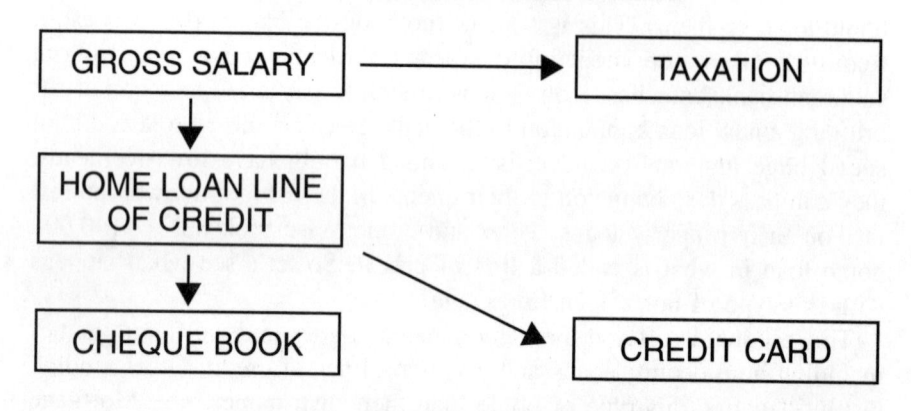

```
┌─────────────────┐         ┌─────────────────┐
│  GROSS SALARY   │────────▶│    TAXATION     │
└─────────────────┘         └─────────────────┘
         │
         ▼
┌─────────────────┐
│ HOME LOAN LINE  │
│   OF CREDIT     │──────┐
└─────────────────┘      │
         │               │
         ▼               ▼
┌─────────────────┐   ┌─────────────────┐
│  CHEQUE BOOK    │   │   CREDIT CARD   │
└─────────────────┘   └─────────────────┘
```

The secret to paying off a home loan in half the time lies in the simple fact that: <u>banks calculate the interest that they charge on a home loan, on a daily basis</u>, regardless of what type of home loan it is. If you understand this key principle, and place as much money into your home loan as possible, then you save interest on a daily basis. The banks have known this for decades. They have made many billions of dollars profit because most Australians take out a twenty-five year home loan, and continue regular monthly or fortnightly payments until the home loan is paid out.

Banks receive deposits in the form of bank savings accounts (like the one shown earlier, into which the Battler Family put their available cash). Banks pay a nominal interest rate (of say 2%) on deposits in these types of accounts and, then, they turn around and lend this same money to people like David and Shirley Battler, to pay for their car lease and for their twenty-five year principle and interest home loan. The banks also lend money to people like the Battlers for credit card purchases, personal loans and other consumer loans. The current interest rate they charge on these other loans is in the order of 6-8% for home loans, 8-10% for leases, 9-12% for personal loans and about an average of 14%-16% for credit cards. These rates will increase as the economic cycle changes (as discussed in Chapter 9).

HOW CAN YOU PAY OFF YOUR HOME LOAN IN HALF THE TIME?

Recently, the banks have experienced intense competition and have been cutting their interest rates for these services. Before this recent competition, banks would have charged higher interest rates for all of these loans. Now, the banks are finding innovative ways of charging additional fees, on all types of loans and services, in order to keep their profits over $1,000,000,000 per annum. This keeps their shareholders happy.

We Australian taxpayers pay for this every time we use a bank's services. The key is not to feel any anger about the banks making enormous profits, but rather, to find ways of using the banks to help you become even richer. I will share some *Strategies* for doing this with you in coming chapters.

Many people understand the principle of paying off their home loan faster, with the most common way being the payment of their home loan on a fortnightly basis. David and Shirley Battler paid approximately $1,000 per month off their home loan (in the above example) as one monthly payment. If they paid $500 per fortnight into their mortgage payment, they would pay, on a yearly basis, $500 × twenty-six fortnights that is $13,000 per annum (instead of twelve monthly payments of $1,000 per month which is $12,000). The effect of making that extra $1,000 payment per year, would reduce their home loan from twenty-five years to about eighteen years and would save them over $60,000 in interest over the life of their home loan. The home loan line of credit Peter and Anne Wise took out, uses this principle, but uses it even more effectively.

Peter and Anne Wise would be able to enjoy exactly the same lifestyle as David and Shirley Battler (apart from the fact that David drove a later model car) and still reduce their home loan from twenty-five years to twelve years. They and you can do this simply by **operating smarter and make your money work harder for you**, by reducing your home loan with every salary payment. In order to demonstrate this, I have summarised the balance of the mortgage owing at the end of each year for both the Wise family and the Battler family on the following page.

After two years of payments, the Wise family's mortgage has reduced to under $124,000 (a reduction of over $16,000 off the mortgage balance) whereas the Battlers will not be able to reduce their mortgage to this level until about the seventh year. By the end of five years, the Wise family's mortgage will be under $95,000 whereas the Battlers will have to wait until the fourteenth year of their mortgage to be at this level.

By the end of year ten, the Wise family will have reduced its mortgage to approximately $30,000, whereas the Battlers will not get to this level

COMPARISON OF A TYPICAL PRINCIPAL & INTEREST MORTGAGE WITH A LINE OF CREDIT HOME LOAN

Mortgage Balance Year Ended	Peter & David's Age	Battler Family 25 Year P & I Mortgage $	Wise Family Line of Credit $
0	25	140,000	140,000
1	26	137,923	132,220
2	27	135,692	123,862
3	28	133,295	114,881
4	29	130,719	105,232
5	30	127,951	94,865
6	31	124,978	83,726
7	32	121,783	71,758
8	33	118,351	58,900
9	34	114,663	45,085
10	35	110,700	30,241
11	36	106,443	14,293
12	**37**	**101,869**	**0**
13	38	96,954	
14	39	91,674	
15	40	86,000	
16	41	79,905	
17	42	73,355	
18	43	66,319	
19	44	58,758	
20	45	50,635	
21	46	41,908	
22	47	32,530	
23	48	22,455	
24	49	11,631	
25	50	0	

HOW CAN YOU PAY OFF YOUR HOME LOAN IN HALF THE TIME?

until somewhere in the twenty-third year of their mortgage. Somewhere in the twelfth year, the Wise family will pay out their mortgage completely, but the Battlers, if they stick to their twenty-five year mortgage (as many Australian families do), will have to wait until the twenty-fifth year when David is fifty years of age, before their loan is paid off.

This effect looks even more dramatic in the form of a graph, which follows. Along the bottom of the graph I've put the age of both Peter and David, starting their mortgage at $140,000, when they are both twenty-five years old, and progressing until both men are fifty, when David Battler will finally pay out his $140,000 home loan.

When Peter Wise is aged thirty-seven, his $140,000 has been paid out, in less than twelve years. The Wise family will have made total repayments to the bank of $208,440, (making the total interest paid on this mortgage $68,440). By the time David Battler is fifty years old, the Battler family will have paid $302,227 into their home loan, representing $162,227 in interest, and the same $140,000 in principal, to the bank. The total saving in interest that the Wise family makes is $93,787. Not only has the Wise family saved itself a tremendous amount of money in after-tax dollars, they also have another thirteen years of paid salary to use in a more tax effective manner, towards building riches for their family.

Another way to look at this is to work out the before-tax cost that the Battler family pays, compared with the Wise family, in making the extra interest payments to the bank over the differing terms of their loans. Over the coming twenty-five years both Peter and David can expect their salaries to rise with inflation. This rise in salary will push them into a higher taxation bracket. For this example, I will use the after GST taxation rates, after 1 July 2000, for incomes between $20,000 and $50,000 per annum, which attracts taxation at the marginal taxation rate of 31.5% (including Medicare levy as detailed in on page 54). Using this taxation rate, the total extra cost that the Battlers paid, by not working smart with their money, is almost $137,000, as shown in the calculation below:

$$\text{Before-tax additional cost of the Battler family mortgage} = \frac{\text{Additional interest paid}}{(1 - \text{Marginal Tax Rate})}$$

$$\text{Total extra before-tax dollars} = \frac{\$93{,}787}{(1 - 31.5\%)}$$

$$\text{Battler's lost before-tax income} = \$136{,}915$$

HOW TO BUILD RICHES

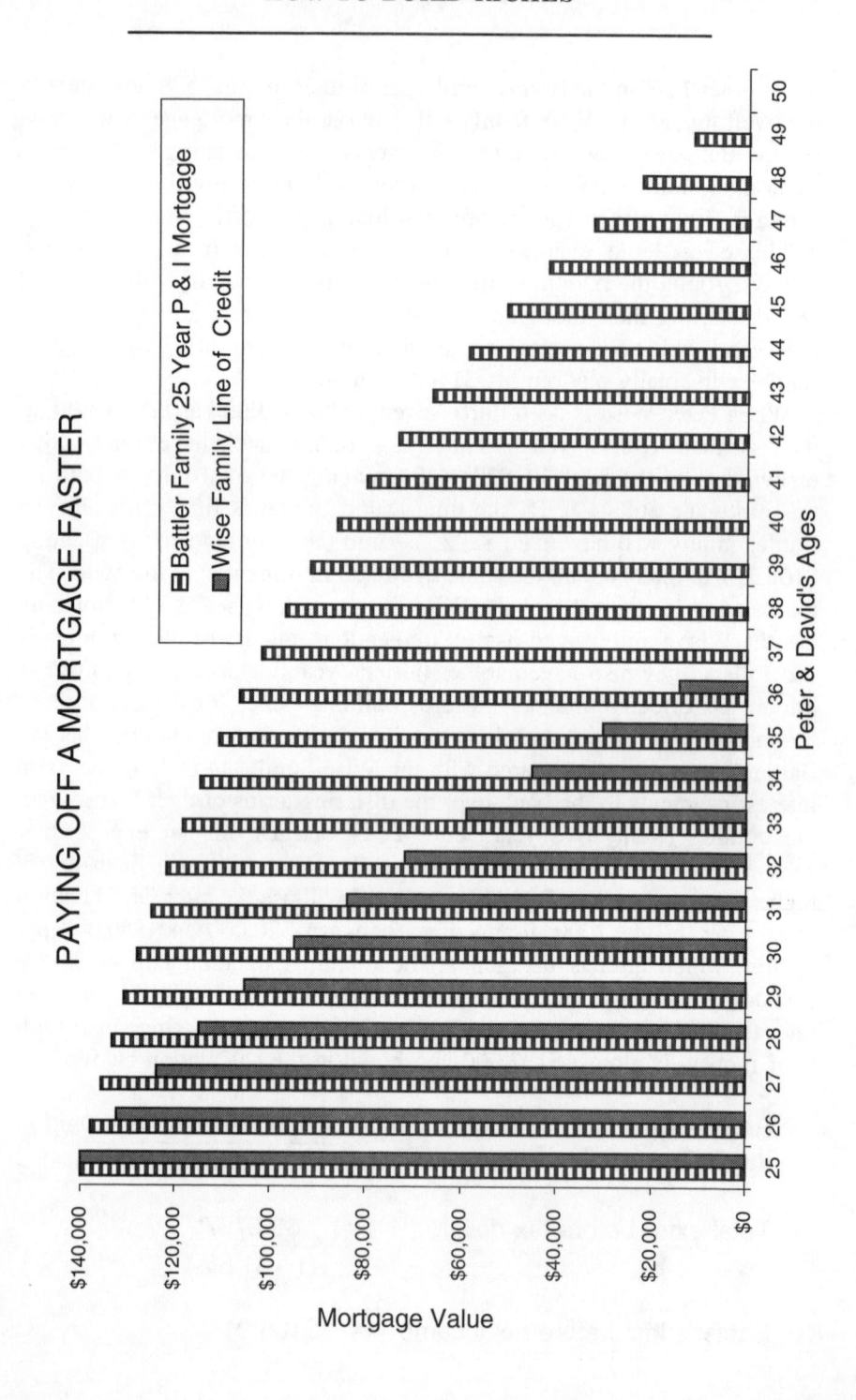

PAYING OFF A MORTGAGE FASTER

Legend:
- Battler Family 25 Year P & I Mortgage
- Wise Family Line of Credit

X-axis: Peter & David's Ages (25–50)
Y-axis: Mortgage Value ($0 – $140,000)

HOW CAN YOU PAY OFF YOUR HOME LOAN IN HALF THE TIME?

The Wise family's saving was almost $137,000. If the Wise couple invest this money carefully, to build riches for their family, this difference can and will amount to an accumulation of several millions of dollars throughout their working lives, as you will discover later in this book.

The GST will have little effect on this example of how to pay out a home loan faster. Interest and bank fees are 'input taxed' under the GST which results in no GST being charged by the lending institution. GST will be charged on legal and accounting advice to do with a loan or taxation advice.

The rich get richer while the poor get poorer. Fortunately, you do not need to start rich in Australia in order to build riches. You can help yourself, your family, and Australia by spending less than you earn, building equity in your home, and then using your home as security to build riches.

Chapter 6

HOW DO LOANS AND TAXES AFFECT YOUR BUSINESS?

'It is in the interest of the community that a man in a competitive business, shall have the incentive to make as much money as he can.'
~ **Louis Dembitz Brandeis.**

Business owners were given a tremendous incentive in September 1999 with the adoption by the Howard government of the report prepared by John Ralph. It gives major reductions in **Capital Gains Tax (CGT)** on the sale of businesses with a net worth of less than $5 million.

Tax laws change regularly. Compromises are also made to get legislation approved and once adopted they can still be changed by subsequent governments. The proposed CGT changes as they relate to investments, is detailed in Chapter 24. For now, I will outline how these changes if adopted will benefit business owners.

What New CGT Relief is Now Available to Business Owners?

After 21st September 1999, the previous fifty percent capital gains tax goodwill exemption is to be replaced with a fifty percent general CGT exemption for all 'active assets' (detailed below). When combined with the general fifty percent exclusion (detailed in Chapter 24), individuals owning small businesses will be liable to tax on a maximum of 25 percent of their capital gains tax when they sell business assets (which can include land and buildings). Up to 100 percent CGT exemption can also be available under certain conditions. This will encourage business investment which will contribute to economic growth and jobs creation.

The CGT incentives relate to '**active assets**' which require the assets to be:-

1) a business, company, unit trust or other membership interest where the taxpayer is a controlling individual of the entity carrying on business;

2) those which can include land and buildings, goodwill and intellectual property. These assets may be used in a business that is operated by a connected entity. It does not include share portfolios or rental properties;

3) not more that $5 million as a net value that the taxpayer and entities connected with the taxpayer own.

As well as a seventy-five percent CGT exemption for active assets, it is proposed to allow generous roll-over deferrals of CGT if the tax payer who sells a business buys other replacement active assets.

If a business owner sells active assets and then retires, up to $500,000 used to fund retirement is exempt from CGT.

One hundred percent CGT exemption is proposed if all of the following criteria are met:

1) the active assets are held continuously for fifteen years and are sold after 20 September 2000 (i.e. fifteen years after the CGT commenced) and the taxpayer has reached age fifty-five or more and is retiring or has become incapacitated;

2) the asset must be an 'active asset' at the time of disposal; and

3) the asset has been active for at least half of the previous fifteen years.

Assuming the new CGT laws are adopted as law in the format that the government proposed above, it provides great incentive for Australians to build businesses and in the process provides employment. When sold, the business owner will be rewarded by minimal CGT so that they can achieve financial freedom and provide security for their loved ones.

HOW DO LOANS AND TAXES AFFECT YOUR BUSINESS?

Why Build Your Own Business?

Before I move onto the exciting world of investments, I will briefly give you one example of the wisest ways to use a business loan. The running of your own business is a challenging, sometimes risky, yet often very rewarding experience. Several years ago, I used to sell businesses, and over the years, I have owned and run several businesses myself as well as being a consultant to many dozens of clients, in the capacity of accountant and financial adviser.

Many people who wish to become self-made millionaires can achieve their objective, with much less risk, by being an excellent employee. They can achieve this by wisely using the money that they earn as wages, through the reduction of consumer and security loans (previously covered) and the use of investment loans, which I will share with you in later chapters. Before anyone considers giving up a well-paid position, as an employee, and starting a business on their own, they would be well advised to get very clear on their goals and the reasons they have for wanting to own a business. Look at the alternatives available (which I will cover in the following chapters), before embarking on a new business. Assuming you are considering buying a business, or expanding, or upgrading your existing business, the following information on using business loans may be of use to you in making such a decision.

Most small businesses, started from scratch, fail. Figures from both the USA and Australia confirm this dramatic fact. Research from the USA shows that, during the first five years of operation, more than 80% of self-started businesses fail. In fact, of the businesses started by people who thought of an idea and then raced out and set up a business, less than 5% are still in existence after ten years. However, if the person who starts the business, has already worked in and run another successful business, and buys into a successful franchise, the chance of success in the first five years of operation is more than 90%. This dramatic difference is based on the successful systems that the operator of the business runs. If you wish to learn more about this, an excellent book on the subject is *The E Myth*, by *Michael E. Gerber* (published by Harper Business Publications, USA).

How Do Business Loans Affect Your Profit?

Let me demonstrate how business loans can affect your profit. Let us assume:

1) that you have $50,000 to invest in a new business. This initial investment capital may have come from the sale of another business or from other sources;

2) that you have a good credit rating and the ability to borrow in order to buy into a new business if you wish to;

3) that you have already worked in other successful businesses; and

4) that you have a proven track record in business systems and working with employees, banks and customers.

Let us suppose that there are two video stores for sale in the town or suburb in which you wish to establish your business. One is a thriving large store, located in the main shopping centre, well-positioned for easy access to passing trade, open seven days a week, and close to other convenience stores. The other video shop is a small establishment in a back street, that has been trading for a short period of time. It is much less expensive to buy. Both stores have a long-term lease over their business premises, with a five year lease and a five year option to extend.

The smaller of the two video shops is for sale for $50,000, which represents fifteen hundred video tapes valued at $25 each ($37,250), plant and equipment (i.e. cash register and shopfittings) valued at $5,000 and goodwill of $7,250. This store will earn, after paying wages to all outside employees, $40,000 per annum for you. You will need to organise book keeping, a staff roster, and take over all responsibility for employees (when they are sick and don't come to work) and all the other important priorities that are required of a business owner. For all this work you will receive $40,000. The chances are great that anyone who has the initiative to run a store like this, and put in so many hours a year, would probably be able to earn $40,000 working for someone else who owns another successful business. Therefore, you may assume that the real earnings of the smaller video store of $40,000, less the wages that you could earn somewhere else ($40,000), are nothing. The net return on the invested cost of the store of $50,000 (to purchase it in the first place), means that the store is really returning no profit, after allowing for wages for the proprietor. If you buy this store you have really only bought yourself a job and all the responsibilities that go with owning your own business.

The larger video store is for sale for $150,000, which represents three

HOW DO LOANS AND TAXES AFFECT YOUR BUSINESS?

thousand video tapes valued at $25 each ($75,000), $10,000 worth of shopfittings and $75,000 for goodwill. It is assumed that this larger business earns $100,000 per annum, after allowing for interest on a business loan of $100,000 (the cost of the business being $150,000 less the equity invested of $50,000, wages to outside employees and all other costs). If this store was bought, and you subtracted, from the $100,000 of annual profit, $40,000 of wages that you could earn working somewhere else, then you have earned $60,000 for each year that you run the store. Preparing the effective return, on the hard-earned investment of $50,000, to be made in either business can be assessed with the aid of the table on the following page.

The table shows that the larger video store gives a return on invested funds of 120%, after allowing for owner's wages. The smaller video store gives no return on investment at all, after allowing for wages. The decision, of whether or not to invest in a particular business, requires more attention than I have available in this section. The key to success in business is like the key to success in building riches. I call this *ASK*ing your way to riches by taking *Action* only after you have a detailed and working *Strategy*, and this is determined by the amount of specialised *Knowledge* you acquire and use, prior to the decision to buy any business.

		Smaller Video Store $	**Larger Video Store** $
Net Annual Gross Profit		40,000	100,000
Less: ~ Wages to Owner	=	(40,000)	(40,000)
Net Profit to Owner		0	60,000
Purchase Price of Business		50,000	150,000
Less: ~ Business Loan		0	(100,000)
Equity Invested in Business		50,000	50,000
RETURN ON INVESTMENT (after wages to Owner)	=	\multicolumn{2}{l	}{Net profit to Owner / Equity invested in Business}
Return on Investment (ROI)	=	0 / 50,000	60,000 / 50,000
ROI	=	**0% pa**	**120% pa**

The question arises as to whether the owner of the larger video store, earning $60,000 per annum after wages, should use this money to reduce the business loan of $100,000. Many would think that the first thing they should do is to pay out this business loan in total, and then own the business without any loans whatsoever. This is a very conservative *Strategy* and is one that would best be applied if the business was likely to encounter any new competition from, for example, other video stores opening in the area, Pay TV, Cable TV networks that could possibly erode this business's income; or if there was only a short lease.

If the business is stable, with a long-term lease (ideally, in the order of ten years), with limited competition and the ability to maintain, or even increase its net annual profit, then you may work in it for ten years and then re-negotiate a new lease on the business premises for another ten years. You may then sell the business for an equal, or greater amount of money than you paid for it initially. The business loan can then be repaid out of the proceeds of sale, sometime in the future. If this method is used, then the loan will not need to be reduced at all and you may choose to take out an interest-only loan, which means that you will only pay interest to the bank. You will not need to repay any of the $100,000 principal of the loan to the bank under these conditions. You will then have an annual income stream of $60,000 a year, (after your wages are paid), to invest in other investment assets outside this business. If this money is wisely and carefully used, it will make you rich.

The exciting and rewarding use of investment loans will be covered in Chapters 13 and 17. It is now time to move on, to discover how to compare investments in order to derive maximum riches from them.

Chapter 7

HOW DO YOU COMPARE INVESTMENTS THAT CAN MAKE YOU RICH?

'The more extensive a man's knowledge of what has to be done, the greater will be his power of knowing what to do.'
~ **Benjamin Disraeli.**

If you are to succeed in giving yourself both security and financial freedom, your aim in building riches needs to be to accumulate significant valuable assets outside your home. These assets can then provide you with an income stream that will fund your lifestyle, any emergencies or needs for money that may arise in the future, and allow you to support other people whom you wish to benefit from your riches. Once you have a sufficient income stream and asset base outside your home, you can choose whether you wish to work, or not work, and what you want to do with your time. In being ambitious and striving for this goal, you also make it easier for the government, because the governments of the future will not need to fund retirement and health benefits for people like you and me. Our ambition and striving allow us to be independently wealthy, with no need to rely on government or family members for handouts. One of the key principles behind achieving this objective, is learning how to make our invested funds grow at the fastest possible rate.

Albert Einstein is regarded as one of the most intelligent people who lived in the 20th Century. Einstein proposed the theory of relativity and many other amazing concepts that led to our current understanding of atomic physics. Einstein was once *ASK*ed what was the most powerful concept or principle that he was aware of. His reply was that:

> **'the most powerful concept or principle in the world that I am aware of, is that of *compound interest*'.**

We all know that if you put your money, say $1,000, into a bank or an investment, at 10% per annum simple interest return (after-tax), and allow that money to generate interest or to grow (capital growth), then, at the end of the first period, or the first year, you will have a larger amount of money than when you started, this being $1,100 (i.e. $1,000 invested and $100 interest). In the next year, you will not only earn returns (and possibly capital growth) on your initial amount of money invested, being another $100, but you will also receive a return of another $10 on your interest earned in the first year (i.e. in the second year you receive $110 interest on invested funds of $1,100). As the years go by, you earn interest upon interest upon interest. This effect is called *compounding* and it is the essential ingredient that allows people to rise from a starting place of some assets, to eventually become millionaires or billionaires.

Compound interest has worked for countless people over many thousands of years and it can work for you, if you harness it. You've probably heard the statement that the second million dollars is easier to make than the first million dollars. From personal experience, and from the advice I have learnt firsthand, from dozens of self-made millionaires and the hundreds of wealthy people whom I have read about, this is an absolute truth. So, you might well *ASK: 'how do I make my first million dollars?'* The trick to making your first million is the same as for the making of your second million. It relies on compounding the assets and income that you have now, in a way that will produce the greatest capital growth and still supply the safety required, so that you will not put your invested funds at too much risk. Before you explore this exciting world, it is worthwhile having a comprehensive understanding of how compound interest works, simply so that you can use it to decide between comparable investments.

The Awesome Power of Compound Interest

What is the impact of putting a small amount of money away on a daily basis to build a future nest-egg? Let's assume that the person who is making this investment has read this book and has the *Knowledge* to make

HOW DO YOU COMPARE INVESTMENTS THAT CAN MAKE YOU RICH?

their money work hard for them thus earning 16% per annum. By the time you have finished reading the coming chapters you will know how to achieve such returns. What difference will it make, over time, if the amount you invest is $2 a day, or $5 a day, or you become a really big investor and invest $10 a day? The table below shows the effect of compounding a small investment of money on a daily basis, over a long time.

REGULARLY COMPOUNDING A SMALL AMOUNT OF MONEY OVER TIME:

Value at the end of year	$2 a day at 16%	$5 a day at 16%	$10 a day at 16%
5	$5,564	$13,910	$27,820
10	$17,931	$44,828	$89,655
20	$106,526	$266,315	$532,630
30	$544,263	$1,360,658	$2,721,315
40	$2,707,069	$6,767,673	$13,535,345
50	$13,393,236	$33,483,090	$66,966,180
Millionaire Year	34	28	24

A study of these numbers will give us a couple of useful principles.

The first is that the more money you put in per day, the more money you get back on a proportional basis. That is, if you put $2 a day aside, at the end of five years you have a little over $5,500, whereas if you invest $10 you will have accumulated over $27,800 (five times the lump sum for five times the daily investment).

The second, and more relevant principle obvious from these figures is that of the impact of time on the amount of money you have accumulated. At $2 a day, it takes twenty years for you to accumulate a little over $100,000, then in the next ten years your lump sum has grown to over $500,000, more than four times the amount of money in half the time! In the next ten years, an additional profit of over $2,000,000 is accumulated, and from the fortieth to the fiftieth years, at only $2 a day, your lump sum has grown to over $13,000,000. The same trend develops for the larger amounts of money invested per day, on a proportional basis. What this shows us is that **it takes a while to build your original investment**

HOW TO BUILD RICHES

up to a certain lump sum, but after that, your riches increase very rapidly.

For example, let us assume that Anne Wise started putting away $2 a day from her twentieth birthday, until her seventieth birthday. At seventy, Anne would have over $13,000,000 invested (see the first column on the table on the previous page). Let's assume that Anne had also been investing other money and decided to give this $13,000,000 to her children. Anne's children may well be aged in their thirties by this time. If she had two children, they could receive $6.5 million each. This could pay for the educational expenses of any of her grandchildren, as well as help her children to buy their dream homes and give them other investment capital. I guess you wish your parents had read a book like this many years ago and had started investing for you at, or before the time you were born, so that you could receive some of this $13 million! It is never too late to start investing for your children, or your grandchildren, or yourself.

Shirley Battler, at the same age, twenty, decided that it was too much like hard work to start putting aside $2 a day, so she put it off. At age forty, Shirley was too busy with her children to start investing, so again, she decided to put it off. At the age of fifty, Shirley thought it was time to start putting aside money to invest for her children, so she invested $10 a day for the next twenty years, until she reached seventy years of age. The lump sum she had accumulated at $10 a day for twenty years would be a little over $532,000 (from the previous table). If Shirley Battler also had two children, then they would receive a little over $260,000 each. The awesome thing is that Anne Wise has only contributed a total of $36,500 of her regular savings to accumulate over $13,000,000, whereas Shirley Battler (who procrastinated and put off investing) had contributed twice as much money, i.e. $73,000, to accumulate a total nest-egg for her children of a little over $500,000. Anne Wise had accumulated **over fifty times as much money for every dollar she invested** as Shirley Battler. The principle and the message are straightforward. Start saving and investing as soon as you can, to make your money accumulate to a lump sum, which will build you riches.

A simple, yet powerful way of easily understanding and calculating how compound interest can work for you is to understand the principle that is called **The Rule of 72**.

The Rule of 72 says that: if you take the magic number 72 and divide it by the compound interest rate of return that you receive on your invested

HOW DO YOU COMPARE INVESTMENTS
THAT CAN MAKE YOU RICH?

funds, the answer is <u>the years it takes for your money to double</u>. This formula also works in reverse. If you take the magic number 72 and divide it by the years it has taken for your money to double, the answer is <u>the compound interest rate of return you have received on your investment over this period.</u> Following is a table that demonstrates, for differing compound rates of return, the amount of time it takes for money to double. It also shows how the Rule of 72 operates in reverse:

'RULE OF 72'
The principle behind compound interest

72	Divided by	Compound Interest Rate of Return	=	Years for Money to Double in Value
72	Divided by	4%	=	18
72	Divided by	8%	=	9
72	Divided by	16%	=	4.5
72	Divided by	24%	=	3

RULE OF 72 IN REVERSE

72	Divided by	Years for Money to Double in Value	=	Compound Interest Rate of Return
72	Divided by	10	=	7.2%

At 4% return it takes eighteen years for your money to double. At 8%, only nine years, at 16% only four and a half years, and if you can get your money to compound at 24% per annum, it takes only three years for your money to double!

Let us assume that you, or your parents, have owned a house for ten years and at the end of ten years, the house had doubled in value. The Rule of 72 (in reverse) says: that 72 divided by this ten years means you received 7.2% compound growth on your real estate.

In Chapters 23 and 27, I will share with you the findings of my research on historical rates of return on different types of investments, including fixed interest, real estate and shares (these being the three main investment categories open to most of us).

How Much Richer will You Become by Compounding Your Money at a Higher Rate of Return (After Inflation)?

In order to demonstrate how compounding your existing riches at differing rates of return and how inflation will effect the spending power of your money, I have set out the following example. I will assume, for this example that, in the future, the rates applying will be:

1) Interest rates will return you 4%;

2) Inflation will also be 4%. This is the increase in the cost of goods and services, (which may seem a little low now, but over time, has proved to be fairly accurate);

3) Real estate and shares will increase in value at 8%;

4) Using leverage (the use of borrowed money) to buy real estate and shares will increase your return to 16%;
(The ability to earn a greater return using borrowed money will be detailed further in Chapters 13 and 17).

5) Investing in a variety of investments over time, these being shares, real estate and fixed interest, will return you 24% (how this operates will be demonstrated in later chapters).

The specific details of which investments perform best over time, are detailed later in this book. For this exercise, it is simply assumed that you may be able to earn a return of 16% or 24% on your invested money by applying the material covered later in this book.

To demonstrate the effect of increasing the rate of return on your money, I'll assume that you have $10,000 to invest and that you wish to invest this money for eighteen years. You will want to know how much money you will have invested, at the end of the eighteen years. However, you will also want to know what the amount is in real terms, that is, after you have allowed for the decrease in spending power, resulting from inflation eroding the purchasing power of your money. The principle I wish you to understand is that: as you increase the rate of return on your

HOW DO YOU COMPARE INVESTMENTS THAT CAN MAKE YOU RICH?

<u>invested money, you more than proportionally increase the effective profit you make after inflation.</u> Following is a table that demonstrates the application of the Rule of 72 and how it can work for you:

APPLYING THE RULE OF 72

Amount Invested $10,000

Rate of Return	4% Fixed Interest/ Inflation	8% Property/ Shares	16% Leveraged Property/ Shares	24% Extra- Ordinary Returns
Years to Double Your money	18	9	4.5	3
Year Ended	$'000	$'000	$'000	$'000
0	10	10	10	10
3				20
4.5			20	
6				40
9		20	40	
12				80
13.5			80	
15				160
18	20	40	160	320
Less: Inflation 50%	(10)	(20)	(80)	(160)
Year 18 Current Dollars	10	20	80	160
Increased Spending Power in Current Dollars	0	1	7	15

If you left your $10,000 sitting in a bank account at 4% interest (assuming that there are no taxes on your invested money, which is obviously not the case), then, at the end of eighteen years, you would have $20,000, i.e. your money would have doubled. However, if inflation has also been at 4%, the $20,000 on hand at the end of eighteen years will only buy you the same amount of goods and services as $10,000 would have bought you at the time you first invested your money.

For example, if a car costs $10,000 today, in eighteen years time at 4% inflation, a car will cost you $20,000. So, your $20,000 after eighteen years only has a purchasing power in today's dollars of $10,000. This means the effective profit of your investment at 4% for this eighteen years, after inflation, is $0 and the times your money has doubled in current dollars is again zero. The effective returns from investing in cash or interest bearing investments will be detailed in the next chapter.

Inflation does the opposite of Robin Hood!

Robin Hood took from the rich to give to the poor. Inflation robs the ignorant and pays dividends to the well-informed. Inflation robs the poor (or savers, who put their money into the bank) and pays dividends to the investors (the rich), who borrow money from the bank, to invest it at a higher rate of return. Inflation is our enemy if we don't know how to make friends with it and how to apply it to build riches. This concept will be explored later in more detail.

What is Your Likely Return if You Invest in Shares or Real Estate Using Only Your Own Money?

By putting your $10,000 into real estate or shares, without the use of any borrowed money (no leverage), you might expect to earn in the order of 8% compound capital growth return, (excluding dividends), for the next eighteen years. At the end of nine years your investment would have grown from $10,000 to $20,000, and at the end of eighteen years your investment would be worth $40,000. If you reduce this investment for inflation (that is half of the purchasing power), you would have $20,000 worth of spending money in today's dollars, or an effective profit of $10,000 in today's dollars. This means that your money has doubled once in today's spending power. The actual historical returns from both shares and real estate and fixed interest will be detailed and compared later in this book. The returns used in this chapter are purely for demonstration purposes.

What is Your Likely Return if You Invest in Shares or Real Estate Using Borrowed Money?

By investing in real estate or shares, using money borrowed from a bank, you may expect to earn a greater return (as will be detailed later). Let us say that you will earn 16% on your invested money. Whenever you borrow money to buy an investment, you can increase your chance of greater returns on investment. Caution needs to be exercised when borrowing. Borrowing to purchase shares is a significantly greater risk than borrowing against real estate (and this area will be covered in more detail in Chapter 13.)

It is assumed that, by investing in shares or property using borrowed money, you can increase the return on your invested $10,000 to 16%, compound capital growth. If you invest at 16% then at the end of four and a half years, your money will have doubled. It will continue to double, so that at the end of eighteen years you will have $160,000. This is the same spending power as $80,000 in today's money (as detailed above, due to inflation having eroded the purchasing power of your money). Your money will have increased in spending power by a total of seven times over this same eighteen year period. Increasing the growth rate (in the above table) from 8% to 16%, i.e. <u>doubling the growth rate once, results in a compound return of seven times the spending power</u> at the end of this eighteen year period.

What is Your Return if You Wisely Invest in a Combination of Shares, Real Estate and Fixed Interest Using Borrowed Money?

If you invested your $10,000 at a 24% compound growth rate, your money would double after three years, and continue to double every three years until, at the end of eighteen years you would have $320,000 or $160,000 worth of current spending power. Your effective profit (in today's spending power) is $150,000 ($160,000 less your original investment of $10,000). This would mean that you would have increased the spending power of your initial $10,000 by a total of sixteen times over this period, and that you also have an additional amount of fifteen times the money (in today's dollars) on hand to spend any way you want.

Compound interest will make you very rich, in a shorter period of time, if you invest as large a lump sum as you can, and then continue to re-invest it for the longest period of time available, at the highest rate that you can safely earn on your money. It is through applying the principle of compound interest that many of today's billionaires have been able to accumulate their fortunes. Like many of us, they started with little or no money, and had to work hard (or smart) to accumulate their first amount of investment money. They then invested their initial money and continued to invest this money, allowing it to compound at the fastest rate possible. Warren Buffet (the second richest man in the USA) is a walking advocate of the principle of compound interest. Warren Buffet made his fortune through investing in shares, and owning and controlling certain key businesses that gave him the cash flow and the control, to build his fortune. This money, he continued to invest in the share market.

In Australia, the second richest family (after the Packer family) is the Lowy family, which owns a major holding in Westfield Limited and the Westfield Shopping Centres. What Frank Lowy and his family have done, is to use their specialist expertise to invest in real estate and shopping centres and then allow their money to continue to compound, using the share market as a means of raising money, to buy and build new shopping centres, and this continues to increase their wealth. The principle that these billionaires use is the same principle that you and I can apply in amassing our riches. Let us now look at how *you* can apply this principle to build riches. There are three main areas to invest in directly, these being:

1) Fixed Interest
2) Shares
3) Real Estate

It is time to examine the application of compound interest in these three main areas of relatively safe investment, open to us in Australia (or overseas for that matter). Earning interest on our current riches is one of the available alternatives. To find out how this will effect your riches you need to know . . .

Chapter 8

WHAT IS THE REAL RETURN ON CASH AND FIXED INTEREST INVESTMENTS?

'Rich men die but banks are immortal.'
~ **Wendell Phillips.**

The safest investment is generally considered to be to deposit money and earn interest income from a bank or other financial institution. This can take the form of cash management, savings, fixed interest, or other deposit accounts.

Very rarely, in a politically and economically stable country like Australia, do people run the risk of not getting back their money when it is deposited with a bank. It rarely happens in so stable an environment, that financial institutions go broke, or go into liquidation. Occasionally this happens, as was the case with the Pyramid Building Society in Victoria and Estate Mortgage in NSW. These are very rare occurrences in Australia.

There is, however, an increasing trend of bank failures overseas, from the *Savings and Loans Crisis* in the USA to the recent run of bank failures in Asia. Where these failures occur, in every case, it has been relatively easy to see in advance, that the banks that went broke were making unintelligent, or greedy lending decisions. It may well happen here in the future, but if you learn the principles set out in this book, then you will be able to protect yourself from such bank failures. In Australia, when a bank collapses, frequently the government will intervene to make good depositors' monies (out of the income that they generate from taxing the rest of the community).

How effective have fixed interest investments been in recent decades? The following graph illustrates the actual return on money invested with the banks (and building societies in earlier years) on sums between $5,000 and $100,000 for one year fixed rate returns. It also shows the comparable inflation rate, often referred to as the Consumer Price Index, or **CPI**, from the Australian Bureau of Statistics (**ABS**), for the years from 1976 until 1999 inclusive.

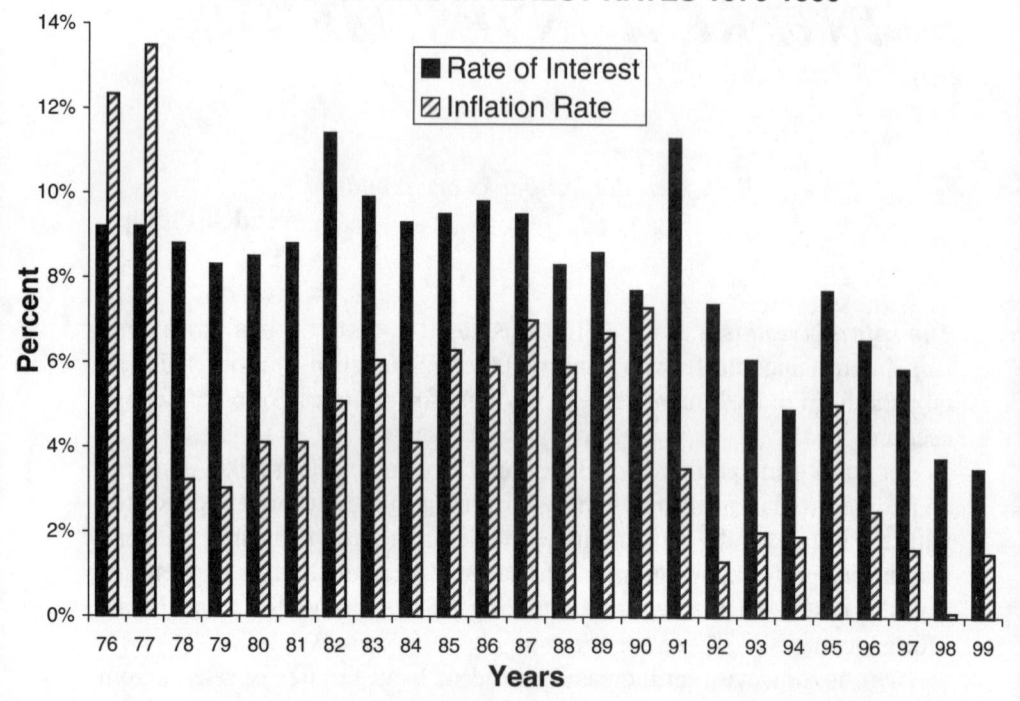

INFLATION AND INTEREST RATES 1976-1999

Source: The Reserve Bank of Australia & the Australian Bureau of Statistics

In 1976 and 1977, there was the rare occurrence of inflation actually exceeding the rate of interest paid by banks. This, in economic terms, was the beginning of what economists call **stagflation**, an economic term that indicates there is high inflation and high unemployment occurring at the same time. It is easy to see from the graph above that interest

WHAT IS THE REAL RETURN ON CASH AND FIXED INTEREST INVESTMENTS?

rates go down, and go up, and continue to go down and up, over time. This occurs in a cycle (which will be detailed in the next Chapter).

Interest rates are effected by Commonwealth Government policy. The government in Australia controls interest rates through the Reserve Bank. Interest rates are, increasingly, becoming the primary tool used by the government to affect the economy as a whole. I'll cover the reason why governments do this, and the impact it has on us as investors, in the next Chapter. Inflation, in the graph on the previous page, also moves up and down in cycles, in line with the economic cycle.

What Effect Do Taxes and Inflation Have on Fixed Interest Investments?

As an example, let us assume that the interest rate you would get by depositing your money in the bank, at present, is 3.75%. The assumed inflation rate for the next year is 2%. What effect does earning interest have, on people in different income brackets? If your income is $30,000, you will pay 31.5 cents in tax (including the Medicare levy) after July 2000 for every dollar of interest you earn. Whereas, if your income is over $50,000, you will pay 43.5 cents. If you earn in excess of $60,000 per annum income, you will pay 48.5 cents tax for each dollar of interest you earn, as detailed on page 54, for the reduced taxation rates after the Goods and Services Tax is introduced.

The table on the following page shows the interest income from a $10,000 investment in a fixed interest account, less taxation, less the inflation reduction in the purchasing power of the invested cash, over a one year period. This effective, after-tax and after-inflation, return, divided by the $10,000 fixed interest investment, gives us a percentage return after-tax and after-inflation, on these invested funds. Notice the impact of taxes and inflation on a fixed interest investment in the following table.

HOW TO BUILD RICHES

EFFECTIVE RETURN ON A FIXED INTEREST INVESTMENT
after taxes and inflation

ASSUMPTIONS	
Assumed Interest Rate Return (average)	3.75%
Assumed Inflation Rate (average)	2.0%
Amount Invested in Fixed Interest	$10,000

Calculation of the effect of Taxes and Inflation on an amount invested in Fixed Interest or a Cash Management Account:

	Different Pre-Tax Incomes		
	$30,000	over $50,000	over $60,000
Marginal Taxation Rate	31.5%	43.5%	48.5%
Before-Tax Interest Earned	$375.00	$375.00	$375.00
Less Tax at Marginal Rates	($118.13)	($163.13)	($181.88)
After-Tax Return	$256.87	$211.87	$193.13
Less Inflation on Invested Cash	($200.00)	($200.00)	($200.00)
Effective After-Tax & Inflation Return on Cash Deposit	$56.87	$11.87	($6.88)
ROI (Return on Investment) equals the Effective Return divided by amount invested in Fixed Interest	$56.87 / $10,000	$11.87 / $10,000	($6.88) / $10,000
Return After-Tax and Inflation	0.57%	0.19%	(0.07%)

After allowing for the effect of taxes and inflation, someone earning $30,000 would earn 0.6% return on their money for the year ~ this is just over one half of one percent effective return. Someone earning over $40,000 per annum will earn about 0.2%. Someone else earning in excess of $50,000 per annum, investing their money in a bank in this way, will actually lose $6.88 for the year ~ i.e. they will lose about 0.1% of the effective value of their $10,000 over the year. You may think that fixed interest investments are very ineffective investments over the long-term for building riches, and I agree. Fixed interest investments, however, are a useful part of an overall investment *Strategy* at certain times in the economic cycle, for reasons that I will cover in Chapters 9 and 27.

WHAT IS THE REAL RETURN ON CASH AND FIXED INTEREST INVESTMENTS?

The graph below shows the effect of taxes and inflation on an amount of $100,000, had you invested it from 1976 to 1999 and allowed it to compound in a bank account until the end of 1999.

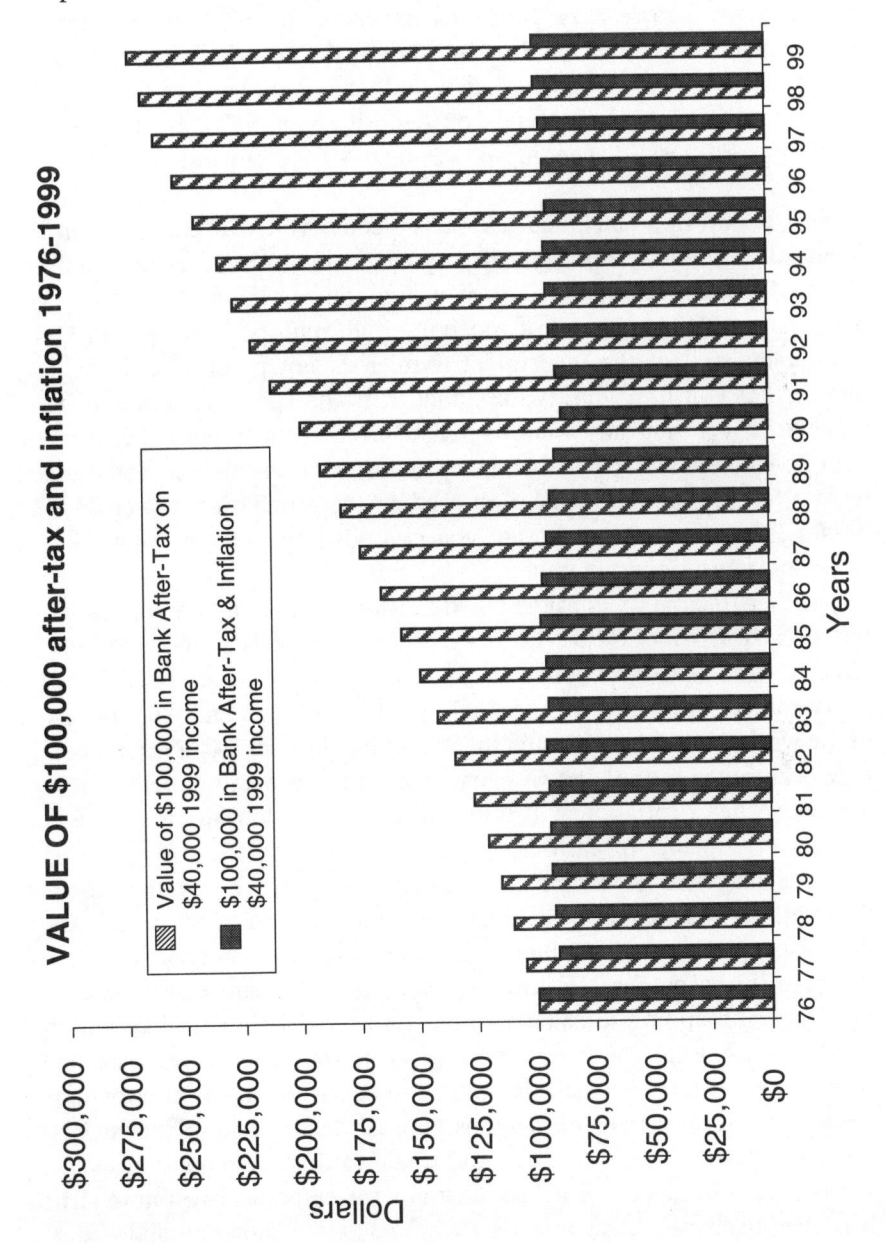

If you looked solely at the bank account (assuming you were earning $40,000 of income per annum over this period) the balance would have increased from $100,000 to over $272,000 during that twenty-three year period. Many people may think that excellent, if they were ignorant of the effect that inflation has had in eroding the spending power of their money. After I deduct both inflation and taxes, you can see that in 1999 the effective value of the funds on deposit (over $270,000 in 1999) is actually worth less in spending power than $100,000 would have been in 1976.

This is an important point, as many people you will encounter in the financial community will appeal to your desire to build riches, and are prepared to take advantage of your ignorance. Frequently, they will promise you the likelihood of receiving high returns. You need to know that, at the end of the investment term, it is not purely the amount of money that you have that is important, it is the spending power of your money. So you not only want to make sure that the projected returns on your investment are achievable, but you also want to calculate for yourself what effect inflation will have on eroding the purchasing power of your money. Then, and only then, are you in a position to know what the real return on your money may be.

Another factor to consider is **deflation**, which is the opposite of inflation. Deflation is the decrease in cost of goods and services. It affected the world economy in 1998 (after the spread of the Asian economic collapse) and will be likely to affect Europe and the other parts of the world including Australia in the coming decades. As it is a relatively new occurrence in the 20th Century, many people wrongly believe it will always be here. Inflation will return and over the long term will reduce the spending power of cash.

Using the Rule of 72 I demonstrated in Chapter 7 (for the eighteen year period), you will be able to calculate a projection of what you expect to make on your invested funds. You can also learn to approximate the decrease in the purchasing power of your invested funds over time, due to inflation. Learning to calculate your future riches is a bit like building a habit or a muscle, the more often you do it, the easier it becomes. What is important is to grasp the principle and get into the habit of applying it.

One of the most valuable lessons you can learn, is to understand how financial markets move upwards and downwards on a regular basis. This *Knowledge* will be one of the foundations for building your future riches. It is time to learn . . .

Chapter 9

WHAT AFFECT WILL THE ECONOMIC CYCLE HAVE ON YOUR INVESTMENTS?

'Tough times never last, tough people do.'
~ **Robert Schuller.**

Most people are aware that the overall economy moves in what is called an **economic cycle**. Sadly, few use it to become rich. During every economic cycle there will be times when you can make high returns from differing types of investments, be they fixed interest, shares, real estate, or other investments. For well over one hundred years, this has been referred to as an economic cycle. Until recently, it has been reasonably easy for people to understand where they are in the economic cycle and, also, to predict, based on historical experience, what is going to happen next, and when this cycle will change. Certain factors, today, are making it more difficult to accurately predict, where we are in this cycle and, what will happen next. This original model is still useful however, and forms an essential part of your riches building *Strategy*. A diagram of one interpretation of this economic cycle follows on the next page.

If you are investing for the long-term (i.e. longer than a five year period), then this model gives you an understanding of how to make greater-than-average profits from your investments. At the peak of a **boom** (confidence is at an all-time high), share prices, real estate prices and wages are all increasing at a rapid rate, fuelled by people borrowing large amounts of money to invest. Many including myself will say this occurred in the first half of 2000.

ECONOMIC CYCLE

BOOM
Inflation Increases

Rising Property Values ↗
Government increases Interest Rates ↘

↑ Banks make Borrowing Easier
↓ Falling Share Prices

UPTURN
Rising Overseas Reserves ↑
↓ Falling Overseas Reserves
DOWNTURN

↑ Rising Share Prices
↓ Banks Tighten Lending

↑ Government decreases Interest Rates
↓ Falling Property Values

← Rising Unemployment ←
GLOOM

In boom times, some people in the financial community, who also desire to build their own riches, appeal to investors' greed and ignorance by telling them how much money they will make (usually based on past information, and usually on a few exceptional investments). These fast-talking salespeople (popularly known as sharks) also play on the fears of the general population, by telling potential investors that if they don't invest their money, then they run the risk of missing out on this 'once in a lifetime' wonderful time to invest (or some other sales pitch).

WHAT AFFECT WILL THE ECONOMIC CYCLE HAVE ON YOUR INVESTMENTS?

I have observed this pattern for decades. As soon as people are investing and saying that these boom times will go on forever, the smartest investors in the market are usually selling down their shares, refinancing their real estate and holding it, and putting their money in safe places, like fixed interest or cash management accounts. **This is when it is prudent to use fixed interest type investments in your riches building Strategy**.

What Happens in a Boom?

Historically, boom times cause increase in prices and spending. As this inflationary pressures mount, the government increases interest rates (with what is called **monetary policy**), through the **Reserve Bank of Australia**. This increase in interest rates affects the available spending money for people, like the Wise and Battler families, and all other members of the community, who have a home mortgage, or other borrowings. As consumers have to spend more money to service their borrowings, they spend less money on consumer goods and services. Selling less goods and services, because of the decrease in demand from consumers, reduces profits. Higher interest rates also mean that companies, particularly those listed on the share market that have a high percentage of borrowings, have to pay more interest on their borrowings.

Combined, these factors result in a decrease in company profits that produces a corresponding decrease in their share price, which relates to company earnings. While this is happening, people get scared and take their money out of shares, which exerts more pressure on share prices and they fall. This is when share values can frequently fall by 10% to 20%, or more. It is about this time in the cycle that people frequently put more of their money into paying down mortgages on their real estate investments or deposit it in fixed interest investments.

2000 is predicted to be a year when the effect of the Asian economies beginning to recover from their financial crisis, and the US economy slowing down, combined with worldwide deflation may well cause a similar effect. Even though interest rates are at historical low levels in Australia, the fear of people losing their jobs can cause them to spend less. This can reduce companies' profits. If people also choose to buy less shares or not to buy them at high prices, the sharemarket will fall and a downturn occurs even though interest rates are low.

What Happens in a Downturn?

As the economy starts to slow down even more, governments raise less taxation revenue as companies make fewer profits and less Capital Gains Tax is paid by investors. Add to this, low consumer confidence, and tighter lending criteria from banks for investors to borrow money. Banks lend less in downturns as they realise they have many bad loans from their boom time lending habit. Also, about this time real estate prices stagnate, or even fall. This particularly applies to non-residential properties and sometimes, to residential properties. The decrease in real estate prices is usually much more dramatic for industrial, retail and commercial properties. The reason for this is that these properties are much more linked to the general business climate and that of their business tenants. These types of properties are ones that fund managers invest in. If the tenants can't pay their rent, the property owner has a cash flow problem. A fall in people wanting to buy these properties results in falls in the value of some real estate trusts and superannuation funds (that do not have quality long term tenants). **For this reason, it is important to have the choice to be able to move your superannuation and other investments into fixed interest type investments during these times in the cycle** (as will be detailed in Chapters 25 and 27). It is better to make a little money after-taxes and inflation, than lose money in the sharemarket or a bad choice of real estate trusts. Residential real estate (particularly well-positioned real estate) is less likely to decrease in value as much as shares may, during these times, for reasons that we will cover in more detail in Chapters 15 to 18.

Some property trusts can be a good place to invest in downturns because they pay a much higher return (7% to 13%) than do bank deposits. Care must be exercised in buying into quality property trusts when prices are relatively low. I did this myself during late 1998 and during 1999.

What Happens in the Gloom?

In the gloom, as the economy slows right down, and business confidence is at an all-time low, unemployment rises. Companies tighten their belts and sack existing workers. They fail to take on new workers or expand their businesses. Governments are particularly sensitive about unemployment and the economy as a whole, perhaps because it is one of the key platforms upon which they will be judged when they seek to be re-elected.

WHAT AFFECT WILL THE ECONOMIC CYCLE HAVE ON YOUR INVESTMENTS?

Governments will decrease interest rates as a means of encouraging confidence and investment in the economy, and also to help companies make profits and employ more people. This is the time when prices of real investments, shares and real estate, are about to increase in value and it is the best time for people to invest.

What Happens in an Upturn?

This decrease in interest rates means consumers have more money on hand, as they are paying less money on their twenty-five year principle and interest home mortgages and other consumer borrowings. This extra money starts to flow to providers of goods and services and companies listed on the stock exchange again. This increases company profits, as they are paying less interest on borrowed money and, at the same time, starting to earn more profits from extra sales. The result is that their operations are more profitable and their share prices rise again. More people then wish to buy into the share market, with the expectation of earning profits from this increasing share prices. Most people start investing in the sharemarket in times of **upturn**.

The best times to buy shares are in the gloom, or at the time when governments have just begun to decrease interest rates. Generally, there is a tendency for interest rates to move in a trend. When they start to decrease, there is a tendency to remain in a downward trend for a while (and vice-versa). Governments continue to decrease interest rates to stimulate the economy until there is an improvement in the economy. This will result in improved company profits and increased share prices.

Once share prices have risen, there will be a general flow-on effect and the whole economy will start to pick up and go into an upturn. A usual result is that the banks relax their lending criteria which leads to easier access to money. At this time, there is usually an increase in real estate values. Employees get higher wages and buy bigger, or better homes, or renovate their homes. At the same time, the investment community puts more money into investment real estate, residential, industrial, commercial and retail. After a while real estate prices often start to increase too rapidly ~ people become over-excited and pay too much money for real estate. This, in turn, raises real estate prices, unrealistically. This contributes to the next shift in the economy and results in another boom time. Inflation soars and governments slam the brakes on the economy by increasing interest rates, and the cycle continues to repeat itself. It amazes me, that even though this has happened for hundreds of years (and it's easy to understand how it has happened in the past), people, on the spur of the moment, lose sight of this trend. Then, when times are booming, they expect them to continue to boom forever! It has never happened in the past and will never happen in the future. There are a few irregular trends, which will change the markets for a period of time, and I will cover these shortly. It deserves repeating: being aware of the economic cycle and buying real investment assets in the gloom and either selling in the boom, or never selling, is the way to build riches much faster.

The wealthiest people in Australia and the USA, people like Kerry Packer and Warren Buffet, have accumulated a major portion of their wealth in the share market by **buying shares when most people are fearful**, and then **selling these same shares when most people are greedy**. The identical wisdom is used by astute real estate investors also.

Mr Buffet says it this way:

'Be greedy when everyone else is fearful, and be fearful when everyone else is greedy.'
~ **Warren Buffet.**

Another way to say this is to *buy in the gloom and sell in the boom.*

There will be times when you will leave your money in fixed interest investments and see the effective return after-taxes and inflation, as being rather low. This is far better than having your hard-earned, after-tax dollars invested in the share market, or non-residential real estate in boom times, and seeing these shares and properties losing significant amounts of your money. It is much wiser to wait to invest, if the cycle is very near the top of a boom. To build even greater riches, wait until interest rates have increased for a while and demand is at an all time low, then, use your capital to buy quality investment real estate and shares, at lower prices. You can then hold these investments and, when the market prices increase, make the greatest profit in the shortest time. One of the two main ways to get rich is to invest in the share market. Let us explore the exciting opportunities that exist in the wonderful world of building riches through investing in shares. It is time to learn more by *ASK*ing ...

Chapter 10

HOW DO YOU BUILD INCOME BY INVESTING IN THE SHARE MARKET?

'Someday the ethics of business will be universally recognised, and in that day Business will be seen to be the oldest and most useful of all the professions.'
~ **Henry Ford.**

Almost every working Australian has an investment in the share market, whether they know it or not. Australian workers have their compulsory Superannuation Guarantee Charge (SGC) payments invested by the managers and the trustees (the people who control each superannuation fund) in the sharemarket. The major places that superannuation fund trustees invest, is the share market. The Australian share market is co-ordinated by an organisation, which has become a company itself, this being the Australian Stock Exchange Limited (**ASX**). Before the ASX was able to be owned by members of the public, it was owned by a number of shareholders, who were all **sharebrokers**. Sharebrokers are licensed by the Australian Securities and Investment Commission (**ASIC**) and sharebrokers (often termed brokers) follow stringent guidelines set for them (often termed brokers). Sharebrokers have to hold a **Security Dealer's License** with the ASIC. They must lodge security deposits and annual audited financial statements with the ASIC, to continue to comply with their regulations. I have a Security Dealer's License and security deposits with the ASIC for most of the last ten years. Being the holder of a Security Dealer's License, I also have to abide by this code.

Sharebrokers buy and sell shares through a computer system called **SEATS** (Stock Exchange Automated Trading Systems). **Shares** used to be called '**stocks**' many years ago, hence the term '**Stock Exchange**'. Clients of sharebrokers phone their broker and make enquiries about buying or selling particular shares, and the broker is able to give them accurate, up-to-the-second information over the phone as to what is happening with their shares. This enables the client to make an informed decision about whether to buy or sell. The buyer or seller can place an order, and can have purchased or sold their shares, sometimes within minutes, depending on whether they are buying or selling at the same price as other people in the market.

The share market exists for two reasons. One is that large companies raise money for expansion by the issuing of shares to members of the public. The other is for owners of shares to be able to have a market place in which to sell their shares to others who wish to buy into companies. There are two share markets in Australia, one called the **Main Board** and the other the **Second Board**. The Main Board comprises the major public companies in Australia ~ household names, such as ANZ, Westpac, NAB and the Commonwealth Bank ~ as well as the major insurance companies AMP, National Mutual, and hundreds of other companies including Telecom, BHP and Coles Myer. There are stringent requirements with which companies must comply in order to remain listed on the ASX. The Second Board lists smaller companies than the Main Board, and it has less stringent listing requirements. The Second Board is really a stepping-stone for many companies that are not large enough yet to be listed on the Main Board. There is far less trading of companies on the Second Board and these shares are considered to be less saleable (liquid).

Why Buy Shares?

The main benefit of the share market as an investment medium is that owners of shares are entitled to a proportion of the company's profits. The shareholder receives **dividends**, which are a distribution of profits to shareholders, usually twice a year, at the end of the taxation year for the company and usually halfway through the company's tax year. As well as receiving dividend income, shareholders in companies are entitled to any increases in price, in the value of the shares, from the time they buy their shares to when they sell them. These increases are called **capital gains** (or capital profits). Any asset that can go up, can also go down. Therefore, ownership of shares also carries with it the risk that shares may decrease in value. If the owner of the shares sells them while the price is down, the result is a **capital loss**. The taxation of capital gains and losses is taxed under the **Capital Gains Tax (CGT)** legislation which is detailed in Chapter 24. The government halved this tax rate in late 1999 which provided much greater incentive for people to sell shares and realise their profits.

How long you hold shares depends upon the likelihood of you making a capital gain, or capital loss. This generally depends upon whether you buy shares in the boom times, or in the gloom times.

The proportion of Australians who directly own shares, particularly those listed on the Main Board in Australia, increased from 10% of the population in 1991, to 16% of the population in 1994, to 20% in 1997 and by 1999 is said to be between about 35% and 40%. Other surveys show that over 30% of these direct shareholders hold only one company's shares. The reason for this extraordinary increase in shareholders has been partially attributed to: the boom conditions that existed in the Australian Share Market in 1997 and 1998; the success of the Australian Government in selling part of the shares in the Commonwealth Bank and Telstra to a huge section of the Australian public; and the two largest insurance companies, National Mutual and AMP, being converted into public companies. Many Australians have been inspired to invest in the share market and have been encouraged by the massive increases in direct share ownership in the USA and Europe in recent years.

What is Dividend Imputation?

Former Labor Government Treasurer and then Prime Minister, Paul Keating, made a major change in the tax effectiveness of owning shares in Australia, when he introduced the **dividend imputation** system in the 1980's. Dividend imputation allows shareholders to receive a credit, for taxation paid by the company in which the shareholder owns shares. Prior to dividend imputation, the company would pay tax on its profits, distribute dividends to the shareholders and, then the shareholders would again be taxed on their dividends (the same profit) at up to top marginal rates! This system was grossly unfair and the current system has encouraged many more people to invest in the share market.

If a company distributes a dividend to shareholders <u>without having paid any tax on the profits</u> that are distributed, these are called **unfranked**

dividends, and the shareholders will pay tax on the full amount received.

Dividend imputation operates when companies pay tax at the company rate of tax on their taxable profits. If the company pays this full rate of company tax at 30% after July 2001) and distributes dividends to the shareholders with a credit for the tax paid by the company, these are called **fully franked dividends**.

Sometimes the company may make a partial tax payment, in which case shareholders receive dividends called **partly franked dividends**. This is when a credit arises only for the proportion of the tax that the company paid. Shareholders then are liable for the balance of tax, on the dividends that they receive, that have not had tax paid on them.

Most public companies tend to distribute their dividends to their shareholders as fully franked dividends. The shareholders then have to include in their taxation returns, as income, both the dividends they receive and their share of the tax paid by the company on those dividends (called the **franking credit**). The shareholder then receives a tax credit (i.e. a tax deduction) for the tax paid by the company. As a result of this tax credit, the taxation payable on dividends received, as a consequence of investing in shares, is very low.

The table on the next page demonstrates the taxation effect of dividend income from shares. Taxpayers will pay differing amounts of tax on the receipt of these dividends, depending upon their taxable incomes from other sources (which means they will be taxed at different marginal rates of tax, as detailed on page 54).

Assuming that you received a fully franked dividend after tax rates change in 2002 of $7,000 (i.e. the company has already paid $3,000 in tax), and had an existing income from other sources, of $10,000 (as shown in column one of the table) the taxation requirements are that you add the fully franked dividend of $7,000 *and* the imputation credit of $3,000 to your existing income. This totals a new taxable income of $20,000. The franking credit of $3,000 is greater than the tax that would have been payable by you, the taxpayer, on the total income (i.e. $2,680) so no tax is payable by you. After 2000 the tax system changed to allow people on low incomes to carry forward a credit for the difference between the imputation credit ($3,000) and the lesser amount of the tax they would have paid $2,680. This results in a refund from the Tax Office of $320. Once the tax on the $10,000 income before the dividend is deducted the total tax credit that is refunded from the **Australian Tax Office (ATO)** is $1,150.

HOW DO YOU BUILD INCOME BY INVESTING IN THE SHARE MARKET?

If you were earning $25,000 income after mid 2001, you would pay an extra $150 at the end of the year, as a result of owning these shares (column two in the table). In essence $7,000 of franking dividends, less an additional $150 worth of tax paid. The third column shows the situation if your income from other sources was $60,000. You would pay $1,850 in tax out of the $7,000 dividend income received.

DIVIDEND INCOME FROM SHARES AND THE EFFECT OF DIVIDEND IMPUTATION IN 2000/2001

It is assumed you are a Shareholder, and your share of total company profits is $10,000. The company pays $3,000 tax on your share of this profit and pays a fully franked dividend of $7,000 to you. The tax adjustment on this dividend in your hands, based on different levels of existing income for you, would be:

Marginal Taxation Rate on Existing Income (before GST)	**18.5%**	**31.5%**	**48.5%**
Assumed Pre-Tax Other Income (A)	**$10,000**	**$25,000**	**$60,000**
Add: Fully Franked Dividend	$7,000	$7,000	$7,000
Imputation Credit $6,000 × 30 / 70	$3,000	$3,000	$3,000
Taxable Income (with Dividend)	$20,000	$35,000	$70,000
Tax on Taxable Income	$2,680	$7,405	$21,330
Less: Franking Rebate	($3,000)	($3,000)	($3,000)
Tax Payable/(Credit)	($320)	$4,405	$18,330
Less: Tax on Other Income (A)	($830)	($4,255)	($16,480)
Net Tax Payable/(Refund)	**($1,150)**	**$150**	**$1,850**

It is easy to see from the above example that, if a couple with differing incomes, one earning $60,000 a year and the other earning $10,000 or $25,000, it would be better for the taxpayer on the lower income to be the owner of the shares. If the partner with the lower income received the dividend income, they would receive all of the income (and possibly a taxation refund). Whereas, if the higher income earner owned the shares they would pay some of the dividend proceeds as tax. Another reason for the taxpayer on the lower income to own the shares would be that he would also pay less CGT when he sold the shares. (CGT will be covered in Chapter 24 and Appendices 3, 4, and 5).

The only exception to this rule would be if someone were entitled to a spouse rebate and the dividend income did not provide a benefit greater than the spouse rebate. Please consult a Certified Practising Accountant (**CPA**) or a **Chartered Accountant**, to discuss your particulars if you are in this situation. These accountants have to pass rigid entry examinations and undergo regular courses and training to keep up with current trends (I have been a member of the Australian Association of CPA's for over nineteen years, and am a fellow of this organisation).

What are the Costs Associated with Investing in the Sharemarket?

The two main costs associated with buying and selling shares are **brokerage fees** and government stamp duty. When you buy or sell shares through a sharebroker, the broker will charge you a fee for each transaction. The amount of this fee will depend upon which broker you use (as some discount their fees) and the volume of shares you buy through the broker. The more money you invest with one broker the more likely it is that you will be charged a lesser percentage on your share transfers.

Fortunately share brokers fees as well as legal and accounting fees for issuing or transferring shares do not attract GST. They are input taxed and thus exempt of GST.

Most sharebrokers will charge between 1.0% and 2.0% of the value of the shares traded, for investors who do not buy or sell shares regularly or who do not sell many tens of thousands of dollars worth of shares at a time. For smaller share trades, brokers may charge a sliding scale fee that is often 2.5% on the first $5,000 of shares; 2.0% on the next $10,000; 1.5% on the next $35,000 and 1.0% thereafter.

Sharebrokers, who charge full fees, will caution you against the use of some **discount brokerage firms**. Discount brokers will sell shares for a flat fee, or a greatly reduced fee. In some instances, various sharebrokers I use tell me they sometimes see transactions for selling (or buying) shares, well outside the range that others are trading at, at the time. When they look at

HOW DO YOU BUILD INCOME BY INVESTING IN THE SHARE MARKET?

which broker made the trade, they often tell me it is a discount broker. The client will incur this loss of profit (which is usually much greater than the brokerage fee). There are some excellent discount brokers. The trick is to phone around. If you are just getting started and do not trade often, a discount broker may be a good place to start.

If you are an experienced share trader and do not need the benefits and other services a shareholder can provide (detailed below), then buying and selling shares over the internet is something to consider. **Internet trading** of shares can reduce your total brokerage fee to less than $20 per trade.

Sharebrokers offer a range of services to their clients. Generally speaking, the more money you make in the share market, the more commission your broker makes, and the better the service you receive.

State Government stamp duty is not charged after June 2001 on listed shares bought or sold. This is one concession to compensate for the GST introduction. For shares that are not listed on the stock exchange, the government stamp duty is 60 cents per $100 of shares bought or sold.

What are the Other Services a Sharebroker can Offer?

The larger sharebrokers can offer you services including:

1) Access to research that they conduct on companies and make available to their clients;

2) Access to share floats ~ these are shares in companies offered for the first time, before they are listed on the stock exchange. Once these shares are traded on the stock exchange, other buyers often have to pay more to purchase these same shares in the share market;

3) Up to date information on shares that they advise to buy or sell;

4) Access to a person who will trade for you when the market is very busy. When there is a share crash and prices drop very rapidly (which happens every few years), many people become fearful and sell their shares. This drives share prices even lower. At some time during these regular crashes, there is often an opportunity to buy shares at a bargain price (although with some share crashes the market may drop for years). If it is a great time to buy shares (in companies with good management, or companies whose assets exceed their selling price) you need to be able to have access to a sharebroker who will take your buying orders and act on them. If you

haven't already established a relationship with a broker, it is likely that you will have to wait until they are ready to deal with you (as they look after their regular clients first). When the broker gets around to your order, the market may already have increased and you may have to pay much more for the shares you wanted.

Frequently, the total of these services can be more profitable to regular share investors (or even first time investors) than the tax deductible fees you pay a broker to help get richer. Consider choosing the right sharebroker and getting rich together.

The saying is that the rich get richer and the poor get poorer. In the Bible it is said that: *'to those that have, more will be given, and to those who have not, even that which they have, will be taken away from them.'* In context, this refers to much more than just money. However, those people who make things happen, by investing in their education (people like us), and then apply their *Knowledge*, will be rewarded later. Rewards from having the ability to *ASK* (take *Action* on *Strategies* based on specialist *Knowledge*) will eventually include being rich in more ways than just making money. When you become a person of *Action*, you develop confidence, courage, enthusiasm and many other riches that give you as much pleasure or more than monetary riches ever will.

You may well *ASK*: *'How do I decide what shares to buy?'* That is an excellent question and it leads to the next topic, which is . . .

Chapter 11

HOW DO YOU MAKE DECISIONS ABOUT INVESTING IN THE SHARE MARKET?

> *'It is not the will to win, it is the will to practice to win that makes the crucial difference.'*
> ~ **Bobby Knight.**

There are two different schools of thought commonly used to analyse shares. The aim of both is the same: to predict share prices with the intention of making a profit. One is called **Technical Analysis** and the other **Fundamental Analysis**.

A detailed description of these two schools of investment criteria for the share market could easily cover several books, so in the space available now, I will simply introduce you to these areas. There are many books written on the share market and they are readily available from good bookshops including the ASX in major capital cities.

What is Fundamental Share Analysis?

This school of share market thought believes that the best way to compare shares in one company with shares in other companies is to study and compare the published information available on the respective companies. Information on companies that are listed on the stock market is available from various sources. Companies themselves put out annual returns (glossy colour publications) outlining the company's financial and other progress over the past year and any expected plans for coming years.

Additional information about companies is often published in newspapers, magazines and trade publications. The more information you gather, the more informed the decision you can make as to which company you invest with, when to purchase shares and when to sell shares.

Share investors like Warren Buffet spend large amounts of time reading companies' published annual returns. Warren Buffet reads about ten annual returns a day, looking for specific information that will give him clues as to whether a company is likely to make future profits or not. Warren Buffet has made over $60,000,000,000 AUD (Australian dollars) so far by investing in the share market (without using other fund managers) by using this Fundamental Share Analysis. In Australia, it's not as easy to gain access to the annual returns of great numbers of companies. Phone and *ASK*.

Warren Buffet has amassed tens of billions of dollars by seeking out information then buying in the gloom and selling in the boom. He also has made his billions by accumulating enough money to entirely control the ownership of companies that generate profits. He then reinvests these profits to buy shares, or other businesses.

Many stock market theorists and university lecturers (some of whom taught me when I studied for my Security Dealer's License), advocate a principle which is called the **Efficient Market Theory**. This basically says that all information known on companies will filter into the market and the share price will accurately reflect the value of all this information. Advocates of the Efficient Market Theory say that successful investors like Warren Buffet only make their money because of their contacts and not through the information they acquire from published information. I disagree. It is interesting to see critics (who are not rich) criticising many ethical, prudent, rich people. Would you rather follow the advice of someone who is rich, or a salaried critic? Many people find the Efficient Market Theory inadequate, because it has never been able to predict when the market is too hot or when the next share crash is going to wipe out major sections of shareholders' equity. If the Efficient Market Theory were as efficient as its advocates claim, then shareholders would know when the market was too hot and wouldn't buy in at that time. Warren Buffet's reply to the Efficient Market Theory is: *'if you're so smart, why am I so rich'*. Smart work is better than abstract theory.

Tracking through company literature, the annual returns, the financial press and even the Internet are good ways of finding information about

HOW DO YOU MAKE DECISIONS ABOUT INVESTING IN THE SHARE MARKET?

companies. People who buy and sell companies (including Australia's richest people, Rupert Murdoch and Kerry Packer) all assess the same financial information that is available to the rest of us. The difference is that they have trained themselves to be able to make better decisions, as a consequence of their analysis of when is a good time to buy shares, and when is a good time to sell. Another *Strategy* of the mega-rich is to buy enough shares in a company to gain directorship (either they or one of their representatives will become a director). These people have the financial capability to buy large numbers of shares and do so in order to gain more information on a company's performance, as well as to protect and direct their investments. Small shareholders do not have the luxury of this advantage.

What are the Financial Ratios You Would Use to Invest in Shares?

The information that is published on shares is frequently converted into financial ratios arrived at by dividing one figure, such as, annual earnings of a company, by the number of shares, to determine the earnings per share (EPS), which is one ratio printed in financial publications. The share market produces large numbers of jargon words and abbreviations. The first time you converse with a major sharebroker you possibly may think he is speaking a foreign language!

Some of the terminology, commonly used in assessing whether to buy or sell a share, includes the following:

Last Sale $:
This refers to the price at which the last shares in the company were traded (sold) in dollars;

EPS (Earnings per Share):
This is calculated by dividing the annual earnings of the company by the numbers of shares in the company (and is represented usually in cents);

P/E (Price to Earnings) Ratio:
This is calculated by dividing the share price by the company's earnings per share;

DIV (Dividends) Cents per Share:
This is the annual dividend for the company and may be written as either six months (which represents the last six months dividend paid) or twelve months. It is usually represented in cents;

DIV (Dividend) Yield:
This ratio is calculated by dividing the annual dividend by the last sale share price and ignores the purchasing costs of buying the share. As last years dividend is not an accurate reflection of the company's likely future profit and dividend, it is only really useful as a guide to what the dividend yield may be in the future. It can be quite misleading because of the fact that some companies will purposely issue a dividend, even when they record a loss. They do this so that this ratio looks healthier, with the intention of encouraging their shareholders to keep their shares and continue to buy more shares, by virtue of the fact that they are receiving dividends, even if the company is losing money;

NTA (Net Tangible Assets) per Share:
This ratio represents the net tangible assets of the company, divided by the number of shares. The result is expressed in cents. Even though they are called tangible assets, you have to be wary and look at the financial reports of the company, to make sure that large amounts of money are not being attributed to brand names or such things as television or radio licenses, which can be taken away by regulatory authorities if they are not complied with;

D/E (Debt to Equity) Ratio:
This ratio represents company debts divided by the value of shareholders equity funds (that is the total share capital of the company), expressed as a percentage.

The NTA and D/E ratios are useful to calculate what is the worst that can happen, (a down-side analysis of the company), if the company is liquidated (or wound up). If the company is wound up, then the value of the assets and brand names will be all that can be sold off and recouped by shareholders. The trouble with this, is that by the time the court fees, liquidators' costs and litigation fees are handled, (if the company has been badly managed), there is frequently nothing left for the shareholders. If there is something left, it's only a few cents in the dollar for every share purchased. Many companies that have gone into liquidation in recent decades, were considered, at one time or another, to be amongst the strongest companies in Australia, including Bond Corporation, Quintex, and Estate Mortgage. Rarely do major Main Board companies go broke and lose all of the shareholder's money, but this is a possibility and has to be considered as a risk, if you are going to invest in the share market. It is highly unlikely that well-managed companies will go into liquidation. It is usually when the forecast returns of the company are projected to be too high and are based on growth by acquiring other companies, that caution needs to be observed. One of the key ratios to watch in such cases is the P/E ratio. If the P/E ratio starts, consistently, to get very high in relation to other companies in its industry, it is a definite sign that boom times are happening. Whenever there is a boom, there is cause for caution, because those companies' share prices may dramatically decrease if there is a downward correction in the share market.

All Ordinaries Index:

A commonly used term is the '**All Ordinaries**'. This is used in share market conversation and also is an Australian Stock Exchange ratio. This is an Index (or average value) of shares in the stock market as a whole. The All Ordinaries Index is also referred to as the '**All Ords**'. It comprises various other composite indices and categories of shares including the All Industrials Index, Investment and Financial Services Index, the Mining Index and the All Resources Index. These composite indices, in turn, break down into various industries' sub-indices, which, in turn, comprise information on various companies that are listed on the share market. If you thought of the All Ordinaries Index as a huge pie, and if you cut out a slice of the pie, that slice may represent the 'All Resources Index' that would be comprised of a group of other indexes such as Oil and Gas, and Diversified Resources and, within each of these sub-categories, would be companies listed on the share market. These companies are all on the Main Board of the Stock Exchange. Numerous publications including Shares Magazine, and the weekend edition of the *Financial Review* newspaper, are readily available and have excellent breakdowns and analysis of these ratios and the companies that comprise them. You can also surf the internet to find an increasing number of Web sites that will provide useful information on ratios and company details for a monthly fee.

What is Technical Analysis?

Technical analysis is frequently used by people to track what share prices have done in the past, and then to predict what is going to happen with them in the future, based on these past trading trends. People use these trends, not only to track shares directly, but also, to track share indexes, options, futures and commodities. Share indexes are combinations of share prices that are average, as an index. Options are rights to buy or sell shares with only a small amount of money expended. Some of these other indexes are listed and traded on the Futures Exchange (which is in discussions to merge with the ASX). Chartists are Technical Analysts, who use charts of previous information. They watch for when charts reach a peak and come down in price and when they decrease in value (and vice-versa). They also look for increases and for patterns. They believe that these minor and major movement corrections can be used to predict when the market is likely to go up or go down.

There are many publications written on Fundamental Analysis. I have friends who buy and sell shares (and trade in indexes) based on analysis of enormous amounts of information and on following investment in accordance with of these trends. Most of the time, very few of these patterns are able to be accurately predicted. If you are able to predict it more often than not, you need to develop a system whereby you don't risk all of your money on one trade and you spread your investments into a number of purchases over periods of time. I have other friends who observe yesterday's trading patterns on the (All Ordinaries) Share Price Index and then buy, on the strength of this analysis, the next morning. Their intention is to sell these indexes during that same day and make small margins on these few daily transactions. The challenge, for most people, is that brokerage fees, government charges and taxes will erode a significant proportion of the profit made in this continual trading process. The other problem is the large amount of time and effort required to get you trading profitably. If you are trading with a large sum of money, several brokers will discount their fees if you *ASK* them.

A combination of these two approaches is probably the best policy. Observing past trends (particularly large market trends such as the business cycle) and company ratios, then gaining as much information, as possible, about a company, and its projected performance in the future, is probably the best way to maximise your returns from the share market.

Buying in the gloom and selling in the boom, or never selling your

HOW DO YOU MAKE DECISIONS ABOUT INVESTING IN THE SHARE MARKET?

shares, (until you need to recoup the money, ideally in retirement), will accelerate your accumulation of riches. Traders buy low and sell high. This brings us to the differences between traders and investors.

What are the Differences Between Traders and Investors?

Traders are people who buy low and sell high. Traders are likely to want to make a small profit on a regular basis and have to keep good records of every purchase and every sale and pay tax on their profits. To become a rich share trader, you will need to become the type of person who has excellent skills with numbers and ratios, has access to a computer, and has the time to make detailed share analyses. Share traders usually have a short-term view to holding their shares, perhaps only for a matter of hours, days or weeks. You can make money as a trader and you can also lose a lot of money, if you don't know what you are doing.

If you are experienced in the sharemarket and have over $20,000 in superannuation, it may be worthwhile being a share trader in your own super fund. Your tax rate will be only 15% (versus up to 48.5% as an individual). Share investing in a super fund, if held for over twelve months, drops to 10% (as will be discussed in chapter 24 and Appendices 3, 4 and 5) with individual CGT being half the individual marginal tax rates shown on page 54 (between 10% to 23.5%, plus only half the Medicare levy). Some will say superannuation is a long term investment so they will buy long term stocks. You can do share trading with only a portion of your investment capital. As your experience grows, you may invest more and become more adventurous.

Investors on the other hand are more likely to purchase shares in solidly performing companies, when the rest of the market is selling shares and getting out of the share market. These rich investors then hold their shares for the long-term, or never sell them at all. Warren Buffet has become an extraordinarily wealthy man through using this principle of buying low and selling high (usually holding shares for a number of years). Mr Buffet is a definite long-term investor, whose advice to many is: 'You should buy stocks as if you were prepared for the stockmarket to close for seven years or so'. In certain instances, Warren Buffet keeps all of his shares in certain companies and has held some for decades. It has been this approach which has made him the world's wealthiest share investor.

In the years leading up to the 1987 share market crash, Warren Buffet had sold almost all of his shares, apart from a few companies that he totally controlled. He sensed that the market was too hot and decided not to buy any new shares. During this time, he purchased what are called **Convertible Preference Shares**. He was paid a high rate of return on money advanced to these companies and he had the option, at his absolute discretion, to convert the amount of money that he loaned to that company, into shares in that company, at a certain date. He did the same thing again during 1998. For information about differing types of shares on offer, the ASX bookshops, in your local capital city, have an excellent service available to members of the public. In major centres, like Sydney and Melbourne, the ASX offers free lunchtime seminars giving information about different types of shares and the share market. This may change with the ASX becoming a public company, and wanting to save every dollar they can. Ideally, they will continue to educate future investors (whom they will profit from every time they buy and sell shares).

Both trading and investing are profitable if you do your research first and do it at the right time. Be careful. Many rumours don't turn out to be true. Some people are more prone to invest for the long term and become investors. Others love the excitement of compounding their money faster by trading and taking profits frequently. I do both at different times in the Economic Cycle.

How will Compulsory Superannuation Change the Share Market for Decades?

As mentioned earlier, the Baby Boomer Crisis is a funding nightmare for the Federal Government in Australia. The Government has trouble making welfare payments to the Australian public now. With the percentage of people of retirement age set to double in coming decades, the government knows it is in trouble. This is why it forces individual employers to pay superannuation payments for their employees in order to fund the retirement packages of their employees. The sum total of the amounts of money going into superannuation is predicted to be several times the current size of the whole share market in Australia. There is also predicted to be over $150 billion dollars of new funds being paid into SGC in the next four years, alone.

What this means is that large amounts of money are going to continue to flow into the share market. Fund managers who manage the large superannuation funds, prefer the share market as the major source of their

HOW DO YOU MAKE DECISIONS ABOUT INVESTING IN THE SHARE MARKET?

investment. This preference towards the share market will continue to grow here and overseas. In the USA and Europe, the trend is the same, with large amounts of money going into their respective superannuation funds and flowing into the share market.

Ideally, it would be fabulous if the Federal Government could encourage (or force) more Australians and Australian fund managers to invest this money in the Australian share market. As the Australian share market represents only about 2% of the world-wide share market, however, there is an increasing trend for fund managers to diversify and invest in shares in foreign countries. The problem with this is that although certain profits are made for Australian shareholders, the companies and the economies that really benefit most from this investment are in foreign countries, not here in Australia. With high unemployment in Australia, and the likelihood that this will continue, we need to use every avenue we can to produce bigger and stronger Australian companies, who employ Australians and can compete internationally.

Investors tend to focus on the long-term and encourage growth of the economy. Traders do not have this effect, as they force up markets and force down markets to make short-term profits. Traders appear to have little or no interest in long-term investment in stable companies or for the benefits that such investment would have on the economy as a whole.

Careful investors buy in the share market, particularly in times when there is a lot of pessimism and lack of market confidence, referred to as a **bear market**. They then hold these shares for the long-term. If you do this there will be an inevitable recovery of the share prices in stable investments when confidence returns to the market, and fund managers and others buy these shares again. This is definitely a recipe for future riches. As the share market in Australia is often prone to large downward spirals, it is worth considering being an investor who buys in a Bear Market. To become rich, you then hold and wait until the Main Board market is booming and people are paying very high P/E ratios for shares, referred to as a **bull market**. When the market is booming, then sell some or all of your shares. Afterwards you can use this money to build maximum growth elsewhere, or to reinvest in the same share market, when the market has crashed or corrected and become a bear market again. You can still be an investor and sell your shares when other people are trading irrationally and paying too much money for theirs. The same people who pay too much for their shares are often likely to be the ones who become fearful when share prices crash. Somebody needs to be there to buy the shares again and it might just as well be an investor, like you, a person who takes the time to invest in their education, read books like this and develop *Strategies* for building riches, for themselves and their families.

As a consequence of the large amount of SGC money flowing into the share market, long-term investment in the share market will produce long-term riches. Be cautious and spend time developing your *Knowledge* and *Strategies* before you take *Action* in this profitable yet risky market.

As you start to learn more about the share market you will often see fund managers and others advertising the spectacular success of certain managed funds over a period of time. These articles imply that you should invest in certain managed funds to ensure that you make a similar return. Never have I seen these same people advertise the spectacular crashes and losses of profits that are also made by these same managed funds! Share prices can go up and down very quickly. Every time they go up, there are shareholders who make a profit. Every time they go down, there are shareholders who make a paper loss (or a real loss if they then sell these shares).

How then, do you make money from the growth in value of shares? You will need to know ...

Chapter 12

HOW DO YOU BUILD CAPITAL RICHES BY INVESTING IN THE SHARE MARKET?

'Money attracts money.'
~ **Old Yiddish Proverb.**

If you buy shares low and sell shares high, then you make a real capital profit, which is taxed. If you buy shares high and sell these shares low, you make a real capital loss, which can only be offset against future capital profits, (profits made from selling shares, or real estate, or goods, at a profit), for tax purposes. Shares frequently move up and down in price, which results in some making profits and others making losses. This movement up and down is called volatility.

Volatile markets offer great opportunities for astute purchasers to buy low and to make good profits. The graph on the following page, which uses information published by the ASX, shows the overall increase in value that would have been made, had someone invested $10,000, in 1958 to 1998, forty years later, into all the shares in the All Ordinaries Index and left that money in those shares (spending their dividends elsewhere).

After forty years, the initial $10,000 has increased to just over $185,000 in value. This is a good return, considering that the investor would also have received dividend income, as a consequence of owning these shares. The growth of the shares represents all of the shares in the All Ordinaries Index.

HOW TO BUILD RICHES

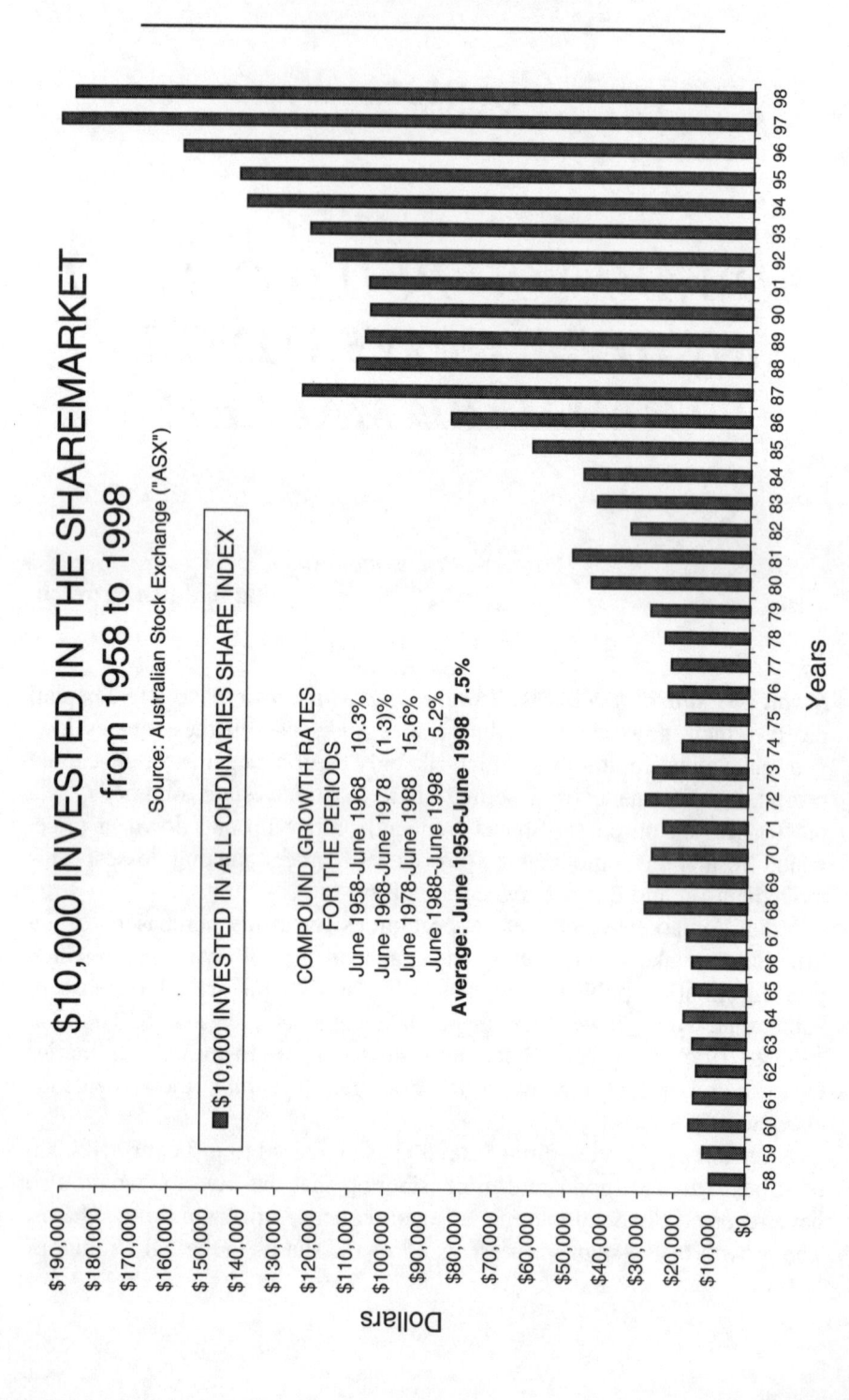

$10,000 INVESTED IN THE SHAREMARKET from 1958 to 1998

Source: Australian Stock Exchange ("ASX")

■ $10,000 INVESTED IN ALL ORDINARIES SHARE INDEX

COMPOUND GROWTH RATES
FOR THE PERIODS

Period	Rate
June 1958-June 1968	10.3%
June 1968-June 1978	(1.3)%
June 1978-June 1988	15.6%
June 1988-June 1998	5.2%
Average: June 1958-June 1998	**7.5%**

128

HOW DO YOU BUILD CAPITAL RICHES BY INVESTING IN THE SHARE MARKET?

Some shares outperform this index. However other shares do much worse than this index. If you had invested in certain shares, such as Bond Corporation Limited, you would have lost almost all of your invested money.

Careful analysis of share investing is a certain way of reducing the likelihood of you losing your money on any particular share.

You can clearly see that in 1960, 1968, 1981, 1987 and 1997, the share markets reached relative peaks. The share increases from 1991 to 1999 represent the largest sustained increase in the share market since the end of World War II, in 1945. Many prudent investors, during 1999, were concerned that most shares in the US share market were overpriced. There is also concern that, as a result of the Asian financial crisis, America, Australia and others are likely to suffer larger-than-ordinary Balance of Payments problems (importing more than we export).

I predict a further downward correction in the share market and a reduction in the All Ordinaries during 2000, for a variety of reasons that I detail in the *Building Riches* audio tapes.

It is also easy to see, from the previous graph, that there are times when you would have wanted to have your money invested in shares, and other times when you definitely would not! The graph shows that, for three of the past four decades you would have made money. If you had your money in the share market from 1968 to 1978, you would have lost 1.3% compound of your riches. The best-performing decade was from 1978 to 1988. If you had your money in shares then, you would have earned a compound growth rate of 15.6% per annum. The average over this forty year period was a compound growth rate of 7.5%. Remember, how we used 8% for both property and shares in our Rule of 72 calculations (in Chapter 8), which meant your money would have doubled every nine years. At 7.5% actual compound growth, your riches will double every 9.6 years (72 divided by 7.5% is every 9.6 years).

The share market has been active in Australia for over 120 years and the ASX will give you access to their extensive records (for a fee). One publication they produce is *ASX Indices & Yields*, and it tracks the All Ordinaries Index (and several others), over time. How has the share market performed over that 120-year period? On the following page is a graph showing the value of an investment of $1,000, in 1878, that is placed in all the shares in the All Ordinaries and left for 120 years (assuming all dividends are spent by the shareholder).

HOW TO BUILD RICHES

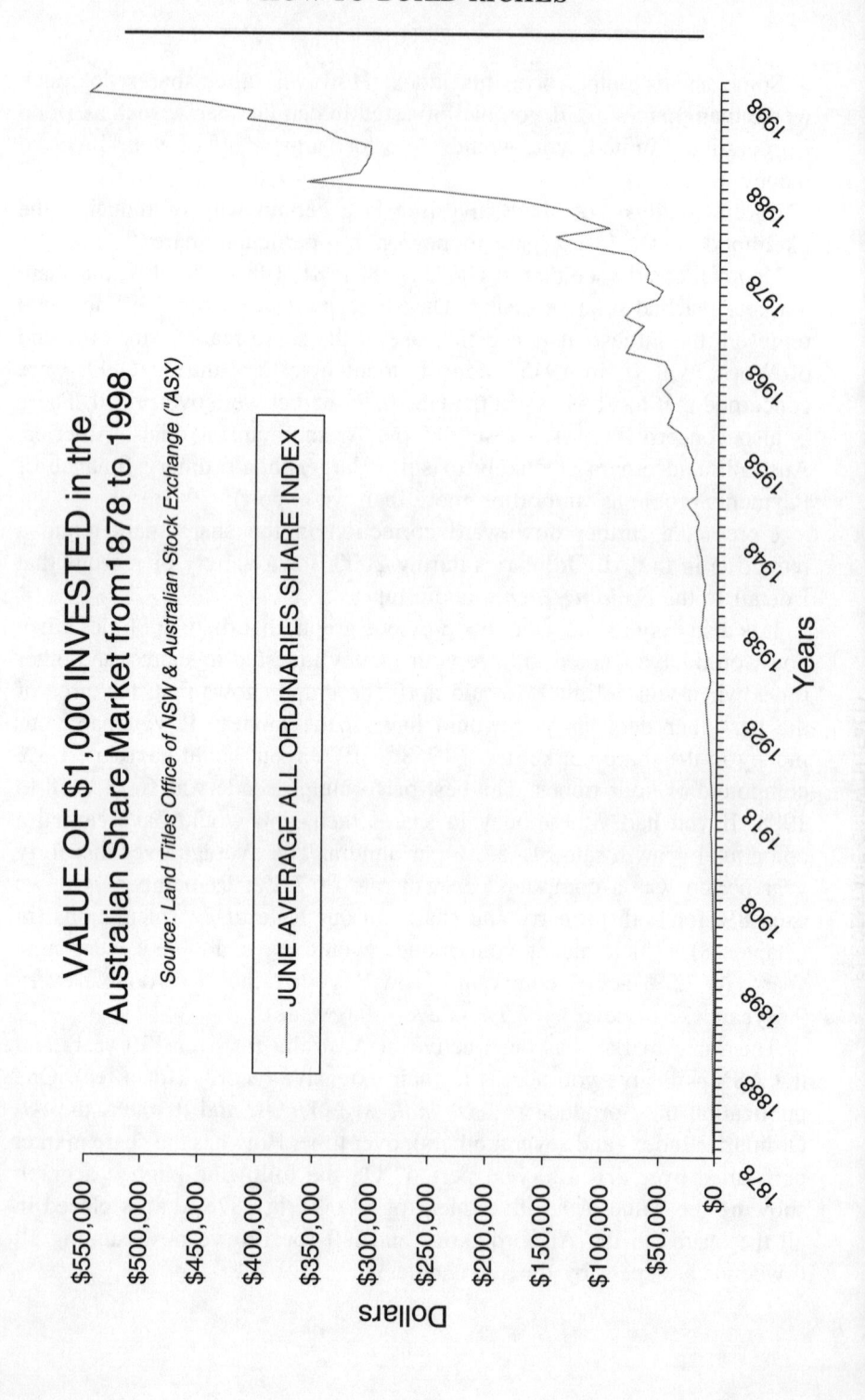

VALUE OF $1,000 INVESTED in the Australian Share Market from 1878 to 1998

Source: Land Titles Office of NSW & Australian Stock Exchange ("ASX")

—— JUNE AVERAGE ALL ORDINARIES SHARE INDEX

HOW DO YOU BUILD CAPITAL RICHES BY INVESTING IN THE SHARE MARKET?

The graph on the previous page, again demonstrates the awesome power of compound interest. It took eighty seven years, from 1878 until 1965, for the initial investment of $1,000 to grow to $50,000. In the next thirty-two years the total investment value jumps to over $500,000 in 1997.

One meaningful way of understanding the volatility and overall performance of shares during this time, is to analyse the compound growth rate of these shares over this period. The graph below shows the compound growth over each of the twelve decades after 1878:

COMPOUND GROWTH (AND FALL)
of the All Ordinaries Share Market Index
for the period 1878 to 1998

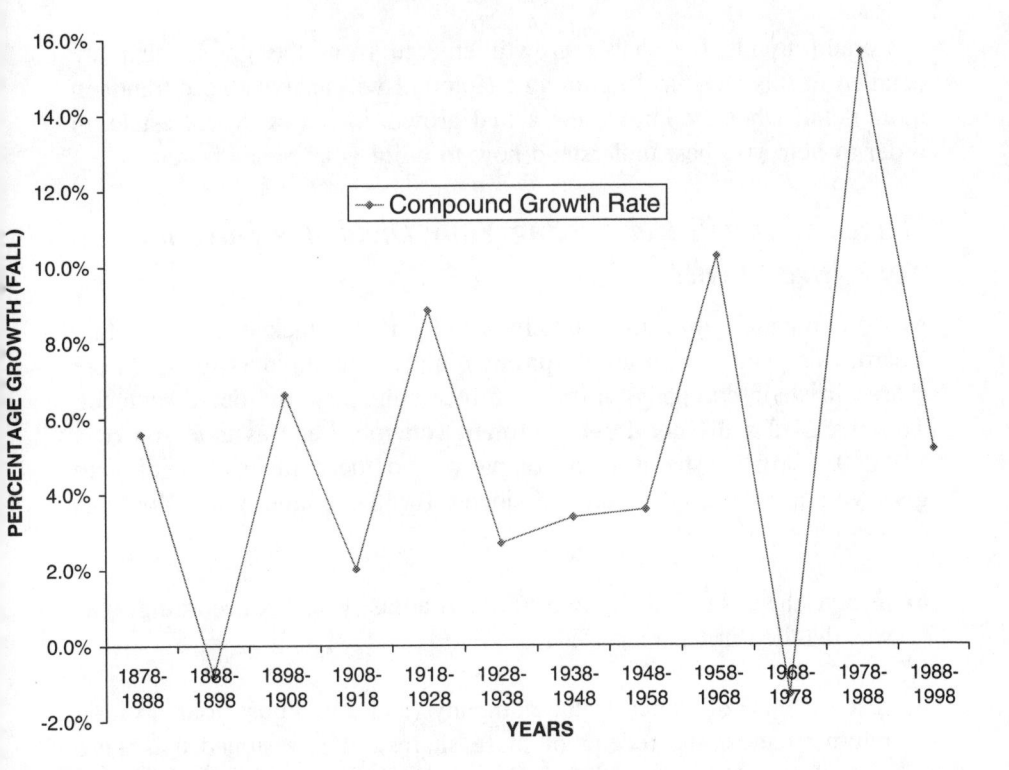

Source: ASX Indices and Yields 1995 and ASX

A closer analysis of the graph on the previous page shows a few interesting features that occurred during this period:

1) The greatest decade of growth was in the 1980's. The compound growth rate was 15.6% in the decade from 1978 to 1988

2) The next greatest growth was 10.3% from 1958 to 1968

3) There were two decades when you would have lost riches, at a rate of between 0.8% and 1.3% (before inflation)

4) The average compound growth rate, over this whole one hundred and twenty years, was about 5.44%.

Certain trends for shares growth emerge from the graphs that are detailed in this chapter. In coming chapters, I will analyse these trends in more detail when I compare the actual growth in shares to real estate, in order to help you best understand how to build your riches fastest.

What Effect will Reinvesting Your Dividends Have on Your Investment?

Many companies that are publicly listed on the stock exchange Main Board, (also called **public companies**), allow shareholders to buy more shares in their company, instead of receiving their dividend payment. This is called a **dividend reinvestment scheme**. Let's assume you own $10,000 worth of shares in a company, and the company is going to give you a 4% fully franked dividend for the whole year. You can either:

a) receive the cash dividend of $400 (and adjust your tax accordingly) as was detailed in Chapter 10; or

b) receive $400 of shares in the company (and still adjust your taxation return to show the receipt of these shares). It is assumed that these new shares and your existing shares grow at an average of 8% per year, that is, 2.5% greater than the compound growth rate for the last one hundred and twenty years.

HOW DO YOU BUILD CAPITAL RICHES BY INVESTING IN THE SHARE MARKET?

What will be the effect over time if you take option (b) and have all of the dividends from your $10,000 investment reinvested?:

1) At the end of year ten, your investment will be worth over $31,000;

2) At the end of year fifteen, you will have over $54,000;

3) At the end of year twenty, you will have over $96,000;

4) In year twenty five, your investment will have grown to over $170,000.

Notice that in the last five years you would have made $74,000 ($170,000 less $96,000) which is more money than you would have accumulated in the first fifteen years of this investment.

The next chapter will show you how to make even greater profits (or losses) by investing borrowed money in shares. Borrowing to buy shares has become very popular and is an important subject to understand. People with little share market experience tend to rush into this area. People frequently do this to generate a taxation deduction for the interest that they will pay, to borrow the money to buy the shares.

Interest on loans to buy assets that are bought with the intention of making a profit (i.e. Investment Loans), is tax deductible in the year in which it is paid. Interest payments can also be paid for up to thirteen months in advance and claimed as a tax deduction when paid.

Borrowing to buy shares (particularly when the share market is in the middle of a bull market) is very risky and you can make or lose a lot of money. It is better for you to be aware of the risks before you invest. There are many people, who in recent years, have had to sell their houses to pay back **margin calls** (explained in the next chapter). This particularly concerns me, as financial hardship in our community accounts for more divorces (and the accompanying damage to young children and families alike) than does drunkenness, and mental and physical abuse, combined. Borrowing to buy shares can make you rich if you approach it cautiously and at the right time in the business cycle (as previously detailed). So how does borrowing to buy shares work? It is time to find out by *ASK*ing ...

Chapter 13

HOW DOES BORROWING MONEY TO BUY SHARES ACCELERATE YOUR CAPITAL PROFIT (OR LOSS)?

'There are two times in a man's life when he should not speculate; when he can't afford it and when he can.'
~ **Samuel Longhorne Clemens (Mark Twain).**

A growth industry in recent years has been the dramatic increase in funds being made available for investing in shares. Only a few years ago there were very few lenders indeed, who would lend you money to purchase shares. Then, and now for that matter, you have to be very careful when you read the fine print on the contracts of these share loan agreements. The reason for care is to avoid having to make substantial contributions when the share market corrects and decreases in value (which it always does).

There are two basic types of loans used when buying shares, **margin loans** and **protected equity loans** (detailed on page 140).

What are Margin Loans?

Margin loans are loans secured against shares. The amount allowed for such loans is between a minimum valuation of the shares that are used as security for the loan (between 20% and 50% of the value of the shares), and a maximum value of the shares that are purchased (usually between 70% and 75% of the value of the same shares).

HOW TO BUILD RICHES

Margin loans are a great way to build riches if used carefully and at the right time, with the right shares. For example, the minimum amount that is usually loaned for margin loans ranges from $20,000 to $50,000. Interest rates are between 8.0% and 9.25% at present, and can sometimes be negotiated to as low as 7.25%, if funds are deposited with the lender and interest on the margin loan is prepaid. Higher interest rates, (between 2% and 3%) may be charged by some lenders if you do not borrow over a certain amount, say $40,000. Let us assume that you are an investor and have $30,000 of your own hard-earned money to invest, and that you wish to consider to use leverage (this being the use of a lender's margin loan money to buy you more shares) of $70,000. This means you are then able to purchase $100,000 worth of shares at the lower interest rate.

The table on the next page illustrates what happens if the shares that you purchase increase or decrease in value by 10%. Your new equity (how much money is yours after borrowings) is compared with what the situation would be if you simply purchased $30,000 worth of shares, without any borrowing.

With no leverage, your shares either rise or fall 10%, depending upon the change in value of the shares. If the shares increased in value by 10%, using leverage, the percentage increase on your equity is 33.3%. However, if your shares decrease in value by 10%, the value of your equity decreases by 33.3%, instead of 10%, if you did not borrow. It is easy to see from this example that it is possible for you to make a lot more money using leverage and also for you to lose a lot more money using leverage.

As the share market is so volatile, it is desirable to be very cautious using borrowed money to purchase shares and when entering into the share margin loans (particularly if you are just getting started in the share market). Early payment penalty fees can be incurred, if loans are repaid before the agreed date (so read the fine print)! Payments have to be made in what is called **margin calls** if the value of the shares drops below a nominated amount. A margin call is a demand, made by the lender who holds the shares, to pay an amount of money, within a specified period, to bring the loan back to an agreed level. If this is not done, severe penalties can apply, as will be detailed on the example in the next few pages. If this happens, the borrower has to either meet a margin call (sometimes in a shorter period of time than twenty-four hours) or have the lender sell the shares to restore the loan to the agreed ratio. This can be very expensive indeed (particularly when the share market has fallen and the value of the shares sold is low at the time of the forced sale).

HOW DOES BORROWING MONEY TO BUY SHARES ACCELERATE YOUR PROFIT OR LOSS?

SHARE MARGIN LOANS

	USING LEVERAGE	USING NO LEVERAGE
Your own Equity	$30,000	$30,000
Loan Obtained	$70,000	$0
Initial Market Value of Your Shares	$100,000	$30,000

10 % Rise in Market Value of Your Shares

New Market Value of Your Shares	$110,000	$33,000
Loan Balance Outstanding	($70,000)	$0
Value of Your Equity	$40,000	$33,000
% Increase in Your Equity	33.3%	10.0%

10 % Fall in Market Value of Your Shares

New Market Value of Your Shares	$90,000	$27,000
Loan Balance Outstanding	($70,000)	$0
Value of Your Equity	$20,000	$27,000
% Decrease in Your Equity	(33.3%)	(10.0%)

How are margin calls activated? I will use an example to demonstrate this. It is assumed that you are borrowing 70% of the value of shares. The lender in margin loans establishes a ratio called a margin call value (or trigger value), which, in this instance, is 77.5% of the value of your shares. If your loan ever becomes higher than this margin call value then you are called upon to restore the value of the shares and funds held (sometimes within twenty-four hours), so that it is higher than the margin call value. If it is not restored, then the lender (who holds your shares) can sell your shares as demonstrated in the example on the next page. In this example it is assumed that your shares fall in value by 5% or 10%.

If your share values fell by 5%, the margin call value is $73,625, (being 77.5% of the new value of your shares, which is $95,000). As this amount is greater than your existing loan balance of $70,000, no margin call is required.

HOW TO BUILD RICHES

If, however, your shares dropped in value by 10%, to $90,000, then the margin call value of 77.5% of $90,000, is only $69,750. This amount is lower than your loan balance of $70,000.

MARGIN LENDING AND MARGIN CALLS

	Shares Starting Position	Effect of a 5% Fall in Value	Effect of a **10% Fall in Value**
Value of Your Shares	$100,000	$95,000	$90,000
Margin Call Value **(77.5% of Value)**	$77,500	$73,625	**$69,750**
Maximum Lending Value on Your Shares (70%)	$70,000	$66,500	$63,000
Your Loan Balance	$70,000	$70,000	**$70,000**
New Value of Your Equity	$30,000	$25,000	$20,000
Leverage Ratio of Shares before Margin Call	70%	74%	78%
Margin Call Required	0	0	**$7,000**

A margin call is required as the leverage ratio is greater than 77.5%.

Even though there is only a $250 shortfall, your loan is in default and the lender will force you to do one of three things:

1) Pay $7,000 cash, to reduce the loan from $70,000 to $63,000 being now 70% of the current value of the shares

2) Sell some of your shares so that the value of your share portfolio is again 70% of the value of your shares. This would require over $23,000 of shares to be sold (which is over 25% of the value of your shares, resulting from a 10% fall in the price). This $23,000 of sales proceeds (plus brokerage and stamp duty), reduces your loan to a new

HOW DOES BORROWING MONEY TO BUY SHARES ACCELERATE YOUR PROFIT OR LOSS?

loan value of $47,000. The new value of your shares is $67,000 (being the new value of $90,000 less $23,000 of shares that had to be sold to make the margin call). The new loan balance of $47,000, divided by the new value of your remaining shares brings you again within that 70% limit. This means your new equity is $20,000 (being your shares value of $67,000 less your new loan balance of $47,000).

For you to get your original investment back to $30,000 again, your shares will have to go up in value by $10,000 on the reduced value of your remaining shares of $67,000. This means you need a 15% increase in your shares price to get your money back.

If you work out the same numbers for a 20% fall in your share values (which is not uncommon when shares are overpriced), then the lender can sell over $46,000 of your shares (plus brokerage and stamp duty). If this happens you will require a 59% increase in the value of your shares to get your money back.

It is easily seen why margin calls can be very risky, particularly if you do not have the available cash to pay the margin call. It is very awkward and painful to be forced to sell a large section of your shares when the margin drops. If the market recovers by the same amount in the coming days, it is too late. The damage has been done as your lender may have already sold your shares.

3) You can lodge additional acceptable shares with the lender, (with a current market value of over $10,000) to restore the overall lending ratio of the total share portfolio to $100,000. This means the value of the loan balance is once again 70% of $100,000.

Margin lending is great when shares are going up and times are good. It can be very expensive when share markets start falling. Be careful not to buy shares with a high margin lending percentage in a bull market (unless you are a risk-taker with plenty of available cash to restore the loan if your share value falls).

What are Protected Equity Loans?

Protected equity loans are share loans for a higher percentage value of the shares than margin loans. The loan value can be between 80% and 102% of the value of the shares purchased. The 2% over the 100% value is used to cover costs. Loan sizes are usually a minimum of $40,000 to $100,000.

Interest rates on these loans range from about 12% to about 28%. The interest rates are often so huge, because the lenders of such loans take all of the risk. At the time the loan is due for repayment, the shares may have decreased in value to the extent that the borrower does not wish to proceed and would rather write-off the interest expense, paid as a tax-deductible loss, than be forced to have to purchase these shares. If the borrower had to purchase the shares, then not only would the borrower lose on the interest paid, but also on having to purchase shares at a lower price than they were originally bought for. In this situation, the lender takes possession of the shares at the lower market price.

If, however, the share market increases, the borrower receives all of the profit on shares, less the interest and set-up costs of the loan. The borrower, in this situation, ends up owning the shares with the loan against them and can either renew the loan or pay tax-deductible interest on it, sell the shares to repay the loan, take another loan with another lender, or repay the loan with money from other sources.

Timing is critical with both margin loans and protected equity loans. It is advisable to buy both when the market is low and likely to increase, or when the market conditions are so strong that there is a definite likelihood of the market continuing to increase in value for some considerable time.

Some people used to borrow to buy shares, and pre-pay interest in May or June, of a given year (when they have made large taxable profits from other sources). This system of pre-paying expenses will not be available to any business or individual who has a turnover of less than $1,000,000 in the last 2 years on average excluding GST (such businesses or individuals will be classed as **'small business'**) after 1 July 2001. People used to receive a tax deduction in that same tax year ending 30th June. If you did this, when your tax return was processed you would receive a tax refund of up to 48.5% of your pre-paid interest. It is still advisable only to do this if it is a good time to invest and you have thoroughly researched your investment. It is amazing how many otherwise intelligent people make rash decisions, in May or June of every year, to avoid paying tax, only to lose more money than they save! If you asked the same people to work for six months of the year for no salary, they would think you were a lunatic, but this is exactly what they are doing when they put their hard earned riches at risk, solely to get a tax deduction. Investing in shares can build riches. You need to invest wisely.

Chapter 14

WHY BUILD RICHES IN THE SHARE MARKET?

'The accumulation of property is no guarantee of the development of character, but the development of character, or any other good whatsoever, is impossible without property.'
~ **William Graham Sumner.**

What are the Advantages of Investing in the Sharemarket?

1) Shares provide dividends income and capital profits (and losses) in the form of changes in share prices;

2) Shares listed on the main board of the stock exchange are readily saleable, at a market price. This allows you reasonably quick access to your money if you need it for an emergency (or opportunity);

3) No tax is paid on the profits realised from an increase in value in shares, until the shares are sold;

4) Individual shares, generally, have a low entry price and it is possible to get started in the share market with less than $1,000;

5) Imputation credits mean that share dividend income can be tax free to shareholders, who are in a relatively low tax bracket.

What are the Disadvantages of Investing in the Sharemarket?

1) Fear and greed drive the share market. When you have invested in shares, and they are going up or down quickly, it can be difficult, at times, to remain objective about your investment;

2) A person in the company in which you invest can commit a major fraud, or can squander large amounts of the shareholders' capital (including your money). This can amount to billions of dollars of the company's profit. This has been the case in recent years, with the Sumitomo Corporation, in Japan, losing over three billion dollars, through one employee mismanaging the company's accounts. Another example was Baring Brothers, losing almost one and a half billion dollars, when one of its traders made a bad decision. If a major fraud occurs, chances are that the shareholders will get very little or even nothing back from their investment in the company. The courts rarely have little left to give to the shareholders, after the lenders, lawyers and accountants have claimed their fees;

3) Small investors are prone to buy when everyone else is buying, at the top of the market. The same people often get scared and sell at the bottom of the market. Prudent research before you invest will minimise the chance of poor judgement;

4) If you are given hot tips from someone who works in the company, you run the risk of being an inside trader, which is illegal. Although charges are hardly ever made for such offences, if convicted, there can be severe penalties, including gaol sentences;

5) Borrowing against shares (margin loans) can be risky, particularly at high lending ratios. If you do want high lending ratios, it is advisable to have large amounts of money (or shares) readily available to repay loan money if your loan goes into default and a margin call is required.

WHY BUILD RICHES IN THE SHARE MARKET?

Are all Large Public Companies to be Trusted?

There are many ethical public companies and directors. There are also quite a few greedy rogues. Take caution when dealing with both large and small companies. Some years ago I lived in Perth and I had negotiated a highly profitable real estate property transaction in Sydney. At the time, I had a friend who was a senior executive with what was then, one of the largest public companies in Australia. This company has subsequently been liquidated with its shareholders receiving almost nothing. The former head of the company was once a yachting hero and many Australians trusted his company and himself and invested many hundreds of millions of dollars with them.

The founder of this company, having lost billions of dollars of Australian hard-earned money, is currently in gaol for fraud on a totally different matter. To the best of my knowledge no charges were successfully made against the directors of this company, who lost billions of dollars of value in this public company (including the losses incurred by the banks' shareholders who loaned this company money).

To this company, I took my real estate investment and *ASK*ed them to fund my project, which was potentially a transaction worth over $700 million. I had secured enough of the project to control this transaction and I offered this company 90% of the profit in this deal, as well as interest on their invested funds (I was young and keen to launch my career by doing one of the biggest real estate projects in Sydney at that time).

Because I knew one of their top executives personally, I thought I would be treated fairly. Unfortunately for me, they cleverly tied me up in an interim agreement, then changed the basis of our original agreement (although they were happy for me to do all of the work). This company had their lawyers push me to get even more control and money from this transaction. I refused to be cheated. The matter went to the Supreme Court in NSW and the company eventually settled out of court as a result of my legal action. However, the deal was lost and I learned a lot.

During this transaction I worked from the offices of these corporate cowboys, (once in the top twenty publicly listed companies in Australia). Having seen how they operated, it is my opinion that there are many people on average salaries who would have done a better job running this company than those I saw in their offices.

Control your own future and avoid losing most of your money by not investing in a Bond Corporation Limited (Allan Bond), Qintex (Christopher Skase), Westmex, or Estate Mortgage etc . . .

The share market is an excellent source of investment if you are thorough in your research and you have the ability to hold your shares for the long-term. Be careful. Buy when everyone else is selling, in a bear market, and be sure to sell when everyone else is buying, in a bull market. Long-term implications of the SGC will mean there will be fabulous opportunities in the share market in coming decades, provided you pick the time when you get in and get out of the market.

Should You Plan Your Affairs to Minimise Tax?

Some people buy shares with an expectation of making a **capital profit** (also referred to as a capital gain). A capital profit happens when shares increase in value, to a price higher than the shareholder paid for them. This profit is only taxed when the shares are actually sold (and the profit received). It makes sense to plan the sale of these shares, where possible, in order to minimise or defer your taxes. For example, if a taxpayer wanted to sell shares on June 15th, it might be better to wait until July 1st. This puts the sale and profit in the new taxation year and gives the taxpayer a whole twelve months to plan how to minimise the impact of the tax on these shares.

Although you can legally arrange your affairs to minimise tax payable, the tax office will rarely, if ever, tell you that if you changed your affairs, you could save tax! The tax office is keen to raise as much tax revenue as it can. Tax laws change regularly. If you are serious about keeping up to date with the latest rulings and are keen to know about tax-saving techniques, you will be interested in listening to the *Building Riches* audio tapes, or attending seminars conducted by reputable and experienced presenters. Many who have purchased our tapes have gained much more than just excellent ways to build greater riches. I encourage you to become a lifelong learner of specialist *Knowledge* which will allow your life to be richer in all areas, including financially.

It is now time to look at the other main area for direct investments and that is . . .

Chapter 15

HOW DO YOU PROFIT FROM INVESTING IN REAL ESTATE?

'Property is dear to men not only for the sensual pleasure it can afford, but also because it is the bulwark of all they hold dear on Earth, and above all else, because it is the safeguard of those they love most against misery and all physical distress.'
~ **William Graham Sumner.**

Real estate comes in many forms. You can buy vacant land, rural land, shops, commercial offices, industrial factories, hi-tech industrial buildings, and residential homes (that range from run-down shacks to luxury, waterfront mansions).

A massive amount of money is flowing into superannuation as a result of the SGC. The fund managers of the main superannuation funds do not only invest in the share market. This money is also finding its way into large commercial buildings, modern industrial buildings and huge retail shopping centres. In the late 1990's, prices being paid for prime, non-residential real estate, by fund managers, were as high and higher than they were in 1989, before the last real estate crash.

Buying real estate, in some ways, is just like buying shares. The trick is to buy low and sell high, or not sell at all. There is not enough space here to explore more thoroughly the areas of non-residential, real estate investment. Non-residential, real estate investment can be more profitable than residential investment, but is far more risky and requires specialist *Knowledge* and specialist management of these properties. In mid 1999 for example, it was not a good time for individuals to be buying some non-residential real estate, because of the relatively high prices being paid at that time. It moves in cycles just like residential real estate and shares. The GST will be levied on non-residential rent. The tenant will get a credit which can usually be included in the service provided which the consumer of the company's products ends up paying for. Landlords of non residential real estate should get specialist assistance when drawing up their next lease to make sure thy can pass the GST on to their tenants.

GST will not be charged on residential rent.
Most people have some understanding of residential real estate, because we all currently live in it and have lived in residential real estate for all of their lives. You may already have a good understanding of how to invest in residential real estate and wisely accumulate riches in this way. If you have specialist information and experience in large, non-residential, real estate, then you can apply the same principles from this section to your other real estate investments.

Real estate is an excellent investment because, as well as receiving rental income (or rent) for established houses and apartments, the owner of the real estate also has the ability to make capital profits when the real estate goes up in value. It is possible to lose money through investing in residential real estate, but it is much harder to do so than through investing in the stock market. It is much harder to lose money in real estate because approximately two out of every three residential properties is owned by an owner-occupier (refer to page 26), who are unwilling to sell their house if real estate prices dropped in value (unless they were forced to sell). This provides a natural buffer that is not available in the share market.

If the share prices in any company go down too much, many people will sell their shares because of the fear of further losses, or the fear that the company may go out of business (which can become a reality). Residential properties do not go out of business! If these properties are well-located and well-maintained, there will always be a tenant for them, so a rental income will always be possible. Buying residential real estate when prices are very high, (and some expect prices to continue to increase at a rapid rate forever), is just as ridiculous as buying shares, when people (many of whom have no experience) are telling you to buy when the share market is too high and these same people say it will never again.

It is interesting to hear some people say that shares are a better place to build riches than real estate. Others will just as actively say that real estate is a far safer investment than investing in shares. Who is right? In my opinion, both investing in shares and investing in real estate are fabulous ways to get rich. If you are a wise investor, then, over time, you may choose to invest in both areas. You may well end up with a preference to put most of your money in either real estate or shares.

It is becoming increasingly popular for people to talk about spreading their risk and diversifying their money, so that they leave some of their equity invested in different forms of investment, such as:

1) shares
2) real estate
3) fixed interest or a cash management account.

As I detailed earlier, there are very wealthy people, including self-made billionaires, who prefer one area of investment to another. If you read through the *BRW Magazine Rich 200*, a list of the wealthiest two hundred people in Australia, you will see that a tremendous number of them have made their money through investing in real estate.

Should You Buy a Home or an Investment Property First?

People often *ASK* me: *'Should I buy a home or an investment property first?'* It is not wise to give advice to people until you first know exactly what their goals and values are in life, and know how much risk they are prepared to accept. From a financial perspective, a key ingredient in this question lies in the tax-effectiveness of borrowings used to buy real estate.

If you borrow to buy a house that you will live in, then there is no tax deduction for the borrowings. As you learnt before, there is a high cost associated with security loans. (You have seen how David and Shirley Battler have chosen to take twenty five years to pay off their family home loan). Due to this high cost of consumer and security loans, my advice to people getting started, is to buy a home that you can afford and to only borrow that amount of money needed to buy it. Buy your home in an area that is affordable and good for you to live in.

Buying a home is probably one of the biggest investment decisions that most people make. The decision to buy any real estate (including your home), should be made not only with your heart, in terms of your emotions, but also with your head. Using your head includes taking the time to *ASK* yourself: *'Where is the best place to buy my home?'*, *'How much money is the best amount to borrow for it?'*, *'What is the best loan to use to secure my property purchase?'* The answers to these questions will have an enormous effect on your future wealth. In the coming chapter, you will see how Peter and Anne Wise, who bought their family home first, were able to borrow against their equity in this home to buy investment real estate (the borrowings on investment real estate are tax-deductible). They were able to build riches much faster using this *Strategy*. For most people, buying a home, that they can afford, and quickly reducing the security loan on their home mortgage, allows them to build up equity. They then can use this equity in their home as the security to borrow against, in order to invest in other assets. Meanwhile, the value of their home should also be increasing while they are reducing the debt, particularly if they buy their home in the right area.

What Type of Real Estate Should You Buy and Where Should You Buy It?

These are two questions I am commonly asked. Both of them will be answered later in this chapter. It is not possible for me to know when you first or last read this book, or when you would want to use what you've learnt from it, so telling you, specifically, to buy real estate in a certain suburb, or street, would be just as foolish as trying to tell you to buy shares in a particular company, irrespective of when you might buy them. Just as share prices go up and down with supply and demand, so too do real estate prices. It is, however, possible to determine, from research into the real estate market, where certain trends emerge and where the areas are that offer the best capital growth on your real estate investment.

There are authors in Australia who recommend buying **median priced properties**. A median priced property is a statistical creation and no such real estate ever exists. As many properties sell above that median price as sell below that price. This figure is derived from a cross section of all real estate in an area ~ old and new, dilapidated and renovated, cheap and expensive. In my mind it is not prudent to race out and buy investment real estate based on figures that have no resemblance to real properties being sold to real people for a real profit.

If median priced properties were the best investment, then most of the richest people in our society would own lots of them! Most of the self-made millionaires, and many of the smarter investors tend to own quality properties, which are always in high demand, and are located in sought after areas. These properties are usually far more expensive than the median priced properties. I know many people who have made many millions of dollars through owning better quality properties.

While building riches through real estate investment, I encourage you to go and look at and consider real properties, that real people would want to rent. (Owning these properties will give you income). It is also important to consider whether your investment choice would be attractive to other buyers, should you decide to sell it. The aim is to invest in property that you can easily sell for the best possible price, and to give yourself the opportunity to make a huge capital gain on the sale. Many people buy real estate and never sell it. Some even accumulate large real estate portfolios that they pass on to their families in their wills. Eventually, most of us will choose to, or need to, sell some of our investment properties. I will discuss this further in the following chapters.

Where are People with Lots of Money Going to Want to Buy and Live in the Future?

If you start *ASK*ing quality questions like this, you are likely to get quality answers (as you begin to train your brain to build your riches). As discussed earlier in this book, the fastest-growing group of people in the Australian population is made up of people aged over sixty-five. The interesting thing is that, these people are the people with most of the money in our economy. Many of these people will sell their family home after the children have moved out. They often decide that they now need a different type of home. When they sell their existing family home (often on the quarter acre block) which has significantly increased in value, they may well receive, in a city like Sydney or Melbourne, an amount approaching, or in excess of, $600,000. They then have this money on hand, to go and buy their dream retirement home.

So What Type of Property are the People with the Money Likely to Buy and How Will This Knowledge Help You Get Richer?

When these people retire, most are going to want to live in a property that:

1) has no steps;
2) is in an area close to amenities; and
3) ideally has pleasant views (if they can afford it).

It is interesting, that many older people will count how many steps there are in a property. They may consider one property with seven steps to be a worse buy than a property with two steps. This indicates that good quality, single level apartments are likely to be a good investment. Be careful not to be tricked into buying very cheap units, in large unit complexes, which may not appeal to older people. Ideal investment properties are more likely to be semi-luxurious (or luxury), single-level, residential homes, or apartments in small blocks with an elevator. These properties will cost you more money initially, but there will always be a strong demand for them in the future. If you are purchasing as a Baby Boomer, yourself, and looking to accumulate wealth for your retirement, then the chances are good that you will want to hold this real estate for some considerable time. Eventually somebody will be the purchaser of your real estate.

One excellent technique I use, to make astute property investment decisions, is to make a mental picture of the type of person (and, even better, remember somebody I know who fits that profile) who will either rent or buy my investment real estate. Be careful to concentrate on those types of people who fit into larger groups in our society (not just a unique type of person). This way you are more likely to select property that will have a broad market of buyers. Once you can do this, you are well on your way to making a good investment decision. I have made millions of dollars through using this visualisation method before designing the properties I have developed, built, then sold or held to make a profit for my investors and myself. Honing this skill is like developing any other muscle, it takes practice. Once you get good at it and continue developing it, you can become a master. From my own experience, I can assure you that developing this skill of visualisation will help you become rich.

How Can You Get the Right Knowledge?

Unfortunately, in most capital cities, in Australia, the only available statistics on residential properties are on median prices. To me, a median price index is useless. A classic example of this is the median price of properties in Hunters Hill, in Sydney. From 1990 to 1995, the median

HOW DO YOU PROFIT FROM INVESTING IN REAL ESTATE?

house price in this suburb showed a substantial decrease in prices. Many people, mistakenly, thought that this decrease in the median price was purely brought about by the increase in noise, from aircraft flying over Hunters Hill. This did have an effect, but was not nearly as big an effect as the fact that, part of the adjoining suburb was included in the boundaries of Hunters Hill, and that suburb included many lower value homes. A look at the median price statistics would never disclose this fact. If you want to buy and own properties for real people, then you want to look at and buy real properties!

In a suburb, in your city, beautiful old character homes may be being pulled down, with cheap, rental accommodation being erected for government-assisted welfare recipients. The sale price statistics, which are used to find the median price, show, in one period, the sales of the large, stately homes and, in other periods, the sales, or transfers, of some of the discounted properties. These median figures, which average these statistics, will obviously distort the whole picture of other figures of real properties, being sold to real people.

A meaningful comparison of properties requires actually going and comparing real properties to other real properties. To get really rich, you may even consider different parts of a given suburb. I decide on the streets that I will buy an investment property in, and other streets in the same suburb, in which I will not buy a property.

I encourage you to handle with caution and trepidation the idea of buying median priced real estate.

Let me give you an example of real properties based on real figures, so you can start to generate the principles that will allow you to decide wisely, where to buy your investment properties. In NSW, (and particularly Sydney) in the twenty years between 1976 and 1996, the government valuer conducted real valuations on real properties, as a means of assessing the rate of increase in property values. This research gives us a clear insight into the changes in values and changes in social trends, that can help you to become rich. They defined inner city suburbs, in their research, as the suburbs within six kilometres of the centre of Sydney. Middle distance suburbs were suburbs between six and twenty-five kilometres from the city centre. Outer suburbs were suburbs more then twenty-five kilometres away from the city centre (where at least half of the population of Sydney lives). From 1997 to 1999 inclusive I have used conservative estimates of the same properties that the NSW Valuer General used from 1976 to 1996.

HOW TO BUILD RICHES

On page 153 is a graph that indicates the amount of money you would have accumulated, had you invested in a three bedroom Sydney cottage in 1976, in each of these three areas. What is easily noticed, is that the inner city suburbs outperformed the middle distance and outer city suburbs.

This graph shows the dramatic difference in the rate of return for the owners of real estate in each of the three areas. In 1976, the average three-bedroom cottage in all three areas was valued at approximately $40,000. By 1999, real estate in the outer suburbs of Sydney had only grown to just almost $240,000. The corresponding property, in the middle distance suburbs, had grown to a little more than $364,000. The average inner Sydney suburban cottage had grown to just under $515,000. A detailed analysis of the actual valuations, shows that over this twenty-three year period, the compound growth rate for the outer suburbs was just over 8%, for the middle distance suburbs, just under 10% and, for the inner city suburbs, over 11%. Using the Rule of 72, you know that 72, divided by the compound rate of growth, tells you that it would have taken nine years to double your money on outer suburban real estate, just over seven years on property in a middle distance suburb and less than six and a half years to double your money on an inner Sydney suburban cottage.

Although the NSW government no longer prepare these figures (and most other states use 'media figures' which are of no real use) the trend that following graph shows holds constant. Historically around the world property closer to the centre of cities grows at a faster rate. This trend will continue in the future.

What are the Reasons for the Difference in Return of Real Estate in Different Areas?

There are several reasons for real property values increasing at different rates in different areas. These reasons include:

1) A tendency for people to want to live closer to where they work. With professional people having to work longer hours and traffic increasing, many professional people desire to live closer to where they work;

2) Many areas close to the city contain real estate that is amongst the most expensive and sought after in Australia. With Sydney hosting the Olympics, in the year 2000, the chances are excellent that properly selected properties, in Sydney, will continue to rise. One reason for this

HOW DO YOU PROFIT FROM INVESTING IN REAL ESTATE?

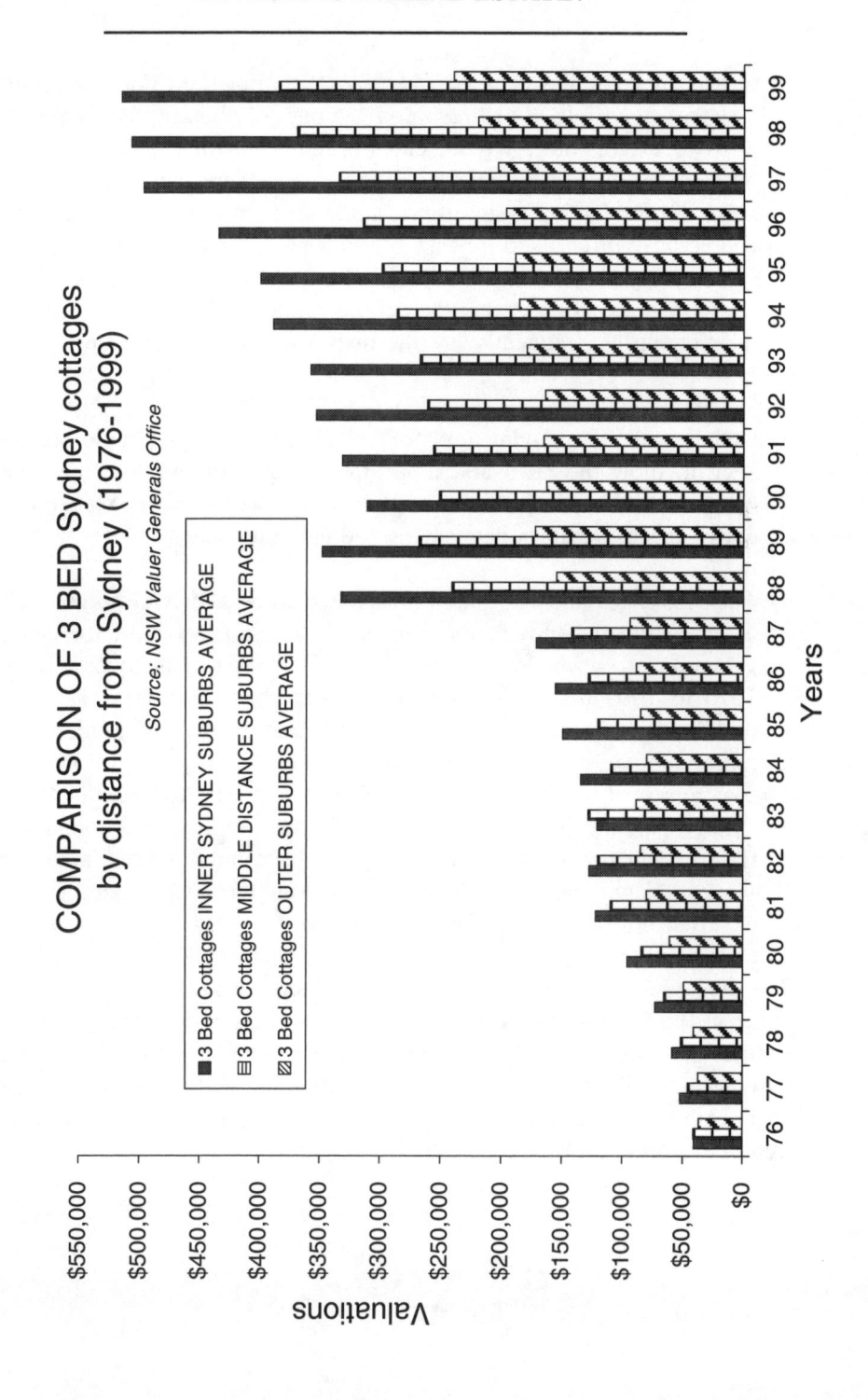

COMPARISON OF 3 BED Sydney cottages by distance from Sydney (1976-1999)

Source: NSW Valuer Generals Office

Legend:
- 3 Bed Cottages INNER SYDNEY SUBURBS AVERAGE
- 3 Bed Cottages MIDDLE DISTANCE SUBURBS AVERAGE
- 3 Bed Cottages OUTER SUBURBS AVERAGE

HOW TO BUILD RICHES

is that most of the professional people coming into Australia from overseas, tend initially to reside in Sydney, Melbourne, Perth and, to a lesser extent, other capital cities around Australia. Many of these overseas professionals have qualified to live here, before they enter Australia, by having a significant amount of financial reserves. These people have often lived in Asia and Europe and seen real estate prices (particularly in Asia) exceed those in Sydney by up to five times! They know from experience, that the people who own the best real estate in their countries, frequently are the ones who build the greatest riches in their society;

3) Couples are now having less (or no) children. Many people are not keen to mow the lawn and look after a big yard in their free time. Many now want to be part of a caf society, able to walk to restaurants, coffee places, retail outlets, shops and entertainment venues;

4) There is a demand for quaint, charming, three bedroom homes built at, or before the turn of the 20th century. An analysis of the actual valuation of two bedroom units, in selected suburbs in Sydney, from 1976 to 1999 reveals that inner city suburban units grew at 9.8%, middle distance suburbs grew at 8.6% and Liverpool, (which is a representative example of outer suburban Sydney), grew at 8.1%. It's easy to see, at once, that the compound growth rates for three bedroom cottages, in the inner city, far exceeds that for two bedroom units. Careful selection of the right quality two bedroom units can, however, yield a significantly greater increase in returns, closer to that experienced for the three bedroom cottages.

The dynamic of supply and demand is another reason for the increase in value in three bedroom Sydney cottages. There are a decreasing number of three bedroom, free-standing cottages, close to the city, in all Australian cities. Having lived for some years in Melbourne, Perth and Sydney, and spent extensive time in Brisbane, Adelaide and Hobart, I've seen the same trend develop in all of those cities.

HOW DO YOU PROFIT FROM INVESTING IN REAL ESTATE?

So Where Do You Buy, to Maximise Your Chances of Building Greater Riches?

The key, from the Sydney experience, is to find suburbs with properties that are in areas yet to be developed to their fullest potential. These suburbs are close to other areas that are very popular now but, for whatever reason, these suburbs have not yet taken off. Buy in these suburbs and wait until the rest of the city catches on to the idea that these properties are well-located. Eventually, higher income people will move into the area and beautify the older cottages, which then will lead to a massive increase in the value of the area and your properties. There are a limited number of three bedroom cottages and semi-luxury apartments and a high demand from people who want to have their own home, close to work. The supply of these properties is far less than the demand from people who would like to buy them. This excessive demand will always push the prices up, particularly if you buy at the right time.

The same trend will exist for Baby Boomers wanting to retire to quality properties near beaches, the harbour, and bushland areas that are also close to facilities and ideally within easy access of the city. There is a difference between the quality accommodation that Baby Boomers will want to live in, and the glut of cheap units that have recently been constructed in many cities around Australia. For example, there is currently a massive over-development in Sydney, Brisbane and Melbourne of high density one and two bedroom units that will not suit many of the wealthier Baby Boomers when they buy their retirement unit. The inevitable effect, if you have a greater supply of cheap units than there is demand for, will force down the prices (over a considerable number of years), as it becomes a buyers' market and people are able to buy these units for a lesser price, if they wait for the right time.

When some people make an investment decision to buy real estate, they may want to buy purely on the basis of price, and buy the cheapest real estate they can. This is often a bad investment decision. My wife owned a property on a busy Sydney main road (in an outer middle distance suburb) that she bought before we were married. It was one of the few properties in the area that she really wanted to live in, that she could afford, at that time. We decided to sell this property and use the money from the sale in another, better-performing, real estate investment. Due to the location of the property, we had trouble selling it quickly and eventually had to sell for less than we believed it was worth. However, we gladly sold it because we were able to use the money more effectively somewhere else. We have compounded her equity very successfully to significantly make up for more than the decrease in that sale price. The moral of the story is, that if a property is in a less than favourable location when you buy it, and you're able to buy it for a cheap price, you may have to sell it for a cheap price at the other end. Ideally, your aim is to buy a very well-located property, when the business cycle is at its lowest and real estate prices are very low ~ when it is a buyers market. Your aim then is to hold this real estate until prices are very high and the economy is booming. People then will be prepared to pay huge amounts of money for your property. The relative rate of return on your well-located real estate will far exceed the rate available on real estate that you could have bought for a much cheaper price, in a secondary location. **Buy quality when real estate prices are in the gloom and sell them when they are in the boom**, (or never sell them at all, which I will cover in the coming chapters).

Last year, I owned, amongst other investments: a three-bedroom property in the outer suburbs of Sydney, a four-bedroom property in the middle distance suburbs, and a two-bedroom luxury townhouse in the inner city suburbs. The actual increase in profit from the two-bedroom property in the inner city suburbs, was greater than the growth of both the middle distance and outer suburban properties combined! For various reasons, I sold the inner city suburban property and used the proceeds to invest in several other properties in Sydney (again within this inner suburb six kilometre radius). Be flexible and consider buying two-bedroom or three-bedroom properties, on their merits.

Be careful when buying one-bedroom and bed-sitter properties in certain places (particularly close to the centre of capital cities at the moment). There is a definite over-supply of one and two-bedroom units looming, in Sydney, in suburbs like Pyrmont, Ultimo, Blackwater Bay and Sydney city itself, as in Melbourne, Brisbane, and Perth. Although there are a lot of people moving in towards the city (particularly young people renting these apartments), there are far more places being built than there is likely to be demand for (in the next few years). Eventually the market will collapse and real estate prices will go down on the poorer-performing properties and will stay down for some years.

The more *Knowledge* you gain and research you do, before you develop your *Strategy* and before you take *Action*, the more dramatic will be the

HOW DO YOU PROFIT FROM INVESTING IN REAL ESTATE?

increase in the riches that you will accumulate later. Wisely selecting the right property investments is likely to make you hundreds of thousands of dollars more, over the life of your investment in that real estate. In assessing the real estate you wish to buy, you want to look not only at the supply and demand now, but also the supply and demand in the future in the areas in which you are buying. You may defer your buying decision if you are in doubt.

One of the greatest benefits of a long-term real estate investment, is that the compound rate of growth significantly exceeds the inflation rate, over the same period (as evidenced in the graph on page 153). The greater the rate of growth of your investment, exceeding inflation, the greater your effective return, in today's dollars, on your investment. This is our aim in investing and this will be covered in significant detail in coming chapters.

How do You Buy Real Estate with Confidence and Ease?

There are a number of techniques to significantly improve your riches by purchasing the correct properties with confidence and ease. The precautions noted below identify some of the most relevant skills for you to develop, to assist you to buy real estate in the best way:

1) How do you avoid being a sales victim?

There are some fabulous real estate agents. There are many more who will only be in the industry for a year or two. Guard against sales techniques that tell you that you have to put in an offer or someone else will buy this property today! About every tenth time I have heard this and other similar techniques they are accurate. In not letting a sales person pressure you into buying, (through a tactic or a lie), you give yourself time to think and compare properties.

When I buy a property (particularly if it is my first in an area) I like to have looked at up to 100 others first. If a great deal goes, so be it, there will be more. Some people will lie to you. Face the facts. Be confident. Keep looking. There are always good buys for a hard-working buyer.

2) How not to pay for value that you add!

If a house is run-down, then I get excited. I love to buy the worst house in the best street. Then, I pay the lowest price in the street (and I don't pay for potential). When I make this property one of the best houses in the street, I keep the profit that I deserve. This is called adding value.

Make sure the house (particularly if it is brick) has what a good friend of mine calls 'good bones'. That is, the basic structure works ~ if the walls and rooms are in the right place, you can cosmetically add a new kitchen or tiling.

Most people will see a poorly presented property and promptly walk out. If there are unkempt lawns, or cockroaches, or a mess in a house, these can easily be fixed. You can offer a low purchase price and buy a property for a discount of $10,000 then only spend a fraction of that to clean it up.

3) *How do you avoid buying a nightmare property?*

There are specialist building inspectors whom you can find in the Yellow Pages (usually under 'Building Inspection Services' or a similar name).

When you identify a property you really want to buy and your offer has been accepted, it is advisable to have a professional building person (unless you are one already) inspect the property and identify any defects. This is worthwhile, even on new properties. Just because one company builds more units than another doesn't mean they build them any better. In recent years I have seen appalling examples of newly constructed buildings where major items have been left out of a property by inexperienced or greedy developers or builders. It does happen.

When you get the report from the inspector, be careful to be objective about it. Often these reports can be quite long and detailed. Be careful to separate the important things that need rectification from minor defects that you can tolerate. Almost every property has defects. It is the major problems, like a lack of proper waterproofing or structural supports, that you really want to avoid! Move on. There will always be another property. Alternatively, make your offer subject to the seller fixing all of the faults, at no cost to you.

4) *How do you find out if the area near where you buy is going to change?*

Local residents know, before a first-time buyer, what is happening in their area. If you go to the local council Town Planning Department

HOW DO YOU PROFIT FROM INVESTING IN REAL ESTATE?

you can find out a great deal about the area in which you are interested. They can tell you if there are any proposed zoning changes (that might allow businesses, units or factories) around your desired area. They can also tell you if there are any applications to build near the property you are interested in and much more. *ASK*ing a neighbour about the area can be a good idea also. You don't want to buy a lovely home only to discover that the local motorcycle gang has its headquarters next door and they party all night, every night. All you have to do is *ASK* before you buy.

5) *How do you further protect and inform yourself?*

Your solicitor, or conveyancer, can do many searches through government departments (for a fair fee) that will determine whether the street is to be widened, or there are building defects, outstanding land tax on the property, or a host of other things you need to know. Better a little caution now. A properly worded contract to purchase can solve many problems. In States where the real estate agent writes up the sales contract (like Western Australia) it is advisable to obtain from a solicitor, or another professional, a list of clauses you want in the contract, before you sign it. If you know in advance what you want included in the contract, the chances are good that you will get it. Your *Knowledge* and *Strategy* will allow you to take better Action

6) *How do you maximise your tax deductions on the purchase?*

If the property you want to purchase was built after 1985, you can get a tax deduction for depreciating the building itself. *ASK* the seller if they have a depreciation schedule on the property (from when they bought the property) or from the builder. If you can't get one from them, then a quantity surveyor can prepare one for you for a fee. This fee will usually be saved in tax, in a short period of time and is tax deductible if you purchase the property as an investment property. If it is to be your home you will not need such a report. Further information on tax deductions will be covered in the next two chapters.

7) *Keep learning what you know to develop mastery!*

As a Black Belt karate instructor, I have taught many people self-defence, confidence and inner peace. The people who become great at martial arts (or anything else) are people with enough discipline to keep learning the basics. The more often you read this book, the greater mastery of the basics and the principles you will develop, to become your own master of building riches. One saying that they use at the head dojo (training hall) of my style of karate (Chito Ryu) in Kumamoto, Japan is:

> *'Reward comes not from perfection,*
> *but rather from its unending pursuit.'*
> ~ **Soke Sensei.**

In your quest for riches, it is not one particular transaction that will secure your financial future. Rather it is the combination of all of the transactions, experience and skills you develop along the way that makes you ready for any opportunity when it arises.

Are You a Real Estate Trader or a Real Estate Investor?

Real estate traders are people who buy run-down old properties, renovate them and then sell them for a profit. I have friends who do this, quite successfully. The majority of my wealthy friends and clients tend to be real estate investors. They buy their properties when everybody else is fearful and selling their properties, and hold onto them for the long-term, mostly never selling them. The more my wealth increases and the more properties I own, the more likely I am to keep more and more of the properties I buy, for the long-term. My long-term aims include passing on an estate to my family and to charities that I will establish to provide educational and motivational services to Australians. Taking the long-term approach to real estate investing, and investing in a way that is consistent with your long-term goals and values, will bring you the most satisfaction and, ultimately, the greatest amount of financial return.

It is time to discover the *Knowledge* you need, to be able to multiply your riches and the number of properties you will own. In order to do this, you will want to know . . .

Chapter 16

HOW DO YOU BUILD INCOME BY INVESTING IN REAL ESTATE?

'I don't think you can spend yourself rich.'
~ **George Humphrey.**

The type of residential real estate that will make most people rich comprises properties that people will want to rent. When it comes to selling your investment properties, it is also important to have owned properties that others will want to purchase from you at a high price (that maximises your profit). The last chapter gave you some insights into the types of properties and the locations to select, to maximise your capital profit from your investment properties. This chapter is concerned about the rental and purchase aspects of properties that will make you rich.

Are You Investing for Several Years?

Residential real estate can go up very quickly in value. In Chapter 27 you will see that in some boom years, growth of over 20% a year, in cities like Sydney, can be common. However, the costs associated with buying and selling properties, including government taxes, will steal a lot of your profit, if you are not careful.

If you invest for over five years and have arranged your affairs so that you have a regular income and will not need to sell the property in the short term, then residential property becomes a better investment. Even though your initial costs are higher than for most other investments, (shares, managed funds, trusts, etc.), your expected returns are higher and your risks are lower. The next two chapters will give you the power of more *Knowledge* to better compare alternative investments. Further on, in the *Strategy* section you will see how, over a working lifetime, a well thought out *Strategy* will make you rich.

Assuming you are buying to become rich over a period of time, your initial costs to buy a property will soon be recovered. The benefits over the long-term will be worth it. Be careful to buy at the right time in the economic cycle, when property is likely to increase in value. This will be covered in more detail later.

Are There Any Benefits to Owning Real Estate Using No Borrowed Funds?

Owning real estate without using any borrowed money can, in the long-term, make you rich. It will, however, take a lot longer and require more money to get you started. Most people, when they acquire the *Knowledge* contained in the next chapter, will think it ridiculous to own real estate without using savers' money to make them rich. Owning real estate, without borrowing, is frequently used in three situations:

1) *In Retirement:*
Once you are rich you may choose to repay your borrowed money and live off your rental income and other investment income.

2) *Superannuation:*
Some people own properties in their own superannuation funds without any borrowing. At present there is a much easier way to get rich and provide for your own retirement (a goal the government, supposedly, also wants). This can be achieved through using borrowings by investing in a Unit Trust that you control. The Howard government wants to prevent you doing this, and I will be covering this in Chapter 27.

3) *For the Fearful or Paranoid:*
Knowledge is a powerful antidote to fear. There are people you meet who allow fear to drive their lives. They will not use other people's money to make them rich, because of their fear. They have a propensity to concentrate on anything, and everything, that can go wrong. Soon you will be able to dispel any old fears to build even greater riches.

HOW DO YOU BUILD INCOME BY INVESTING IN REAL ESTATE?

How many people would ever be able to afford to own their family home if they had to wait to pay cash for it (particularly in more expensive cities, like Sydney and Melbourne)? Very few indeed. They would probably be retiring about the time they bought it (due to the deposit gap which I mentioned in Chapter 4).

It is worthwhile understanding how property works, without borrowings, so you can decide how much to borrow and how to arrange your borrowing to get rich sooner. Having read Chapter 15, you are already well on your way to knowing how to buy, and how to research to buy the right investment property. It is also important to know how much it costs you personally to build property riches. To illustrate this throughout this chapter, we will use the purchase of a brand new strata titled property as an example. It is assumed the purchase is made after the introduction of the GST in 2002.

What Are the Cash Inflows and Outflows of Owning Property?

It is assumed that you are buying this property, for $249,000 plus purchasing costs. The relevant income and expenses are:

Weekly rent	$300
Weeks vacant p.a. (tenants moving in and out)	1 week
Real estate agent's management fee (full service)	6%* rent+GST
Initial fee to real estate agent to find a tenant and advertising	$500 + GST
Accountancy fees in relation to property	$300 + GST
Annual water rates and council rates	$790
Body corporate levies (including insurance and maintenance)	$800
Insurance (contents and malicious tenants damage)	$300
Repairs and Maintenance	$100 + GST
Other expenses (phone calls, travel, stationery, etc.)	$100 + GST

HOW TO BUILD RICHES

The expenses listed are quite conservative. Chances are, you can spend less than this on these items in many areas. It is assumed, however, that you have purchased your property in an excellent area with great capital growth prospects. Often I see people convinced to buy a property because the rent is high or expenses low and the buyer can easily afford it. In the last chapter we saw that between 1976 and 1999 in Sydney, the owner of an outer suburbs property might have earned a few thousand dollars more in taxable rent, but missed out on almost $300,000 of capital gain (which attracts no CGT until the property is sold, and even then, this tax can be reduced). Borrowing against this increased value means an even greater profit for the person who invested in the inner suburbs.

For this example, after the GST is introduced, in the first year of ownership, the property (without borrowings) will earn the following return, on a cash inflow and outflow basis. GST is calculated at 10% added to some relevant costs. the payer remits 1/11th of the total fee to the Tax Office. The GST will slightly increase the cost of owning properties. Over time rents will rise to pay for this extra cost. Fortunately rent and interest for residential properties is not covered by a GST.

Rent received (51 weeks x $300)		$15,300
Less: deductible cash expenses	$ 550	
Real estate agents letting & ad.'s & GST		
Real estate agents management fee	$1,018	
(6.0% of $15,300) (including GST)		
Water & council rates	$ 790	
Accounting fees (including GST)	$ 330	
Body corporate levies	$ 800	
Insurance	$ 300	
Repairs and maintenance	$ 110	
Other expenses (including GST)	$ 110	$ 4,000
Net cash inflow/(outflow)		**$11,300**

HOW DO YOU BUILD INCOME BY INVESTING IN REAL ESTATE?

What Are the Non-Cash Tax Deductions that You Can Claim?

As well as being able to claim a tax deduction for expenses that have been paid, property owners are also able to get a tax deduction for certain non-cash expenses. The most common are:

1) Depreciation of fixtures and fittings (carpets, blinds, etc)
2) Special building write-off
3) Borrowing costs (covered in the next chapter)

The **fixtures and fittings** in the property when you buy them can be depreciated (i.e. claimed as a tax deduction over the life of the asset). The cost price of these individual items is the amount available for **depreciation.** There are two methods of depreciation, these being:

1) Prime cost method (only for those with a turnover less than $1 million)
2) Diminishing value method (which will no longer be available)

The **prime cost method** allows an asset to be depreciated by a set percentage of its cost each year. An annual deduction is allowed at the same rate until the asset is fully depreciated to $0 or is written-off.

If the prime cost method is not nominated with the tax office, the **diminishing value method** used to apply. However from 22 September 1999 this method of depreciation is no longer available to property used predominantly for leasing or related activities, i.e. investment properties. For those of you that had real estate before October 1999 and elected to use this in your tax returns the diminishing value method allows a higher rate of depreciation, but this is applied annually to the depreciated value, i.e. the original cost, less what has already been allowed for depreciation.

Let me demonstrate for a property owner using the prime cost method. In the first year, the amount is proportioned for the number of days that the asset was owned (in the taxation year ended 30th June). In the second year of ownership, the balance of the value, less the purchase price is again multiplied by the depreciation rate, to get the second year's depreciation allowance. This amount is reduced each year until the asset value is reduced to zero or the asset is sold or written off.

For example, say one of your items for depreciation is carpet that cost $2,000: If the prime cost method is used, the rate is 17%.

PRIME COST

	Opening Value	Depreciation at 17%	Closing Value
Year 1	2,000	340	1,660
Year 2	1,660	340	1,320
Year 3	1,320	340	980
Year 4	980	340	640
Year 5	640	340	300
Year 6	300	300	0

The prime cost method allows you to depreciate all of an item in a faster number of years (in the sixth year above).

All individual items (i.e. each light fitting) can be depreciated separately, and every item less than $300 can be totally depreciated in the first year of ownership. This increases the first year's depreciation considerably. Make your decision soon after you buy your property.

An owner of investment real estate can also get a tax deduction for most construction costs and renovation expenditure. Residential property built after the 16th of September, 1987, is depreciated at 2.5% per annum. For buildings erected between 18th of July, 1985, and the 15th of September, 1987 the rate is 4%. Included in the amount allowed to be depreciated are such items as architect's fees, other consultant's fees, builder's profit margin, construction materials and labour. You do not receive a report when you buy each investment property a highly qualified quantity surveyor can prepare a report for you to maximise these tax deductions.

Using the property that was purchased earlier in this chapter, it is assumed that the prime cost method is chosen to depreciate the fixtures and fittings. The total value of these fittings is $26,750. The annual depreciation claims for the property will be as detailed on the following page:

HOW DO YOU BUILD INCOME BY INVESTING IN REAL ESTATE?

Depreciation Deduction

Year 1	$6,475	Year 6	$3,088
Year 2	$3,088	Year 7	$3,088
Year 3	$3,088	Year 8	$1,747
Year 4	$3,088	Year 9	$ 0
Year 5	$3,088	Years 10 onwards	$ 0

The assumed construction costs that can be depreciated are $74,000. At 2.5% per year, you can claim $1,850 as a tax deduction for the next forty years of ownership. Properties purchased after 1997 have to add the allowable tax deductions for depreciation of the building to the sale price, at the time of the sale.

Your accountant will do this for you with the records you keep of each year's depreciation claim.

The effective taxable profit of your property, in the first year of full ownership, is:

Net Cash inflow (from page 164)		$11,300
Less: Non-cash Allowable Tax Deductions		
Depreciation of Fixtures & Fittings	$6,475	
Depreciation of Construction	$1,850	$8,325
		$2,975

Therefore, even though you have $11,300 cash in your hand, at the end of the year (rent, less cash expenses), you only pay tax on $2,975 of this income, at your marginal rate of tax.

Your net cash received, after tax, on the property depends on your tax rate. If you earn $40,000 from other sources during a year after June 2000, the tax you will pay on $2,975 at 31.5% (including the Medicare levy) is about $937 (after the GST). Your net cash proceeds from the property will then be $10,363 (being net cash inflow $11,300, less tax payable of $937).

Your after-tax rental return from the property would be about 4% in the first year of ownership (before any capital growth is added). This, alone will not make you rich, but it is still a better return than you will get from a fixed interest deposit at present (before taxes erode this return). Being the owner of real estate, you will also earn capital growth on your investment (which was between 8% and 12% per annum in Sydney for the twenty-one years to 1999, as detailed in Chapter 15). It is this combination of income and capital growth that has the potential to make you rich.

The third section of *Knowledge* you need to build riches, is that of knowing how to acquire the art of investing prudently. By now, you will have an accurate understanding of your current financial position and enough information to start your riches building. Also, you now have an understanding of the three essential investment areas: cash, shares and real estate. It is time to find out how to use your investments to build your riches to fulfil your dreams much faster, by learning ...

Chapter 17

HOW DO SAVERS MAKE INVESTORS RICH?

'Interest makes some people blind and others quick sighted.'
~ **Francis Beaumont.**

Savers, like our couple with the twenty-five year home loan, David and Shirley Battler, leave their excess money in bank accounts to earn a small amount of interest. As you discovered in Chapter 8, after taxes and inflation, they will be lucky to retain the spending power of their money at all (if they haven't spent it on consumer assets and leisure in the meantime).

Investors are smart and borrow this money from the same banks. The banks charge a higher interest rate to the investors than they give to the savers and make a profit on the transaction. This profit is tiny compared to the profit that the investors can make if they invest this borrowed money wisely to build their riches.

In Chapter 5, the other couple, Peter and Anne Wise, had decided to pay off their home loan faster, using a line of credit. If they took out their home loan five years ago, the balance of their home loan now will have reduced from $140,000 to a current balance of just under $95,000 (page 76). Alternatively, the Battlers still have a loan balance on their property of almost $128,000. It is now time to see how the Wise family can use the equity in their home (the difference between what it is worth and what they have as a home mortgage) with the assistance of the banks and the savers, like David and Shirley Battler, to help them get rich.

For this example I will assume that the capital growth rate for real estate is 8%. This is less than what was actual for the inner suburbs of

Sydney over the last twenty years (almost 12% as detailed on pages 151 to 154), but is a conservative rate over the longer term. You will probably earn more than 8% if you apply the principles outlined in this book.

Over the past five years, the Wises' home (and the Battler's home) has increased in value from $175,000 to a current value of about $257,000 (at 8% compound growth per annum). This means that the Wise family now has $162,000 equity in their home ($257,000 less the $95,000 line of credit).

It is assumed that, when the Wise family listened to the *Building Riches* audio tapes, they became excited about building wealth by investing in real estate. Since that time, they have increased their *Knowledge* of the suburbs and area in which they wish to invest. They also applied all the principles covered in Chapter 15 and the tapes on buying the right property in the right area. They have decided to buy the property that was used in the example in Chapter 16. They agreed to buy this strata title unit for $249,000 (which included the GST) and to borrow all of the money required to buy the property.

Peter and Anne Wise's salaries have kept pace with inflation, which we will assume in this example is 4%. Peter's current salary is $40,700 and Anne's current salary is $23,250. Historically, wages growth has exceeded inflation.

Peter and Anne decided to put the investment property in Peter's name only. They did this because Peter had paid more tax than Anne (because of his higher salary) and would get a greater tax benefit from owning the property (which will be shown in this chapter). Even though Peter and Anne are happily married, they decided to write up an agreement that, in the event of divorce, the investment property value would be split evenly as part of any property settlement.

Peter and Anne Wise have the ability to make drawings up to the level of the line of credit (mortgage) on their house, by way of a cheque, any time they like. They could pay for part of the new investment property using the equity they have built in their home.

What are the Banks' Criteria for Investment Property Loans?

Banks are primarily concerned with two things in relation to lending money for investment loans, these being:

HOW DO SAVERS MAKE INVESTORS RICH?

1) the security of the loan;
2) the ability of the borrowers to pay the bank's interest (and principal) on their loan.

Every bank has its own criteria for loans and each varies tremendously. For the same family, one bank may lend $300,000, whereas another bank may only lend $200,000. Do not be upset if one bank will not give you the loan you want. There are over 990 lenders in Australia for investment property loans (excluding solicitors and private lenders, who total in the thousands, but generally want a higher interest rate). Bank managers are just ordinary working people. They will retire poor if they do not invest and, even though they lend money, they are not taught how to get rich themselves. They are dictated to by senior management, who are often dictated to by chief executives who stand to make millions of dollars a year in share options and salary at the shareholders' expense. This creates a pressure cooker environment to squeeze the last dollar of profit for the shareholders and the executive.

If you are a hard-working Australian, with good credit and assets, then another lender will want your business. There are plenty of people who can get you a loan without a fee being paid by you. How can this happen? The banks are closing branches to save money. It is much cheaper for independent people to bring business to the banks than for the banks to get it themselves. These people will come to you and often represent several (or up to dozens of) lenders. You can pay a finance broker thousands of dollars (which are tax deductible) for the same service if you prefer. We deal with several companies that provide this service, free of charge to the borrower, and we often have one of these people do a brief segment with us in the *Building Riches Program.*

How Can You Set Up Ownership of Your Investment Property?

If you are self-employed, own a business, or have income from various investments, then there may be a better way to own your properties (or shares) than in your own name. The reason why you may choose to have your assets owned by another entity, be it a company, discretionary (family) trust, unit trust, or your own personal superannuation fund, is to protect your assets and to reduce taxation legally. It may be best to be bought in a company rather than a trust. Recent changes to the taxation of trusts will see them pay tax before they distribute earnings to beneficiaries from 1 July, 2002. They then distribute after tax earnings with a credit for tax paid (in a similar way to companies distributing franked dividends as detailed on pages 111 and 113). Space does not permit the full explanation of this here. The chances are good that if you have chosen the right accountant (or lawyer), then they personally use this type of structure for holding their own investment assets. Over many years, I have found that professionals who practice what they preach make the best advisers. *ASK* your accountant or lawyer: *'Do you own any investment properties?'* and *'In what type of entity do you hold them? And why?'*.

There are many excellent chartered accountants and CPA's who want to get rich by investing. If your accountant or other advisers choose to get rich by advising you on things they do not do themselves, maybe it is time to consider a new adviser. Over the years I have made many hundreds of thousands of dollars by having the right consultants. I encourage you to consider doing likewise.

In the following example we will assume, for simplicity, that the property is to be owned in Peter Wise's name. If Anne earned more than Peter, then the property would be better held in her name.

How Much Does It Cost to Buy an Investment Property?

It is assumed Peter and Anne Wise buy their investment property in a suburb five kilometres from Sydney (away from the current suburbs that are likely to decrease in value). The total cost to purchase the Wise's investment property, is assumed to be $260,000, as detailed on the following page. Many readers may find a purchase price of $249,000 high. Throughout much of Australia, units and houses can be bought for around half that amount. Certain authors promote buying such cheaper properties. Sydney and Melbourne are the two main business capitals of Australia. The limited supply of land close to these two cities, and strong demand will secure long term capital profits if you buy the right property. Buy carefully and get richer.

The GST does not apply to previously lived in residential real estate. Building works and profit on new constructions will attract a GST. The total increase in cost has ended up being about 6% for new properties built after the GST.

HOW DO SAVERS MAKE INVESTORS RICH?

Contract Price of Property (including GST)		$249,000
Add: Acquisition Costs (including GST)		
Purchasers Conveyancing Costs (includes GST)	$ 770	
Stamp Duty on Purchase (NSW)	$7,205	
Property Inspection Service (includes GST)	$ 250	
Other Out of Pocket Costs (full search fees, etc)	$ 175	
		$ 8,400
Add: Borrowing Costs (including GST)		
Loan Application Fee to Bank	$ 0	
NSW Stamp Duty on Mortgage $190,000	$ 705	
NSW Stamp Duty on Line of Credit (see below)	$ 350	
New Loan Lender's Solicitors & Valuation Fee	$ 850	
Line of Credit Bank & Legal Fees for Increase	$ 350	
Other Mortgage Costs & Lawyers Expenses	$ 105	$ 2,600
TOTAL PROPERTY COST (To be borrowed)		$260,000

    Peter and Anne Wise had to decide how to arrange to finance this $260,000. They first spoke with their bank, and their bank manager said she wanted security over both properties for each loan. Peter and Anne decided they did not like this idea. They preferred to keep each of their future investment property loans independent of each other. This is preferable for you also, as you then have greater ability to sell or refinance individual properties without putting all the control with one loans officer from one bank.

    Most banks will lend from 90% to 95% of the cost of a residential home to owner occupiers, providing they have enough income and they agree to pay **mortgage insurance**, which pays out the bank if they cannot pay the loan back. The insurance company then pursues the owner for the money. Such high ratios are only advisable on your first home if you are buying at the right time of the cycle and you know property prices are set to jump in your area by 20% or so. If you don't buy, then you will pay a lot more later. If prices aren't set to jump, be careful not to borrow too much money.

    For investment property loans like the one the Wises want, all lenders have their own criteria. They assess differently what they will lend, and how much of the rental income they will include in the analysis of the borrowers ability to service the loan as well as many other factors.

Many banks will lend up to 75% or even 80% of an investment property cost without mortgage insurance, taking the investment property as their only security. Other lenders, like mortgage originators (Aussie Home Loans and RAMS), will require the borrower to pay mortgage insurance on over 65% of the money bought as a ratio of the purchase price, which is called the **Loan to Value Ratio (LVR)**. If you have to pay mortgage insurance, it is a once only fee ranging from 0.24% to over 3.0% of the purchase price of the property. It is tax deductible for investment properties and is generally considered to be a sound way of maximising the return on your money (as we will cover shortly).

What Peter and Anne Wise decide to do is to borrow $190,000 (or about 75%) of the value of the cost price of the investment property, secured against the property as the bank's only security (apart from a guarantee). The lending bank requested that both Peter and Anne guarantee the loan, even though Peter was the only borrower. They did this because the family home was in the name of both Peter and Anne and this increased the bank's evaluation of the guarantee.

Peter and Anne then needed to find the difference between the total property cost of $260,000 and the investment property loan of $190,000, this being $70,000.

Peter and Anne knew that their existing line of credit only allowed them to access the difference between their existing mortgage and the limit of the line of credit ($150,000 less $95,000) being $55,000. As they required $70,000 they needed to find an extra amount of $15,000.

Peter and Anne's home is now worth $257,000. They increased the available line of credit limit secured on their property to $200,000 with their bank <u>before</u> they applied for the other loan. As Peter and Anne's incomes had both increased and they had been good customers of the bank, reducing their line of credit regularly and always making their payments on time, their bank had agreed and kept their interest rate at the same rate of 7.25%.

So, when it came time to put a deposit on the investment property (usually 10% of the purchase price) and pay the acquisition costs and borrowing cost, the Wises' had the ability to draw cheques for it all from their line of credit. After settlement of the new investment property, the Wise's had increased their home loan from $95,000 to $165,000 and paid

$70,000 from it into their other property and costs. They also had access to an additional $35,000 from the line of credit on their revised home loan in case of an emergency or a fabulous investment opportunity.

So what are the Loan to Value Ratios (LVR) on the two properties after settlement?

Wises' Line of Credit LVR $= \dfrac{\text{Loan}}{\text{Value}} \times \dfrac{100}{1}$

$= \dfrac{(\$90{,}000 + \$70{,}000)}{\$257{,}000} \times \dfrac{100}{1}$

Home LVR $= 64.3\%$

Wises' Investment Property LVR $= \dfrac{\$190{,}000}{\$249{,}000} \times \dfrac{100}{1}$

Investment LVR $= 76.31\%$

Both of these individual ratios are conservative and the banks are content with their security on each loan.

Which Loans are Tax Deductible?

Loans to buy investments are deductible when the purpose of the loan is to gain income from the investment (the rental income being taxable).

This is a key principle that can make you rich. It is for this reason that we should aim to keep consumer loans and security loans to a minimum, as they are generally not tax deductible.

When, however, a loan (like the Wise's line of credit) is split into two components, part may be tax deductible. The $95,000 that is remaining as a borrowing to buy their home, is not tax deductible. However the additional $70,000 used to finance the new property (which will generate rental income) is tax deductible. In the future, the Wises' will need to make sure they keep good records to separate these two loans.

The new loan on the investment property is to attract an interest rate of 7.25%. Peter and Anne Wise decided interest rates were about as low as they expected them to go and so they borrowed this money on a fixed rate of 7.25% for five years on an interest only basis (meaning they do not need to repay any principal over this five year period).

Why is an Interest Only Loan on an Investment Property Probably the Best Loan for You?

Most astute long-term property investors go for interest only loans (and not principal and interest) for three main reasons, these being:

1) *Interest on the loan is tax deductible:*
Interest payments are tax deductible. Paying out principal (the loan) is not tax deductible. Paying out the investment loan will reduce the balance and hence the tax deductible interest on the investment property;

2) *Loan repayments are not tax deductible:*
Every dollar used to repay debt is not tax deductible. Therefore on the top tax rate it costs about $2 in income to repay $1 in debt;

3) *The security position keeps improving:*
Over time, the loan on the investment property becomes even less of a concern to the banks. In five years, the value of the investment property has risen to over $365,000 (at 8% growth) and in ten years, the new value will be about $537,000. As the balance of the loan remains constant at $190,000. The LVR will drop to 52% in year five and further drops to less than 36% in year ten (refer to graph on the next page). At these low LVR's the lender will be very happy with its security, providing the interest payments are met. Most banks only start getting nervous when they don't get paid or the LVR's go above 80%.

So the bank is happy. What about the Wise family? To see how they have performed (at only 8% compound growth on all properties) let us compare their financial position with that of the Battler family. The graph on the previous page does just that. In five and ten years after the Wise family invest in their first investment property what will be their relative assets and loans? The Wise family continue with their line of credit, and the Battlers with their twenty-five year principal and interest loan (Chapter 5).

HOW DO SAVERS MAKE INVESTORS RICH?

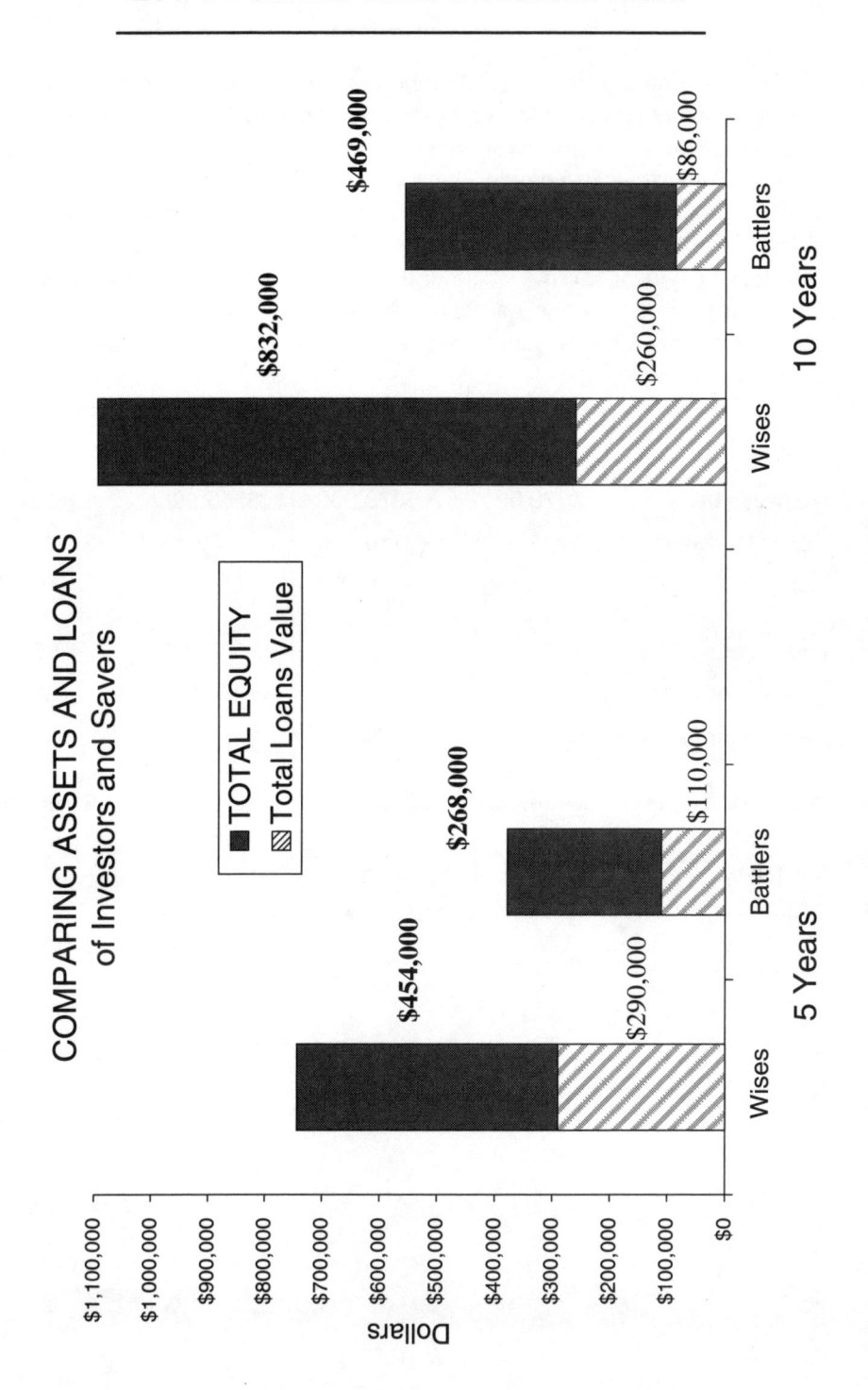

COMPARING ASSETS AND LOANS
of Investors and Savers

	Wises (5 Years)	Battlers (5 Years)	Wises (10 Years)	Battlers (10 Years)
TOTAL EQUITY	$454,000	$268,000	$832,000	$469,000
Total Loans Value	$290,000	$110,000	$260,000	$86,000

HOW TO BUILD RICHES

The Wise family has over $180,000 more equity in five years and over $360,000 more equity in ten years than the Battlers. This is assuming that the Wise family has not invested again (which they obviously will do, as I will demonstrate in coming chapters). What is more, the Battlers still have a home loan after this ten years and will be paying it off at over $1,000 per month for another ten years. The Wise family stopped paying mortgage payment seven years after they bought their investment property (thirteen years before the Battlers). The difference is even more obvious if we look at a table of their Assets and Liabilities (shown below).

	5 YEARS		10 YEARS	
	Wises	Battlers	Wises	Battlers
Home Value	$378,000	$378,000	$555,000	$555,000
Home Mortgage	($ 30,000)	($110,000)	$0	($ 86,000)
Home EQUITY	$348,000	$268,000	$555,000	$469,000
Investment Value	$366,000	$0	$537,000	$0
Investment Loan	($260,000)	$0	($260,000)	$0
Investment EQUITY	$106,000	$0	$277,000	$0
TOTAL EQUITY	**$454,000**	**$268,000**	**$832,000**	**$469,000**

But how much has it cost the Wise family in after tax payments to get this much richer? This will be answered when you find out . . .

Chapter 18

HOW CAN YOU GET RICH AND HELP THE ECONOMY?

*'There are three ingredients of a good life:
yearning, learning, and earning.'*
~ **Christopher Morley.**

What is the Government Housing Dilemma?

Two in five people in Australia cannot afford their own homes and so live in rented housing. Public housing waiting lists are increasing all the time. This is bad news for people who genuinely need government assistance. As mentioned in Chapter 1, the Federal Government, in the 1997 budget, stopped paying the States public housing costs and, instead, gave them an amount and made the States take responsibility for how they used this money to house the poor. Most informed people see this as the thin end of the wedge, with the Federal Government likely to pay less in real terms (i.e. after inflation) to the States in coming years. Most State governments are spending more money than they earn now and will be forced to cut back services in coming years, or raise taxes, or both.

With forty percent of the population renting, the government needs to either provide housing for that many people, or have investors own additional investment properties to house these people. Obviously, governments are less efficient (due to the overhead costs of huge numbers of additional people and offices they require) than average working Australians, at owning and managing investment real estate.

The governments need to encourage average Australians to have the ambition to own more than one property and help house their fellow

Australians. They do this by allowing investors a tax deduction for all expenses including interest and some non-cash deductions (discussed in Chapter 17). If interest and expenses are greater than rent, then the investor can write off this loss against other income. This has been called **negative gearing**. I believe this term has served it's 'used by date' and will introduce you to a better way of understanding this concept, later in this chapter. Before I do, I'll show you an example of the real cost of owning an investment property using Peter and Anne Wise's first investment property that was outlined in the last chapter. (It is assumed that this investment takes place after 1 July 2000 and occurs during the GST tax system).

What Affect will the GST have on Real Estate Prices?

Residential properties that have been lived in are not taxed under the GST. If property developers buy residential land and construct new buildings, the land cost does not attract GST. GST at one eleventh ($1/11$) of cost price is paid on materials, subcontracted labour and profit on all works done after 1 July 2000. The net affect will be an increase of about 6% of a property totally constructed after June 2001 or later. As the Australian economy is likely to slump in late 2000 or 2001, current land prices will probably fall soon after the introduction of the GST. The net initial effect on residential real estate prices may be negligible. Over time real estate prices will increase again.

Peter and Anne decided that property prices were too high in 1999 and early 2000 to buy a property. They ignored the sales pitch by the developer and agents. They decided to wait until after the boom (Chapter 9) and decided to buy after the next fall in real estate prices. They figured that this would more than cover any extra cost associated with the GST effect on new residential properties.

How Much Does It Really Cost to Own an Investment Property After Rent and Tax Refunds?

Peter and Anne Wise have decided that they like the idea of making over $275,000 in the next ten years from owning their first investment property. They are excited about the fact that they can make this money, using the equity they have built in their home (by eliminating their security debt faster). They do, however, want to get an accurate understanding of how much their first investment property will cost them, after the tenant pays rent and they get their taxation refund for owning the property.

As most of the figures for the cash expenses and the depreciation on the fixtures and construction are the same as the ones already covered (on pages 164 and 166), I will concentrate on the new deductible expenses now. The major additional tax deductible expense is interest and another is the ability to get a tax deduction for the costs involved in setting up the investment loans.

How is the Interest Paid?

There are two amounts of money borrowed in this example. One is the 75% loan on the investment property itself, of $190,000. The other is the increase of $70,000 in the line of credit secured on the Wise family home. As the purpose of this loan is to buy a property to generate rent, then any interest paid on this $70,000 is tax deductible. The total tax deductible interest for each year (on an interest only basis) is detailed below.

Interest on Loan on Investment Property:	= $190,000 × 7.25%	= $13,775
Interest on Line of Credit Increase:	= $70,000 × 7.25%	= $ 5,075
Annual Tax Deductible Interest Expense		= $18,850

The interest on the investment property is usually paid monthly.

The Wises have arranged to set up a bank account specifically for this investment property. Each month the real estate managing agents receive the rent, pay all cash expenses, and put the balance into the Wise's bank account on the first working day after the end of the previous month. They have arranged for their interest payments on the investment property loan to be taken from this same bank account on the tenth day of each month (allowing time for the agent's cheque to clear). The Wises will pay any shortfall into this new account at the beginning of each month. They do this so that any money they receive from salary and tax refunds remains in their line of credit for most of the month. This has the effect of reducing their line of credit as soon as possible (as described in Chapter 8). The Wises have their taxation refunds (detailed later) paid, with their salary, directly into their line of credit every pay day.

This more than covers the line of credit payments. At the end of the year, they simply give their bank statements, on their line of credit, and their other investment property bank account, to their accountant. He knows that the annual interest from the line of credit that is tax deductible is $5,075 (as calculated above). This interest is not subject to GST.

Some lines of credit will allow for a different statement on the home loan and the investment property loan ($70,000) amounts. When the home loan part of the line of credit is fully paid out, the Wises will continue to allow the $70,000 balance to appear until they sell their investment property and then finally pay it out. If they buy another home it is possible to transfer a line of credit to this new property. In this way you may only ever need one line of credit mortgage, which can be transferred to any property you move to in the future.

What Tax Deduction Do You Get for Borrowing Money?

The costs of borrowing money are tax deductible when the amount borrowed is used to buy properties with the purpose of generating rental income. This is clearly the case for the Wise's investment property loan and also for the costs in increasing their line of credit to allow them to buy the investment property.

The costs to put two loans in place are again assumed to be incurred in NSW. It is possible to save on the legal costs by buying a conveyancing kit, and arranging all of the legal requirements associated with buying or selling a property yourself. If you do the searches yourself, the Land Titles Office in most States makes it easy to organise searches through them and other government departments all at one time, and in one place on one form. For the first property you buy, you might choose to use a solicitor. If you do, *ASK* for copies of all documents and *ASK* to look at the conveyancing and mortgage files after the transaction is settled. You will learn a lot about the procedure and the various searches required.

Most conveyancing work in legal firms is done by a senior clerk and not a lawyer anyway. The lawyers are available however, if it becomes complicated. A good lawyer is almost as valuable a resource as is a good accountant. If you find a good lawyer, it may be worthwhile giving them the conveyancing work and paying a few hundred (tax deductible) dollars for the peace of mind it gives you, knowing that they will assist you if a problem develops. In most States other than NSW (where the lawyers have monopolised most of the conveyancing this century) most of the conveyancing will be done by settlement agents or conveyancers. These specialists are also available in NSW.

Peter and Anne Wise used a solicitor for both the mortgage and the property acquisition. They also spent $250 on a full inspection report on their property (even though it was new). The seller gave them a schedule of depreciable items so they did not need a quantity surveyor.

The borrowing costs totalled $2,600, as detailed in Chapter 17. These borrowing costs can be claimed as a tax deduction, over the length of the loan if it is a fixed rate, or five years, whichever is the sooner. The Wises opted for a five year fixed rate loan (as they thought interest rates would rise soon). Therefore, they were entitled to a tax deduction of $520 per year, for each of the next five years, for borrowing costs.

How Does Inflation Affect Property Costs Over Time?

Over time, inflation increases the costs of goods and services. It is no different with investment property costs. The cash property expenses for the first year of ownership are projected to be $4,000 (as detailed on page 164). The rent is projected to be $15,300, being fifty-one weeks at $300 per week (as detailed on page 163). The cash expenses of $4,000 divided by rent of $15,300 is approximately 26%. It is assumed, as rent increases each year, the property expenses will increase at the same rate of 4%. Rent probably increases more than inflation, but a conservative amount is included in this example. These assumptions are used in cash flow analysis in Appendix 2.

Peter Wise's salary is also assured to increase at 4% per annum (the assumed inflation rate). The fixtures depreciation and construction depreciation are also the same as in the example used in Chapter 16.

What is the Cash-Flow Situation Before Non-Cash Allowable Deductions?

The cash flow projections after inflation of the property (before non-cash expenses) in the first three years is detailed on the following page.

Year	1	2	3
Rent	$15,300	$15,912	$16,548
Less: Cash Expenses (26% rent)	($4,000)	($4,137)	($4,303)
Less: Interest Expense	($18,850)	($18,850)	($18,850)
Annual Cash Flow Pre-tax	($7,550)	($7,075)	($6,605)

It is easy to see that as time goes by it is even easier to fund this cash flow, even if the property is funded 100% by borrowed money.

How Do Taxation Refunds and Non-Cash Deductions Make Property Ownership Easier?

The Wise family's investment property is made more affordable over time as rent increases more, in total dollars, than do cash expenses (which are 26% of rent in this example).

Over the first year of ownership the effect that this property has on Peter Wise's income and his annual tax refund is detailed below:

Peter's Income (gross salary)	40,700	
Tax BEFORE property (I)		**$9,200**
Add Rent	15,300	
Total Income with Rent	56,000	
Less: Total Tax Deductions (including GST)		
Interest	(18,850)	
Cash Expenses (26% of Rent)	(4,000)	
Depreciation on Fixtures	(6,475)	
Depreciation on Construction	(1,850)	
Borrowing Costs Amortised	(520)	
Total Property Tax Deductions	(31,695)	
New Taxable Income	24,305	
Tax AFTER Property (II)		**$4,036**
TAX REFUND [(I) — (II)]		**$5,164**
Less pre-tax Cash Flow (at top of page)		(7,550)
After-tax Profit/(cost)		($2,386)
WEEKLY PROFIT/(COST)		**($45.89)**

After the tax refund that Peter Wise receives, the property only costs $2,220 in the first whole year of ownership, (that is less than $46 per week or about $6.50 per day). Remember that after GST, Peter will save over $1,500 in extra tax that he used to pay. This money helps to pay for this investment property. To get a better understanding of who pays what percentages of the property it is often best to see it graphically. A graph depicting who pays the expenses associated with this property follows:

HOW CAN YOU GET RICH AND HELP THE ECONOMY?

WHO PAYS FOR Mr & Mrs Wise Investor's Investment Property in the First Year of Ownership?

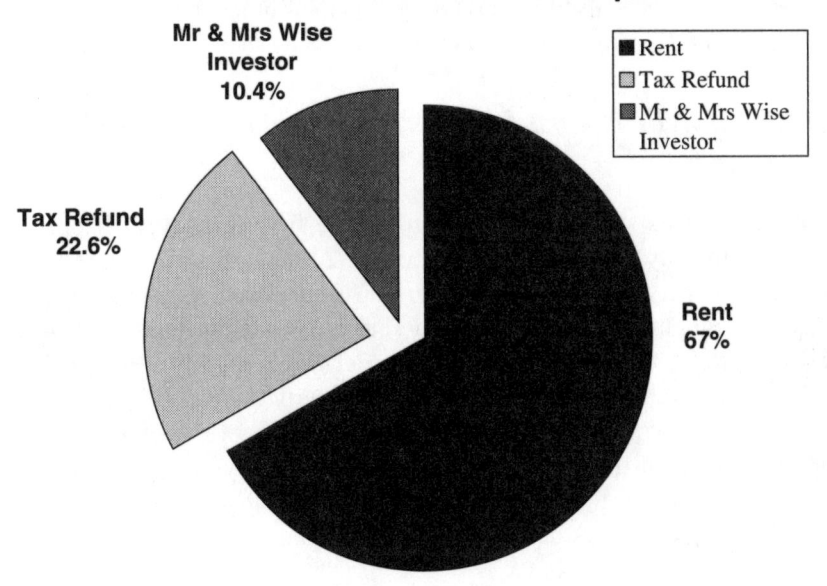

- Rent: 67%
- Tax Refund: 22.6%
- Mr & Mrs Wise Investor: 10.4%

How Can Owning Real Estate Be Made Even Easier for You?

The tenant pays a huge 67% of the cost of owning the property in year one. The tax refund pays 22.6% and Mr Investor only pays 10.4% of the cost of the property in after-tax dollars. It gets even better if you fill out a simple, single, A4 double-sided application, called a 2036 form (under section 1515 of the Tax Act). The Tax Office will instruct your paymaster, in writing, to reduce your annual tax and to reduce your tax payments for the year on a proportionate basis by each pay period. For example, Peter Wise will receive $5,164 from the Australian Taxation Office in the first full year of ownership of the property. By filling in a 2036 form (or having his accountant do it) he will receive this tax saving at the rate of almost $100 in his pay packet every week (assuming he is paid weekly). If he is paid monthly then it would be a bit over $430 a month.

Obviously, to make the most of this money, you will want to put it somewhere where you will not spend it. Peter and Anne Wise chose to deposit this money in their line of credit and only draw on it monthly, to pay the interest payment on the investment property (via their bank account described above). This also reduces interest on their home loan and helps to pay it out even faster (as detailed in Chapter 5) using their line of credit.

How Much Will It Cost in After-Tax Dollars to Get Rich in Property?

The above analysis shows what happens in the first year. What happens after that with only one property? Appendix 2 shows that, over the first ten years of ownership, the cost to Peter and Anne Wise, after tax, ranges from about $60 per week in the second year of ownership to about $14 a week in the tenth year! The total cost in after tax dollars is $19,169. On page 178 you saw that this <u>one</u> investment property increased in value by over $277,000 over that same ten year period. The effective return on investment (ROI) of the after-tax money that physically comes out of the Wises' pocket, before the property incurs capital gains tax (which I will refer to in Chapter 24), is detailed on the next page.

$$\text{ROI} = \frac{\text{Investment Property Equity}}{\text{After Tax Cost}} \times \frac{100}{1}$$

$$= \frac{\$277,000}{\$19,169} \times \frac{100}{1}$$

$$= 1,445\%$$

That is 145% growth per annum. Obviously the compound growth will be less, but you can see that the return on invested dollars is huge.

Our goal in getting rich is to compound our invested dollars at the fastest rate and still have our invested dollars safe. The above example is an excellent way to achieve your objective.

How Does Borrowing Money Increase Your Profit?

If you can earn about the same profit (on shares or property) safely, and receive this profit with less of your money invested, then obviously, your actual invested dollars are producing a greater return.

HOW CAN YOU GET RICH AND HELP THE ECONOMY?

In the above example, the same property was bought and held as I demonstrated in Chapter 17. If this property was purchased without using any borrowed money it would cost $257,400 cash (being the purchase price of $249,000 plus acquisition costs of $8,400). Over the next ten years the effective rental return, after allowing for tax paid on this rent returns just over $97,800. In ten years the property has increased in value by about $279,600 (being $537,000, (refer page 178), less the total cost to buy the property of $257,400).

If the property is financed by the use of 100% borrowed money, the property value still goes up by over $275,000, (but no cash was invested by the borrower). In this situation, the actual cost to own the property in the first ten years is $19,169 (the specific cost for each of the first ten years is detailed in Appendix 2).

The table on the next page compares the return on invested dollars on the same investment property, with no borrowing or 100% borrowing.

$$\text{ROI} = \frac{\text{Capital Gains} + \text{After-tax cash received}}{\text{Initial Investment} + \text{After-tax cash paid}}$$

	No Borrowing	100% Borrowing
=	$\frac{279{,}600 + 97{,}854}{257{,}400 + 0}$	$\frac{277{,}000 + 0}{0 + 19{,}169}$
=	$\frac{377{,}454}{257{,}400}$	$\frac{277{,}000}{19{,}169}$
ROI =	147%	1,445%
Compound ROI =	8.8%	29.8%

Thinking back to the Rule of 72 it is easy to see that compounding your money at almost 30%, doubles your money almost every two and a half years. Careful use of borrowed money (as in the example above), will make you **rich much faster** than if you simply double it at about 9% (doubling every eight years), by investing in real estate or shares without the use of any borrowed money. Remember the example on page 93, in which I demonstrated that, applying of the Rule of 72 with a compound return of 24% on invested funds dramatically increases the return on investment (returning an effective return after inflation of 15 times the return of an investment returning only 8%). Investing at almost 30% compound simply accelerates the growth of your riches at an even faster rate.

What is the History of Negative Gearing?

In the 1960's and 1970's taxpayers paid significantly more tax on their incomes than we do today. In the section on shares, you learned that share dividends were taxed twice in those days (once on the company profits and again on the taxpayer, without any franking credits).

In those bad, old days, taxpayers on the top marginal rates paid tax of 64 cents in the dollar (which is much worse than today's top rates of 47% plus Medicare levy). At the same time, no capital gains tax existed and any profit made on the sale of shares or properties was not taxed.

What this led to was high-income earners buying properties with high borrowings and incurring losses by the expenses being higher than rents. 64% of this loss was funded by diverting money that otherwise would have been paid in tax. If any profit was made on the sale of the asset then this was a bonus. The term negative gearing meant that:

1) The expenses exceeded income so that a 'negative' cash flow, or loss, was generated;

2) Through 'gearing' or borrowing money, the interest paid to finance the transaction to buy the property resulted in the loss.

A loss is still a loss. I see many, otherwise intelligent, people throwing money into all manner of schemes at the end of the financial year to get a tax refund or to avoid paying tax. Very few of these schemes actually show a profit. Most of them are simply contrived to prey on people's desire to avoid paying tax. The tax office is forever increasing its scrutiny of these schemes and you may lose your money and run the risk of not getting a tax deduction. Worse still, the Tax department can rule these schemes illegal, and penalise you by over 50% of the tax payable. If you want to fight the matter in court, you may have to fund a court case for years (and risk up to $100,000 or more to get your money back). The glamour can quickly disappear as fast as the operators of these tax schemes. Be careful with these schemes.

HOW CAN YOU GET RICH AND HELP THE ECONOMY?

Many so called property consultants sell property investments (usually in low-priced, outer suburbs and poor investment areas) by promising you a tax refund as a result of owning the property they are selling. Frequently they will encourage people to buy interstate at seemingly cheap prices. Don't be fooled. You only profit when the property goes up in value. Buy well in the better suburbs.

Another area of negative gearing that is taking off in popularity, is that of share margin loans. If you go into these heavily just to get a tax deduction and hope you may make a profit, your hope and greed may turn into despair if you can't make the margin calls, and the lender sells your shares, and maybe your house as well.

So with the desire to make profits, what is a better way to look at and define investments which have a short-term cash shortfall?

What is Positive Leverage?

Is *positive leverage* your answer? The Macquarie Dictionary defines these two words as:

Positive
'*measured or proceeding in a direction assumed as that to increase, progress, or onward motion.*'

Leverage
'*the effect of using borrowed funds rather than capital in a venture.*'

The principle of how leverage works is demonstrated in the investment property example earlier in this chapter. The $249,000 property (plus costs) owned over a ten year period, will cost the owner only about $37 per week in after-tax dollars. The cost is about $19,200. The profit before tax is $277,000 as detailed on pages 187 to 188.

The concept of leverage is not new. Archimedes, the Greek mathematician, coined the use of the word lever more than two thousand years ago. He said that: '*if you can give me a lever long enough, and a place to stand, then I can move the world*'.

HOW TO BUILD RICHES

loan of $257,400

$40 per week

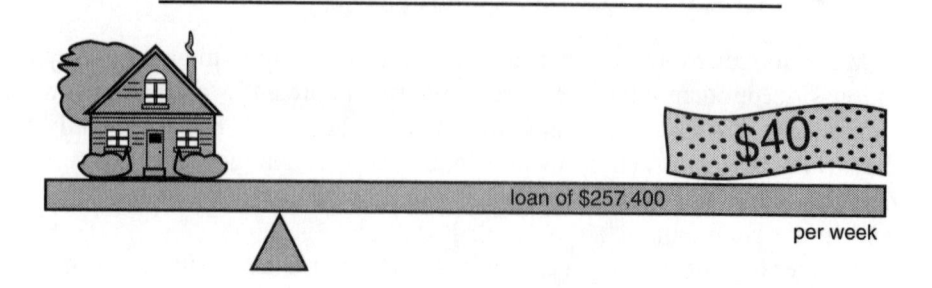

A lever is a bar which when acted upon by one force (the power), will cause the other force (the object) to tend to rotate in the opposite direction around a fixed support (the fulcrum). In our example;- the power is less than $40 per week; the object is the cost of buying the investment property (that can make you rich); and the fulcrum is the process of you *ASK*ing your way to riches. The longer the bar (i.e. the more borrowings) the less force (your own money) it takes to own your investments.

I define *positive leverage* as the ability to invest money in a way that generates a profit after allowing for both *taxes* and *inflation*.

This differs from the traditional negative gearing which ignores inflation and assumes tax deductions will be allowed and continue to be allowed for the schemes they enter into.

Your investments use *positive leverage* best, to the extent that your actual cash investment is small, relative to a larger return of capital profits (which are not taxed until later). If you can outlay $40 a week to generate over $275,000 in ten years, your investment is highly positively leveraged. In the *Strategy* Section I will show you how to make even greater riches using this concept.

Any concept or principle usually has an opposite effect. What is the opposite of *positive leverage*?

Is Negative Leverage a Trap for Fools?

The Macquarie Dictionary defines Negative:

'*measured or proceeding in the opposite direction to that which is considered positive.*'

I define **negative leverage** as being the situation where invested money generates a return that is negative after allowing for both taxes (including Capital Gains Tax) and inflation.

Investments can make money and still generate negative leverage if, you pay too much tax and your money does not grow sufficiently to keep pace with the decrease in spending power that occurs every month due to inflation eroding your cash. The most common form of negative leverage is leaving your hard-earned money snoozing in a bank account. Over the long-term you will actually have less spending power than you do today (as shown in the graph on page 101 from 1976 to 1999).

It is quite possible to invest and achieve negative leverage. People, without the *Knowledge* that you now have, do it all the time. Don't let it happen to you. Protect yourself by keeping your *Knowledge* current after you finish reading this book. Track the business cycle in its broad movement and invest at the right times. Put your money in your line of credit or even in the bank at the right times. Invest your money to work harder for you when the economy has slowed for a while, which it will always do again, and then profit when shares and property increase in value later.

How Could You Lose Your Money?

The secret to losing your money is to fall prey to several recurring problems. The major ones are:

1) Ignorance (no specialist *Knowledge*);
2) Lack of direction (no specific *Strategy*);
3) Greed (*Knowledge* overcomes greed);
4) Allowing others to manipulate you by using guilt;
5) Being driven by fear instead of directing your finances.

1) *Ignorance:*

People who do not develop specific *Knowledge* and expertise fall victim to ignorance often. They see property, or shares, as good, bad, or better than one another. This is ignorance. Shares and property are both good investments at different times in the economic cycle (and your life-time).

Continue to LEARN and you will continue to EARN higher than average returns. Continue to invest some of this in your future education and you will compound your money even faster and get even richer. This book is a good start, keep it up. People often wonder why we promote other people's books and materials. We do it to help give our clients as much specialised *Knowledge* as we can, to accelerate their ability to design better *Strategies* for better *Action*.

2) **Lack of Direction:**
Just about everyone would like to be rich. Only one in one hundred actually achieve it. Use this book and the *Strategy* section to set your direction, get committed to your goals and make a plan. Know what you want. Pay the price. Take *Action*. Enjoy your rewards.

3) **Greed is the con person's primary weapon:**
If you are greedy, you make it easy for any unscrupulous person to part you from your money. They will tell you that the sharemarket will go up forever, and now is different from the past years, and it has changed forever. If you believe this aspect of human behaviour, and that the two primary drivers of the sharemarket being greed and fear no longer operate, you are in for an expensive education!

When things have been too good for too long it is time for caution. Take profits by selling your shares. Do what made Warren Buffet one of the wealthiest self made people on the planet: Be greedy when everyone else is fearful, and be fearful when everyone else is greedy. Fools do it the other way. They hope it will go on forever, and part with their money on some share borrowings at the wrong time in the economic cycle, when the masses (who don't get rich) are buying. They then follow the other sheep and sell when everyone else does because fear enters the market, causing the inevitable stock market fall, to become a stock market crash.

You can be greedy with property also. Borrow big when prices are high (without doing the proper homework) and don't leave any extra borrowing power (remember that the Wise family had access to another $35,000 in their line of credit in the example used on page 174 and 175). If you buy low, when the prices rise, you benefit. When they stay steady, or increase and then drop at a later time, the drop is usually only a fraction of your increase in value. You are still ahead in the long-run.

4) **Some people manipulate others with guilt:**
It is often said there are guilt throwers and guilt catchers. An unscrupulous salesperson or con person can, by a series of questions, trap you into feeling guilty for not buying their product. Don't be a guilt catcher. If you sense someone manipulating you with guilt say:

HOW CAN YOU GET RICH AND HELP THE ECONOMY?

'*You're not trying to make me feel guilty are you?*'. They will often say: '*no*'. You say: '*good*'. Once they start doing it again, repeat the question. After two or three times, they will stop. A tactic shown is a tactic blown. People can only manipulate you if you let them. Don't let them.

5) *Fear:*

This is the big one. It stops many people from achieving much of their potential in life. I will cover even more solutions to FEAR in Chapter 30. It is now time to find out how fear stops many people from getting rich with property. This subject is so important it forms the basis of the next chapter.

Knowledge destroys fear. It is time to find out . . .

Chapter 19

HOW DOES KNOWLEDGE DESTROY FEAR?

'"Come to the edge", he said. They said, "We are afraid".
"Come to the edge," he said. They came.
He pushed them ... And they flew.'
~ **Guillaume Apollinaire.**

Have you ever noticed that bullies (or for that matter con people) usually pick on weak or fearful people? Probably all of us witnessed it in school. Many adults in today's society are afraid, and increasingly violent TV shows and movies only add to that climate of fear.

As a Black Belt Karate instructor I have witnessed people come to their first class full of fear about the local neighbourhood bully or thugs. These same new students can also be fearful about a new learning skill (being Karate manoeuvres). After practising the techniques I teach them, within a few months, or even a few lessons, their confidence increases. As they become more confident they work harder and smarter at their techniques and their fear falls away. The more you practice the better you become. If you practice every day, you will become better, in a month, than someone who practices once a week will become in a year.

It gives me great pride to see people being able to defend themselves against bullies in a short period of time. Keeping your skills secret, and using them powerfully has great effect. The element of surprise allowed David (from the Bible) to slay Goliath, marry the princess and become King. I have seen thin people overcome one hundred plus kilogram bullies. The interesting thing is that bullies rarely attack confident people. Con people have no influence over people who are not greedy or fearful.

Knowledge is the answer. Continue to learn and you will continue to earn.

Your *Knowledge* of *How To Build Riches* will overcome and destroy fear if you use it wisely.

Using common sense as to when to buy, combined with specialist *Knowledge* on individual stocks and properties, will increase your chances of getting rich. It takes time, but the rewards are worth it. If shares excite you, then re-read that section of the book again later, and continue your journey to riches. The more specialist *Knowledge* that you acquire before you act, the better. In Chapters 27 and 28, I will demonstrate how by investing in shares, real estate, and cash, you can get richer faster.

Where Are You Spending Your Time?

A good friend of mine, a man who is highly successful in his chosen field, takes regular *Action* on concepts and principles that excite him. His willingness to pick up something new is inspiring. He has really applied many of the concepts I am sharing with you, in this book, in his life. At a time when he hadn't focused much on money, I *ASK*ed him:

'*How much time do you spend worrying (being fearful) about money?*'

While he was thinking about this I interrupted his thinking to *ASK* him another question:

'*How much time do you invest in acquiring specialist Knowledge on* **How to Build Riches?**'

He estimated that he probably spent about three times as much time being fearful around money as he did learning specialist *Knowledge* to make him rich. What about you? If you are like most people, you spend less time working on solutions to becoming rich than you could.

My friend now spends some time each day (I suggest starting with thirty minutes and working up from there) reading and learning specialist *Knowledge* to make him rich. It is possible to read information in one week from a book that took a millionaire twenty years to learn (like this book and many others). Within a year, you can have a huge number of skills. Faster again, is to listen to audio tapes, attend seminars, to read, and then apply what you learn. This compounds your new knowledge and reinforces it.

What do they call people who study riches for an hour a day? RICH! That is what people will be calling you in years to come.

If you spend time on finding solutions to problems when fear raises its head, instead of focusing on the fear, you will become rich. You will also become more confident in the process and also become a better role model for everyone you meet and influence.

Why Do Most People Remain Poor?

Most people allow fear to drive them. They do this by spending much of their time thinking of all of the things that can go wrong in a particular investment. Instead, spend time finding solutions to problems and then apply what you learn. Your riches will multiply.

Once you master this concept, you can actually welcome problems and even the experience of fear. What I do, is rename problems as challenges or even better, opportunities. When most people think of fear they react to it. In reacting, the fear controls them. By converting the fear into an opportunity, you are challenging your brain to find a solution. My friend, studies Aikido, a Japanese martial art. In Aikido, when an opponent charges at you, it is possible to move aside and use their aggression to have them defeat themselves (by effortlessly throwing them to the ground or by deflecting their attack). Over time, they cool down and you can actually make friends with an opponent. The same is true about fear. We will deal with this more in the *Action* section (Chapter 30). The more you do any skill, the better you become, like martial arts, love making, cooking, being self-confident or any other skill that you apply yourself to.

Let us look at typical fears that stop many people. We also want to spend most of our time on solutions to overcome and transform such fears, in a way that allows us to *ASK* our way to riches. The same approach can be used to transform any fear into an opportunity.

1) What if you can't find a tenant?
The easy solution is to drop the *ASK*ing price of your rent. If you have applied the *Knowledge* in this book you will have bought the right type of property in the right area. Demand will always be there for this type of property. A short-term decrease in rent will allow you to get a tax deduction for part of it anyway. A better way is to get creative with your ads and generate enough interest to lease it. Either way will bring you a tenant.

2) What if interest rates increase?
Interest rates will always go up and down, usually in trends that last

for years, as detailed in the economic cycle. With all good investment loans you can change your interest to a fixed rate (at market rates) and protect yourself from future rises. It is an easy, and cost effective way of protecting yourself against future cost increases.

3) **What if property prices fall?**
Once you apply all the *Knowledge* in this book about buying in the right area, at the right time and choosing the right property, you protect yourself. Again, *Knowledge* destroys the fear. Residential property prices will fall occasionally. They will fall much less than shares will, and far less frequently, because homeowners own two in every three properties. When prices do stall, or fall, they only ever fall a fraction of the last increase. Be patient, another boom in your investment property's value(s) will happen again.

4) **What if you buy the wrong investment property?**
If you have applied the *Knowledge* in this book, it will be difficult to buy the wrong investment property. Over time, your property will rise in value.

If ever you did make a bad decision, the best advice, usually, is to wait until the best time to sell your property, and then buy in a better area. However, this is expensive. It is much better to get specialist *Knowledge* and buy the right property the first time around.

It takes courage to sell a property that is under-performing, often near the peak of a boom, and put that money in your line of credit, or a bank. However, you can then use this money to buy a great property when the market falls and before the market rises again. Over a longer period, the difference this decision makes can make you much richer. Stubborn pride supporting a bad decision can cost you a lot, in terms of what you could be making. If you were willing to cut your losses, then you could get out of it. Put it down to experience. Learn from it and never repeat it.

5) **What if you lose your job?**
If you learn specialist *Knowledge* in your employment, and do what you love to do, you will always be employed. What if you don't like what you do now? Pretend that you love it and you will do it better. Learn specialist *Knowledge* to get a better job (*Strategy*) that you would rather do and take *Action* when the time is right. Most important

HOW DOES KNOWLEDGE DESTROY FEAR?

is to use what you currently have and get it working for you. Once you have built enough riches in your investment properties, you will be able to use them to generate money to support yourself in the short-term until you get a job again.

Don't buy a property if you cannot afford to have an additional amount that you can access in times of an emergency (a buffer).

If you are really insecure in your job, then maybe you should work harder to improve your security, or find another job, before you buy an investment property.

Once your assets build, they will support you. Without a buffer, or investments, you may have to sell your house to support yourself. Buying at the right time protects you, rather than putting you at risk. Develop a winning *Strategy* to combat this fear.

6) *What if you get sick and can't work?*
The answer is often the same as the above. Once you have begun to invest, insurance can protect you against this risk.

The best insurance for this is Income Protection insurance, which is fully tax deductible. This insurance is one that I have and recommend. Get a broker to shop around for you. It is worth considering. Get healthy. *ASK* your way to health and improve your chances of enjoying the benefits of having excellent health.

7) *What if the government changes the rules on negative gearing (positive leverage)?*
The Labor Government under the influence of Paul Keating, did this in 1985. Within two years, rents increased over 75% in Sydney (and other major cities). The same people that the government was trying to help (by taxing the rich to pay the poor) were harmed. They realised their mistake and re-allowed negative gearing again in 1987. This, combined with the stock market crash of 1987, was the reason property prices soared by over 90% for the next two years in many areas.

If a government does change the laws again, it probably would be a hasty decision that may well cost them the loss of power in the next election. Chances are:
i) the next government will again reverse the mistake, or
ii) if it ever was abolished again, it is highly unlikely ever to be retrospective. It may be just the reason you need to buy in the next downturn.

Most intelligent people doubt any Australian government will ever tamper with the tax deductibility of interest in the next few decades.

8) What if you get a 'tenant from hell'?

If your tenant won't pay rent, or damages your property, you can protect yourself. There are several excellent insurance policies (in all States) that will cover your contents from 'malicious tenant damage'. If your fittings or fixtures are damaged by tenants (which is rare), the correct insurance policy will allow you to replace them. This will give your property a better look which may increase your rental income.

If a tenant won't pay rent, your managing agent (or yourself) can evict the tenant, and when that tenant moves out, have any rent shortfall taken from their bond. The same insurance policy mentioned above will often pay for some of the cost of evicting such a tenant and repay you your lost rent.

Many people, including myself, and probably you, have been tenants in the past. Most tenants are good people. Choose your tenants wisely and the problem will not arise in the first place. If you think it might, insure yourself.

You can begin to generate solutions to any other challenges that arise. Do most of your solution focusing before you invest, and you decrease the chances of most things happening. John Paul Getty said he would do all of his worrying before he entered an investment. If he could not live with the worst outcome, he would ignore the deal, no matter how good it looked. If he could handle the risks, he would invest and, once in the transaction, spend most of his time stopping any obstacles arising and focusing on his desired outcomes. Good advice! We can do this also.

Be creative. Be careful. Transform fear into opportunities. You will become a more confident person. Cynics may be accurate, however optimists who *ASK* their way to riches live longer, have better relationships with other people and enjoy better health. It has been said that 'cynics are romantics who have lost hope'. Ignite your hope, have it spark a flame that illuminates your path and provides inspiration for others to follow your example. Dare to build riches.

Many people decide to give their money to others to invest for them. Let us look at the most common way they do this by *ASK*ing ...

Chapter 20

WHAT ARE MANAGED FUNDS?

*'If I have but enough for myself and my family,
I am a steward only for myself and them, if I have more,
I am a steward of that abundance for others.'*
~ **George Herbert.**

Managed funds are large pools of money made up of money from small and large investors alike. These monies are controlled by fund managers who direct the investment of this money on behalf of the investors and take various fees from the pool for providing this service.

Most Australians have money invested in managed funds through their compulsory superannuation (whether they know it or not). The calibre and performance of fund managers changes as does each manager's performance itself from year to year. Some provide consistently good returns and others do not.

In the category of managed funds it is convenient to put **property trusts**. They are different from the traditional managed funds in that all of their assets (apart from some cash) are in property alone. Managed funds usually have a blend of Australian shares, overseas shares, fixed interest, and some non-residential property.

What Types of Managed Funds Are There?

1) Income Trusts (mostly interest investments);
2) Equity Trusts (mostly shares or property);
3) Multi-Sector Trusts (those which are not Income or Equity Trusts).

1) Income Trusts

These trusts come in different forms and are sometimes called:

I) **Cash** (100% of assets are able to be converted to cash within one hundred and eighty days);
II) **Enhanced Cash** (liquidity above a certain ratio, i.e. 80%);
III) **Capital Guaranteed** (over 75% of the fund is fixed interest);
IV) **Mortgage Funds** (over 50% of the fund is in mortgages).

Fund managers are able to trade in bonds (a form of deposit) and yield capital profits (or losses) as a result of the sale of these bonds, as well as receiving fixed interest. Like direct investments in cash, these funds are good to invest in, prior to a share or property crash. Over the long term, (over five years) property and shares generally will out-perform income trusts. More details on this comparison will be given in Chapter 27. Historically, these funds may earn from 4% to 20% per annum before entry or exit fees.

2) Equity Trusts

These trusts include:

I) **Overseas Equity Trusts** (over 75% of assets are invested in overseas shares);
II) **Industrial Equity Trusts** (over 75% of assets are in industrial type shares);
III) **Resources Equity Trusts** (over 75% of assets are in resources shares);
IV) **Property Securities Trusts** (over 65% in listed (on Stock Exchange) property investments);
V) **Unlisted Property Trusts** (over 65% in unlisted trusts or direct property).

The fund managers of these respective funds invest in these asset classes to maximise returns within the restrictions of their investment guidelines. Over the long-term, they will provide greater returns than income trusts. As shares and non-residential properties are both volatile investments (they change as the economic cycle does), returns can be either high or low over different periods.

Over a five year period, returns on these funds can vary from 2%

WHAT ARE MANAGED FUNDS?

to 25% per year. The range is huge. Because the sharemarket is so volatile, you can see positive returns of anywhere up to 40% in one year and negative returns up to as much as 40% in another year. It is because of this that it is important not to be greedy or to be romanced by past performance in returns. The past (particularly in the short-term) is no guarantee of what will happen next year. The pattern is more important to observe (as was detailed in Chapter 9). Compare managed funds to other funds in the same time period. The financial magazines like *Personal Investment* or the *Weekend Financial Review* can be a good starting place. From there you can send away for prospectuses (formal publications put out by the fund managers that comply with ASIC regulations).

3) *Multi-Sector Trusts*
These trusts include:

I) **Multi-Sector 30 (50) (70) or (70+) funds** (with the number dictating the maximum percentage of funds in shares);
II) **Capital Guaranteed** (initial capital is guaranteed but it still invests in various areas);
III) **Regional (or Global) Funds** i.e. USA, Japan, European, South East Asia or Global (where 70% or more of the assets are invested in shares in these regions).

You will know before you invest in each of these funds what they will be investing in. This gives you the ability to buy and sell, or transfer into another fund, depending upon how you think each one will perform in the future.

Over a five-year period the returns on these funds will vary, depending upon where the investment was made. As funds are primarily in shares, there is a good chance for a profit or a loss if you invest in a given area, depending upon when you buy and sell. Returns of between 8% and 15% over a five year period (before entry or exit fees) are common. Be careful. Don't invest at the peak of a boom, expecting these returns. If the market crashes it can take you some considerable while to get your money back.

What Are the Benefits of Buying into a Listed Trust?

Trusts that are listed on the share market are more liquid (i.e. they are easier to sell). Unlisted trusts are harder to sell and very hard to sell for a fair price when markets take a downturn.

The larger the listed trust, the easier it is to sell some of your units in this trust without affecting the unit price. Large institutional investors (other fund managers and companies) also invest in these larger trusts providing more stability (in almost all cases) to investors.

What Fees are You Likely to Be Charged?

The **prospectus** (which is a legal document outlining benefits and risks that is approved by the ASIC) for each fund outlines the fees you are charged by the fund manager. Usually there will be a substantial entry fee with no exit fee or visa-versa. This fee is usually around 3% to 8%.

On top of this, there may be a fee charged by the fund manager on the assets of the trust, of a nominated percentage per year. For example, the fund manager may take 2% of the value of the fund each year. Be careful of this because it is fine for someone who makes you 20% in a year to take 2%, but if they lose 20% of your money, you do not want them charging you 2% for not reading the market well. Sometimes, if they have to have 70% in shares (in a given area) and the sharemarket is going to crash, then, you should move your money (even if you get hit with an exit fee) and put it in another safer place until it is time to invest in shares or property again. Chapter 26 outlines master trusts that have low fees (if you have substantial fees to invest). However there is another solution.

Can You Transfer Your Money Between Different Types of Funds?

Most large institutional fund managers have different types of funds under their control. For a fee, generally called a switching fee, you can transfer from income to equity to property or balanced funds. Some funds will charge no fee if the funds are only switched once a year.

Transferring your money between different funds with the same fund manager is an excellent way to improve your return. From mid 1999, all Australians will be given the choice of where their superannuation

WHAT ARE MANAGED FUNDS?

payments are made, as well as being able to move their super. Look at doing so if you are not currently getting the returns and the service you desire.

If your existing fund manager charges more than, say, 0.5% or 1% to switch between funds, then maybe you should change to a fund manager who will let you do what you want with your money! The larger the fund manager (sometimes), the easier it is to switch between funds. More benefits of this will be covered in Chapter 27.

Managed funds may also have all manner of account keeping and, seemingly, hidden fees like banks do. They have huge offices of professional people to pay and as they become public companies, the likelihood is that they will charge more, rather than less, indirect fees. Be careful. Read the documents.

Unfortunately, the vast majority of Australians leave their superannuation money in a certain type of managed fund and then look at the performance once a year (when they get their annual statements). Taking a more active role in moving your money from one fund to another can make you richer. This exciting area will be covered more in the *Strategy* section in Chapter 27.

The next chapter deals with this critical area of superannuation. It is a fabulous source of riches ...

Chapter 21

HOW DO YOU BUILD SUPER RICHES?

'With all the alluring promise that someone else will guarantee for a rainy day, social security can never replace the program that man's future wealth is, after all, a matter of individual responsibility.'
~ **Harold Stonier.**

Have you ever noticed how many people have lost interest in superannuation? Many are disenchanted, and others are concerned with what seems to be change after change after change to superannuation legislation. Some say it has changed on average every six weeks for the last ten years (or more). Despite the changes, it is still a fabulous area to build wealth and I encourage you to get interested and build super riches (i.e. riches that are yours in your superannuation fund).

Super riches are a great area of investing for five primary reasons:

1) The tax rate is only 15% (reducing to 10% for capital gains, refer to chapter 24);
2) You can't get at it until you are aged over fifty-five or more (with some exceptions);
3) After retiring you can earn profits tax free (if structured correctly) and have a rebate (i.e. a discount) on tax when you receive a distribution from an approved annuity fund;
4) You can control your own super riches;
5) It is, after all, your money!

These issues are worthy of further analysis:

1) *Why are your Super Riches taxed at only between 10% to 15%?*

The Australian government knows it cannot afford to pay the retirement pension to all the Baby Boomers. The Hawke Labor Government introduced the SGC as a means of people self-funding their own retirement. A low tax rate, 15%, is a key towards encouraging people to fund more than the minimum into their super.

In years to come, don't be surprised if the rate goes up to 20%. Many politicians make many promises to get elected into power. They then have to come up with the money.

The government only allows the 15% tax rate to super funds that are called complying funds. That is, they comply with government legislation. To keep this tax status it is worth complying. If you choose to run your own superannuation fund (which I encourage people to do), then your accountant can help you comply. If not, find another accountant. There are many excellent accountants who specialise in superannuation and have their own super funds. From my experience, it pays to use one of these accountants for your super riches.

2) *Why is it good if you can't get at the money?*

If you don't intend to live beyond fifty-five or sixty then I encourage you to set new goals. If you intend to live to be eighty or one hundred years old or more (in vital health) then you will have twenty or forty years to enjoy your riches.

Not having the chance to spend your super riches allows them to compound longer (which is a key to build riches as shown on pages 89 and 90).

If you compound your riches longer, at a low tax rate, you will earn more money. The only other ingredient is getting the highest return. At present you can do all of the investing that we have covered in this book in your own super fund.

3) *Can you receive a tax rebate and pay no tax on your profits?*

Once your super riches have grown and you have retired, you can transfer some of your super riches into an annuity. An annuity is a fund that pays you money each year. It is like your own pension fund.

The good news is that profits earned in this type of fund are not taxed. The other good news is that when you receive income from this type of fund you get a 15% rebate (that is, a 15% discount on your marginal tax rate).

HOW DO YOU BUILD SUPER RICHES?

You have to pay above a certain minimum amount from your annuity and less than a maximum amount each year. The formula is complicated and depends on your age and amount of funds. Your accountant can help work it out as part of your annual tax planning.

If you die, your annuity reverts to your spouse and can actually be used to pay tax-free money to your children. Use a professional to plan this while you are alive. The first step is to build substantial super riches in the first place.

4) Can You Control Your Super Riches?

From July 2000, all Australians will be able to choose their own super fund. That means you will be able to pay your SGC and other super payments into a super fund of your choice. Obviously, if you set up your own fund, then you will choose it. If your employer is not flexible in this regard there are certain low cost super accounts (run by banks and others) where you can put your super contributions and move it to another account later. Many employers currently let you choose where your super payments go.

If you have a reasonable amount in super now, you can 'roll it over' (i.e. transfer it) to another complying fund that you set up and control. Some people say that this is only for rich people. People become rich by doing the things covered in this book. If you are not yet rich, do things to become richer. If you are rich now then keep learning, investing and become richer. You can always give the money to charities, which will allow you to help other Australians have a better life after you have kicked the bucket and carked it! Why wait? You can make a difference while you are alive also.

Changes to the tax laws from 1 July 1999 allow you to gift money in your will and get a tax exemption for such gift (so it will not effect your beneficiaries). Also, gifts of property that are over 12 months old and are over $5,000 are now tax deductible (i.e. gifting real estate or art works to other people or an art gallery or charity). It is now possible to also set up private charitable trusts to assist others in a tax effective manner.

Most employed people have little real sense of the value of superannuation. It passes through their hands and remains very abstract and distant when all they receive is an annual report about it. It can seem as if it has nothing to do with them! By now it must be obvious, not only that it is your money but that you do have a say in what is done with it and can, in fact, use it to increase your riches substantially.

Why Would You Want to Run Your Own Super Fund?

Running your own super fund gives you control. If you do not have control, you run the risk of losing some or all of your super riches. In the shares section I noted a few of an increasing number of multi-billion dollar frauds and corporate collapses that have happened in recent years. If someone else controls your money and they commit a fraud or just lose your money, then what are you going to do? There are a limited number of cunning people who have more ways to hide this money, or themselves, than you or I can imagine. Corporate cowboys are a real threat to your riches. By the time the solicitors and receivers have made millions of dollars unravelling their carnage, you will be lucky to get any money at all. Controlling your own super reduces this risk.

In describing the above, I want to stress that con people are usually only a very small minority of money managers. Most professional fund managers are honest and hard-working. Even so, I encourage people to consider building their own riches and learn to make more money than the fund managers (as will be detailed in Chapter 28).

How Much Can You Make in Super Riches?

In the tax year ended 30th June, 2002, you can earn over $529,000 and take this money out as a lump sum when you retire. You can also set up a pension fund (or annuity) with another $529,000. That means you can tax effectively accumulate over $1,058,000 in super riches. This is also indexed each year in line with the increase in **Average Weekly Ordinary Times Earnings** (AWOTE) so it will increase to be over $1 million per person very soon.

For a couple in early 2002, if you don't have plans to accumulate over $2.11 million in super riches (in today's dollars) you are not using the system the way it has been designed.

The good news is that you can continue to build super riches well over $1 million each and still only be taxed at 15% on your profits. When you access your super riches later, only then will you will pay a higher rate of tax. So you still have the money and you have built it in a low tax environment.

How Much Can You Contribute to Build Super Riches?

Tax effectively you can contribute more to your super fund than the SGC. Depending on your age you can have your employer pay the following amounts in the year ended June 2002 (at the low tax rate of 15%):

Under 35 years old	$11,912
35-49 years	$33,087
50 and over	$82,054

These amounts will be indexed each year also. Your accountant or the Tax Office (phone 132 864) can give you current information, or visit the ATO website on: ato.gov.au.

The government does alienate high-income earners by charging the **Superannuation Surcharge**. It increases the contribution levy of 15% by 1% for every $1,219 of taxable earnings (i.e. after all deductions for interest and depreciation etc.) you earn from $85,242 to $103,507 in the 2001/2002 tax year. (These amounts increase every year after 1999). That means, if your income is under $85,242 you pay 15% tax on your contribution to super. If you earn over $103,507 you pay 30% on your superannuation contributions. In between, it depends on your income. This is stupid. High income earners should have the same incentive to invest in super riches as anyone else. At 30% tax, though, it is still better than 48.5%. It is also another example of foolishness, that the government does not round these amounts to even amounts, and has people concerned about doing complex calculations to pay extra tax instead of providing incentives to fund their own retirement.

If your taxable income is over $85,000, then maybe with careful use of *positive leverage* you can reduce it legally and still make large super contributions (without paying these higher contribution rates). Salary packaging is another way of reducing your taxable salary. Your accountant can help you organise this efficiently.

When Can You Access Your Super Riches?

If you were born before 1st July, 1960, you can access your super riches at age fifty-five. If you were born after 1st July, 1965, you have to wait until you are sixty. If you are somewhere in between, it increases by one year over fifty-five for each year or part year, after July, 1960, that you were born.

What Should You Do to Get Super Rich?

Start now. The younger you are the better. Put in a bit more SGC, control your own funds (if the idea appeals to you). Develop the ability to track the economic cycle. Move your super money in line with the economic cycle and get out of shares when they are too hot. The awesome power of compounding will work for you ONLY if you invest, make your money work hard and give it time to work.

You can start building super riches with as little as $400 if you have other assets. We go through this in our *Building Riches* tapes or your accountant can help you. My advice on managing your super, is to use an accountant who actually uses his or her own super fund to invest in and builds their own riches.

For most people it is advisable as a rule of thumb to only set up your own super fund if you have over $50,000 in super already. It should cost you from $350 to set up your own super fund ($1,300 if you require a company to act as trustee, which is not required for an individual's fund). Your annual fees to have this fund audited, and lodge all forms will be over $600 per year. As your super funds grow, these amounts become smaller in comparison to a fund manager. For example, when you accumulate $100,000 in super, a fund manager charging 2.5% annual total fees will cost you $2,500 per year compared with maybe $1,000 if you manage it yourself.

It is now time to move on to the *Strategy* section. Once you start to think strategically, your riches and life will improve dramatically. Let's get started right now by *ASK*ing . . .

3

What Strategies Do You Need to Build Riches?

Chapter 22

HOW WILL YOUR STRATEGY MAKE YOU RICH?

'Failure to prepare is preparing to fail.'
~ **John Wooden.**

Strategy: 'Skilful management in getting the better of an adversary or attaining an end.' ~ *Macquarie Dictionary.*

If you do not have a Strategy for building riches, then chances are high that you may be taken advantage of by someone else. There are many people you will meet who will try to get the better of you and con you out of your riches. I do not wish to be negative by warning you of the fact that many people treat making money as a battle. For them, there are winners and losers. This is called a Win/Lose game. The best way to defend yourself from these people is to have a *Strategy* of your own.

It has often been said, and I agree, that the only person a con-artist cannot take advantage of is an honest man or woman. When you combine honesty with a *Strategy* for success, you eliminate much uncertainty and make it much easier to build your riches (i.e. attaining your end).

It is easy to play a Win/Win game with yourself and your business associates if you build this into your *Strategy*. Do you currently have *Strategies* in various areas of your life? We all have *Strategies* whether we recognise them or not. You have a *Strategy* for cleaning your teeth, getting out of bed in the morning and answering the telephone as well as how you either increase or decrease your riches.

A good question to *ASK* yourself is: 'How is my financial Strategy making me rich?' If it is not, then it is time to replace it with a more effective *Strategy*.

You already have detailed specific *Knowledge* on the components necessary to build riches. Throughout the rest of this book we will add to that *Knowledge*. When you control *Knowledge* with the information you already have and then continue to add to it, you begin to compound your *Knowledge* quickly. Is this enough to make you rich? Generally not. What you need is enough *Action* and confidence to take *Action* in order to convert your dreams into investments that will make you rich. A *Strategy* provides a framework for your success. You learn from, and continue to get better at, those things you concentrate your attention on regularly. *Knowledge* is important and it forms the foundation of your riches.

The next essential ingredient is your individual *Strategy*. The more comprehensive your strategy, while remaining easy to understand and use, the faster will be your progress to the riches you desire. Once your *Strategy* is in place, it is time for *Action*. Do you remember the *ASK* model framework (from the Introduction)? It is so useful and easy, that it warrants repeating. The formula for riches looks as follows:

ASK Your Way to Riches

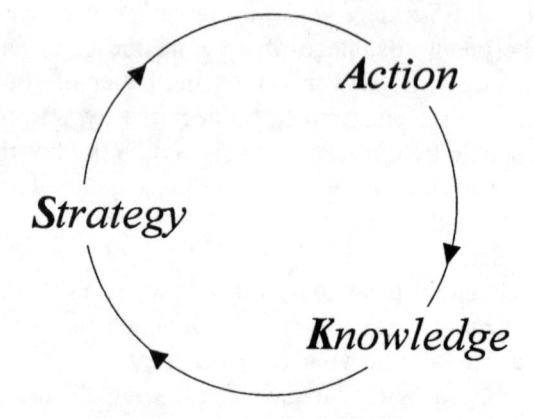

Strategy → *Action* → *Knowledge* → *Strategy* (cycle)

Knowledge allows you to form better *Strategies* so you can take better *Action*. So how does every unique person design their own *Strategy*?

We are all different. However, you know that almost everyone wants the same things in life. All sane, well adjusted people want to be healthy, happy, prosperous, have great interpersonal relationships and feel that our

HOW WILL YOUR STRATEGY MAKE YOU RICH?

life is filled with fun and enjoyment. It is possible to start to define broad *Strategies* in life to achieve these objectives. Money and riches cannot guarantee happiness and health, but they can give you more security and the freedom to achieve these objectives.

You may develop a lifetime *Strategy* to build riches so that you have greater freedom and security. Within this lifetime *Strategy* you may develop various financial *Strategies* for investing in cash, shares and real estate. And within each of these *Strategies* you might have various other *Strategies* involving investing in your name, your superannuation fund, and in other entities like companies or trusts (which I will deal with later). The different sub-levels of *Strategies* and who you use to implement them, will have a direct relationship to the results you achieve. The more sophisticated and detailed you make your *Strategies*, the greater will be your chances of success (providing of course you take *Action* on these *Strategies*).

To demonstrate how a lifetime financial *Strategy* can work, let us look again at Peter and Anne Wise. The Wises decided to write out a *Strategy* for their financial life. The framework of their *Strategy* was based on the following 7 steps.

What are the 7 Steps to a Richer Life?

1) Make an accurate and detailed assessment of your starting place;

2) Define exactly what you want to achieve. Do this from as far out into the future as you can (50, 60, or even 70 years!) and progressively work back to the present until you have a goal for the next 90 days;

3) Determine what specialist *Knowledge* you will need to achieve this goal and get that *Knowledge*;

4) Set a *Strategy* in place for achieving each individual step in your plan. It is difficult to have a *Strategy* with too much detail;

5) Take decisive *Action* on the first and most important priority that will make your plan be realised soonest and keep taking *Action*;

6) Observe the results you are getting and compare them to your plan.

Refine, adjust, or change your plan, as circumstances dictate, to achieve your objectives if you get off track;

7) Remind yourself regularly of the reasons why you are doing the things required to build riches.

For example, if family happiness is important then make regular time to be with your family and tell them all how much you love them.

In the next three chapters you will see how the Wise family implemented these 7 steps.

Your *Strategy* will be based on your particular circumstances.

Once you have decided on these steps and made a written plan, you are ready to set sub-*Strategies* in place. Your individual *Strategies* will be determined by the investment profile you set for yourself. You may choose to take acceptable risks. You might be perfectly happy borrowing money and letting savers make you rich. This *Strategy* allows you to buy investment real estate at the best time and in a good location. Alternatively, you may feel shares are a better place to invest and you may do this with or without borrowings. Or you may invest in shares, real estate and cash to build your riches faster.

In our *Building Riches* audio tape series I we go through a detailed process where participants plan their lifetime financial *Strategy*. Many people, within a few weeks of doing this exercise, find they are confident about getting rich and achieving their goals and are well advanced in the achievement of their most important step. Feedback from people who have done this exercise reveals that they accelerate their financial goals dramatically.

In order to develop superior *Strategies* you need to continue to refine your original *Strategy*. In the next chapter I will examine the actual performance of various investments in order to help you define your own personal *Strategy* to build riches faster, You need to decide ...

Chapter 23

WHAT ARE YOU GOING TO INVEST IN?

'Brains first and then Hard Work.'
~ **Eeyore. (A. A. Milne.)**

Opportunities abound to get rich. For the person who has done their planning (*Strategy*) it is relatively easy to find opportunities to get rich.

In order to develop a successful *Strategy* for building riches you will need to know how various investments have performed over time. This will allow you to fine tune your *Strategy* in the future by taking a long-term approach to building riches. You now know that cash and fixed interest will only protect your riches for a while. Over the long-term, leaving your money in interest bearing deposits will not make you richer because of the two ravaging effects of taxes and inflation. It is more relevant then to see how you can build riches by investing in shares and real estate for the majority of the time. Interest investments offer a safe haven for your money in uncertain times.

How do Shares and Real Estate Values Compare over the Long-term?

Let us assume that one of your relatives was living in Australia in 1878 and they had some money to invest. What would have been the capital growth that they would have achieved, had they invested in a full brick terrace house or the share market and then enjoyed spending the net rent or dividends? For this example I will use a terrace house located in

HOW TO BUILD RICHES

Goodhope Street, Paddington. I saw this property for sale in 1995 (and it was almost one hundred and twenty years old). After it sold, I searched the previous actual sales figures on this property. These figures are on public record at the Land Titles Office in your respective capital cities and, for a fee, you can gain access to records on any real estate sales in Australia. This is useful *Knowledge* to assist your own research of a given property or suburb. Using this information has saved me tens of thousands of dollars.

The ASX has prepared financial indices on the Australian share market going back to 1875. From 1875 to 1936 they used the Commercial and Industrial Index. This was then adjusted to correspond with the All Ordinaries share index (described earlier) from 1936 until today's index.

The actual sale price of the Paddington terrace in 1878 was $910 (£455). For simplicity the following chart has used figures that are based on initial investments in both shares and real estate of $910. A graph comparing the same amount invested in shares and this property from 1878 to 1958 follows.

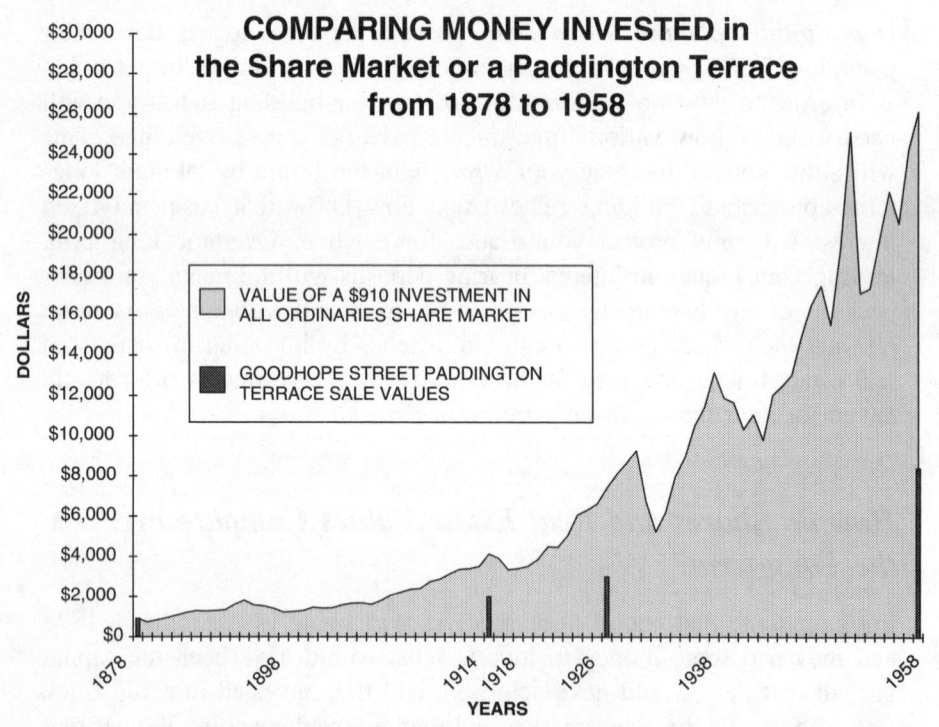

COMPARING MONEY INVESTED in the Share Market or a Paddington Terrace from 1878 to 1958

- VALUE OF A $910 INVESTMENT IN ALL ORDINARIES SHARE MARKET
- GOODHOPE STREET PADDINGTON TERRACE SALE VALUES

Source: NSW Land Titles Office and the Australian Stock Exchange

WHAT ARE YOU GOING TO INVEST IN?

The $910 investment in the share market over the eighty year period performed better than the Paddington terrace. Paddington was not a popular area for much of that time, and real estate in the leafy family oriented suburbs performed better over that time. There are properties near Sydney's harbour and its beaches that also performed much better than this property during this period.

The Paddington terrace sold in years 1914, 1926 and 1958. We can assume that this gives an accurate value of the property. In 1958, if you received the shares from your ancestor, handed down in a Will, they would have been worth $26,144. If you received instead the Paddington terrace, in 1958 it would have been worth $8,400.

What about the next forty years?

The graph on the following page shows the continuation of the same property and shares for the period from 1958 to 1998 inclusive. The values in 1958 are the same values as detailed in the above paragraph. The Paddington terrace, when sold in 1979, was worth $137,500. In 1979, the value of the shares would have been $78,569. During this time Paddington had become a sought after location and the price of the terrace house had increased to more than the value of the shares. What then? In 1995, if you sold the Paddington terrace, you would have received $1,700,000 (after selling and legal fees). In 1995, your shares would have been worth $406,653.

We can see that, over this one hundred and twenty year period, you would have received much more money by owning the property than the shares.

There were periods earlier in this time when shares were a better investment.

Some would say that the terrace house may have needed renovations to sell it at $1.75 million. They would be right, but I think you can see that in 1995 you could have done a lot of renovations for over $1.3 million (being the additional value that the property was worth in comparison with the shares). Alternately, if you had shares you would have wanted to make sure all your shares were not in one company in case it went into liquidation taking all your money with it (like Bond Corporation or Quintex did). If that happened, your shares investment would have been worthless. Shares and real estate both offer good investment returns at different times.

HOW TO BUILD RICHES

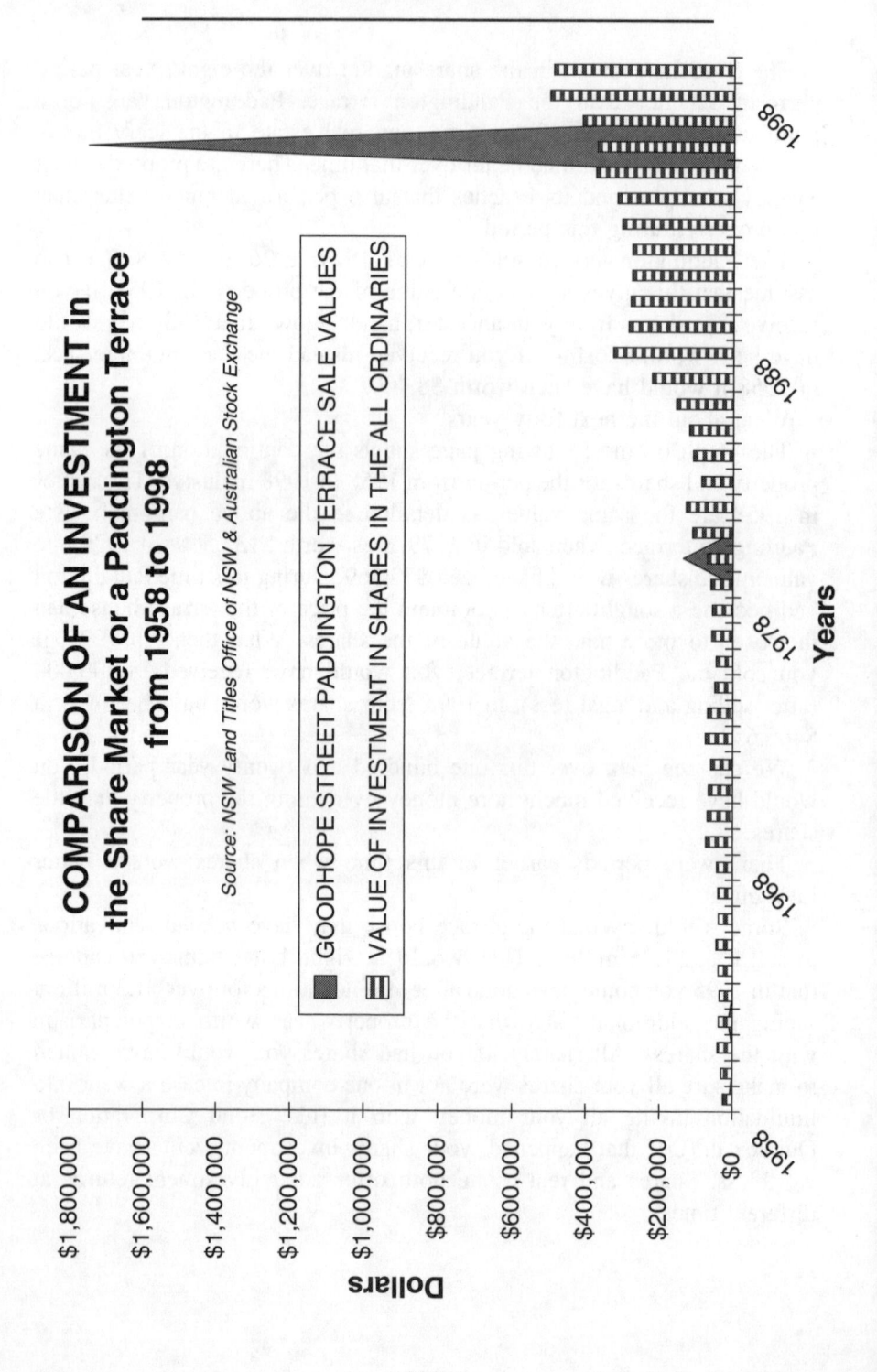

COMPARISON OF AN INVESTMENT in the Share Market or a Paddington Terrace from 1958 to 1998

Source: NSW Land Titles Office of NSW & Australian Stock Exchange

- GOODHOPE STREET PADDINGTON TERRACE SALE VALUES
- VALUE OF INVESTMENT IN SHARES IN THE ALL ORDINARIES

WHAT ARE YOU GOING TO INVEST IN?

Let us now compare shares and real estate in more recent times. Again we will use real properties and the All Ordinaries share index and this time I will also include fixed interest (after tax).

How Have Different Types of Investment Performed Over the Past Twenty Years?

The graph on the following page shows what your increase in capital would have been from 1976 to 1999, if you had invested $100,000 in either:

1) Shares in the All Ordinaries share index;

2) Inner Sydney real estate. An average of both inner Sydney actual three bedroom cottages and two bedroom units. Chapter 15 detailed facts and reasons why the cottages outperformed the units over this period. It may be that you used your money to buy both units and cottages. For this reason I have included both sets of figures (even though the cottages only would have improved the relative real estate return);

3) Fixed Interest in one yearly investments, with the taxation on the interest being charged at 44.5% (because tax on interest is unavoidable).

In comparing the absolute increase in capital it is easy to make these observations:

I) Inner Sydney properties exceeded shares in value, for twenty of the twenty-three years;

II) Both shares and property were much better investments over the period, than was interest income;

III) Shares and property both moved upwards and downwards in line with the general economic cycle.

HOW TO BUILD RICHES

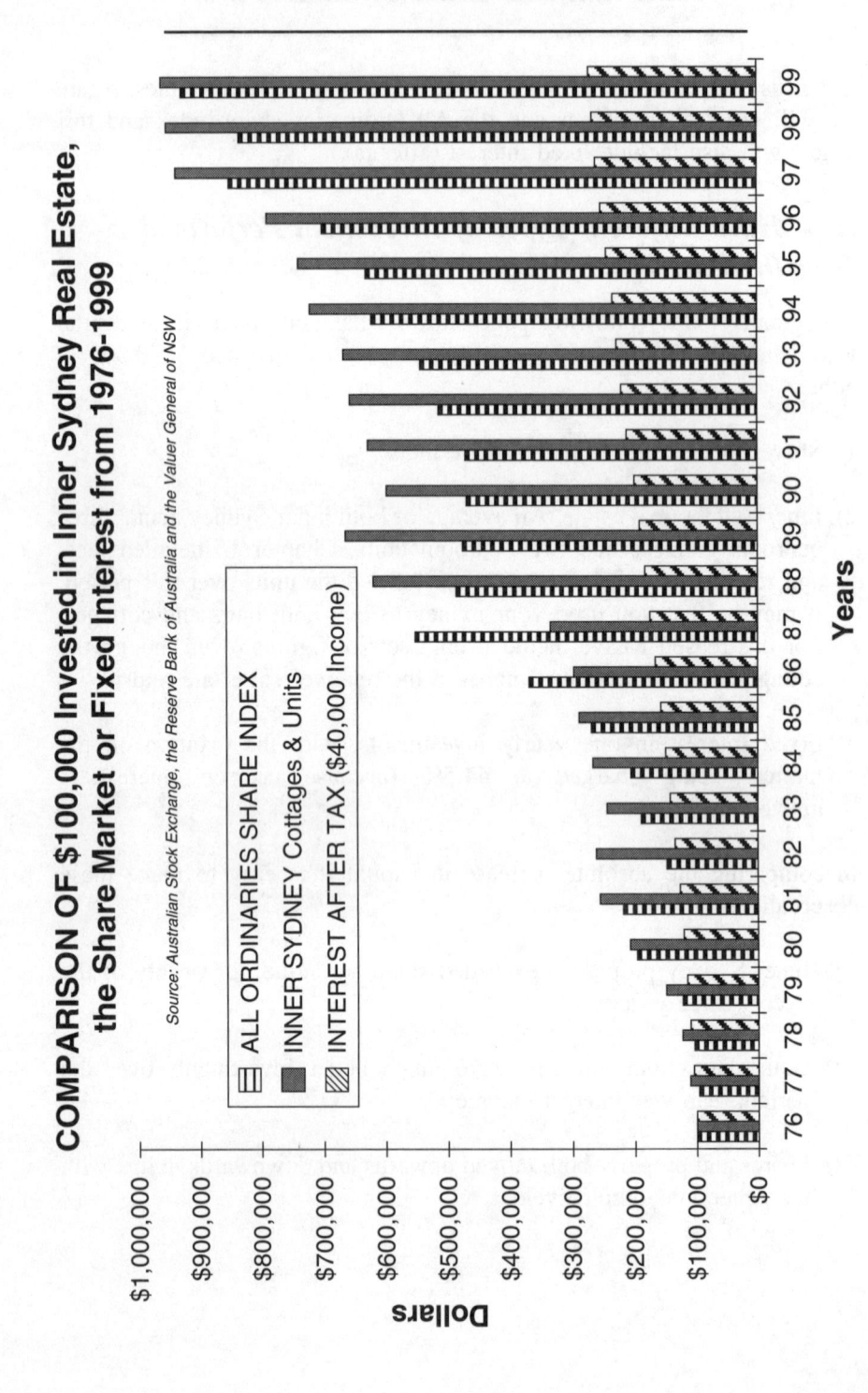

COMPARISON OF $100,000 Invested in Inner Sydney Real Estate, the Share Market or Fixed Interest from 1976-1999

Source: Australian Stock Exchange, the Reserve Bank of Australia and the Valuer General of NSW

Legend:
- ALL ORDINARIES SHARE INDEX
- INNER SYDNEY Cottages & Units
- INTEREST AFTER TAX ($40,000 Income)

WHAT ARE YOU GOING TO INVEST IN?

How are Most Shares and Property Comparisons Biased?

Generally, most comparisons you see between shares and property will be biased in two main ways:

1) Most property comparisons use the Median Priced properties data. This data is useless in analysing real properties (as discussed in Chapter 15). For a meaningful understanding of property you want real valuations (such as the ones used in the graph on the previous page);

2) Shares have an inherent leverage, which is not mentioned in any comparison I have ever seen. For example, in mid 1999 the following top Australian companies ratio of Total Debt to the Total Value of the company was:

Company	% of Debt
1) News Corporation Ltd	31%
2) BHP Ltd	55%
3) National Australia Bank Ltd	72%
4) Westpac Ltd	75%
5) Telstra Ltd	41%

You can see that a large proportion of the assets of these top companies have been bought using borrowed money. As detailed in Chapter 9, on the economic cycle, the more borrowings a company has, the more likely its share price is to decrease, when interest rates rise. This applies to banks also. Even though banks pass on the cost of interest rate rises to their borrowers, they have more loans default in times of higher interest rates and, accordingly, a lesser profit and a lower share price.

Shares have more indirect borrowing than property. This occurs as a result of the high proportion of borrowed funds as a proportion of the company's assets (as shown above). Most people are ignorant of this fact. They buy their shares in a public company, and assume that if they do not borrow to buy the shares, then there is no borrowing. If the company itself has 50% (or more) of its assets bought with borrowed money, the shareholder, indirectly, is responsible for this risk. If the company gets into financial trouble or is eventually liquidated by its lenders, then it is the shareholders who suffer. The shareholders only get what is left after all lenders, employees, creditors are paid, as well as the lawyers, court costs and the liquidators. In cases like Bond Corporation Limited and others, this is usually very little, if anything.

If you see comparisons of shares and real estate in financial publications, it is worthwhile to remember that the shares have a greater amount of indirect risk (as a result of the company's borrowings). This gives shares an unfair advantage when comparing to real estate without any borrowings (leverage). In the following example I will disregard the advantage that shares have in such a comparison.

If you invested $100,000 in 1976 in either shares, inner Sydney real estate or fixed interest and let your investment compound until 1999, how much would you have in each of these three investment classes? As at June 1999 the value of your $100,000 invested in these three areas would be:

Inner City real estate value	$960,140
Shares value	$927,781
Bank deposit value	$272,065

It is assumed that the interest after tax was left in the bank. For real estate and shares, the net rent or dividends are not included (and are assumed to be spent or invested elsewhere).

Which investment category would you prefer?

Are Shares or Property More Risky Over Time?

Owning shares is more risky than owning property if no borrowings are used. The reason for this is that shares already have an inherent leverage as noted above. The other reason, which I covered earlier, is that two in every three properties are owner occupied. Owner occupation means that property prices are less likely to fall. Likewise, property may not rise as quickly as some shares do at certain times. But, as we can see above, real estate still outperforms shares.

In the chapters on shares and property, I covered the aspects of borrowing to make these investments. For most people it is easier and less risky to borrow to buy property than it is to buy shares. Any local bank manager can generally organise a property loan for you. If you want a share loan, it will have to be processed through a specialist section of the bank. If you borrow against shares (which are already inherently

WHAT ARE YOU GOING TO INVEST IN?

geared), you increase your chances of large profits, or losses, depending upon when you make your investment.

If you have experience at analysing company financial reports, and understand when to buy and sell individual shares, you can earn significantly more than the All Ordinaries Index. For people with this experience, shares can exceed the returns from real estate without any leverage. Tracking shares does render you liable to CGT each year. Calculate this in any comparisons between shares and real estate.

Shares and property are both excellent investments if you are careful and invest at the right time.

Peter and Anne Wise felt more comfortable investing in property because they understood it more than they did shares. In Chapter 17, I demonstrated their investment in a single investment property (when Peter was aged thirty and Anne aged twenty-five). What will happen to the value of this property over time? It was bought for $249,000. Borrowing to cover all costs was $260,000 (as detailed on page 173). Remember that, over the first ten years, the property cost just under $37 per week after-tax (as detailed in Appendix 2). After ten years, the property returns a regular monthly cash flow(after-tax) to the Wise family (as well as their capital profit).

The value of the property, comprising both borrowed funds and equity that belongs to the family, is shown in the graph on the next page.

The investment loan of $260,000, after thirty-five years, looks almost insignificant next to the Wise family's equity of over $3.4 million. An 8% capital growth rate is assumed for this graph. This is much less than it has been for the last twenty years in suburbs close to the centre of the major capital cities around Australia.

The after-tax cost of this property is very low. The capital growth is substantial. It is for these reasons that it is considered unwise to bother reducing the investment loan on properties like this.

When should the Wise family sell their investment property? The next chapter deals with capital gains tax. Once you understand how capital gains tax works you can substantially reduce the tax you pay.

HOW TO BUILD RICHES

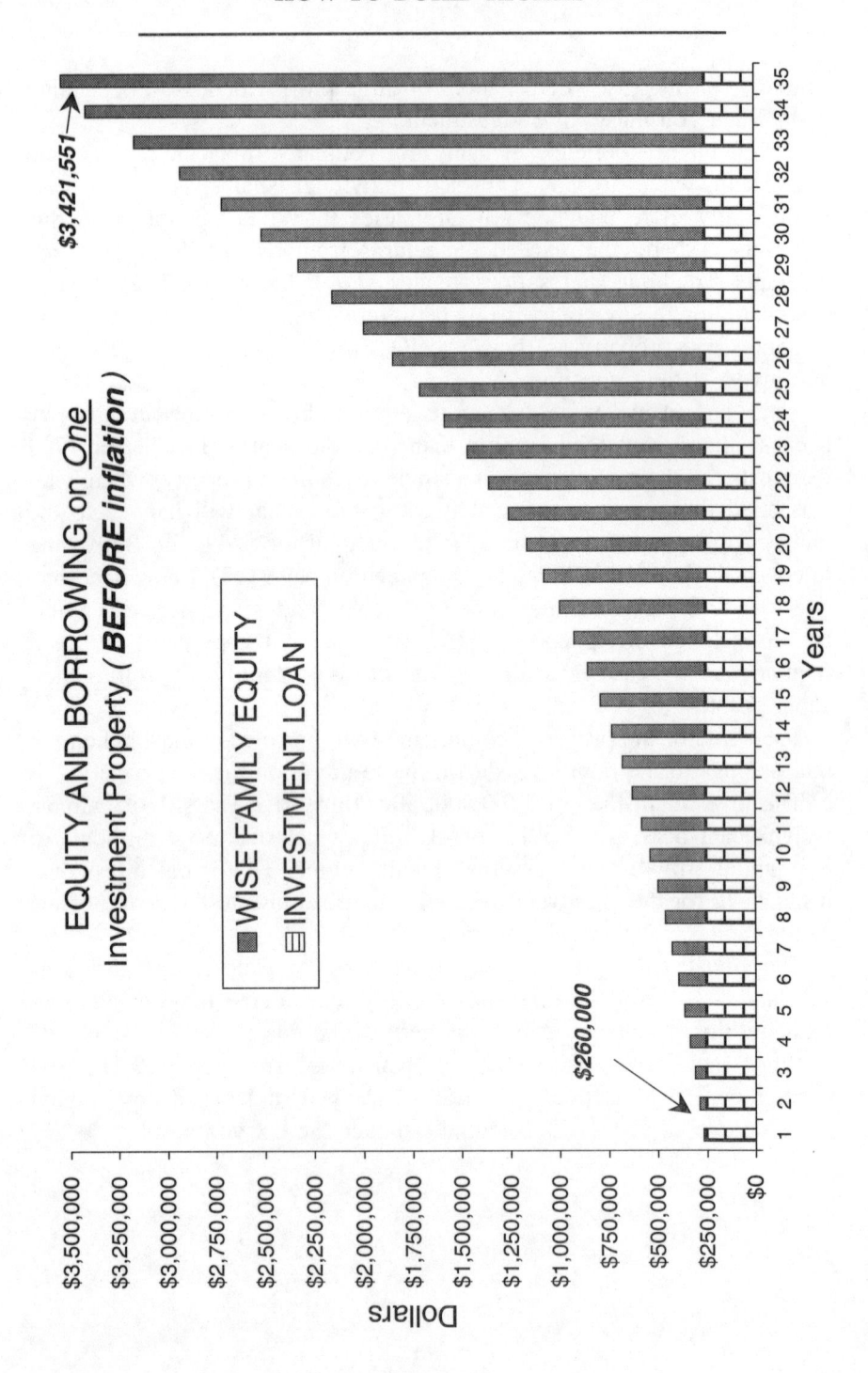

EQUITY AND BORROWING on *One* Investment Property (*BEFORE inflation*)

■ WISE FAMILY EQUITY
☐ INVESTMENT LOAN

$3,421,551

$260,000

Years: 1–35
Dollars: $0 – $3,500,000

Chapter 24

HOW DOES THE NEW CAPITAL GAINS TAX AFFECT YOUR RICHES?

'Taxes: a grave discouragement to enterprise and thrift.'
~ **W. C. Fields.**

Capital gains tax ('CGT') is the biggest expense an investor will encounter. Planning its impact and affect on your investments is critical to consider before you invest. The major overhaul of the CGT structure in September 1999 by the Howard Liberal Government makes planning your investments even more relevant.

The CGT has proved to be one of, if not the biggest revenue earners for the government, of all times. When the CGT was first introduced in September 1985 it was expected to bring in $25 million of revenue after five years of operation. Instead it raised about $100 million in its first year of operation. In 1996-97 it raised $2.1 billion of revenue. The CGT is seen as a 'sleeper' by accountants and future CGT will increase even more, as a result of the huge increase in people owning shares (as discussed on page 111).

Prior to October 1999 the CGT only taxed profits that exceeded inflation and gave generous concessions to people on low incomes. After September 1999 the CGT for individuals is reduced (by one half) and super funds (one third), but no allowance is given for inflation. Companies and trusts get no benefits from the new CGT.

There is a general misconception that CGT is only a tax on the rich and that the new tax changes will especially assist the wealthy only. This is incorrect. Although people on taxable incomes over $50,000 in 1996-97 paid 80% of the CGT, the majority of the CGT taxpayers, almost 450,000 people, earned less that $50,000 (over 72% of the workforce from page 22). With about 4.5 million Australians directly owning shares, more taxpayers on lower incomes will incur CGT. Over time, these capital profits will assist more average Australians to build riches irrespective of their current incomes.

How Do the New CGT Laws Operate?

The fundamental changes in the CGT laws that have been proposed (subject to parliamentary approval) will apply after 11:45am on 21st September 1999 are:

1) For all assets that were acquired after 1st October 1999 and were owned for at least one year, the CGT payable will be based on the **'nominal gain'** and will not reduced for inflation (as explained later in this chapter). The taxable amount becomes the difference between sale price and cost price. Individuals and superannuation funds will pay CGT on a reduced proportion of their realised nominal gain as detailed below;

2) Indexation of the cost base for CGT (used under the old CGT legislation) will be frozen at 30th September 1999;

3) Averaging of capital gains (used under the old CGT legislation) will not apply to any assets that were sold after 11:45am on 21st September 1999;

4) Individuals who bought assets before 1st October 1999, that were owned for at least one year, will have the choice of including in their assessable income either:
   i) one half of the nominal profit realised on sale; or
   ii) all of the difference between the sale price and the indexed cost base (that is frozen at 30th September 1999);
   As time goes by (and particularly after the one-off inflationary effect of the GST in mid 2000), alternative (ii) will become less appealing. Without the ability to average CGT, alternative (ii) will also be less appealing for Australian lower income earners and the retired;

HOW DOES CAPITAL GAINS TAX AFFECT YOUR RICHES?

5) Superannuation funds which bought assets before 1st October 1999 that were owned for at least one year will have the choice of including in their assessable income either:
   i) two-thirds of the nominal profit realised on sale; or
   ii) all of the difference between the sale price and the indexed cost base;

6) Capital losses (the sale of assets for less than cost) will be able to be offset against capital gains that include the indexed cost base, up until 30th September 1999. Capital losses can only be offset against capital profits;

7) Revenue losses will continue to be allowed to be offset against capital gains (as detailed above);

8) Depreciable assets will now be taxed for CGT at the difference between the sale price and the indexed cost price, after 21st September 1999;

9) The CGT on the sale of small business assets was discussed on pages 81 to 82. These changes allow taxpayers: to reduce their CGT on the sale of a business by up to three quarters; roll any tax liability over if they buy a new business; or pay no CGT if they use the proceeds to retire, or as a result of the business owner being incapacitated.

Tax laws change. Even once enacted by parliament they are subject to change by regulation far easier than it was to bring in the original legislation. For example, once the GST or CGT is law, the government of the day can change the taxation rates, e.g. GST from 10% to 12%, by regulation overnight. Before or after the CGT tax rate deductions for individuals and superannuation funds become law, they also can be changed. The above proposed changes to the CGT laws may also be watered down as a political compromise with the Democrats or Independents. If you treat this chapter and book and similar books as a guide, you will be well advised. Your accountant or the ATO can give you precise rates that apply at the time of selling any significant Investment Assets that are subject to CGT.

Let's assume the CGT legislation is enacted by parliament as proposed. The rate of CGT for individuals after the introduction of the GST from

1st July 2000 will halve that shown on the table for personal taxation rates detailed on page 54, being:

Taxable Income	**OLD** CGT Tax Rate Before October 1999 (after inflation)	**NEW** CGT Tax Rate After September 1999 (including inflation)
$0-$6,000	0	0
$6,001-$20,000	17	8.5
$20,001-$50,000	30	15
$50,001-$60,000	42	21
over $60,000	47*	23.5#

* add 1.5% Medicare Levy
\# add 0.75% Medicare Levy

Will the New CGT Suit Everybody?

Most people will choose to elect to use the new CGT regime on the sale of their assets, particularly those who have followed the investment criteria outlined in this book, i.e. buying in downturns (Chapter 9) and buying quality shares and well located real estate (pages 152-154). If you invest and sell quality assets at the right time, your compound rate of return will be maximised (Chapter 7) and your capital gain will significantly exceed inflation. Under these criteria the new CGT laws will benefit your sale and will result in less CGT.

The old CGT rules may suit those who have owned assets for many years and owned these assets during periods of higher inflation (late 1980's and early 1990's) or those who own poorly performing shares or real estate. For example, if someone owned a country property (in many areas) or some under performing mining shares, their capital gains may be only equal to inflation up until 30th September 1999. If you still own under performing assets, you may consider selling them and reinvesting the money into shares or real estate that will compound to give you a better long-term return.

In order to decide which CGT regime to choose, I have enclosed in the Appendices, details and examples of both CGT systems. Appendix 3 details the inflation figures used by the government from the date of the introduction of the CGT system on 19th September 1985 until it was

HOW DOES CAPITAL GAINS TAX AFFECT YOUR RICHES?

frozen on 30th September 1999. Appendix 4 shows the method of calculating the CGT using the old system, after the averaging system has been removed for sales made after 21st September 1999. If you contracted to sell an asset before 22nd September 1999, you can get the ATO or your accountant to mail you the procedure for lower income taxpayers to reduce your CGT using the averaging process.

In order to compare the two CGT systems, I have set up an example in Appendix 5 that uses both systems to cover the sale of an investment property that is assumed to occur in late 2000 using the new taxation rates. In this example the property (excluding depreciable fittings) was bought in October 1985 (CPI Index 72.7) for $200,000, plus $8,000 purchase costs. The property was close to the centre of Melbourne and experienced a compound growth rate of 10%. From the Rule of 72 (pages 91 to 93), the property will double in 7.2 years and again in the next 7.2 years. In late 2000 (15 years after purchase) it is assumed to be sold for $850,000. Using the old tax system the taxpayer (earning $40,000 p.a.) pays tax on the capital gain after inflation, being $471,944 at her marginal tax rate. She would pay $226,493 in CGT. Under the new CGT system the taxpayer would be taxed at 50% of the nominal gain being $308,500 (after selling costs). The CGT under the new system is $147,223. This taxpayer by choosing to use the new CGT rules will pay over $80,000 less tax than had she elected to be taxed under the old CGT regime election (as described in point 4) at the bottom of page 230.

How Will the New CGT Affect Your future Capital Profits?

To demonstrate the long-term effect of the CGT, I will use the example of the Wise's first investment property that was detailed in Chapter 16. What if the Wises sell the property 36 years after they bought it, when Peter retires and is aged sixty-six. The property at that time, at the ridiculously conservative compound rate of eight percent, will have grown to say $3.6 million. Remember the Rule of 72, (72 divided by eight percent equals nine years to double). In the first nine years the property will double to about $450,000, then redouble to $900,000 and again to $1.8 million and finally redouble again to $3.6 million. These figures are very conservative compared to the real estate within six kilometres of Sydney's centre (where our companies develop apartments for our clients). The CGT payable will be about $785,000. The total cash on hand from this sale will be almost $2,440,000 after repaying the loan on this property, the line of credit on their home and paying selling expenses and taxes (refer Appendix 6).

There are ways to legally reduce the CGT even further. Individuals pay about two-thirds of all tax paid in Australia. With the new GST and CGT, this is unlikely to change. Something that I find most ridiculous and highly offensive is the fact that taxpayers are treated more harshly than criminals in the eyes of the law. This occurs as the law places the onus of proof on a taxpayer, to have to prove that they are entitled to any taxation deduction. This onus of proof puts a legal responsibility on the taxpayer. This, in essence makes the taxpayer guilty until proven innocent. Conversely, the onus of proof for a criminal is on the person accusing them. Thus a criminal is considered innocent until proven guilty.

> *Taxpayers are considered guilty until proven innocent.*
> *Criminals are considered innocent until proven guilty.*

A murderer or a rapist is given greater legal rights than hard-working taxpayers. Unfortunately, it is the way our laws have been structured. You can access various methods for legally reducing your taxation. It would be unwise for me to state in this book how to do so as the Australian Taxation Office ('**ATO**') may change the laws to prevent you from legally arranging your affairs to do so. Our *Building Riches* seminars identify concepts to legally reduce CGT which still apply. Our new seminars show people how to reduce their taxes using the new tax system. Please complete the form on page 365 if you would like us to inform you on the availability of such a seminar or audio tapes resulting from it. In paying taxes we provide roads, hospitals, schools and other services for our families and our fellow Australians. In minimising taxes we provide for our families and our own retirement needs. Both are important.

It is time to see how *Strategies* can be set and how they can make you rich by learning ...

Chapter 25

HOW CAN YOU GET RICH ON AN AVERAGE SALARY?

'Getting there isn't half the fun ~ it's all the fun.'
~ **Robert Townsend.**

To demonstrate how it is possible to get rich on an average salary, I will expand the examples of Peter and Anne Wise, and how they made the decisions that made them rich, and how David and Shirley Battler, who failed to make decisions, remained poor.

The purpose of using the examples of these two couples is to show you just how huge is the difference you can make by applying the *Knowledge, Strategies* and *Action* principles outlined in this book.

Our starting point was when these couples were in their early twenties and I have projected their decisions, and their results, through to their retirement. By looking at these projections as *if* these couples had already taken these steps, *you can clearly see just how accessible building riches is for you*.

One of the main reasons for the enormous difference in results ~ the Wises would retire with income from investments of more than $4 million dollars (in today's spending power), compared with the Battlers' $500,000 ~ is the difference in their Strategies.

The Wises decided that they wanted to have more than financial riches, they also wanted rich lives. They wanted riches in health, loving family relationships, satisfaction in their work and great friends. You will remember they prepared their own 7 steps to a rich life (on pages 217 and 218) and they wrote their *Strategy* in a bound *Personal Riches Journal*: I encourage you to keep such a journal that you can add to as your *Strategies* develop. You can see your progress in it. You may even give it to your children or grandchildren to help them follow in your successful footsteps, so they too can build riches. As previously discussed, I have provided pages 372 to 380 so you can start your own *Personal Riches Journal* today. A summary of the Wises' 7 steps to a rich life comprised a detailed *Strategy*. This has been included on the following pages to give you the opportunity to use it as a template. I have also interspersed it with what David and Shirley Battler did for the contrast of people who just go with the flow of life. You can adjust, change, or refine this to fulfil your own goals.

Step 1: What is your starting place?
The Wises first detailed their personal spending plan (in Chapter 3) and recorded this in a Cash Payments Journal (available from newsagents). Then they recorded their own Statement of Assets and Liabilities (like the one provided in Appendix 1). The Battler family thought it was too difficult and put it off.

Step 2: What do you want to achieve?
The Wises decided to set a seventy year plan. At the time of doing this Peter Wise is twenty-five and Anne is twenty: their long-term outcomes are to be healthy, happy, and active when they are aged in their nineties. (Studies, including my own research and observing my own grandparents and others, show that people who desire to be alive and make a difference later in life, have a much greater chance of achieving their goals.)

In their nineties, the Wises want to have a net worth outside their home of over $10 million in today's spending power. They figure that they have plenty of time to achieve this goal and decide that that will be quite ambitious for a couple on an average income. They plan to arrange their affairs so that, at their deaths, their money will be left to family members in a tax-effective structure.

Understanding how the Rule of 72 worked, they calculated that they will need to have about four million dollars when they retire. They decide that they will work until Peter is sixty-five and Anne is sixty.

They decide also that, in order to keep young after retiring, they will have an active life filled with the sports they enjoy, tennis and golf. They also decide to spend extensive time with their future grandchildren. They will take them to Disneyland and Europe as well as treating the whole family (children and grandchildren) to an island resort holiday in the

HOW CAN YOU GET RICH ON AN AVERAGE SALARY?

Pacific at least every two years. In between, they decide they want to travel the world themselves every other year. The Wises think they will travel outside the tourist season, spend time in out-of-the-way local villages, and learn these languages at night school in Australia before they travel, to allow a greater appreciation of the different cultures.

To support their lifestyle in retirement they decide to have after-tax income at that stage of at least seventy-five thousand dollars a year in today's spending power (more than they are earning now). They plan to have their retirement income increase as they get older, as they want to have extra medical help available if needed, to keep them feeling young. They also want the best doctors, masseurs, fitness instructors and beauticians.

To increase their future retirement income they decide to invest in shares as well as property and have a superannuation annuity income (when they retire). They make the conscious decision to support themselves in retirement. They want NO government assistance. They decide that they will be happy paying their fair share of taxes on their future retirement income to help people who are not able to support themselves. They decide to live in a modest family home during their working lives and have two main investment *Strategies*.

The Wise Family's two main investment *Strategies* are:

1) They prefer to invest in real estate rather than in shares. They believe it will be a better investment and that they will make more money investing in real estate than in shares. (If you are an expert in how companies operate and want to invest primarily in shares, you may prefer to invest in shares instead of real estate. I do both, but put most of my money in real estate.);

2) They decide to run their own superannuation fund and actively build super riches. They will send letters to any government that tries to affect their right to build super riches. They consider that they are average working Australians. They don't want any government assistance in retirement and will actively fight any government or individual who violates their rights. Their aim is to have their own super fund wholly own a unit trust that they control. Their accountant has one of these structures and set up one for them for $2,000 which included the cost of buying a company to act as a trustee, a super fund,

and a unit trust. Be sure to read pages 269 and 270 before you set up such a structure. Their unit trust is then going to invest in both property and shares using positive leverage. They love the idea of investing in different areas at different times in the economic cycle. The idea of making more money than highly paid superannuation fund managers appeals to them enormously!

They project that owning four investment properties outside their home will enable them to achieve their goals. When they retire, they calculate that they will be able to sell one property and repay most of the borrowings on the other three properties that they plan to buy, and have money left over. They will then enjoy being in the enviable position of having the net rent from three properties. These three properties of course will continue to increase in value and provide them with security.

To achieve these real estate goals they bought their first investment property as soon as they had reduced their home loan to a low enough amount (as detailed in Chapter 18). After they made conservative calculations they realised that they could afford another investment property about every seven years. If their salaries increase faster or the real estate market increases by more than their conservative projections, then they will be able to afford more properties.

The Wises want two children and decide that Anne will work only part-time for the first ten years of their first child's life. During that time their own parents (who are already well on their way to riches having also listened to the *Building Riches* tapes) will have retired and have offered to look after their grandchildren as often as they can. The Wises' parents have already started investing money for their future grandchildren. They plan to help pay for overseas travel and a university education for their grandchildren.

In order to get started, the Wises first bought a home (being the worst house in the best street) in a suburb six kilometres from the centre of their city. This suburb was not trendy when they bought it. However, the homes in it were lovely old full brick character homes and Peter and Anne renovated over time. Meanwhile, the Battlers decided to buy a new brick veneer home on the outskirts of town with a huge yard. They paid a high price at the top of the market and bought the best house in the best street in suburbia.

The Wises decided upon a line of credit and committed to paying out their non tax-deductible home loan as soon as possible. The Battlers bought instead one new car and then another and took a twenty-five year home loan with the local bank. Five years after the Wises had bought their home, they had also bought their first investment property. These details were covered in Chapter 5.

The Wises invested one full day every week looking for their first investment property. They saw two hundred and fifty homes and put in over one hundred offers between 80% and 90% of the asking price on the properties. They had also bought their own home for less than 90% of the value of a comparable home. They learned from experience that the harder you work, the luckier you get. This idea appealed to them so much that they used it to become lucky and to start their journey towards riches.

Step 3: What specialist Knowledge do you need?
In the month that the Wises first read this book, then listened to our *Building Riches* tapes, they learned more about finances than they had learned in over twelve years of schooling each! They also bought some more books and devoured all the material contained therein. They learned to develop the habit of going to book shops (and second-hand book shops) to buy financial books. Their aim was to spend half an hour each day reading these books and looking for at least one idea that they could use.

Step 4: What Strategies will help you achieve your goals?
In order to become even richer, the Wises formed a group with some of their friends who also read books and listened to tapes and met once every three weeks. They discussed new ideas for building riches, swapped books, and spent time discussing specific shares and the general economic cycle. They also decided to use their own super fund to do some of their own share trading. These meetings took about two hours each.

Step 5: What decisive Action will fastest realise your goal?
The Wises looked for their investment property most Saturdays for a few hours between 11am to 3pm. They held their first shares group meeting at Anne's parents house. Anne's father had a share portfolio and he wanted to be a part of this discussion group. Anne and Peter had already learned much from his experiences.

The Wises' accountant set up their super fund and showed them how to have their existing super monies rolled over into their own fund. Peter and Anne both encouraged their employers to pay their future SGC payments into their own super fund. Their employers were so impressed by their *Knowledge* in this area that they wanted to find out more. Peter and Anne bought them a copy of this book and encouraged them to buy their own *'Building Riches' tape series.*

Step 6: How are your results comparing to your plan?
The Wises monitored their results. It took them a while to get used to saying 'no', to certain social outings on the weekends with some of their friends. They were having so much fun planning their riches, that they weren't prepared to spend most of their time and money with people who didn't have any written goals. They then were able to increase their reading to an hour a day.

Anne decided to enrol in an evening course on bookkeeping and basic business skills. She completed a computer course and after that designed spreadsheets for recording their spending plan and mortgage reduction. Later she will be able to use these skills to plan their property and share portfolios. With these skills, Anne was able to do the books at the hairdressers, where she worked, to make extra income (and add to her job security), which helped make them rich by providing the cash flow to support their property investment *Strategy.*

Peter enrolled in a part-time builder's course and his employer agreed to give him some time off work for this purpose. Since listening to the audio tapes, he had become a better employee, who came in a bit earlier and stayed a bit later than his colleagues. Peter told his boss he wanted to build a career in this company and was serious about his job. Peter was given a pay rise and earned more once he had his own builder's licence. With his new skills he was able to renovate his home and did some of the renovations on their investment properties.

Step 7: Why are you building riches?
Peter and Anne Wise decided to spend every Sunday together having fun. They also decided that their marriage and love for one another was their greatest asset. The Wises decided that health was their next most important priority. They started reading about health and exercise. They planned a regular exercise routine and bought some second-hand weights so they could work out at home together. They cycled or walked at least twice a week together. Later they involved their children by jogging while their little ones cycled, so they could spend time talking together.

So why are you building riches? Once you know the answer to this question you can make sure you spend time achieving your ends. Money and riches will not buy you happiness. You have to find happiness along the way. (This topic is covered more in Chapter 33.) Take time every day to love yourself (warts and all) and do the things that make you happy.

Let us now compare the riches that the Wise family and the Battler family accumulated as a result of their different *Strategies*.

How Much More Money Do Investors Make?

You have already seen (in Chapter 5) how Peter and Anne Wise reduced their home loan from $140,000 to $95,000 in the first five years and how David and Shirley Battler had only reduced their similar loan to about $128,000 over the same time.

When Peter was aged thirty, the Wises bought their first investment property in his name. Anne planned to leave the full-time workforce to raise their children so it would be easier with the bank and with the tax refunds if Peter owned this property. The details of the purchase and funding of their first investment property were covered in Chapters 17 and 18. David Battler, at the end of this five years, paid out the lease on his van (using borrowed money) and then bought a new car for Shirley (again on a lease for five years).

When Peter will be aged about thirty-seven, they plan to buy their second investment property. This will again be bought in Peter's name as Anne plans to have their first child after this time when she is thirty-three. She will drop back her work to two and a half days a week. Anne's parents say they will help with the baby (and later with their planned second child). By this time, their first investment property is planned to only cost them about $26 a week after tax. By Peter's fortieth birthday, it is projected to cost them only $14 per week. The Battlers will still be paying out their home loan and will have less spending money and no investments by that time.

By Peter's thirty-eighth birthday, they will be able to pay off their non-tax-deductible home loan. David and Shirley Battler will still be paying $1,007 per month after-tax, on their mortgage, for another thirteen years.

During this time, Peter and Anne Wise will actively use their money in their own super fund to earn them 12% compound return after all taxes, accountancy, audit and lodgement fees (as detailed in Chapter 26). David and Shirley Battler will leave their SGC payments in the super funds managed by their respective industries. After all fees and taxes, they will on average earn 7% compound.

HOW TO BUILD RICHES

In the next chapter, you will see how the Wises were able to beat the Battlers' fund manager's returns. You will also see that, over their respective working lives, this will equate to over two million dollars extra super riches (before inflation).

So what will inflation do to this money? If they work for a little over thirty-six years and assume a rate of 4% inflation, inflation will cut the spending power of their Super Riches by four. Remember the Rule of 72 (on page 91): $72 \div 4\% = 18$ years. In the first eighteen years, inflation will rob the spending power by one-half. In the next eighteen years, it again decreases their purchasing power by a further one-half of one-half or, one quarter. Thus, $2 million extra, equates to only about $500,000 in today's dollars ~ an amount that most retirees (or anyone else for that matter) would love to have on their Statement of Assets and Liabilities in today's dollars.

When Peter turns forty-five, the Wises plan to buy their third investment property in both their names. Anne plans to then re-enter the full-time work force when she is aged forty-three. The Battlers will both have to work full time to manage their mortgage payments.

When Anne is forty-five, the Wises plan to buy their fourth and final property in Anne's name only. By contrast, David and Shirley Battler will have only paid out their home loan in this year. David and Shirley may decide to spend their after-tax income on having a good time and living it up, after having spent so much time paying out their home loan. They may continue to spend up big for another five years until David reaches fifty-five. At this time, it is assumed Shirley will decide on her fiftieth birthday that she will quit smoking and get serious about starting to save for their retirement. Anne Wise gave up smoking thirty years earlier (when they went through their 7 step life riches plan).

Over the next ten years, when Peter and David are aged fifty-five to sixty-five, the Battlers will contribute an extra $40,000 per year to their superannuation. Peter and Anne Wise will keep contributing the minimum SGC amount (but their super fund will be worth several million future dollars more than the Battlers).

At age sixty-five, both men plan to retire from work. Interestingly enough, by that time, David and Shirley Battler will have contributed more to super and their mortgage than Peter and Anne Wise paid out after-tax on their home loan and all four of their properties in after-tax dollars! That means, on average, both couples had about the same disposable income and lifestyle throughout their working lives, after allowing for the money that each couple invested, in reducing loans and investing for the future.

HOW CAN YOU GET RICH ON AN AVERAGE SALARY?

So how do their riches compare?

A graph on page 244 shows the difference in the riches of these two couples. The figures used in this graph have been reduced for inflation, to convert this money into its current dollar amounts (assumed inflation at 4%). Many people in the financial community fail to do this when they try to sell you a product but, rather, they will try to impress you with the size of the projected investment value. Probably you will want to calculate how much money you will have in today's purchasing power of goods and services.

The projected comparable values of the Wises' and Battlers' riches (excluding their respective homes) is as follows:

1) At the end of their working lives the Wise family will have assets outside their home of over $4,200,000 (in today's dollars). The Battlers, however, will have less than $650,000.

2) In future dollars the Wises will have over $16.5 million, and the Battlers over $2.5 million before both families pay tax when they cash in their superannuation.

3) An interesting thing may happen about Shirley Battler's fiftieth birthday. **Even though she becomes motivated to start saving her way to retirement, she vows she will never mortgage their family home to provide security to buy any investments.** After all, it will have taken them so long to pay it out she won't let someone else have a mortgage on their home. **This is one decision that will ensure the Battlers' poverty.**

4) Meanwhile the Wise family will still have the same $200,000 line of credit that they took out forty years earlier. The difference is that they will only have a $70,000 mortgage on their home, which has been tax-deductible for the last thirty-five years. In the future, when the Wises have extra money, they will be able to use this money to reduce the loan on their home and pay down this $70,000. There will be no point in them putting it in the bank, getting 3% interest and paying tax on it, if they can save 7.25% on their line of credit! **The Wises never will use their home as security for any of their four investment properties. They will use the increase in value of their first investment property to buy their second investment property and so on.**

HOW TO BUILD RICHES

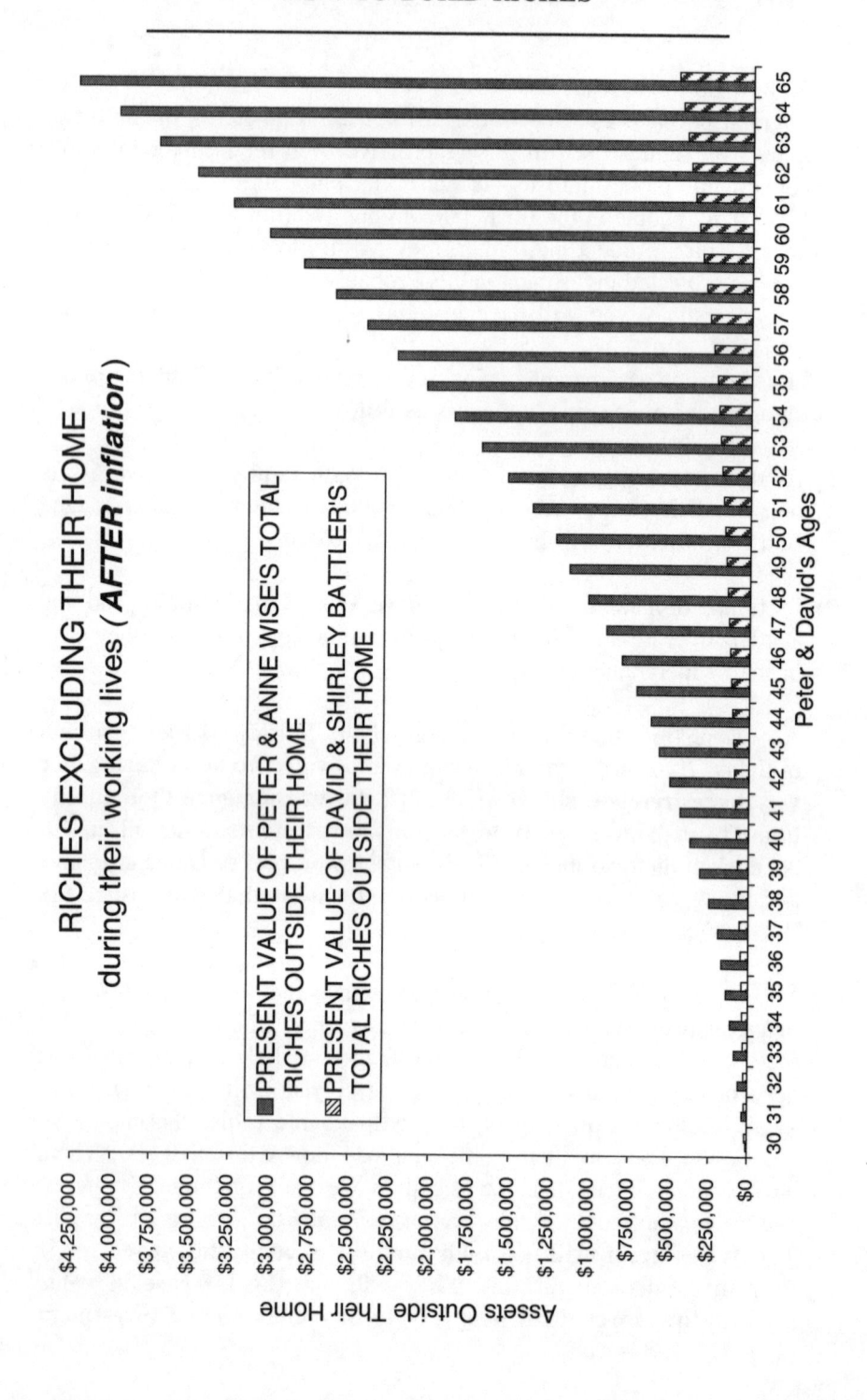

RICHES EXCLUDING THEIR HOME
during their working lives (*AFTER inflation*)

■ PRESENT VALUE OF PETER & ANNE WISE'S TOTAL RICHES OUTSIDE THEIR HOME
▨ PRESENT VALUE OF DAVID & SHIRLEY BATTLER'S TOTAL RICHES OUTSIDE THEIR HOME

Peter & David's Ages

Assets Outside Their Home

5) These two investment properties then provide the security that will allow them to buy their third investment property. These three investment properties provide the security for their fourth property.

How Does Positive Leverage on Real Estate and Shares Compare to a One-off Investment?

Anne Wise has become quite skilled at using her home computer over the years. She projected the capital growth of their four investment properties and compared it with the capital growth they would have received if, instead, they had left their money in the share market, and had not sold or traded any shares.

In her analysis she assumed a constant 8% capital growth rate for both shares and property (as detailed in Chapter 17), until they retire, this being a period of thirty-five years. She assumed that the shares would provide dividends of 4% per annum. The money to buy the shares would be the same $70,000 that they borrowed through their line of credit on Peter's thirtieth birthday (page 174). The cost of this line of credit was predicted to be an average of 7.25% interest per annum. If they bought shares, their dividends would be used to pay for this interest. For the property analysis, she decided to compare what would be the case if they only ever bought one investment property. The cash flow for the first ten years of this property is detailed in Appendix 2. The net rent and tax benefits, from the one property, are projected to be similar to the shares/dividends income. It is assumed that any income from rent or dividends will be retained by the Wises, and not re-invested once the cash-flow became positive.

The graph on the following page demonstrates the difference in capital growth of this single investment of $70,000, in property, or shares. It is not reduced for inflation, but Anne and Peter Wise were still happy with understanding how these two investment choices compare.

It is projected that, at their retirement, the Wises will have a little under $965,000 in shares or a little more than $3,400,000 in real estate equity. It was this analysis, more than any other, that convinced Anne that real estate investment was her preferred alternative to shares investment, while they were working so that they could easily use the positive leverage benefits that real estate affords. The figures of how to calculate this comparison exactly are reasonably detailed. They are covered in the *Building Riches* tapes. Anne decided to take it one stage further, to convince herself.

HOW TO BUILD RICHES

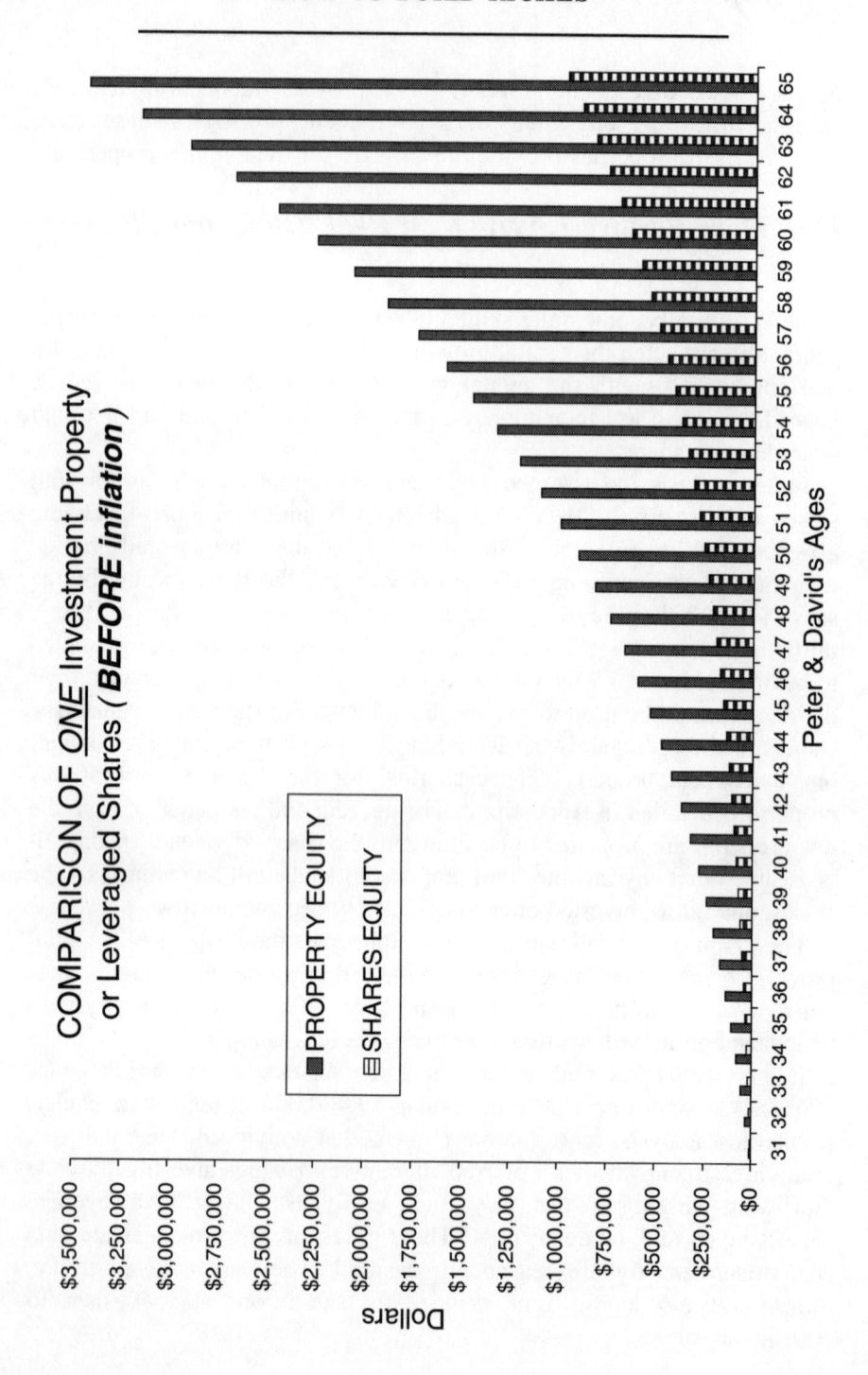

COMPARISON OF <u>ONE</u> Investment Property or Leveraged Shares (***BEFORE** inflation*)

■ PROPERTY EQUITY
▤ SHARES EQUITY

Peter & David's Ages

How Does an Ongoing Real Estate and Shares Analysis Compare when Using Positive Leverage?

Anne Wise learned about margin loans and borrowing to buy shares. She was concerned about the volatility of shares and the fact that margin loans were very risky unless the borrowing levels were acceptable. She thought the maximum margin loan that she would ever consider entering into would be 50% of the value of the shares bought. Even then, she thought she would want to become an expert shares investor before she could consider on-going borrowings against her share portfolio. She was concerned about the risk of a major share crash (which happens every ten years or less) wiping out her share portfolio and leaving her with a loan to repay. Chapter 13 details the effect of margin calls.

Anne made her calculations, based on a 50% margin loan *Strategy*, for the thirty-five year period. As there were many numbers involved in doing such a thorough analysis, of comparing shares and property, she decided to put her analysis in the form of a graph, which is detailed on the next page. The results of her findings are summarised on the following two pages.

What is most important is that you make an accurate comparison of what investments **you** prefer, <u>before</u> you invest. You can learn through books and audio tapes from various people including us how to do this for yourself before you take *Action*.

The Wise family's choice of investment *Strategy* was to invest in the four investment properties detailed above. All of these investment property loans were secured against the investment properties alone. The only loan on the Wise family's home was the original $70,000 loan used to assist the purchase of either their first investment property or their share portfolio.

Anne decided that this analysis would be the *Strategy* upon which she and Peter would make their future investments. She wanted to reduce their investment equity for inflation, because she wanted to know what the real purchasing power of their future riches would be in 1999 dollars (when she did her analysis). The graph on the next page is reduced for inflation so that the equity riches they generated are in today's dollars.

At the end of their working lives, it is projected that the Wises' total net equity from investing in properties will be over $12,000,000 in future spending power, (that is, before inflation), whereas the total net projected equity if they had invested in shares would be less than $4,000,000 (that

HOW TO BUILD RICHES

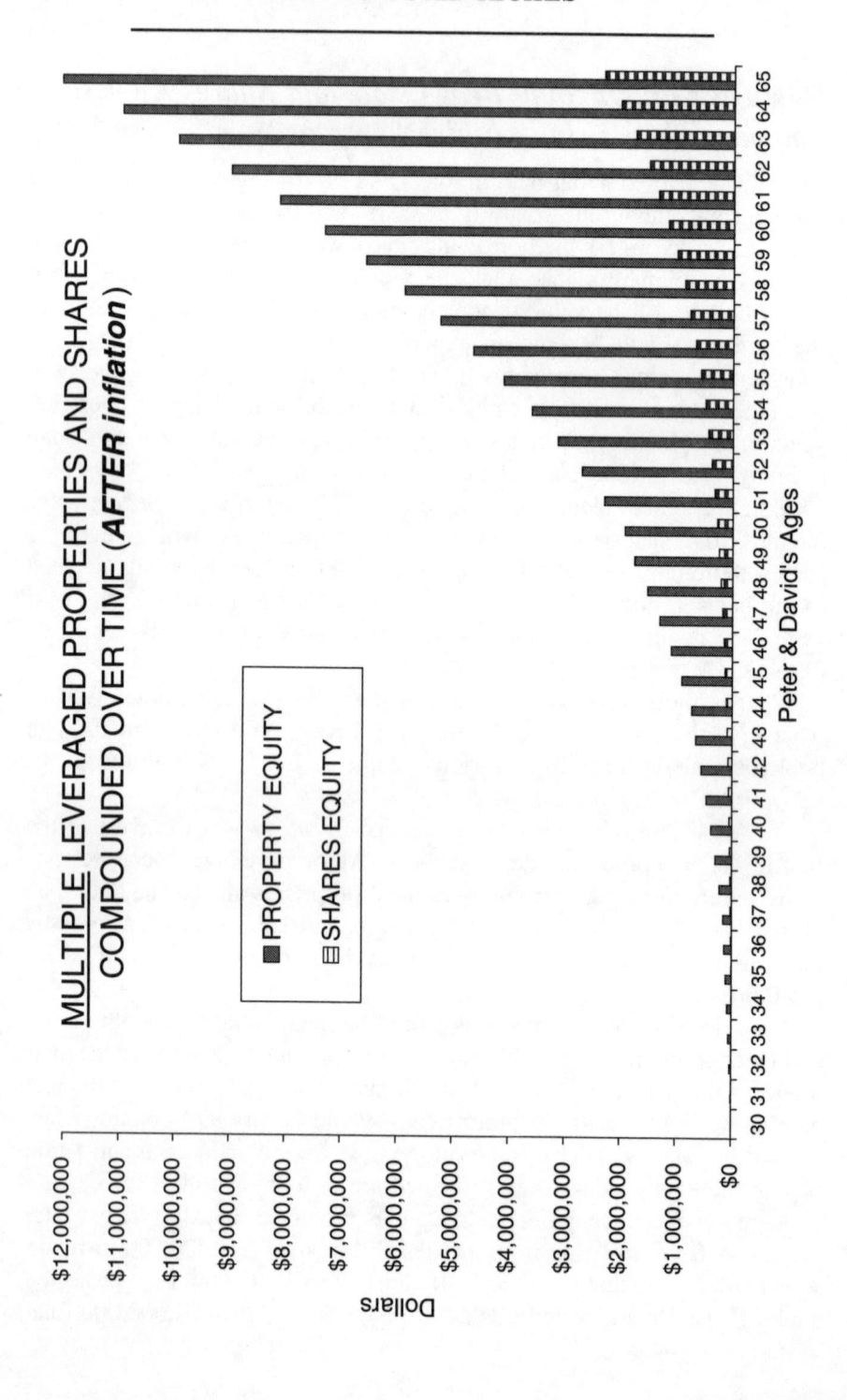

MULTIPLE LEVERAGED PROPERTIES AND SHARES COMPOUNDED OVER TIME (*AFTER inflation*)

- ■ PROPERTY EQUITY
- ▤ SHARES EQUITY

Peter & David's Ages

Dollars

HOW CAN YOU GET RICH ON AN AVERAGE SALARY?

is, before inflation). They considered a *Strategy* of borrowing to purchase shares to be far riskier than borrowing to purchase property. The Wises confirmed that investment real estate was to be their preferred investment area.

If you invest $70,000 of your equity in the same way as the Wises did, then you will receive $12 million after repaying your $70,000 equity contribution. Your compound growth return will be over 15% per annum. There are very few, if any, managed funds that have ever been able to consistently return almost twice the growth of shares or properties, over several decades, after their management fees.

The other investment area that the Wises and the Battlers had easily available to them during their working lives was that of superannuation. This is where the Wise family decided to make their share investments.

It is now time to see how to make your super investments return more by learning ...

Chapter 26

HOW CAN YOU MAKE MORE MONEY USING SUPERANNUATION FUND MANAGERS?

> *'Riches amassed in haste will diminish, but those collected by little and little will multiply.'*
> ~ **Johann Wolfgang von Goethe.**

Fund managers can make you richer. All working Australians have money put into superannuation funds (as detailed on page 52). If you are not yet confident enough to trust yourself to make more money than fund managers, then **how do you get richer by using fund managers?**

From mid 2000 (and earlier if you have a co-operative employer) you can choose where your SGC payments are made. You can also have your new fund manager (if you decide to change) help you 'roll' your existing super into your new fund. This is an easy process, but it takes a few weeks. Before you choose a new fund manager, you want to carefully identify what they will charge you for their services, what flexibility they offer you, and how good they are at managing other people's money.

How Much Will It Cost to Have a Manager Do the Work?

Let us get clearer on how these fees are charged.

How Do Entry and Exit Fees Work?

Usually fund managers will charge either a hefty **entry fee** or a hefty **exit fee** (or both). If you are charged an entry fee, it means the fund manager generally takes between 4% and 6% of your hard earned money before they do anything for you. Most or all of this money is paid to your financial adviser. If you ask them to disclose what they are being paid, they have to do so by law.

If you are investing for a period in excess of five years, this may well be acceptable to you. You can always *ASK* for a fee reduction.

Most fund managers will not charge entry fees if they charge exit fees. Read the fine print and don't choose a fund that hits you for fees both ways. An exit fee is a fee that fund managers charge you against the value of your investment, when you take the money out of their institution. There are certain reputable fund managers who will charge less, or even no exit fees, if your funds are invested with them for a certain period of time (usually a minimum of three years).

Once your super balance increases to a sizeable amount (usually over $50,000), there are wholesale fund managers who charge much lower fees for larger amounts invested. You can also negotiate with your financial planner to charge a lower fee for example, 1% or 2% commission instead of a fee of 5% or so, if you *ASK* for the discount.

At the present time there is intense competition between fund managers to attract a bigger piece of the superannuation market (which is projected to increase by over $600 billion dollars in the next ten years). If you move your super at the right time, you may be able to minimise these fees!

What Are Administration, Asset Management and Trustee Fees?

The major ongoing fee charged by fund managers is generally called an **administration** or **asset management fee**. It is charged as a percentage of the whole fund (which includes your money). The amount of this fee is usually about 1.5% of the fund value, but can range from 0.5% to 1.75%.

If your fund manager is going to perform well, then it is perfectly normal that they receive a fee for supplying all of the expertise to make you richer. The problem I find with these fees, is that they will always charge you the same fee, say 1.5%, even in years when they may lose

HOW CAN YOU MAKE MORE MONEY USING SUPERANNUATION FUND MANAGERS?

20% of the value of your super! This loss situation usually occurs when the fund manager, in certain types of funds, is forced (by the fund type) to keep 75%, or more, of assets in a falling investment type in that year i.e. shares. Understanding the Economic Cycle (chapter 9) you will over time know when to move your money out of shares. Fund managers cannot do this. You can by moving your funds to another type of fund (as discussed later in this chapter).

Trustee fees are charged by an independent trustee who scrutinises the performance of the fund manager. It can be gratis if the trustee and fund manager are part of the same company. It is usually closer to 0.5% per year. If you do have an independent trustee, it can sometimes give you more peace of mind. If the worst happens and the fund manager fraudulently loses the fund's money then, if you are lucky, the trustee or their insurance may make good some of the losses. Be patient, the courts take years! By the time the lawyers and receiver managers have charged their huge fees, you may only get some of the money back. It is highly unlikely but this sometimes occurs (for example Estate Mortgage, Baring Brothers, Sumitomo Life). It has happened to several people that I now advise. Forewarned is forearmed. Choose wisely before you invest.

What Are the Smaller Hidden Fees?

Other fees, such as Investment Fees, can apply. It helps to read the fine print to see if you pay anything to the fund manager whenever they invest. The amount of such Member Fees generally average about $50 per year. When your super funds grow, these fees lose some relevance if your fund manager performs well.

If you only have a small amount in super now, you may want to shop around. Some of the banks have low fee super schemes that may stop your profits from being totally eaten up by fees.

How Much Is It Going to Cost You to Get Super Rich by Choosing Where to Put Your Investments?

A critical feature in choosing a fund manager is to find out how much and how frequently you can change your investment categories. This is called switching your money. You want the ability to be able to switch your money from shares, to cash, to property (or a combination of them), at least once a year.

HOW TO BUILD RICHES

From earlier chapters you know that the economic cycle moves in a predictable pattern. If you look for indicators in the media, you can easily determine whether the market for a particular investment class is overly optimistic and/or over-priced. There is not available space to go through all of these specifics here. This area is covered, however, in detail in our audio tapes and there are plenty of other books and experts who can assist you to learn how to follow the economic cycle. Now that you have the *Knowledge* that it exists, and knowing that moving your super can make you up to seven or eight times as much money (as detailed in the Chapter 27), you will probably take a greater interest in it. As your interest and *Strategies* grow, all you need to do is take considered *Action* and you will learn quickly.

Super funds are generally set up with what is called a **master fund**, in which your super fund buys units. Under this master fund are individual funds like equity and cash funds (that you read about in Chapter 20). As you prudently switch your money between these various funds, you are still holding units in the overall master fund. This is important, as it means that you are not going to incur any CGT on the ownership of your managed units until you transfer them to another master fund. Even though super riches only incur a low 15% tax, you don't want to have to pay it until you take the money out. You may decide to stay with one fund manager in one master trust for over twenty years and move your money to a different type of fund once every year. You do not want to pay any CGT until you take your money out at the end of the twenty years. Each time you switch funds you may incur a **switching fee**.

Many master funds will allow you to switch your money between funds once a year at no fee. Any additional switches in a given year may incur a fee which generally is up to 0.5% of the fund value. These master funds are well worth investing in if you want to move your money to get rich. Shares are volatile. Share funds (or Equity funds) make up the major part of most fund manager's fund types. When share markets crash, it is often a good time to start buying more shares or moving super money into an Equity fund. You may then leave this money in the Share fund for a few years and move it into a Cash fund when the share market gets too hot again. Switching back and forth every few years can dramatically increase your super riches.

HOW CAN YOU MAKE MORE MONEY USING SUPERANNUATION FUND MANAGERS?

How Do You Choose a Fund Manager?

This is a tricky exercise. There are many excellent Australian fund managers and institutions. As the people in these companies can transfer or retire, it is impossible to recommend one company or another. Do your research and gain *Knowledge*. Compile your own *Strategy* based on available *Knowledge* of their fees and flexibility before you take *Action*.

Beware of the trap that many investors fall into. Past performance alone, of a fund manager, does not guarantee future success. Comparing one fund manager with others in the same market, over as long a period as possible, will give you a better basis of comparison. In isolation, it is easy for one fund manager to earn a 20% return for two years especially if the share market itself has increased at 20% for the last two years. If the share market is due to crash, you want to see which fund manager actually predicted and performed well in the last share crash. There are magazines like 'Personal Investment' and 'Shares' that compare different funds' performance. Ask them questions about their predictions and procedures before you consider changing.

Sometimes leaving your super money with your existing fund manager can be the best idea if your money begins to work hard with them.

Over your working life, how will moving money between various funds effect your super riches? Let's see how this effected the Wise's and the Battler's. Peter and Anne Wise decided to run their own super fund and were going to invest in shares and bank deposits directly. Meanwhile, David and Shirley Battler put their super into the same funds that most of their work colleagues did, i.e. two industry superannuation funds. The gross return on these two funds averaged 11% per annum before fees and taxes (this is similar to the average return of many other funds over an extended period of time). This return looks good at first, but the effective return to the Battlers however, is much less. An analysis of the typical costs and net returns that the Battlers received from their fund is detailed on the next page.

When the Battlers saw their super fund's return advertised at 11% they thought it was a good return. They thought no more about it though and just looked at the annual super statements when they came in the mail. As they were contributing each year, the balance went up almost every year (excluding the occasional year when the fund manager's fees exceeded the profit made. Remember, these fees are still charged in years when a loss is made). Over their working lives, their net after-tax return was only 7% after fees and taxes.

HOW TO BUILD RICHES

After 1 July 2000 the tax rate on transactions held for over twelve months will drop to ten percent for both the Wise's and Battler's fund managers (as detailed in chapter 25).

Battler's Superannuation Funds

Entry Fee		5.0%
(When every contribution is made)		
Gross Return of fund (as advertised)		11.0%
Less: Ongoing Fees and Charges		
Asset Management	(1.75%)	
(or Administration Fee)		
Trustee Fees	(0.5%)	
Investment Fees	(0.2%)	
Expenses	(0.3%)	(2.75%)
Profit Before-Tax		8.25%
Less: Superannuation Tax (15% of Profit)		(1.25%)
After-tax Net Profit of Fund		7.0%

Member Fees of $50 per annum for David and Shirley Battler are not included.

The Wises on the other hand found a low-fee fund manager and a master fund that charged lower fees, and also allowed them to switch between Cash and Equity funds once a year, without fees. Also this fund did not charge entry or exit fees. Peter and Anne Wise both put their SGC contributions into the same low-fee super fund and they both occasionally switched between cash and equity funds. They decided to switch funds no more than once a year (unless a share crash occurred and they could switch into an Equity Fund when share prices were much lower. In this case a 0.5% fee applied, which would be offset by extra profits when share prices came back). By switching funds most years, Peter and Anne Wise earned a much higher return (as shown in Chapter 25) and avoided switching fees. Peter and Anne Wise also occasionally took some of their money our of both cash and equity trusts and bought Property Trust units that were listed on the Stock Exchange. Their costs and net returns are detailed on the next page.

HOW CAN YOU MAKE MORE MONEY USING SUPERANNUATION FUND MANAGERS?

Wises' Superannuation Funds

No Entry Fee (Exit Fee is nil) Dealing Cost on Entry & Exit		0.4%
Gross Return (as a result of switching to best funds)		15.0%
Less: Ongoing Fees and Charges		
Asset Management (or Administration Fee)	(0.5%)	
Trustee Fee	(0.2%)	
Investment Fees	(0.1%)	
Expenses	(0.1%)	(0.9%)
Profit Before-Tax		14.1%
Less: Superannuation Tax (15% of Profit)		(2.1%)
After-tax Net Profit (Average of Wises' Chosen Funds)		12.0%

Peter Wise only contributed his SGC payments to his super fund. His SGC payments were made on his full-time salary from age twenty-five to sixty-five. Anne Wise worked full-time until age thirty-two (the same year they paid out their non-deducible line of credit home loan). She then had the first of two children and chose to work part-time for ten years. She then re-entered the full-time workforce at age forty-three. Anne's SGC payments were contributed for all of her working years at the minimum amount. The Wises' combined total SGC contributions during their working lives were just over $502,000.

David Battler and Peter Wise made the same SGC contributions, from age twenty-five to sixty-five. Shirley Battler at age thirty-two had the first of her two children. Shirley kept working full-time (with her parents looking after her children) as their home mortgage was not paid out until she was aged forty-five. As mentioned in Chapter 25, Shirley Battler got serious about their retirement on her fiftieth birthday. She and David did not use positive leverage and did not invest in their education. They made $40,000 of extra superannuation payments every year for the last ten years of their working lives. The Battler's total SGC contributions over their working lives were just over $920,000. On the following page is a graph comparing the superannuation balances of the Wises and the Battlers over their working lives.

HOW TO BUILD RICHES

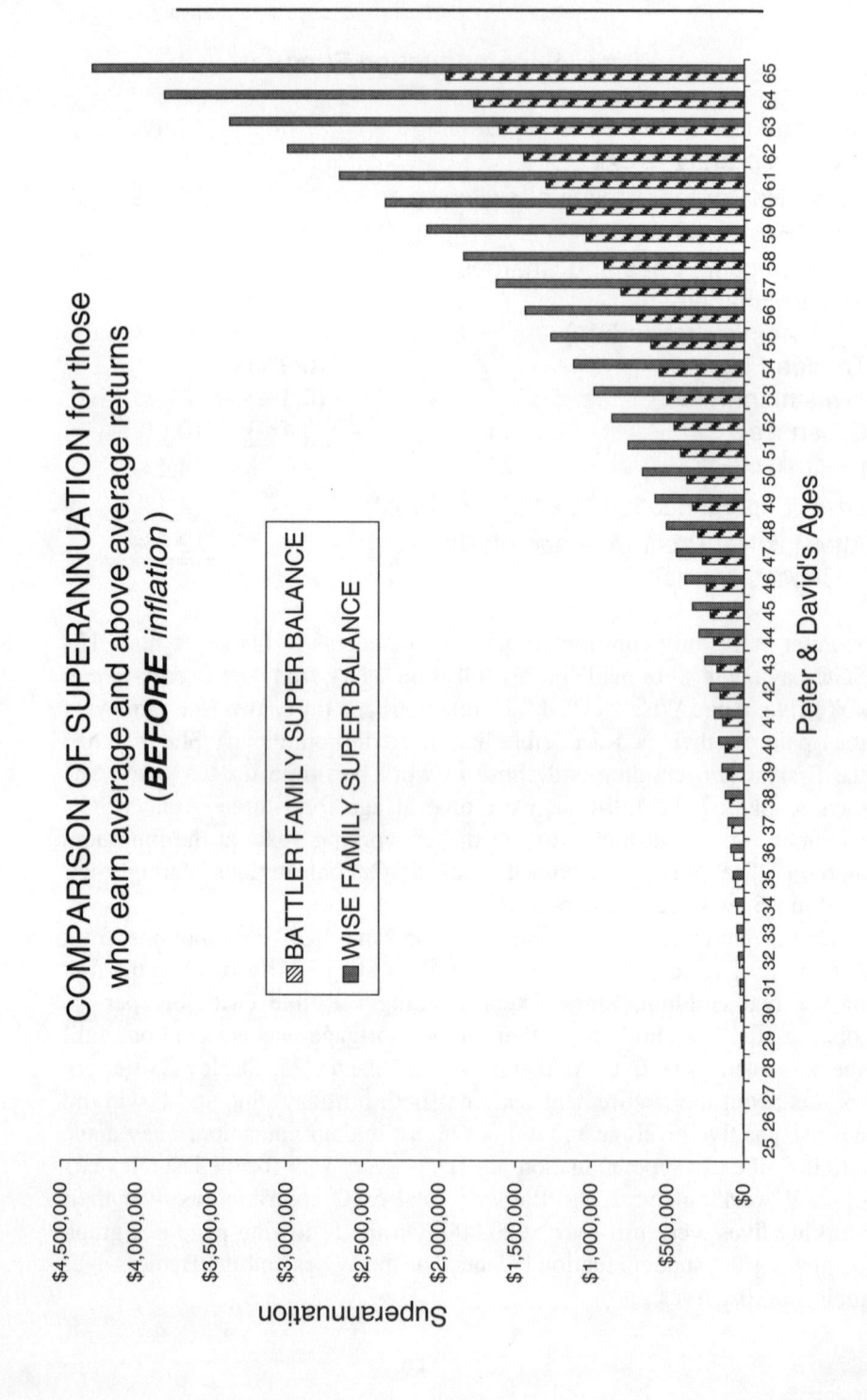

COMPARISON OF SUPERANNUATION for those who earn average and above average returns (***BEFORE*** *inflation*)

Legend:
- BATTLER FAMILY SUPER BALANCE
- WISE FAMILY SUPER BALANCE

X-axis: Peter & David's Ages (25–65)
Y-axis: Superannuation ($0 – $4,500,000)

HOW CAN YOU MAKE MORE MONEY USING SUPERANNUATION FUND MANAGERS?

The Wises made their money work smarter (and harder) than the Battlers, by switching to better performing funds during the course of their working lives and although they contributed only $502,000 (over $400,000 less than the Battlers did), they accumulated a total of over $4,280,000 in super at retirement.

The Battlers contributed over $920,000 but left their super in two average funds and accumulated a total of just over $1,840,000 at retirement.

These figures however are not reduced for inflation. On page 242, using the Rule of 72, I demonstrated that the after-inflation value at their retirement will be only one-quarter of what it is today. Therefore the present value of the Wises' super would be a bit over $1 million and the Battlers would have about $460,000 in today's dollars (including their extra contributions).

Once again, the awesome power of compound interest combined with *Knowledge*, *Strategies* and *Action* produces riches.

The next chapter will detail what the future holds for the Wise and Battler families in financial terms.

What If Your Situation is Different?

What if you are not as young as these couples? What if you want to accumulate more money? What if you have more assets or less assets to start with?

Everyone is unique. If your situation or goals are different from anyone else's that is understandable. The principles to *ASK* your way to riches, however, are the same. You can apply them no matter where your starting and finishing places are. Even though I have made, and continue to make, millions of dollars of profit a year, I am still applying and using the very same principles I share with you in this book. You can *ASK* your way to riches.

In order to achieve your goals, you may require additional *Strategies* or more refinement on your existing *Strategy*. This will become easier with the more *Knowledge* you accumulate and the more *Action* you take. Life is a journey. Always be learning and growing.

Had this book included all of the things I want to share with you, it would have been thousands of pages long and too much for most people to comfortably carry, let alone read! The first step to building your riches is having relevant, useable *Knowledge*. This has been the aim of this book and this aim continues through to the final chapter. There are many authors and thousands of books published every year that can help you get rich. The best consultants will probably charge you in excess of $300 per hour for advice. If you need advice at the time, this too may be a good investment. Even though I have over twenty years experience I frequently use specialists to assist me to keep pace with ever changing legislation. The benefits far outweigh the costs. Learn as you go and eventually you will become your own expert.

As well as books and consultants there are also audio tapes and seminars. Over the years I have invested over $200,000 in audio tapes and seminars that other people have produced. Much of this has been from American speakers and has little relevance and application in Australia, though there are small snippets here and there that have made my investment in them worthwhile. The best investment you can make is in Australian books and tapes by people who practice what they preach. Keep developing your *Strategies*. The chances are good that we may meet. It will be fabulous to hear about your successes and learning experiences. Keep learning more and you will keep earning more. Please write to me and let me hear about your successes.

Some of you may have the desire to control your own super fund and to make more money than the money managers. How can you maximise your superannuation riches (super riches), to make more money than the professionals? This is the subject of the next chapter which is ...

Chapter 27

HOW CAN YOU GET SUPER RICH?

'The man who succeeds in life above his fellows is the one who, early in his life clearly discerns his object, and towards that object habitually directs his powers.'
~ **Edward G. Bulwer-Lytton.**

A couple on an average salary can become multi-millionaires during their working lives (as detailed in the last chapter). They can achieve this by allowing their home equity to acquire assets that compound at a faster rate than inflation does. This was a practical example of the demonstration of the Rule of 72 and the awesome power of compound interest that was discussed in Chapter 7.

How can you harness this awesome power of compound interest in your investments, to make more money for yourself than professional money managers can? In order to see how you can do this it is important to have an understanding of how different investments perform in different years (of the economic cycle).

How Much Richer Can You Get When You Make Your Money Work Harder?

On page 226 you saw the comparison of actual returns from money left to compound in real estate, shares or interest from 1976 until 1989. You saw from the example that real estate performed best over the whole period. It is relevant however, to look at which investments performed best in each of the twelve month periods, ending in June, over that twenty-three year period.

If we look at the percentage change from one year to the next, and compare each of the three investment classes with the year before, a fascinating chart emerges. This chart allows us to easily see the changing nature of each of these three investment areas. A graph of this trend is shown on the next page.

A few trends which are easy to spot emerge from the graph, these being:

1) Real estate performed best over this whole period. There were five years, out of twenty-two, where it approached or exceeded 20% return in one year;

2) Shares had seven years when their return approached or exceeded a 20% return in one year;

3) Property had a negative return for two years, whereas shares had a negative return for six years out of these twenty-two;

4) Shares, generally speaking, went through a rapid growth just before real estate prices increased at their fastest rate. Then share prices fell at a rapid rate;

5) After the real estate prices grew at high rates and then corrected, fixed interest offered the best returns for a couple of years, and then, property prices stagnated. At these times, having your money in cash would have been a smart investment decision. A wise person would not have done this for the long-term. But, in these years, the main aim is to preserve your cash. This is all consistent with the economic cycle theory covered in Chapter 9;

6) There were nine years, of the twenty-two years diagrammed, when growth in value of shares or property exceeded 20%.

An analysis of this graph produces a fascinating trend that has the potential to make you rich, if you use it. To get rich much faster, your aim is to have your money working, earning you the highest rates possible every year. If you do this, your riches grow much faster. The table below demonstrates the highest performing asset class in each of these twenty-two years.

HOW CAN YOU GET SUPER RICH?

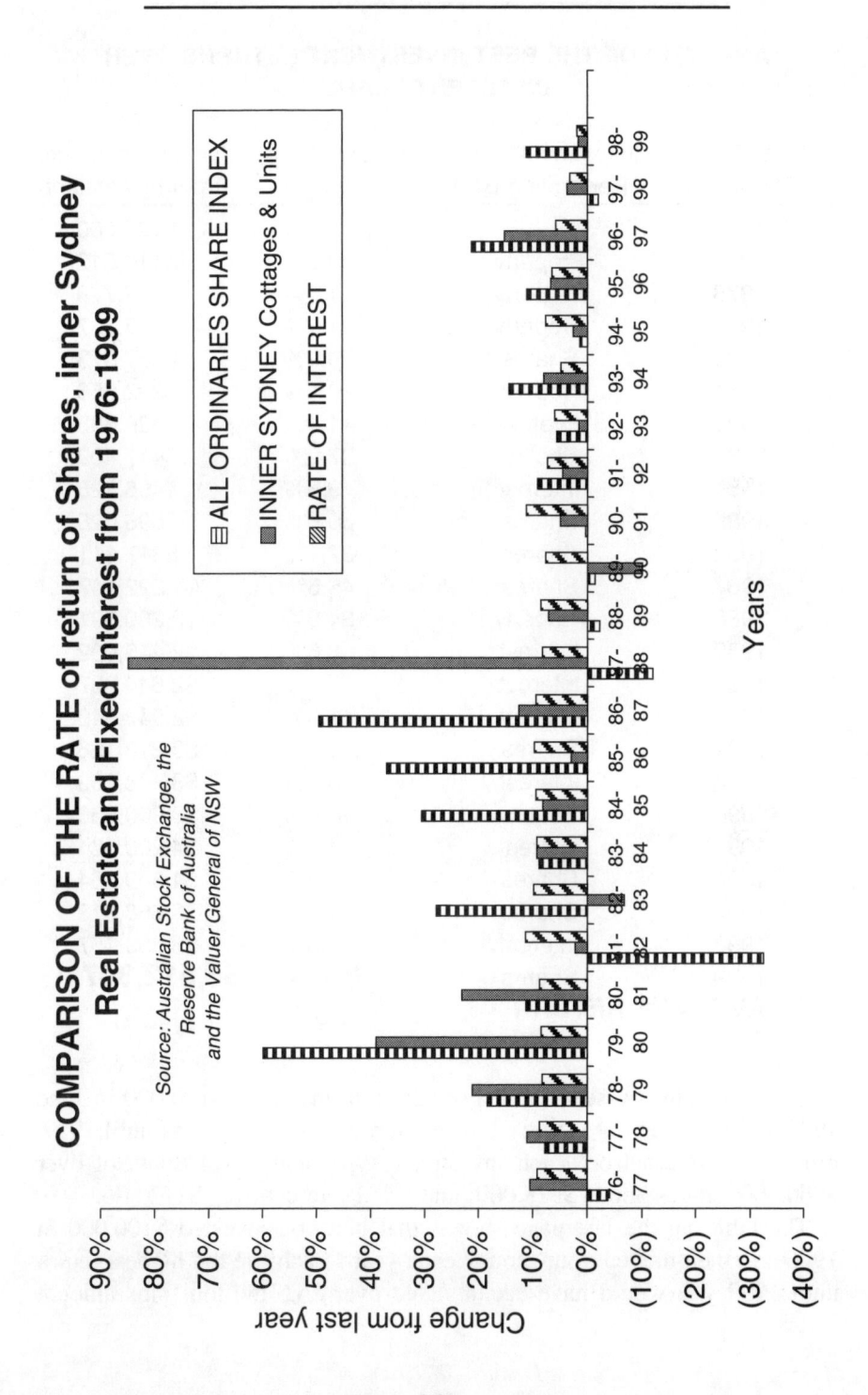

COMPARISON OF THE RATE of return of Shares, inner Sydney Real Estate and Fixed Interest from 1976-1999

Source: Australian Stock Exchange, the Reserve Bank of Australia and the Valuer General of NSW

- ALL ORDINARIES SHARE INDEX
- INNER SYDNEY Cottages & Units
- RATE OF INTEREST

263

ANALYSIS OF THE BEST INVESTMENT RETURNS OVER DIFFERENT YEARS

Year Ended 30th June	Investment Performing Best	Annual return %	Cumulative Return From Investment
1976			$100,000
1977	Property	10.5%	$110,512
1978	Property	11.1%	$122,778
1979	Property	21.2%	$148,767
1980	Shares	59.9%	$237,913
1981	Property	23.1%	$292,956
1982	Interest	11.4%	$326,353
1983	Shares	27.9%	$417,409
1984	Interest	9.3%	$456,228
1985	Shares	30.6%	$596,025
1986	Shares	37.1%	$817,111
1987	Shares	49.6%	$1,222,447
1988	Property	84.9%	$2,260,591
1989	Interest	8.6%	$2,445,002
1990	Interest	7.7%	$2,644,037
1991	Interest	11.3%	$2,942,549
1992	Shares	9.2%	$3,213,126
1993	Interest	6.1%	$3,408,163
1994	Shares	14.4%	$3,900,338
1995	Interest	7.7%	$4,200,664
1996	Shares	11.2%	$4,669,464
1997	Shares	21.4%	$5,668,918
1998	Interest	3.3%	$5,853,157
1999	Shares	11.3%	**$6,512,307**
AVERAGE RETURN		**21.3%**	

You have already seen in Chapter 23, that investing $100,000 in June 1976 and then leaving it in each of the three investment areas until 1999, produced a return from each investment type being: real estate of over $960,000; shares about $928,000; and fixed interest over $272,000.

The table on the last page shows, that had you invested $100,000 in 1976 and then moved your money each year to achieve the highest return until 1999 you would have accumulated over $6.5 million. This amount excludes CGT which, as discussed in Chapter 24 will be reduced from 1 October 2000. If you had made your money work harder, by choosing the best performing asset class in each year, how would your profit compare (with a passive Strategy of leaving it in one asset category)?

1) You would have earned just under seven times the return from just leaving your money in real estate (with no positive leverage);
2) Over seven times the return from just shares;
3) About twenty-four times the return from just fixed interest.

Who retained the extra profit exceeding $5,500,000? You did, if you understood the economic cycle, and moved your money on less than an annual basis, for maximum return.

How Do Professional Fund Managers Compare?

In Chapter 20 you started to learn about managed funds. You learned that different types of managed funds have to leave differing amounts of their invested capital in only one of the three investment areas. Income Trusts, retain over 75% of funds, to be only invested in fixed interest type investments. Equity trusts require the fund manager to maintain over 75% of the fund's assets in shares and likewise, Property Trusts require that the majority of funds be held in property.

It is easy to see that if a fund manager had to have over 75% of invested money in one investment type, then as the prices of this investment went down, so too would the value of the fund.

On average, good fund managers consistently return a capital growth on invested funds, in excess of the average growth of the investment in which they put their money, before they charge their Management Fees. Once you take off the total cost of all fees and charges incurred when you invest your money with a professional fund manager, you get a different picture.

Fund managers represent large financial institutions. Their capacity to charge a variety of fees is almost as clever as that of the banks to find fees! Both institutions earn hundreds of millions of dollars from fees every year.

The types of fees you are charged when you invest in a managed fund include:

Types of Fees	Amount of Fee
1) Contribution Fees	0–6%
2) Exit Fees	0–6%
3) Administration Fees (also called Asset Management Fees)	0.5–1.75% p.a.
4) Trustee Fees	0–0.5% p.a.
5) Switching Fees	0–0.5% (after 1 p.a.)
6) Investment Fees	0.2–1.4% p.a.
7) Member Fees	$30 to $70 p.a.
8) Other Fees	0–0.5% p.a.

When you add these fees up, they can be substantial. Generally you will pay about 4% to 5% when you enter or leave a fund (if you do so less frequently than three yearly). Ongoing fees are likely to be between 2% and 3% per annum.

The published returns on most managed funds are generally published before all of the fees mentioned above are charged. A published return of 12.5% (before fees) may only provide an effective return, in your favour, of 9.75% (after all of the trustee's fees, fund manager's fees and other fees are deducted, which can easily total 2.75% p.a.). Be careful to adjust any published figures and to reduce them for such fees. Do your own calculations. These fees are discussed in more detail in the next chapter.

Fund managers also have limits placed on them as to the amount of borrowed funds that they can use. All income funds and most equity funds will not use any positive leverage. Property Trusts will offer the maximum amounts of leverage that they can employ i.e. 45%.

Why Is a Diversified Portfolio So Popular?

Academics and many market commentators talk about having a **balanced portfolio**. By this they mean having some of your money in shares, some in property and some in fixed interest. They say, that if you do this, then you decrease your risk. Your risk does decrease because when one of your areas of investment is losing money (or growing very slowly) another type of investment will make you money.

There is an opportunity cost in this portfolio approach. The cost is that you are not getting as rich as you can. Instead of having some money in an investment area that is performing well and other money in an area which is performing poorly, what if you moved all of your money to one particular well-performing investment? If that investment type, e.g. shares, performs well in that year, you make more money than you would have if you had a balanced portfolio. Next year you might move your money to property, which historically goes up after shares (as you saw in the economic cycle) and the next year you might put your money in fixed interest, if shares and property are too hot or bullish.

Earlier in this chapter you also learned that, had you been able to choose the best performing investment category, and put all of your money in that investment, you would have earned over an additional five million dollars from 1976 to 1999. A diversified portfolio might be less risky, but, I would rather have the five million as assets in my name and experience a few risks. We are all different in this area of risk tolerance and you have to determine if you would rather get rich more slowly, and with less risk by having a diversified portfolio.

How Can You Make Even More Money by Managing Your Own Funds?

Throughout this book you have accumulated a lot of *Knowledge* and *Strategies* to help you get rich faster. Using a combination of all of these skills will allow you to build riches faster than professional money managers could build your riches. One of the key reasons why you can do this is that you are not limited by the restrictions that are imposed upon money managers.

Restrictions are imposed on the money managers in order to protect smaller investors. As you become more knowledgeable, you can accept greater risks and as a direct consequence, make greater returns.

You can make more money than professional money managers for the following reasons:

1) You can invest in residential real estate.

As you have seen in various graphs in this book, well positioned residential real estate has performed better than shares and fixed interest over time. Most fund and money managers are not permitted to invest in residential real estate under their fund guidelines;

2) *Your portfolio investment choices are not limited.*

Where a fund or money manager may be forced to retain 75% of its assets in shares by the fund guidelines, an intelligent investor like yourself is not limited by such restrictions. If you know shares are too hot, then you can sell all of your shares and put your money somewhere safer.

Being able to put 100% of your money in one investment allows you to take full advantage of the profits from this area. Once you are practised at moving your money it will become easy;

3) *You Can Use Positive Leverage To Get Richer*

By now, you know (from the earlier chapters on real estate and shares) that careful use of positive leverage allows savers' money to help you, the investor, get rich. Careful use of share margin loans will rapidly accelerate your wealth (if you pick the times and shares and if you buy and sell carefully). This opportunity is currently only available until 2001 as discussed later in this chapter.

Using leverage to buy residential real estate, rapidly accelerates your riches. As you follow the principles previously detailed on buying the right property at the right time, you will get better at maximising your future riches. I have made many millions of dollars in net profit for my investors and myself in less that ten years. It works.

Most professional money managers are prevented from borrowing. This alone gives you an advantage over them. You can make your invested money work much harder than money put in a managed fund. Your use of positive leverage not only increases your riches, but allows you to become more confident and able to do more, as a direct result of your successes. The better you become the easier it is for you to win again;

4) *You can use your money in a way that helps you in other areas.*

If your money is under your control, then every time you sell shares, or property, or units in a trust, you can put the money anywhere you like. If you have a mortgage on your home, you can deposit this money against your mortgage (like you saw the Wise family do to pay out their home loan in half the time of the Battlers). If you have children or relatives, you can deposit money with them.

When my parents divorced, my mother had a mortgage on her new home. It worried her tremendously. By depositing some of my profits

HOW CAN YOU GET SUPER RICH?

into a bank account that reduced her mortgage (an offset account) and also paying money into her mortgage, I was able to help her to pay out her mortgage, years sooner. It is difficult to put a monetary value on certain joys that riches can provide. Had I had my money tied up in a managed fund, I would not have had the ability to help my mother as I did. Is there someone you want to help financially?

Using all of these benefits, and others you have learned from this book, you can make more money than the professionals (who are limited by the restrictions they operate under). As time passes and you learn to develop greater skills and more confidence in yourself, you can and will become richer.

How Can You Make More Money than the Superannuation Fund Managers?

In Chapter 21 you learned that you can set up your own super fund. If you control your own super riches, you can choose to invest in a way that indirectly uses positive leverage. This is done by having your own personal super fund (which can also include your spouse or partner and up to a total of five people) own a unit trust that you control. It is diagrammed below.

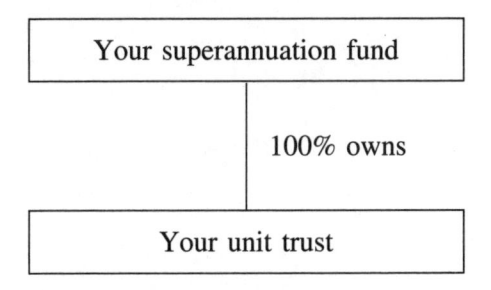

```
┌─────────────────────────────┐
│  Your superannuation fund   │
└──────────────┬──────────────┘
               │
           100% owns
               │
┌──────────────┴──────────────┐
│       Your unit trust       │
└─────────────────────────────┘
```

You can use positive leverage in your unit trust to own real estate and shares. You can literally make many hundreds of thousands (or millions) of dollars more in superannuation, by taking it out of the hands of the fund managers, and applying the principles discussed in this book so far. The example of the Wise family's investments in real estate can also be used by you in your own super fund.

There are other great advantages I could demonstrate for this structure but tragically, the government is changing the super laws from May 2001 to prevent us from building riches to fund our retirement. Please write a letter to:

'The Assistant Treasurer, Parliament House, Canberra ACT 2600'
and demand that our super funds regain the right to invest in any unit trusts that allow Australians to build riches. Once our legal rights are secured, I will demonstrate examples of building riches using this method, in a later book. Be careful. Don't rush out and set up this structure. Wait until the government in power undertakes not to take away our legal rights. To preserve our legal ability to arrange our affairs, in a way that allows us to support ourselves in retirement, I urge you to take fifteen minutes and write a letter to your local Senator and the Assistant Treasurer.

There is a window of investment opportunity until May 2001 to use this structure. Only if you had it already set up before November 1999. Ask your accountant if you had such a structure set up before 2000. It is time to explore the way you can become even richer after you stop working. Your aim should be to have your money working for you, many years after you stop working for it. You can learn this skill once you know . . .

Chapter 28

HOW CAN YOU KEEP GETTING RICHER AFTER YOU STOP WORKING?

'Compound interest is the eighth wonder of the world.'
~ **John Pierpont Morgan.**

Less than 6% of Australians who reach sixty-five, retire and earn over $330 per week after tax. For most of them, their money runs out before they do. If you look after your health, you can aim to have a fulfilling rewarding life into your eighties and even nineties. This means twenty or thirty years of retirement or more.

How Rich Are Your Elderly Relatives?

When I started this book, my father's parents were in their nineties and my mother's parents were in their eighties. Tragically, my father and his father and mother both died in the last two years. The others are alive and well, but their money ran out before they did. They are reliant upon the government for a pension to survive.

My paternal grandparents retired with the savings from their working lives. As I mentioned before, my paternal grandfather worked for the same company for fifty-six years (from age fourteen to seventy) and worked his way up from office boy to general manager. At seventy, the company wanted him to stay on, but he decided to retire. He and his wife lived well but their money gradually ran out. My paternal grandmother developed a debilitating case of arthritis and over the years had both

HOW TO BUILD RICHES

ankles, both knees and both hips replaced. These operations, combined with a case of shingles on her face and eyes, nursing care, plus trips to Queensland (where it was warmer in winter) ate up their life's savings. Their house overlooked a popular beach and is surrounded by million dollar homes. Their home was falling apart now from lack of maintenance. My grandparents were too proud to accept financial assistance from their family, and did not want to move because of the memories of over sixty five years of living and raising their family in that home. This is often the case with many older people. In his last two years, my paternal grandfather lived in a nursing home. He died before his ninety-seventh birthday. They were a loving couple.

Government rules encourage people to dissipate or hoard their assets. If older people earn extra income in retirement (above a minimal amount), they become heavily taxed. Other rules also force the elderly not to sell their homes or personal assets as the receipt of this money will effect not only their pension, but also their entitlement for other government services, like health care assistance. The desire to leave an inheritance to their family, combined with ever decreasing payments to the elderly from the government, are eroding the quality of life of our elderly. With an ageing population and the Baby Boomer Crisis looming, it has to get worse.

My maternal grandmother lives in a suburban home alone and has survived on a war-widow's pension after the death of her second husband. She is a remarkable lady and lives a very frugal lifestyle so that she can give presents and assistance to her many grandchildren and great-grandchildren. My maternal grandfather lives in a nursing home and struggles to budget on the pension. he still offers generous gifts to myself and his other grandchildren and great-grandchildren although with only $5 a week left after all of his expenses, it doesn't go as far as he would like.

I love my grandparents dearly. It would be wonderful if I could go back in time and teach them the *Knowledge* that I am sharing with you in this book, when they were young enough to apply it. A couple of years ago I spoke with my paternal grandmother and video-taped our conversation so I can share it with my great-grandchildren and future generations. As I mentioned previously, she told me she wished she could have had her time over again, as she would have loved to pluck up the courage to buy some investment properties. When they bought their family home in 1933, it cost them $700 (£350). Today, if it was renovated and

HOW CAN YOU KEEP GETTING RICHER AFTER YOU STOP WORKING?

added to, like both neighbouring properties, it would be worth over $1 million. If only they had bought another property or two using positive leverage! They would have enjoyed the last few decades of their lives with more freedom and security. It may be too late for them, but we can do something about our futures.

How Do You Make Your Retirement Income Grow?

The first step is to get rich now. Don't put off getting rich until later. *Action* overcomes many problems with our initial starting places and personal challenges. Use what you have now and accumulate as many riches as you can, ethically and wisely, before you retire.

Upon preparing for retirement, it is worthwhile doing some planning. You will need to generate *Knowledge* of the retirement system, *Strategies* to work within it and take *Action* to arrange your affairs to work within the retirement regulations. Far too many Australians choose to earn less, or give away assets, so they can qualify for a pension or the health card. This is an example of aiming low and achieving their goal. I have met financial planners who show their clients (who are millionaires) how they can still get a full pension! This is aiming high and conning the government and hard-working tax-paying Australians. There is a better way.

My personal aim is to continue to compound my riches so I will not need any financial assistance in the form of a pension, health card or anything else. Even more, I want to be able to leave my family millions of dollars in tax-effective assets, as well as donate millions of dollars to charity so that I can help under-privileged Australians well after I am no longer living. If you set your goals high, you too can *ASK* your way to riches.

What does retirement hold in store for the Wise and Battler families? The Battlers have not set any financial goals and believe that their superannuation will look after them. The Wises set and achieved their goals. The Wises plan to enjoy their retired lives in style and also to allow their riches and income to grow in real terms (that is after inflation). They want to have more money when they need it most because in retirement they have more time and possibly more need of health professionals. Peter and Anne Wise also want their riches to increase so they can leave assets to their families and help their grandchildren and great-grandchildren advance their education or in buying their first home and/or investment property. What is one scenario for these couples?

Firstly, the Battlers decide to take all of their superannuation as a lump-sum on retirement. They will pay tax, each at 16.5% (being 15% tax, plus 1.5% Medicare allowance) on any lump-sum over $90,000 (in 1999 dollars). The figures have been kept at today's rates. On their approximately $1.84 million lump-sum, they will pay tax of about $200,000 leaving them $1.64m. It is assumed that the Battlers do not spend this money on having a good time or give it away to qualify for the aged pension (which many people do). The Battlers also have paid out their home mortgage and it is assumed that they have no other loans or debts to repay.

The Battlers decide to take their money and live on their interest and bank deposit. Shirley and David Battler decide to spend just over $30,000 between them a year in today's dollars ($125,000 in retirement dollars). That means, an after-tax income of less than $300 per week. They intend to increase what they take each year for inflation and still live as long as they can on this reasonable lifestyle.

Anne and Peter Wise have a lot more choices as a result of their investments during their working lives. At the same time that David and Shirley Battler retire, Anne and Peter Wise have almost $4.8m in superannuation as well as four investment properties in which they own a net equity of over $12 million (before selling any of these properties) and they have extra cash in their bank. The day after they retire, the Wises sell one of their investment properties. When the property is sold, they pay out all of the of the loans on their remaining investment properties, pay their reduced CGT and pay themselves an income of over $1,000 a week after-tax (in 1999 dollars). The Wises CGT was calculated in Chapter 24 (and Appendix 5). During their first year in retirement the Wises leave their superannuation working for them and do not cash in any of their super.

In the Wises' second year of retirement, they decide to take as a lump-sum, just under $3 million, (less tax of about $390,000) giving them an after-tax amount of over $2.6 million. The Wises take this money and some of their extra cash (including the extra proceeds from the property sale) and cautiously invest in $2.8 million worth of shares at the next downturn in the sharemarket. These shares will go up in value over time, while providing them with an annual dividend income (that goes up as their shares increase in value), and taxation benefits from the dividend imputation on these shares (as detailed in Chapter 10). This provides one income stream for the Wises which will start with an initial income of $112,000 per annum (assuming a 4% dividend).

HOW CAN YOU KEEP GETTING RICHER AFTER YOU STOP WORKING?

Peter and Anne Wise still have another $1.8 million left in their super fund. They do not take this money out as a lump-sum as it is above their lump-sum limit (and they would have to pay tax at the top marginal rate otherwise). The Wises set up their own superannuation annuity with this money. An annuity is a private pension that allows them to receive an annual distribution (within certain maximum and minimum limits). The good news for the Wises is that the income produced in the annuity (which is assumed at 10% per annum because they know how to make this money work for them), is tax-free. The annual distribution they choose to receive has a 15% discount (a rebate) off their marginal tax rates. This second income stream will start at $180,000 a year (before-tax). If they leave their $1.8m annuity and live off the annual distribution of $180,000 then this $1.8m will be able to be left as an asset for their children, or cashed in if the need arises. Most annuities bought from life insurance companies have no value on death. The Wises set up their own annuity. Their kids benefit.

The Wises' third income stream, which continues from the date they retired, is the rental income on the three investment properties that they own without any borrowings against them. This rental income starts at over $140,000 a year and increases each year with inflation.

In comparing the after-tax retirement income of the Wises (who invested) and the Battlers (who did not), I have adjusted the future incomes to relate to the current values (as at 1998). Their after-tax incomes in graphic form is detailed on the next page.

The Wises' income jumps from $1,000 a week after-tax to $1,500 a week in their second year of retirement. Each year thereafter it goes up as their rents and dividends increase (due to the underlying value of the shares and property increasing). The Wises can pay themselves more in their first year (or any other year of retirement from their annuity). The graph is shown in the ages of Anne and Shirley as, statistically they are more likely to live longer than their husbands. It's about time more men started taking better care of themselves so they can enjoy a full and rewarding life and aim for the big one hundred (years of age)!

Meanwhile the Battlers live modestly off their savings and interest at a bit under $600 a week after tax. At this rate, their life's savings run out when Shirley Battler is aged seventy-three. However, she may have up to twenty years or more of life left (and hopefully her husband will too). If they are anything like my grandparents, then they will require substantial money for medical and other needs.

HOW TO BUILD RICHES

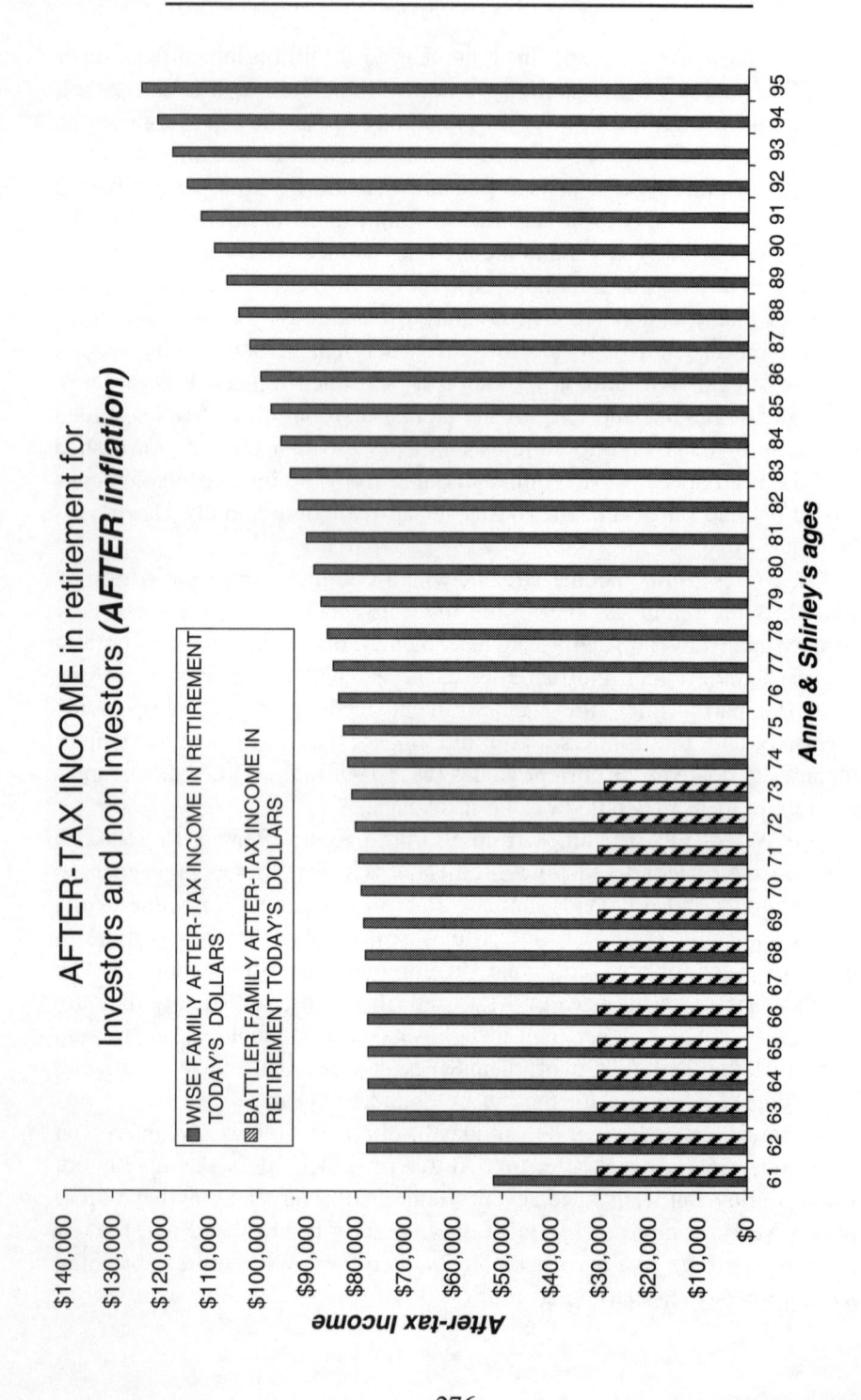

AFTER-TAX INCOME in retirement for Investors and non Investors (AFTER inflation)

■ WISE FAMILY AFTER-TAX INCOME IN RETIREMENT TODAY'S DOLLARS
▨ BATTLER FAMILY AFTER-TAX INCOME IN RETIREMENT TODAY'S DOLLARS

Anne & Shirley's ages

After-tax Income

HOW CAN YOU KEEP GETTING RICHER AFTER YOU STOP WORKING?

If the government cannot afford to pay the pension or their medical expenses, things will look grim for the Battlers. Their quality of life is a lot tougher as a result of not having enough security to support themselves, let alone giving them the freedom to travel, have professional care and enjoy all of the riches our beautiful country has to offer.

How Do You Make Your Retirement Assets Grow?

Again, the secret is to generate as large an asset base as you can while you are working. There are many ways of investing your riches in a more conservative, tax-effective way, once you have accumulated them.

Peter and Anne Wise chose to invest in shares, their own super annuity and kept three of their investment properties. There are all manner of managed funds, superannuation alternatives and financial products available. The Wises' *Strategy* was to allow their assets to grow over time, as a hedge against inflation. By doing this, their assets grew by more than inflation and this increased their riches in today's dollars. If they ever need any extra money they simply sell some shares, a property or pay a bigger annuity payment to themselves.

The Battlers, by playing it safe and leaving their money in the bank, faced the ravages of both taxes and inflation (as detailed in Chapter 8). Their capital was eroded simply to maintain a reasonable lifestyle and it finally ran out.

A graph showing the retirement riches of the Wise and Battler families outside their homes follows on the next page.

The Wises' riches increase from over $4 million in today's dollars to over $8 million when Anne reaches eighty and Peter eighty-five. They have set goals of living healthy lives in their nineties with the support of health professionals. The way they have arranged their affairs means they can live on a higher after-tax income in retirement than they had when they were working. Not only that, but their assets increase in value at the same time. They can either sell their assets and live in luxury, or assist their family or community with their riches.

Tragically, the Battlers' money in the bank is only a fraction of the value of the Wises' riches. It runs out gradually, assuming there are no emergencies. The Battlers (whose savings disappeared within 13 years) are unable to provide financial assistance to their family or community and have to hope and pray that the government can continue to pay the pension (which provides only a survival existence as shown on page 33).

HOW TO BUILD RICHES

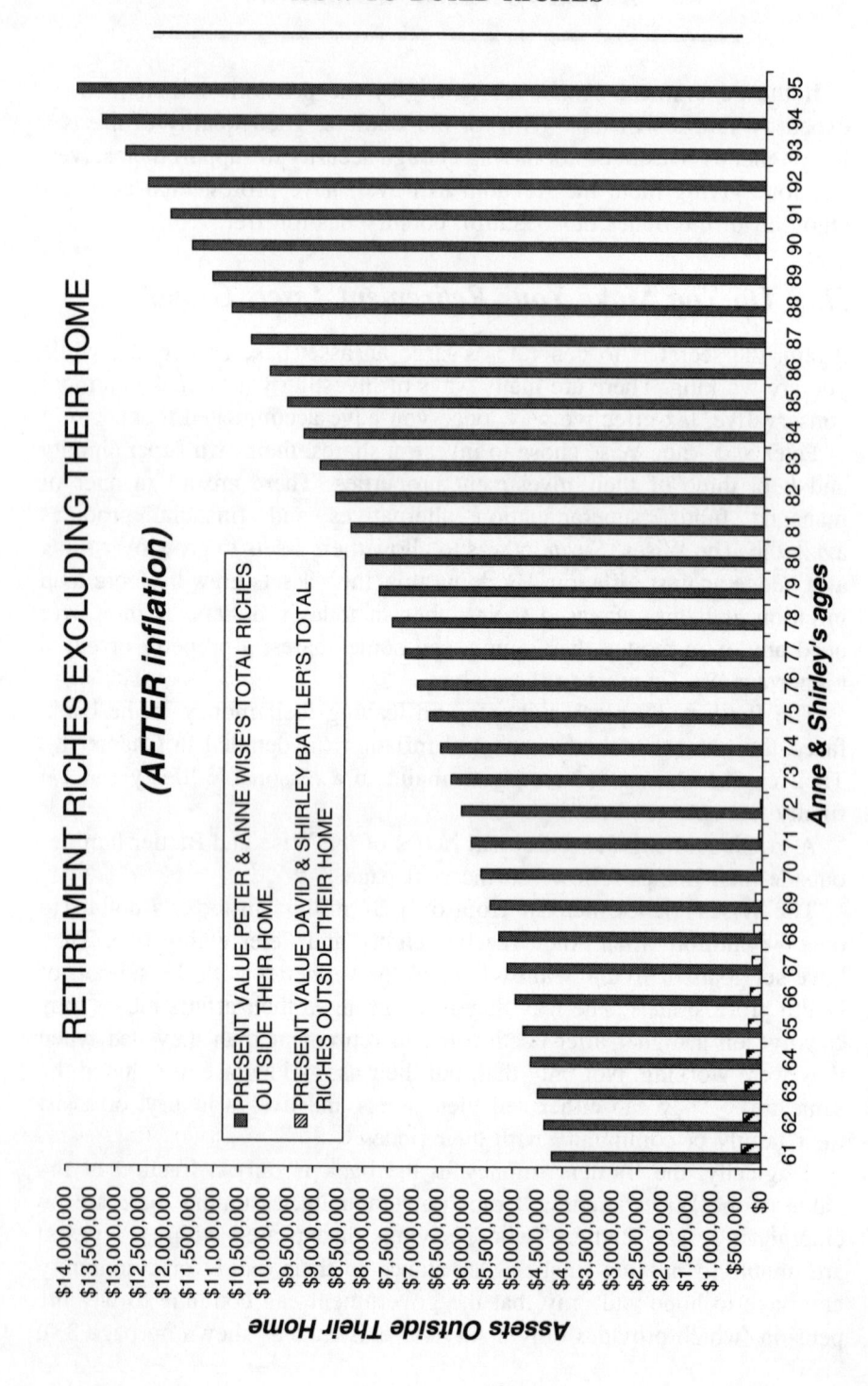

RETIREMENT RICHES EXCLUDING THEIR HOME
(AFTER inflation)

■ PRESENT VALUE PETER & ANNE WISE'S TOTAL RICHES OUTSIDE THEIR HOME

▨ PRESENT VALUE DAVID & SHIRLEY BATTLER'S TOTAL RICHES OUTSIDE THEIR HOME

Assets Outside Their Home

Anne & Shirley's ages

HOW CAN YOU KEEP GETTING RICHER AFTER YOU STOP WORKING?

They are lucky to live in a fabulous country like Australia where our taxes support a basic standard of living for all Australians. Hopefully our children, the children of the baby boomers, won't mind paying enormous amounts of tax to support twice as many retirees, when everyone born before 1963 retires.

How Do You Continue to Create Wealth After Your Death?

The Battler's can leave their family home to the children to sell. Ideally, it will pay off their mortgages and provide additional equity for their children to invest and build wealth.

The Wises chose to organise their assets to assist their children and grandchildren while they are alive. While living, we can set up our financial affairs to provide for the most tax-effective transfer of our riches to the next generation. Without planning, too much may go to the government in the form of taxes. There are various ways you can achieve this objective. Your accountant or a specialist retirement planning professional can assist you in this planning.

The Wises can set up their affairs in a number of different ways to assist their family's riches. These include:

1) Will a Family (Discretionary) Trust Outlive You?

Discretionary trusts (often called 'family trusts') have a life of eighty years. They continue after the death of the people who set them up. The Wise family could have bought (or transferred) some of their assets into a family trust. The primary use of family trusts is to protect the assets in the trust, while giving the trustees (person or entity that controls the trust) freedom to distribute income or capital to any beneficiaries. If you work in a litigation environment, i.e. accountants, lawyers, etc., this may suit you.

If the Wises used such trusts, they could simply pass on the powers of trusteeship to a family member in their wills. These trusts give substantial powers to a person called an Appointor. The Appointor can replace the trustee of the trust (this new person actually controls the assets of the trust, and can appoint a trustee who is able to run the trust as the Appointor wants). The Wise's will also be able to pass on the powers of the Appointor in their wills.

Unit Trusts operate in a similar manner but with less flexibility. From 1 July 2001 trusts will be less appealing as they will get taxed at the same rate as companies. Companies offer another means of asset ownership. Companies continue to exist indefinitely.

2) Will a Company suit you better?

After the change in CGT laws from 22 September 1999 there will be no more indexing of assets for inflation after 30 September 1999. This will have the overall effect of making companies better than trusts for the great majority of people.

Under the new CGT laws it will be better for most people to hold their assets in their own names and not trusts or companies. Top CGT rates for individuals will be 24.75% which is less than company and trust tax rates (both at 30%) with possible extra tax when funds are eventually paid to you as shareholder.

3) What is a Testamentary Trust?

You have probably heard the term 'last will and testament'. A **Testamentary Trust** is a legal arrangement, whereby a person's assets can be used in accordance with a will, for the benefit of the people referred to in the will.

There are tremendous benefits from having your will prepared by a solicitor or other professional. The Wises can will their properties, shares and annuity to their family directly. When the assets are resold, CGT will be incurred from the date of original purchase by Peter and Anne Wise. This tax is not imposed until the assets are actually onsold. If they are not sold, they can be used as security for borrowing against, to make their family members rich.

The Wises' family home would probably be best sold as it will have no tax paid on it. If it is capable of becoming a development site, the Wises' children could sell it to a property developer for more money than they might achieve to another home owner, and pay no tax on the extra proceeds if contracts are exchanged within two years of their parents death. It is something that should be started as soon as the funeral is over. I have organised and negotiated to buy properties this way myself and have been able to pass on great benefits to the families of the deceased who would have wanted their family members to benefit from their life's hard work.

Peter and Anne's investment properties could perhaps be used as an

HOW CAN YOU KEEP GETTING RICHER AFTER YOU STOP WORKING?

alternative family home for their children or grandchildren.

A fabulous benefit of Testamentary Trust is that the income given to minors (people aged under eighteen) is taxed at marginal rates. Usually minors are taxed at the top rate of tax 48.5%. This tax saving and income can be used to provide a private school education, or other benefits, to the Wises' grandchildren or great-grandchildren. The alternatives are tremendous. Arrange your affairs well while you are here! Get busy and start building your riches now, but take the time to do your estate planning while you are still able to.

It is time to move on to the third critical element of our *ASK* formula, that is *Action*. You can have the most *Knowledge* and the best *Strategy* but they are useless unless you take *Action*. It is time to learn ...

4

How can You Best Take ACTION to Build Riches and Retain Them?

Chapter 29

WHAT ATTENTION AND INTENTION WILL MAKE YOU RICH?

'Success is when preparation meets opportunity.'
~ **Napoleon Bonaparte.**

Napoleon Bonaparte is widely acclaimed as being the greatest military strategist who has walked the planet. He is also remembered as a legend in his capacity to take *Action*. He was successful in realms far beyond the military. He established a legal system in France which still exists today. He established universities and educational institutions and was the initiator of Egyptology (which led to the deciphering of the writings of the ancient Egyptians). It was said of Napoleon that he: '*won his battles in his tent*'. Napoleon thought through, in advance, the consequences of any possibility, in any battle in which he was going to be engaged, and consequently was able to respond faster than any of his opponents when inevitable disasters struck. This ability is what you are already aware of and we are calling your *Strategy*. Another statement about Napoleon was *for Napoleon, to think was to act'*. Having thought through his battles in his tent he was able to be decisive and quick in his ability to follow through with *Action*.

Some people, regrettably, treat business and the making of money as if it were a battle, where there is a winner and a loser. I have already mentioned the need to avoid doing business with sharks. As long as people play this WIN/LOSE game, there is a need for caution in all your business dealings. There are people you will encounter in your life who will rob you of your money and your dreams, if you let them. When you are about to take *Action* on a major investment (particularly a long-term investment like property) it is time for caution. Retain your ambition and dreams, but temper your *Actions* with prudence to protect your riches. There are also many wise caring advisors. **Knowledge protects you from the few scoundrels, as well as from risk and fear, by giving you an objective ability to design your** *Strategies* **to protect your riches**.

Let me show you ways to understand how to best take considered *Action* on your path to building riches. Only a minority of people have clear, definite, written goals and reasons for building riches. Your reasons for building riches are your **intentions**. Your goals direct where your **attention** is focussed, when you come to invest. It is time to learn how to use your intention and attention on the journey toward your riches.

Using the Wise family as an example, when they bought their investment property, they wanted to pay particular attention to buying well.

How can You BAT Your Way to Riches?

A simple model that I use when I buy real estate is to use what I call my **BAT** formula. This stands for:

B uy Low
A dd Value
T iming or Tax Effectiveness

Buying Low:

One way to **buy low** priced investment real estate is to take the time to put in as many low offers as possible on properties that fit your investment parameters. Your aim is to buy a quality asset at less than market value. It is possible if you take the right *Action*. The Wises did this when they bought their investment properties.

The aim with any investment is obviously to buy low and sell high. Many of the mega rich buy low and never sell. John Paul Getty became one of the world's richest men. In his book *How To Be Rich* he advocated buying low and selling high and, if possible, never selling at all. The Wises did this with three of their four investment properties. The one property that they did sell was sold in a tax-effective way.

WHAT ATTENTION AND INTENTION WILL MAKE YOU RICH?

In the *Knowledge* section you learned that the best type of residential real estate is property that is in strong demand.

My companies look at over one hundred properties, on average, for every property that I actually buy. Nowadays, the properties that I buy are frequently worth several millions of dollars each. However, the principle is still the same and I still purchase properties that I can add massive value to, in order to make a greater return on my investment. I used the same principle when I began my first property investments in Perth. Time and effort were spent on viewing available properties and a thorough analysis of the market was undertaken, before the purchase of a property was made. The choice of Cottesloe with its proximity to the beach and city coupled with its aforementioned research provided a return significantly greater than average. People frequently tell me how lucky I am with the investments that I make. I don't bother to tell such people that the good fortune and riches that I build is a direct consequence of the work that I do before I make any decision.

Adding Value

You can **add value** in several ways. You may have experience at making cost effective repairs. Another way is to find a long-term tenant for a property that is not rented when you buy it. Or you may finance the property in a tax-effective manner. If you claim the full range of tax deductions on the property, then your after-tax cost may be very low (as was the case with the Wise family in Chapter 18). Doing all of these things substantially increases your expected profit from these properties (or shares).

Timing or Tax Effectiveness

Using **timing** to buy well can be done in several ways. In Chapters 9 and 27, you learned that if you buy real estate (or shares) at the right time in the economic cycle, the chances of your investment going up in value dramatically increase. This is one of the concepts I spend more time on in our *Building Riches* tapes. You can also have professional advisers (who ideally have their own similar investments) assist you by providing advice in this area.

How can You Get Richer by Paying Better Attention?

How can you train yourself to pay better attention when transacting business with many people? Some points I recommend you consider in relation to investing include:

1) Is there a hidden agenda?

Have you ever received junk mail promoting a 'get rich quick' scheme? Or have you seen advertisements that promise you an easy way to get rich? Often, behind this facade is a polished, hidden agenda. The classic one is to come along to an information evening and find that the promoters are really selling you a product. Frequently, it is an over-priced, or poorly performing, investment property.

It is fine to attend such evenings, but don't be persuaded into buying from them until you have learned whether or not it will fit into *your* investment *Strategy*. If you do not pay attention, then a $20 evening might result in you being sold a property that is $20,000 over-priced. Even worse, if you are not careful, you might buy an investment that will not perform as well as another property. Some of the biggest rogues I have met in recent years, run seminars on 'how to get rich' and, behind the seminars are some second-rate properties for sale. A handful of professional people also run such seminars. When you have the *Knowledge* and *Strategy*, you can make a more informed decision. Be careful, is my advice.

The reason I take such great exception to these people is that they are basically risking the security of hard-working Australian families. I mentioned it earlier, but it deserves repeating, a leading psychologist told me that financial pressures lead to more family breakdowns (and hence heartache for their children) than does all of the alcohol abuse and physical abuse, in marriages, combined. Many people get talked into buying properties that will not perform anywhere near the promises. If economic times change, which they always do, then some of these people, who bought at the wrong time, may be forced to have to sell, not only their investment property but, also, their home, which could destroy their marriage. Protect the security of your family by *ASK*ing your way to riches.

There are highly reputable Australian-based experts on financial matters, who do not have a hidden agenda for selling you a particular product. Take the time to research any promoted investment independently. Don't be pushed into buying any investment in one day. If they come on with the oldest trick in the book of saying 'if you don't buy now you will miss out', be careful. There will always be another investment away from these high pressured salesmen. Forewarned is forearmed. If you use caution, you will greatly minimise the likelihood of people taking advantage of you in the future;

2) *How do You Find a Good Salesperson?*

Doing business with salespeople is an essential ingredient in building riches. Although I have mentioned different aspects of dealing with salespeople, they warrant mention again. Some salespeople will be amongst the most professional people you will ever meet in your life, particularly the ones who have remained in their industry for at least ten years. There is likely to be a real estate boom and crash about every ten years. The share market crashes (and corrects) more frequently. People who have been in the industry for a significant period of time will understand that markets move in cycles. They will also, ideally, be wise enough to realise when the market is overheated and likely to crash. Professional salespeople will advise their clients accordingly, because they wish to stay in the industry in the long-term. This builds tremendous loyalty with their clients. It also gives them enormous repeat business. These are the type of salespeople with whom you should associate.

Dealing with any salesperson raises the same issues. Is the person building a career or just pushing to get this one sales commission? Having sold real estate, shares and financial planning, I have had over twenty years experience dealing with salespeople. Not all salespeople are created equally. Some will say or do anything to get you to say: '*yes*', so they get their commission. Take the time to find out if they have told you the truth. You may deal with them (because they have a product you want to buy) but you will be well advised to be much more cautious if they do not tell you the truth. If you have *Knowledge* and a *Strategy*, you will protect yourself;

3) *How do You Find a Good Accountant?*

Most accountants are highly reputable. Accountants are widely regarded as one of, if not, *the* most highly ethical and professional group of people in the country. There are very few accountants who take secret commissions (kickbacks from slick promoters of anything from tax-driven investments through to investment properties). Today, being a specialist accountant has never been tougher.

The amount of legislation that our governments produce in this country is ridiculous. It has been said that, since 1980, the superannuation legislation, alone, in this country, has changed, on average, every six weeks. This is why there are so few experts in the superannuation field. There are many accountants who say that they can assist you to run your own super fund, and who really believe that they are accurate in their assertions. A little bit of information can be a dangerous thing, and sometimes it is better to have a specialist accountant handling a critical area like your superannuation. You may even have another accountant who handles just your taxation returns and advice. And you may have a third specialist accountant who advises you on *Strategies* to build wealth. Even though I have been a qualified accountant for over eighteen years, I still use several accountants myself in different capacities. They have proven to be most worthy of the fees I pay them each year. Several of them have become close friends and I respect their opinions, including Simon Whitfield, of Young Barnsdall and Co. in Sydney, who wrote one of the testimonials you read on the cover of this book.

It is my experience that people who practice what they preach are the best people to work with. For example, if you want to find someone to assist you in looking after your own self-managed super fund, then consider using an accountant who has his/her own self-managed super fund. Every time there is a change in the legislation, because it is relevant to their fund, they will research it. Someone who dabbles in superannuation will never be able to give you the best advice as quickly and at the right price.

If you wish to develop a portfolio of investment properties or shares, I suggest that you use an accountant who also has a portfolio of investment properties of shares. Many times I see accountants and lawyers investing in very wise real estate investments, such as real estate close to the city, with good views and great long-term potential. However their clients invest in brick veneer properties on the outskirts of town, with little prospect for solid long-term growth. You can benefit from your accountant's experience. I consider it your right to *ASK* your accountant: *'Do you invest in shares or property?'* Although they probably will not give you the specifics of their personal affairs, it is relevant that you *ASK* this question and benefit from their leaning

WHAT ATTENTION AND INTENTION WILL MAKE YOU RICH?

and experience. It is worth shopping around and getting the right professionals who have similar interests to your own;

4) *How do You Find a Good Lawyer?*

If you have the need to use a lawyer, get one who returns your phone calls. If a lawyer won't return your calls within a reasonable period of time, the chances are that when you really need him, he won't be available. Lawyers, like accountants can be the most professional people you will meet. When you use a lawyer, make sure you find one who is prepared to explain exactly what is happening in the legal affairs of your investments (at your cost). This way, you learn much more quickly.

My experience with lawyers, like accountants, is to use the ones who invest in the area that I am investing in. I have used dozens of lawyers over the last twenty years and have sometimes found the occasional hypocrite, who has had no personal investments and yet has chosen to give me advice on structuring my transactions. I have replaced such accountants or lawyers as soon as possible. The ones I choose to work with are the ones who practice what they preach;

5) *How do You Find a Good Managing Agent?*

Property managing agents are members of real estate firms who look after the management of your property. Look for experienced ones. You should get a managing agent who is pro-active and who will keep you informed of exactly what is going on. A good managing agent can save you an enormous amount of heartache and money later on. You need a property manager who gets incoming tenants to complete thorough reference tests. Otherwise, you could have tenants occupying your properties who are practised rent evaders who know how to use the legal system to get away with not paying you rent for extended periods of time. A good managing agent doesn't allow this to happen. They are definitely worth a fair rate of commission. In NSW, for example, traditionally, real estate agents will do a full service (which includes collecting rents, paying bills, finding and replacing tenants, etc.) for anywhere between 4% and 7.5% of the rental income. You can get a very good real estate managing agent to do a full service for between 5% and 6% of the rent on an individual property. If you have two or three properties, you may ask for a discount. Choose an experienced managing agent as it will save you a lot of money in the long-run;

HOW TO BUILD RICHES

6) *Should You Put All of Your Contracts in Writing?*

It is said in the legal profession that: '*a verbal contract isn't worth the paper it is written on*'. Some lawyers will argue that verbal contracts can be enforced and they are quite prepared to spend your money in litigation to prove that. As a general rule, put it in writing. Once it is in writing, there is much less scope for ambiguity and the parties know exactly what they are agreeing upon right from the start. Learn to understand how contracts work. Everybody has to start somewhere and you will be surprised how quickly you develop competence in this area.

Watch out when doing business with family and/or friends. The reason for being careful when dealing with friends and family is that if the transaction does not work out well, particularly in the early days when you are gaining more specialist *Knowledge*, you could lose either your family, your friendships, or your money. I have been successful in this area and have many friends and family with whom I have done business in the past. Part of the reason for my success is that I work harder than anyone else I know, in all the transactions that I enter into. The harder I work, the 'luckier' I get.

Partnership agreements are really agreements that are set up to determine what happens if the partnership goes wrong. When partnerships go right, and everyone is making profits, there are usually no problems. It is only when problems arise because one party doesn't keep up their end of the bargain, or some other reason, that the parties wished they had prepared a more thorough agreement up-front. If a thorough agreement is prepared, it can save you a hassle and real money if the partnership is to be terminated.

If you are going into a legal transaction with a large group of people (a **syndicate** of investors), be very careful. Someone has to take responsibility for driving the majority of the transactions. I have seen situations where large numbers of people have contributed their money with an understanding that everybody would do a part of the work. Frequently these syndicates, if not professionally run, result in parties losing a lot of their money, or a lot of their respect for their colleagues and friends in the syndicate, or both. My companies run syndicates and make millions of dollars for our investors. The reasons why we are so successful with them, is that my companies take full responsibility for running the syndicate and explain in detail to everybody, what is entailed in the project before they commit to it.

WHAT ATTENTION AND INTENTION WILL MAKE YOU RICH?

This way, everybody knows what is going to happen. Don't be charmed by the allure of combined finances. Syndicates are hard work. They only work profitably if there is a small management committee or group who are highly experienced in what they are doing and who are fairly paid for their efforts.

7) *Should You Keep Good Tax Records When You Invest?*

The Taxation Department can be incredibly inflexible. Keeping good tax records is a vital part of doing business. Take the time to keep detailed tax records. How are you going to find the time to go back and produce all of your necessary records for a taxation auditor, when you are busy doing another transaction and he or she expects all of your taxation records to be presented straight away? I have seen people lose their businesses, their marriages and almost lose their sanity through not keeping tax records. Don't let it happen to you!

You may even consider employing somebody part-time to keep your records in good order. You already know how to do this from Chapter 3. Your administrative assistant will charge less than your accountant, which will allow your accountant to give you better taxation advice, and optimal planning during the year. Many accountants are trained at giving excellent advice in the preparation and planning of your asset records, particularly those accountants who have investments themselves.

8) *What do You Need to Know when Dealing with Bank Managers?*

I have been fortunate to have some of the top bankers in Sydney and other cities as my colleagues. Some bankers are exceptional money men and women and can give you very good advice.

Bank managers, like most people, operate in the best interest of the bank that pays their salary and are not the most flexible people you will meet. The senior management of some major banks go to ridiculous lengths ~ moving bank managers from branch to branch every few years, so that the managers cannot build up a relationship with their clients! No wonder many banks are losing market share and consumer confidence! You can find excellent bank managers, but again, you have to look for them.

Remember, there will always be another transaction or another opportunity. The harder you work, the 'luckier' you will get. Take your time and shop around and don't let people pressure you into making a quick decision. If you find the right investment, whether it be the first or the hundred and first, within your parameters, be prepared to take *Action* when the opportunity arises. Make sure you take full control and responsibility for making that decision.

Clarity leads to power. When you set clear, definite plans and take *Action* on your most important financial priority, your rate of success increases automatically.

Let me now demonstrate how both your intentions and beliefs can assist you to take *Action* that will make you richer.

How can You Get Even Richer by Using Your Intention?

One of the significant areas that affect your reasons and ability to build riches is that of beliefs. Beliefs are feelings of certainty. The two extremes in beliefs are empowering beliefs and limiting beliefs. I will explore some fast, easy, and effective ways to transform limiting beliefs into empowering beliefs.

For many of us, confusion about money, or negative associations with money, developed in childhood, when we were far too young to have any power or mastery over money and riches themselves. As we grow up we tend to be affected by the beliefs of people around us, our parents, grandparents, or other significant people. Many of our parents and grandparents grew up during the Great Depression and World War II, which was one of the toughest economic periods that people have faced in the developed world, in well over one hundred years. People with parents or grandparents who lived through the Great Depression often have a tendency towards focusing on being able to save small amounts of money whenever they buy anything. People who came through the Great Depression adopted sayings such as: '*never buy anything until you can afford to buy it for cash*'. This was due to the fact that a long time ago, money was less freely available, and many people were unemployed for a variety of reasons. It does not need to apply today, to that extent. However, the lesson, in terms of avoiding consumer loans is just as valid today as it was then. It is critical to make the distinction between consumer loans and investment loans. You now know that investing in the 21st Century will take a different mindset than occurred in the first half of the 20th Century. Careful use of investment loans will accelerate your ability to build riches.

Prudent use of investment loans can make you rich much faster. They

WHAT ATTENTION AND INTENTION WILL MAKE YOU RICH?

should be used wherever possible, after careful research and planning, as you learned in the *Strategy* section. When you observe the pattern of any limiting belief and identify where it came from, most of its influence of it will effectively begin to disappear from your life. The more you develop and refine your compelling goals, intentions, and your *Strategy* for the accomplishment of building your riches, the more likely it will be that you will develop the resolve to overcome any limiting beliefs, therefore you will achieve your goals more quickly.

Many people grew up in families where there wasn't enough money to go around. This may have resulted in them being exposed to the negative opinions (and that's all they are) of other people, towards money, at the dinner table, family functions and wherever else people gather. As detailed earlier, Dr. McClelland of Harvard University found that the greatest way to wreck a person's accomplishment and success in life is to be surrounded by others who don't have strong expectations and desires for success themselves. Our parents, as well as virtually every person that we will ever meet in life, will do have done best that they can with the resources and the circumstances that they experience and create for themselves. Books like this were not readily available when our parents and grandparents were bringing us up. There was not as much opportunity for people then, as there is today, to build riches or to build their own personal development. The fact that you are reading this book right now, means that you are desirous of maximising your full potential. The challenge is for you to move beyond those old limiting beliefs and to decide to do something different than was available for your grandparents, or, even, your parents. I will do my best to assist you in realising your objective, right now, and every time we communicate or meet.

Alternatively, other people who may have grown up in rich homes may still associate negatively towards money because their parents may have been too busy focusing on making money to spend quality time with their children. In my case, I grew up in a middle class family where my father had a fixation on money. He was so worried about saving every single dollar that he developed a reputation of being mean with money. In order to build great riches, you should start making money your friend, and associating having lots of money with being able to achieve the things in life that you really want. Unfortunately my father has passed away, and I have lost the opportunity to be able to assist him to transform his beliefs. At least you and I can work together towards you becoming more empowered towards money.

HOW TO BUILD RICHES

Robert Dilts is an international trainer in NLP, and probably one of the most caring person I have ever met in my life. He is committed to assist every person he meets to achieve their magnificence. The more that I associate with Robert, the better I become at modelling his ability to assist people to realise more of their full potential. You will be able to develop this habit and ability once you start associating with more high achievers. Robert assisted me to review my father's limiting beliefs towards money and to form new beliefs for myself, that were not linked to my father's limiting beliefs. Once I identified the limiting belief patterns that my father held towards money, I was able to transform them into something that would empower me more. There is not the available space to detail all of the intricacies of dealing with beliefs here. Rest assured that there are people who can help you if you want assistance in this area. This section may however give you some useful, easy-to-apply techniques that can work for you right now.

Some of the limiting beliefs about money that I hear from people when I speak with them in seminars or consultations include those listed below:

Save the cents and the dollars will look after themselves

Money doesn't grow on trees

You can't earn more than your father

There isn't enough money for everybody

If I have money, people won't like me

You can't have money and be honest too

Money can't buy me happiness or love.

The above statements and beliefs, in isolation, seem harmless enough. Without clearly defined goals and reasons for building riches, limiting beliefs like these can be a cause of self-sabotage that may affect your ability to build riches. You can do something about limiting beliefs. Some of the things you could consider include:

1) *How do you interrupt a negative belief?*

Interrupting the negative pattern means that when you notice a negative belief, you don't just let it pass as this may keep it active and place you at its effect. Interrupt it in some way ~ this renders it

WHAT ATTENTION AND INTENTION WILL MAKE YOU RICH?

inactive and allows a new more positive belief to be substituted in its place. You can even do something outrageous whenever a negative thought occurs (if you are not in an important professional business setting). You could stand on one leg and wave your arms around like a chicken and make chicken noises or any other silly humorous interruption you can think of. This will create a humorous interruption in your brain. If you do this often enough, the humour dissipates any negative power the old belief had. Soon it has no power at all.

A metaphor of how interrupting a limiting belief works is to think of what happens if you were to scratch a record or CD. If you scratched it a number of times, and then played it, you would not be able to hear the original recording. So, too, if you interrupt a negative belief enough times, it will be unable to be replayed;

2) *<u>How do you replace a negative belief with an empowering belief?</u>*

One way to deal with a limiting pattern or belief is to replace it with a more empowering statement. You can do this every time you become aware of a limiting belief. In your mind, limiting statements can be replaced by positive pro-active statements, every time you become aware of them. This will eventually wear out any emotional charge those old, limiting beliefs may have had. For example, you could replace the limiting statements on the previous page with positive statements, such as those ones detailed on the next page.

Replace: *Save the cents and the dollars will look after themselves* with:
<u>*Focusing on saving cents is far too limiting for me. I have mastery over making dollars and I will make the dollars I earn work harder for me.*</u>

Replace: *Money doesn't grow on trees,* with:
<u>*Money grows from my Knowledge and Strategies and goals that I take Action on.*</u>

Replace: *You can't earn more than your father*, with:
<u>*I can earn more than my father, and I know my father wants me to be successful.*</u>

Replace: *There isn't enough money for everybody*, with:
<u>*Once the rich share their secrets, there is enough money for everybody who is ambitious enough to work to achieve their goals.*</u>

Replace: *If I have money, people won't like me*, with:
<u>People like me for myself, not for my money.</u>

Replace: *You can't have money and be honest too*, with:
<u>I can have money and be honest. My goals and intentions are noble and compel me to do the best I can with the money I accumulate.</u>

Replace: *Money can't buy me happiness and love*, with:
<u>Money can buy me happiness and love. Money can supply me with opportunities to share my wealth with others and to use it in ways that will empower me.</u>

You can replace any limiting beliefs you notice in yourself, with any empowering statement you choose. Alternatively, you can make them simpler or funnier, depending upon what works best for you. The main thing is to know that you can do something about them.

Another method to eliminate limiting beliefs or thought patterns, is to use professional help. There are many different techniques available through qualified practitioners, including NLP (Neuro Linguistic Programming) professionals. There are solutions and it is relatively easy and cost effective to get help to eliminate limiting beliefs.

3) *How do you overcome obstacles?*

All great men and women experience obstacles. The reason they become great is that, despite these obstacles, they still take Action. Do you know how they train circus elephants? They take the baby elephant and chain its leg to a post that is concreted into the ground. The baby elephant, like all of us when facing an obstacle or something that stops us going in the direction we choose, pulls against the obstacle, and pulls against it with all its might. Over a period of time the baby elephant comes to believe that it cannot pull the huge concrete post out. After a while, the trainers are able to replace the chains and concrete posts with a piece of rope and a tent peg and, as the elephant grows, a huge, strong elephant can be held by a flimsy piece of rope and a small length of pipe. The reason the elephant doesn't pull out the tiny stake (which it obviously could), is because the elephant doesn't believe it can.

There are plenty of men and women I meet in my life who have enormous potential but who don't take *Action* because they, like the

WHAT ATTENTION AND INTENTION WILL MAKE YOU RICH?

elephant, don't believe they have the ability to do it. The interesting thing about this story is that if there is ever a fire in a circus, the elephant becomes so motivated to flee from danger, that the desire for freedom becomes greater than its limiting belief. Once this psychological barrier is broken, the elephant will escape from the fire pulling the tiny tent peg and rope with it. Once an elephant has realised that the thing that was holding it back was really insignificant, then the elephant can never be held by anything ever again. So, too, is it with men and women who have mastered obstacles and imaginary limitations through taking *Action*. They too can never be shackled to mediocrity again.

'If you think you can do a thing or think you can't do a thing, you're right.'
~ **Henry Ford.**

It would be easy to write at least one book on beliefs but I do not have the time to do that here. If you want to know more about this area I suggest you read a book written by *Robert Dilts* titled: *'Changing Belief Systems with NLP'*.

Emotions have been called the trigger to human *Action*. Emotions do effect human behaviour because they affect people's feelings and what is important to them. How can you use your emotions to motivate yourself? Find out more by *ASK*ing . . .

Chapter 30

HOW DO YOU MOTIVATE YOURSELF TO TAKE ACTION THEN KEEP DOING IT?

'Whatever you can do, or dream you can, begin it.
Boldness has genius, power and magic in it.
Only engage and the mind becomes heated.
Begin and then the task will be completed.'
~ **Johann Wolfgang von Goethe.**

E-motion can be defined as energy in motion. When you use your emotions to take Action, you create energy. You can also use emotion to expand your ability to take future *Action*.

Emotion and emotional states, once you know how to use them, can provide you with the motivation to overcome obstacles and break **financial inertia** (or the tendency to avoid taking financial *Action*) so that you can move in the direction of your compelling goals. It can be useful to consider the concept of which I am sure you have heard before, that of the **comfort zone**. The comfort zone is a tendency for people to operate within a limited range of personal influence that they have become accustomed to. The comfort zone has been referred to as being like the death rattles in relation to success or excellence in any field of endeavour! People who fall into the comfort zone are definitely falling into a state of financial and personal inertia.

In order to achieve all that you can in life, it is critical to use your emotions to break through the comfort zone to bring you and your area of personal influence to greater levels. The comfort zone for many, is a place of procrastination, apathy and ignorance. It is a place that you probably want to avoid or you wouldn't be reading this book right now. In order to break out of the comfort zone and increase your area of influence, it is necessary to use emotions and to realise that any obstacle that occurs in your life can be used as a blessing to give you the motivation to expand your potential. How can this work?

How can you Expand your Personal Effectiveness?

Your current comfort zone can be described as an imaginary area around yourself. In the diagram on the following page, this area is represented by a circle around 'I', which is an imaginary boundary marking the limit of your current personal effectiveness. You can challenge yourself to step out of your comfort zone, by taking *Actions* towards achieving your goals. This will extend your level of personal effectiveness beyond this circle. An example might be by taking the *Action* to research the benefits and then changing your home mortgage to a line of credit. Other *Actions* that might extend you beyond your comfort zone include: purchasing an investment property, or a share portfolio, or setting up your own superannuation fund. If this feels difficult, then what is happening is that you are pushing up against your current comfort zone. Outside the comfort zone is usually a realm of fear, which, as we know, stands for false evidence appearing real.

Once we confront fear yet still take *Action*, we can *ASK* our way to a greater level of personal influence. As we do this, our zone of personal influence expands to the new area which I have put on the diagram as '**ME**'. Once your comfort zone has been expanded to this newer zone of influence it never decreases again.

Another benefit arising from taking *Action* and *ASK*ing your way out of your comfort zone, is that when you have done it once, it becomes easier to do again. Eventually, it becomes a habit and you continue to expand your zone of personal influence in all areas of your life. You can apply this to your health and fitness, loving relationships, confidence in financial matters or any other area of your life. The main thing to do to achieve this mastery, is to take *Action*. This breaks through any barriers that are stopping you achieving more in life. The only thing that will propel your success in life to the maximum, is taking *Action*.

HOW DO YOU MOTIVATE YOURSELF
TO TAKE ACTION THEN KEEP DOING IT?

INITIAL COMFORT ZONE

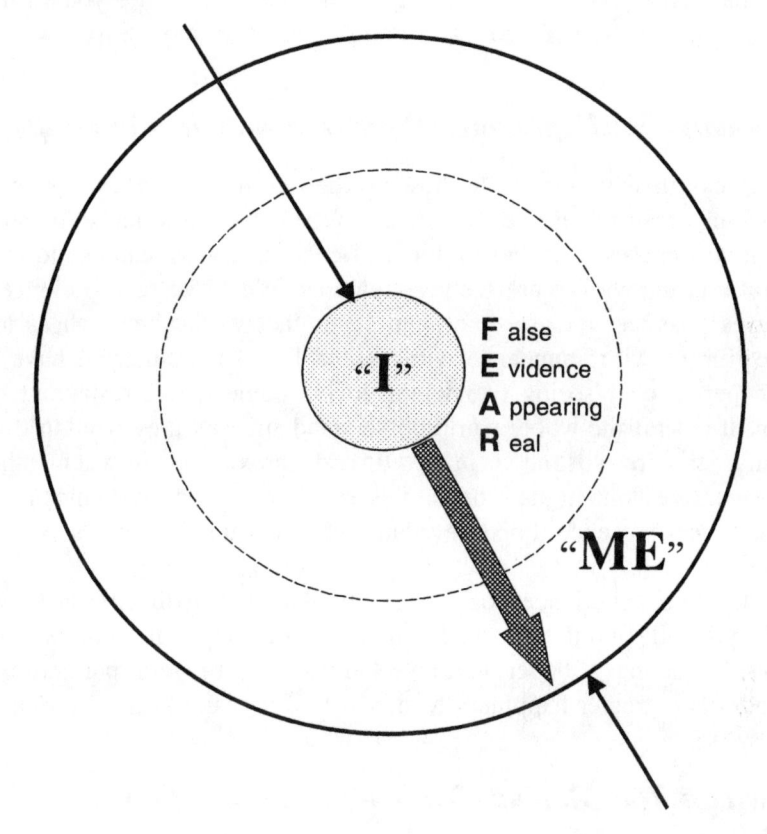

"I"

F alse
E vidence
A ppearing
R eal

"ME"

ENLARGED COMFORT ZONE

Motivation = Motive in Action

Another way to look at the concept of emotion causing motion, is to think about motivation. If you look at the word motivation, it is easy to imagine within it the words 'Motive' and 'Action'.

When you are motivated to do something you have motive in *Action*. The best example of this is, when you have a compelling goal, your motive is to achieve your goal. The only way to achieve your goal is to take *Action* towards it. It is this *Action* and the motive to go towards your goal that gives you a burst of energy. This energy provides you with the capacity to achieve your goal and build your riches more easily.

How can You Experience Positive Emotions more Often?

To achieve their riches in life, how do the rich use *Action* as a means of propelling themselves beyond fear? When we experience a strong emotion, it causes us to have a burst of energy, that we can use to create *Action* and enjoy. We are feeling creatures. We crave to experience, as often as possible, intense emotional states that we desire, such as love. Love fills us with abundance, vitality and life. I am sure you have had the experience of seeing two young lovers come into a restaurant or a room. It is as if the whole world could stand still and they wouldn't care, because they're so much involved and intoxicated in each other's presence. Everyone in the room smiles and lights up, and just enjoys being in the lovers presence. Poets say that when you are in love it's as if you are ten feet tall.

When you experience positive emotions and then link these to your goals, you will find it easy to take *Action*. For example, if you link having riches to having a better loving relationship with your partner, more freedom and greater happiness, you will find it easier to take *Action*.

How can You Motivate Yourself in Line with Your Values?

Values are emotional states that we place importance on feeling. Values include feelings of love, enthusiasm, joy and happiness. Your values are what motivate anything you do, whether you are aware of them, or not. You can use them to motivate yourself to take appropriate *Action* by becoming aware of them in relation to your goals. Just *ASK* yourself what's important to you about achieving those goals. If you keep asking, you'll come up with your values: things like freedom, security, and happiness. You have the capacity to use and to exercise your values any time you like. Have you ever noticed that the easiest way to feel love is

HOW DO YOU MOTIVATE YOURSELF
TO TAKE ACTION THEN KEEP DOING IT?

to be loving towards someone else? If you do this, you radiate love. Your values are positive emotional states, which are fabulous for you to feel. The beauty of emotional states is that you can learn to develop control over them.

Tragically, too many people do not exercise this control, or worse yet, put the control of their feelings with someone else. For example, someone may choose not to express love to another until they feel loved first. This mistake happens in relationships too often. If you first act lovingly, you will feel great, even if your partner does not reciprocate at that moment. You then control your emotional state.

It is possible to train yourself to become motivated, even in the face of adversity. This will accelerate you on your path towards riches dramatically. The way to do this is to develop the habit of learning quickly from experience. It is when you combine *Action* with your attention and intention that you are best able to learn from your experience. Without this combination, or focus, you can run the risk of being like those people you meet who keep making the same mistake time and time again.

How can You Turn Adversity into Something of Value?

Once you have clearly defined goals, you have a direction for your *Actions*. This direction gives you the ability to observe when you are off course. Once you learn how to use your emotions to provide motivation to put you back on course to your goals, your intention and attention will give you the power to overcome any obstacle. People without goals, attention or intentions often do not generate enough motivation to overcome their obstacles. Obstacles and adversity provide us with an opportunity to learn and to gain the experience necessary to achieve our goals. In order to take the *Action* that produces the results, you will want to use your *Knowledge* and *Strategy* to respond to obstacles in the most productive way. Human beings will do more to avoid unpleasant circumstances than they will to achieve pleasant circumstances. This is biological. The fight or flight syndrome is programmed into our neurology and has allowed the human species to survive. You can use this motivation to move away from the obstacles that you do not want, in order to get yourself to an emotional state that causes you to take *Action*. This in turn, activates your motivation and leads to a flow of confidence and self esteem.

Moving away from past failures and adversity can work for individuals, companies and nations.

HOW TO BUILD RICHES

If you are a person who used to lack courage and puts off taking *Action*, you run the risk of being at the effect of circumstances that happen to you and you may eventually become poor and dependent and part of the 95% of the population who do not enjoy financial freedom. You can reverse this trend and develop mastery over fear through the use of your emotion.

Two people can face the same adversity. One may become rich and famous, and the other may live a life of poverty. The difference is in the resolve and willpower of each person, which, when combined with a belief in their possibility and a belief that they can achieve their compelling goals, is unstoppable. One example of this away-from-motivation that I particularly like is that of a young, blind, black man in America, who in the 1960s, applied for a position as a band's drummer. After the audition he was told: *'not good enough kid'*. The young, blind, black kid replied: *'nobody will ever say that to me again'*. The young man's name was Ray Charles and the rest is history. Ray Charles has inspired many millions of people throughout the world by his ability to overcome the adversity of his blindness and that of being from a minority race. Ray has learned how to turn his obstacles to his advantage. He is an outstanding performer and a fabulous role model for his people, his country, and for anyone who has a handicap in life.

It doesn't matter what the adversity is. If there is a big enough desire, a big enough drive and enough commitment to take *Action*, then something valuable can come from every adversity. The rich know how to turn adversity (away-from-motivation) into compelling reasons for them to break inertia and move towards building riches. No matter who you are, you are going to face adversity and fears in life. The difference is what you do with those adversities and fears.

'Do the things you fear and the death of **fear** *is certain.'*
~ **Ralph Waldo Emerson.**

In the process of taking *Action*, particularly in the early days, fear arises for many people. When it comes time to make that final decision or sign that contract, people are often challenged by their past limiting beliefs, or advice from those who call themselves experts. Whatever the obstacle, eventually, you either have to take *Action* or pay the price of not taking *Action*. It is as simple as that. You have to choose between living with the fear or living with the choice of taking *Action*. Poets and authors have

HOW DO YOU MOTIVATE YOURSELF TO TAKE ACTION THEN KEEP DOING IT?

described this process for thousands of years. It has been said that: '*a coward dies a thousand deaths but a brave man but one*'. People who experience fear and don't take *Action* will come close to taking *Action* again and again. They'll experience the fear and won't take *Action*, and may even do this thousands of times. The person who feels the fear and takes the *Action* breaks through the comfort zone barrier and expands their identity to a new level beyond that fear (as we discussed in the comfort zone concept). My wife and I loved the movie 'Strictly Ballroom' starring Paul Mercurio. In this fabulous Australian movie there is a great line where the character Fran says to Paul Mercurio:

> '*A life lived in fear, is a life half lived.*'
> ~ **from the movie 'Strictly Ballroom'.**

How Can You Use Mastery over Fear to Build Character?

Once you know you can take *Action* in one area of your life, you know you can take *Action* in all areas of your life. As you develop greater mastery over fear, you also develop your character and confidence and courage. You become capable of making much larger decisions and become better able to overcome future fears or obstacles.

Fear stops many people from becoming rich. Some of these fears include fears of interest rates going up, or fears of the market going the wrong way, and fears of job loss. Most of these fears are based on old limiting beliefs and on events that generally will never occur. If you carefully read the loan documentation on the average mortgage on a property (or shares), and really understood it in its entirety, you probably would never take a mortgage on your house and would never get rich. Banks have these documents prepared in such a way that they are totally protected. So, a person, who has not read one before, may think that the bank is being unreasonable. In my opinion, these contracts appear to give enormous power and control to the lenders. The reality is, usually, that once the average home loan is entered into, very infrequently will the bank ever enforce the tough clauses within these contracts. I still go through every mortgage with a keen eye, observing the fine print in every document that I sign. But now, I do so with a commercial understanding that is based on the experience of having taken *Action* many times. These days, I sign documents for transactions, worth many millions of dollars, faster and easier than I did my first mortgage, for one hundred thousand dollars. Again, I will say this, *Action* builds character. *Action* also builds the ability to take stronger future *Actions*.

How do People Who Become Rich Respond to Fear Differently?

Obstacles and setbacks in life give you the opportunity to grow as a person, to become rich, and to develop personal mastery as you overcome your fears. When you encounter fear, your life will be transformed into riches or poverty, depending on what you do when you experience that fear.

The rich respond to fear and take a totally different course of *Action* from those who remain poor. They do this because they have long-term goals, and values that provide a structure and a framework for their success, which compels them to take *Action*. People who do not take *Action* remain poor or at the effect of circumstances. They react differently. It is easy for some people to make all types of excuses as to why they did not act. Usually they will tell you that they were right (and someone else was wrong). These people miss the opportunity for building riches, as well as fail to develop personal growth and personal mastery.

The secret is to find or associate enough pain with <u>not</u> taking Action so that you are compelled <u>to take</u> *Action*. I call this the Riches Spiral.

What is the Riches Spiral?

What happens to you in life is not as important as what you do with what happens to you in life. I have developed a model to show how you can turn setbacks into success. This is the Riches Spiral (diagrammed on the next page).

The opposite of transforming fear into riches (the **Riches Spiral**) is taking the soft option of making yourself look right (the **Right Spiral**). Although the words of the two may look similar the results they produce are worlds apart. Do you want to be rich or right? How you use your emotions and resourcefulness, to overcome obstacles, will determine not only your financial riches, but also your quality of life.

The Riches Spiral is most effected by your ability to respond, instead of react, to unfavourable circumstances which I will label fear. It is categorised by the fact that people who remain at the effect of circumstances often 'react' by blaming and complaining. They may then go through a process of acceptance of these unfavourable circumstances, which results, in essence, in them adopting the 'flight' syndrome to fear. As already mentioned, the 'fight' or 'flight' syndrome is an inbuilt protection mechanism in people. The difference with the rich is that they respond to unfavourable circumstances and take responsibility for their future. This leads to a process of using strong away-from-motivation (disgust, rage, contempt etc.) to break any state of inertia. This gets them to the point where they associate to positive long-term compelling goals and values, which in turn takes them to a position of *Action*. This activates the 'fight' syndrome to overcome fear.

At the end of the day, *Action* is a state that follows decision. Decision is a state that follows emotional intensity. *Action* takes courage. When people blame or complain as a reaction to fear, they take no responsibility for their destiny. They place their destiny clearly in the hands of someone else whom they are blaming or complaining about. Alternatively, when the rich encounter fear, they take full responsibility for the way they respond to that fear. The rich may go through a period of reflection or pondering, which leads to a possible chain of emotions diagrammed on the Riches Spiral on the next page.

I have labelled the tendency, for those who are Right, to blame and complain as a capacity to '*react*', and the tendency of the Rich to take responsibility and to go through a period of reflection, as their ability to '*respond*'. Reacting puts people at effect. Responding puts people at cause.

What is the Difference Between Responding and Reacting?

Let me give you an example of the difference between responding and reacting. In NSW, the Labor Government increased Land Tax. What the people who are destined to become poor will often do, is blame or complain about the fact that the government is not being fair. They might even sell or not buy an investment property as a result of this tax. What the rich will do is reflect upon it as a challenge. They will then seek specialist *Knowledge* and develop a *Strategy* that will effect their

HOW TO BUILD RICHES

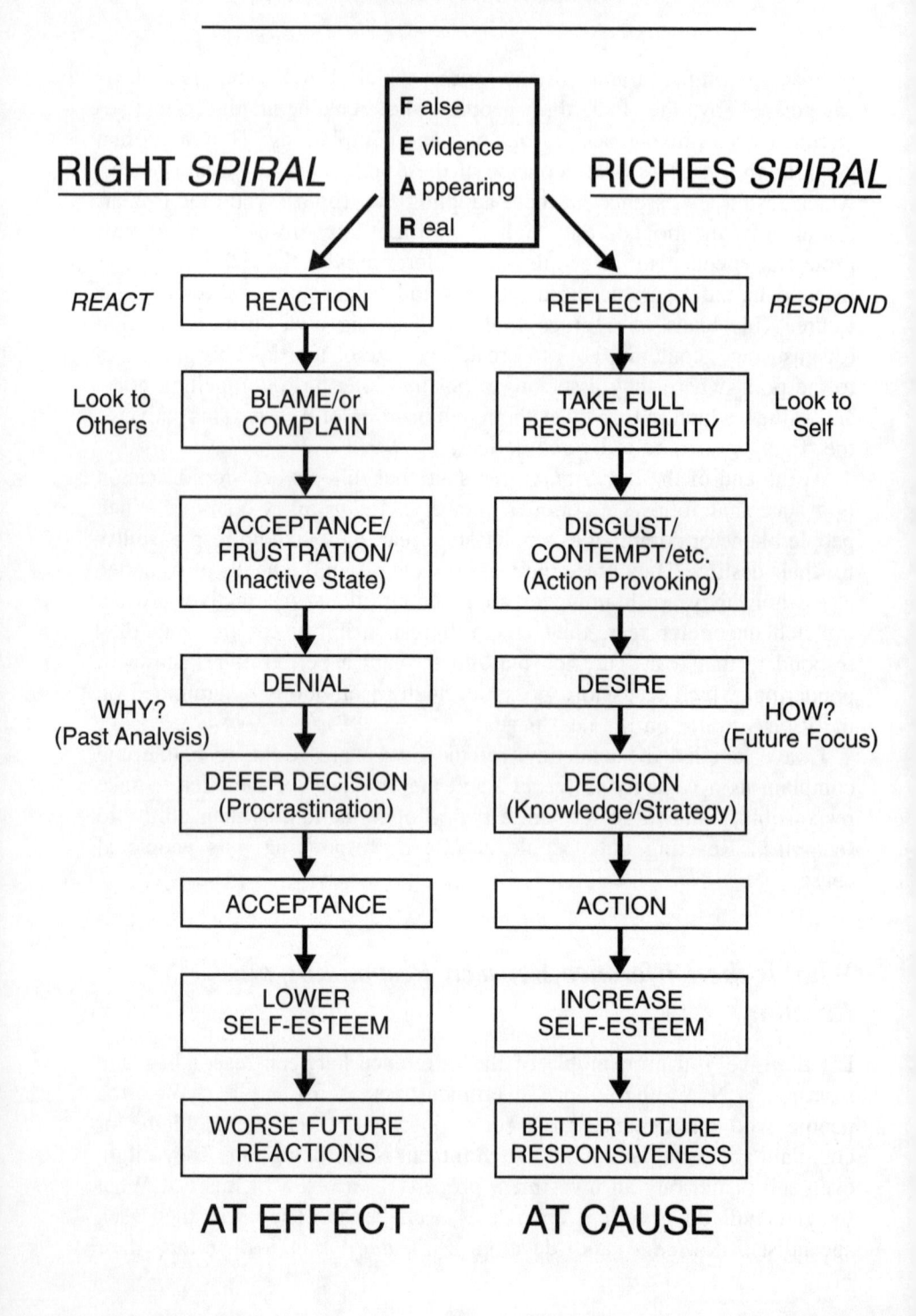

F alse
E vidence
A ppearing
R eal

RIGHT *SPIRAL*

REACT — REACTION

Look to Others — BLAME/or COMPLAIN

ACCEPTANCE/ FRUSTRATION/ (Inactive State)

WHY? (Past Analysis) — DENIAL

DEFER DECISION (Procrastination)

ACCEPTANCE

LOWER SELF-ESTEEM

WORSE FUTURE REACTIONS

AT EFFECT

RICHES *SPIRAL*

REFLECTION — *RESPOND*

TAKE FULL RESPONSIBILITY — Look to Self

DISGUST/ CONTEMPT/etc. (Action Provoking)

DESIRE — HOW? (Future Focus)

DECISION (Knowledge/Strategy)

ACTION

INCREASE SELF-ESTEEM

BETTER FUTURE RESPONSIVENESS

AT CAUSE

investment holdings and will probably increase their rent. This will allow their tenants and the government, (in this case the Federal Government) in the form of taxation benefits, to basically pay for this increase in NSW State taxation. The rich will calculate that the net effect of this tax might be as low as a few dollars a week per property (and that the benefits far outweigh such a fear).

The difference in these two approaches to the same tax is profound. Those who react and make a snap decision, to sell an investment property, or not to buy one, may even base that decision only on a newspaper story sensationalising the tax increase ~ a common ploy to increase the sales of newspapers! When people react, they put themselves at effect, and if they do not step back from this abyss, then they are likely to become dependent later in life.

People who become rich, *ASK* their way to their riches by developing character and self-esteem and by responding differently to the same fears that keep other people poor. They choose to be at cause in their financial future.

The poor may decide to procrastinate and not buy an investment property. Then, they may go through a process of accepting the fact that they don't have the courage to take *Action*. By doing this, they are in fact deciding to believe this is their destiny. This will place them in the category of battlers, or even worse, they may mistakenly believe they have to remain poor. This may eventually lead to them becoming dependent on others, which in turn lowers their self-esteem. With a lower self-esteem and an inability to pluck up the courage to take *Action*, they are likely to picture themselves as people who are indecisive and at the effect of their environment. This will create worse reactions the next time they encounter fear. The solution for the poor, is to discover that they <u>can</u> do things differently, that a different outcome is possible for them, if they learn how to achieve it. Then they might read a book like this one and learn how to *ASK* their way to riches. Once they pluck up the courage to take *Action*, they can put themselves on a different course, that being the Riches Spiral.

How can You Develop Your Action Muscles Around the Kitchen Table?

Place three chairs around your kitchen table. One of these chairs represents *Knowledge*. Another represents *Strategy*. The remaining chair represents

Action. You can go and sit in each of these chairs at will. One way to exercise your ability to *ASK* your way to riches is to use these three chairs in a series of different steps. Let us use them to find a solution to the rise in Land Tax.

Step 1 ~ *Knowledge* chair:
Go and sit in the *Knowledge* chair. In this chair you can experience what *Knowledge* you have available now, and consider what *Knowledge* you can learn in order to make a better decision to combat the problem of the rise in Land Tax (or any other problem).

Step 2 ~ *Strategy* chair:
When you choose to sit in the *Strategy* chair, you can develop a *Strategy* for responding to this tax. From here you can see what will happen with your eventual increases in rent, and eventual increases in tax deductions, and what the net effect and net cost to you will be.

Step 3 ~ *Action* chair:
When you then go and sit in the *Action* chair, you are in an excellent position, having learned from the *Knowledge* and *Strategy* chairs. In this *Action* state, you want to change your e-motions to the extent that you will take the best (or most appropriate) *Action*. All some people need to do to create *Action*, is to imagine their compelling goals and to think and feel about the importance of their values. When they do this, they realise that taking steps towards what they want and taking *Action* on their number one financial priority, will move them towards their goals faster. For people like these, it is relatively easy to make decisions and take *Action*. All of us, however, have within us this *telescopic* capacity to focus on the future and our goals.

How Can You Get Rich by Avoiding what You Don't Want?

Compelling goals will keep you moving towards what you want. Set your goals first. This makes it easy to keep taking *Action* once you have used your emotions to break financial inertia and got yourself to act initially.

As already discussed, we can use the desire to move away from the things we don't want, to create the motivation to propel us to *Action*.

HOW DO YOU MOTIVATE YOURSELF
TO TAKE ACTION THEN KEEP DOING IT?

Away-from-motivation is tremendously powerful and tremendously useful, but only IF you have first established compelling goals and values. Without goals and values, you may create an away-from-motivation and end up anywhere so long as it's not in a place of fear! When you add goals, you are more likely to move towards that direction and closer to what you want. Deciding on a goal is like learning any new habit. Over time, it becomes second nature, and after a while you can do it easily, at any time you choose.

If you do not yet have compelling goals, I encourage you to think of some and write them in your Riches Journal (or the one provided for you on pages 371–378). These compelling goals and your reasons for achieving them, give you the capacity to keep moving in the direction of your goals once you decide to take *Action*. The more frequently you replay, in your imagination, your long-term goals and associate with them, the more intensity you have behind them and the more reasons you will develop to achieve them. The more often you look at the reasons for achieving your long-term goals, the greater will be your e-motional intensity and the greater will be your desire to realise your goals. This creates a greater ability for you to use short-term away-from-motivation as a means of inspiring you to take *Action*.

If You Experience a Limiting Negative Emotion, How can You Use It?

There is a positive use for negative emotions within this framework. It can be highly useful to use a very strong negative emotion to compel you to decide and commit to take *Action*. For example, if you realise just how cynical the nature of the increase in the NSW land tax really is, you may become disgusted with the politicians responsible for it, or treat their move, or them with absolute disdain. The politicians know that the increase in land tax will lead to increased rents. They know that when the rents go up, it will be the renters who will pay for the rise. It is easy for the politicians to point a finger at the landlords and blame them for increasing rents. Voters are seeing through such cheap political tactics faster these days. Another strong emotion that may get you to decide and commit to taking *Action*, is contempt for the fact that these politicians are causing greater heartache and pain to the dependent people in our society who will be paying an increased rent. The government blames the rich and knows the poor will end up paying.

HOW TO BUILD RICHES

Another great away-from-motivation tool, is to generate frustration or anger about the fact that you are currently not heading in the direction of your ideal goals fast enough. You may like to try this exercise at your kitchen table, sitting in your *Action* chair.

Picture yourself twenty or thirty years into the future in a position where you have negligible investments or no investments. In this place you imagine, you may be in need of medical assistance and don't have the money to pay for the best medical help for your children or yourself, or your family, friends or community need money that you are unable to give to them because you haven't taken *Actions* to amass it. If you are younger, you may project fifty or more years into the future and see yourself, like I can see my grandfather, when I go and visit him in his nursing home. For me this feeling alone will do it. When I associate to a picture like this, I vow to myself that this will never happen to me. I am going to take meaningful, decisive *Action* to change my destiny, so that I have sufficient riches, for not only myself and my family but also for my community.

When you experience these negative emotions in this exercise, I encourage you to get that feeling in your gut in a way that your whole body could even begin to shake and you picture horrible mental images out into the future. This could include intensifying the negative emotion in order to get yourself to take *Action*.

Once you have created a negative picture with enough intensity, you can then break free from that cold sweat or that horrible picture. Now, while still in your *Action* chair, desire and determine to make things better. You do not want to take *Action* in the highly emotional state you may have created with the previous exercise, as your judgement may be affected by your emotion. It is useful, however, to use these emotions to get you to a point of decision. Once you decide, you can reduce your emotional intensity.

You may desire to build riches. To do so you may decide to buy an investment property or a portfolio of shares or whatever you consider to be the best form of investment. You decide you're going to do something about it. So you feel the fear and do it anyway.

What Happens After You Decide to Build Riches?

Once a decision is made, you can begin to construct a picture in your mind and think about all of the positive benefits and favourable images and dreams that the riches you desire will bring you, once realised. Another way of increasing your desire and capacity for decision is to read aloud to yourself the benefits that you will achieve for yourself and your family by attaining those riches. When you link those favourable images with the reasons and benefits for achieving your goals, you develop a positive intensity in your e-motions. You can feel this throughout your whole body and you will then be in a position to decide to take definite *Action*.

Whenever you take that *Action* and deal with honourable people, you will raise your self-esteem to the point of actually enjoying taking that *Action*. When you have raised your self-esteem and you do what is suggested in the coming chapters, you will give yourself a clear message that you are a person of *Action* ~ that you are at cause in the creation of your riches in your life. It becomes easy for you to see yourself, in your mind's pictures, as a winner. Once you do this, it dramatically increases your potential to be more responsive in the future, and to generate your ability to respond better to future fears that you may encounter. You are then well on your way towards applying the Riches Spiral, (as detailed on page 310), and continuing to develop your mastery in it.

Can You get Others to Help You Become Even Richer?

Courage is a human quality that you can learn how to generate and that will propel you towards success. We all have to make decisions at various critical times in our lives. Once you employ courage and make decisions, you will be at cause in your life. If you do not yet have the courage to make decisions that will put you in control of your life, you can learn how to access such courage. Courage comes from the heart (from the French word, 'le coeur', means the heart). You can learn how to value yourself. Use your feelings and your heart-felt emotions, to get you to the point of decision, then make wise *Actions*. Become a person of *Action*.

> *'Courage is rightly considered the foremost of all virtues for upon it all others depend.'*
> ~ **Winston Churchill.**

You are either going to become richer or poorer in your life depending upon the decisions you make. Now that you have the capacity to be able to use your e-motions to make appropriate decisions, you can choose. If you have difficulty in using the concepts that have been discussed in this chapter, and in this book, then I encourage you to get some assistance from other people. If you want some help to learn how to develop your belief and trust in yourself, then seek assistance. There are several excellent seminars and courses to help you value yourself more. The more you value yourself, the more successful you will become. There are people who run courses and seminars that can help you to access your courage, to take control in your life to walk the path to mastery.

Once you decide to improve your life, what then? If you are now excited and have decided that you are going to do something, such as buy some investment real estate, I encourage you one more time, to complete this book before you take that important step. It is highly useful to learn everything about retaining your riches once you have created them. You may gain some critical distinctions in the next chapters on how to make even better decisions, in terms of the important areas, like the ownership of your investments. These will help you retain your riches as you build them.

How can You Learn from the Past?

Some people spend a lot of time dwelling on past experiences. Engaging in analysis of the past may reveal to people that they may have avoided past *Action*, or not stood up for themselves at times when it would have been useful to have had more courage, and to have acted or responded differently. This would have put them at cause in their lives. It is useful for observing what has happened in the past and it becomes a learning process for the future. It is highly limiting to keep dwelling on anything that has happened in the past.

Accept your past, learn from it and forgive yourself for any past mistake. It is also useful to forgive everyone else who has ever (as the Lords Prayer says) 'trespassed against you', then move on. I know that in my life I have done many things about which I could wallow in regret. Probably, most people could. However, every new moment is the beginning of the rest of your life. Once you *take control of your life right now* and put yourself at cause in relation to your future, then you need not ever worry about what happened in the past. Living in the past is like trying to get energy or heat out of yesterday's fire. If you have had a fire, all the wood has been burnt up and all you have left is ashes. If you put those ashes in the fireplace and try to light them again, you won't get any

HOW DO YOU MOTIVATE YOURSELF
TO TAKE ACTION THEN KEEP DOING IT?

heat. Treat your past as a source of learning, that allows you to take better *Action*, and it will be useful. *ASK* yourself questions like: 'What did I learn from that experience?' and 'NEXT TIME, how can I take better *Action*, that will move me toward my goals faster?'

How Have Others Overcome Their Past Setbacks to Build Riches?

Everybody faces setbacks. People who become rich or great in life, learn from the past and take future *Actions* to *Build Riches*. Let us look at an example of how people have used setbacks to inspire them to use greater riches in their lives. There are plenty of role models of possibility whom you can use on your pathway towards building riches and developing huge success in the corporate arena and in other areas of your life. One of these people is Tom Watson Senior.

Tom Watson was employed by NCR (National Cash Register) in the USA. NCR and Tom Watson had a difference of opinion and NCR fired him. This gave Tom Watson the opportunity to use this adversity which challenged him to set compelling goals and values upon which he would build his future success. He vowed that he would form a company that would one day be more powerful than NCR (one of America's largest corporations at that time). Tom Watson fulfilled his promise because he had that compelling goal and because he had meaningful values. The company he formed was IBM (International Business Machines) which did become the largest computer company in the world during Tom Watson's lifetime, surpassing NCR. One of the major reasons for Tom Watson's success and his dramatic success with IBM, (one of the greatest success stories of the 20th century) was that Tom Watson instigated in IBM, a set of corporate values which included the importance of the individual employees at IBM and the importance of the company's focus on the customer, as the reason for them being in business.

Again, I'll state it in many different ways with many different examples, the lesson is still the same. If you have long-term compelling goals and meaningful values, then, when adversity or fear confronts you, you have the capacity not only to move beyond the fear and not be at the effect of it, but also to build character and respect while you build riches. It is that long-term compelling goals focus that keeps you moving in the right direction, long after the away-from-motivation has got you started into *Action* (as detailed earlier in this chapter). The away-from-motivation and adversity that you encounter in life, can be used to your advantage if you have the courage to do it. Whether it be the blind Ray Charles, or hundreds of thousands of other inspiring role models, as I said earlier, it is not what happens to you that matters in life, it is what you do with what happens to you.

> *'In every adversity is the seed of equal or greater opportunity.'*
> ~ **Napoleon Hill.**

Napoleon Hill's research into five hundred of the men who shaped the modern USA during and after the great depression, found that all of these great, successful people only attained their success after confronting adversity and continuing beyond it. Character is only developed under difficult circumstances that are often hard, bitter experiences. Steel can only be forged in furnaces under immense heat. Character is the same. Adversity is not to be avoided. Instead, the rich welcome it as an opportunity to be embraced and then overcomed. It is used as a valuable lesson, so that they can build greater character. It is not always easy to step out of your comfort zone, confront fear, make a decision and take courageous *Action*.

> *'Courage is the control of fear.'*
> ~ **Rudyard Kipling.**

How can You Benefit by Taking Action?

There are obvious benefits to taking *Action* and having courage. These include:

1) Every great man or woman has been one who has taken *Action* and developed character. There are hundreds of people I could reference who have used adversity and fear to inspire them to set compelling goals, and live by their values, then build major success.

    You possess the same qualities as all of the great people whom I have described in this book and all of the ones you will read about in your life. The question is, are you going to answer the challenge and set long-term compelling goals, confront every adversity and find a solution to it and build your character in the process? I can't answer

HOW DO YOU MOTIVATE YOURSELF TO TAKE ACTION THEN KEEP DOING IT?

that for you. I'd love to be your shadow every time you faced a challenge, and tap you on the shoulder to remind you that you do possess the seeds of greatness, that you do have the ability to respond instead of react and that you are at cause in creating your future success. Courage is a muscle like any other one and it responds to exercise.

Once you start to take *Action* and develop it as a habit, you are well on your way towards developing riches. Your ultimate success will depend upon how compelling your goals are, and how committed you are to following them through. You too can become great and rich;

2) You can take pride in yourself. Many people intend to start programs to develop themselves or build riches. The difference between them and you is that you have invested the time to read all of this book. You are well on your way to becoming rich and building a rich life. The day you build the habit of taking massive, considered *Action* and doing this on a regular basis, after having developed *Knowledge* and *Strategies*, will be the day your success begins to compound;

3) You are well on your way to building riches. You have faced fear and shown courage in reading this book and being prepared to apply its principles. Once you start taking considered *Action* regularly, you become a winner.

How can You Become an Even Richer Person?

Every decision carries with it the weight of responsibility. The responsibilities of becoming decisive and making decisions include:

1) Every major decision means cutting off from another choice. Take full responsibility for your choice. Rely upon your judgement. Protect your crop (i.e. your investments) from critics, well meaning relatives, and those jealous of your success. Sometimes, even your own family members will not have the same resolve or character that you have. Own your decisions and the total responsibility that comes with them;

2) If you make a 'poor' decision, be willing to accept its consequences ~ don't fall into regret, but rather use it to learn from and move on to

greater success. If the market moves the wrong way, it will eventually recover. All markets will recover. Have a longer-term focus;

3) You can apply your past lessons now! Every millionaire or billionaire I know or have read about, regards their past challenges, setbacks and adversities as a valuable part of their eventual success. Gradually their success grows and every transaction that they make becomes comparatively easier, once they let go of the ghost of the past. Every poor or dependent person I know, lives in the past much of the time and relives their failures time and time again. The problem is that they don't learn from them or use them productively. Choose to become rich. Use the past as a signpost and don't drive towards your desired goal with one eye in the rear vision mirror the whole way. Move on. Keep going in the direction of your goals.

Don't wish life or decisions were easier. Make yourself better, through developing character and investing in yourself, and you will be able to handle tougher decisions faster and more easily. As you do this, life will become easier and you will be able to handle more responsibilities and more decisions. The more responsibilities you have and the more decisive you become, the greater will be the responsibilities you will be given, and the greater the riches you will build.

'No great battle is won on the defensive.' **and**
'Only great battles produce great results.'
~ **Napoleon Bonaparte.**

Napoleon, with whose quotes we started Chapter 29, is truly one of the most outstanding leaders and one of the most courageous men who ever walked the planet. His ability to take *Action* was legendary, and so too was his success. The reason for Napoleon's success was his desire and his drive.

Begin to *ASK* your way to riches. Use *Knowledge* to research the market. Use *Strategies* as a means of determining what your next most important financial priority is. *Strategize* the means to achieve your riches. Commit to taking *Action* and using the methods described in this chapter to compel you to take *Action*. Continue to *ASK* the right questions until you are capable of obtaining the right investment, with people of equal integrity and character to yourself. Take decisive *Action* consistent with

HOW DO YOU MOTIVATE YOURSELF TO TAKE ACTION THEN KEEP DOING IT?

your values and continue to build on that *Action*. Move in the direction of your long-term goals. If you do this, then what may happen for you, is that you develop the habit to:

> *'Do the thing and you will have the power.'*
> ~ **Ralph Waldo Emerson.**

It is now time to investigate the important area of how to retain your riches as you build them, by learning ...

Chapter 31

WHEN YOUR RICHES ARE BUILDING, HOW DO YOU KEEP THEM?

'Put not your trust in money, but put your money in trust.'
~ **Oliver Wendell Holmes.**

Building riches is a skill that is learnable. This book is designed to show you how to *ASK* your way to riches. This is a journey which never ends. You cannot ever be too rich or too healthy or too loving. There is always the ability for you to share your riches with others, or to give to those less fortunate, in our society, who want to improve their lives. This is a major driving force of my mission in life.

It is important for you to begin to think about how you plan to retain your riches, once you have built them.

The Great Australian Dream is to own your own home without a mortgage.

The American Dream used to be, to own your own company and be a self-made millionaire. In America today, the greatest expectation to become a millionaire is to sue somebody else and to take a million or more of their money!

According to the American Bar Association, if you live in California and earn over $50,000 a year there is about a 25% chance that you will have a litigation action taken out against you! Unfortunately, in Australia, we are following the American trend towards increasing litigation. The time to prevent litigation is before it ever arises. Lawyers and their clients are unlikely to take legal action against someone without assets in their personal name. If you are in a profession where litigation is a natural part of doing business, then you may want to protect your assets. I know many people who are lawyers, auditors, accountants, businesswomen, and other professionals, who have taken the steps to protect their homes and investments from litigation.

How Do You Protect Your Assets?

1) *How do your protect your family home?*
The first asset people look for if they want to sue you, is your family home. If your family home is in the name of your spouse, or partner, who is less likely to be sued, then this may protect your home. I say may, as it depends upon how you arrange your other affairs. If your spouse is a director and shareholder in your trading company, then you many not escape litigation. A good accountant or lawyer can advise you if this applies to your circumstances.

2) *Should you own assets in your name?*
If the assets are in your name, or the name of a partnership, you have no legal protection if you are sued. If you are a responsible person, you may choose to own your assets in your name because your CGT is reduced (chapter 24) and you can offset losses against other income, i.e. Positive Leverage (page 190).

In the earlier example of the Wise family, they may have put their family home in Anne Wise's name alone. Any couple can draw up an agreement with their solicitor as to what happens to the home proceeds if they divorce. If one party dies, **a testamentary trust** (detailed on page 280) may offer flexibility, to transfer assets and income with negligible cost to your loved ones, and save them much tax after your departure.

3) *Can Partnerships protect your assets?*
In most cases the answer is NO. However, in some States, there are 'Limited Partnerships'. There are some situations or professions where these cannot be used, e.g. auditors, but for the rest of us, they offer some protection. If this applies to you, talk to your accountant about it.

4) *Should you own investments in a company name?*
Generally, after September 1999, companies are better than trusts,

WHEN YOUR RICHES ARE BUILDING, HOW DO YOU KEEP THEM?

to own capital appreciating assets (i.e. real estate and shares). The reason is that companies do not have to be wound up in eighty or so years, as trusts do, and both will pay the same tax from July 2001.

Discretionary trusts used to be a better choice for holding investment assets, because companies do not offer as much real asset protection. Legal actions can be lodged against a company, as well as all of its directors and shareholders. If your spouse owns all the shares in the company, it may provide you with some protection. The advice of both an accountant and a lawyer may be required, if you really want to avoid taking this risk.

Increased litigation makes all forms of asset ownership risky as courts often 'lower the corporate veil' of trusts and companies.

5) *Are Trusts a good place to own your investments?*

Many people are paranoid about using a trust structure to own their investment assets. This fear stems from the ATO saying they intend making the richest thousand people in the country pay more tax. The ATO claims that these very rich individuals are finding loopholes in the trust laws, in order to avoid tax. These loopholes are being closed. It is unlikely that the main benefits of trusts will be able to be changed. Some people don't pay any tax and abuse the system, yet still want to use our roads and hospitals. Most Australians will agree, that unfair loopholes should be closed. Trusts will still remain one of, if not the best places, to own your investments.

Unit Trusts are trusts where unit holders have a proportional ownership of assets, depending upon the units they hold (very much like a company). Unit Trusts will only protect your assets if the units are owned by different classes of unit holders (e.g. a husband owning income trusts and the wife, capital units), or by a super fund. Seek advice if you want to use a Unit Trust.

Discretionary (or 'Family') **Trusts** used to be the best structure for owning assets, be they businesses, real estate or shares. Any action against a beneficiary, has no right against the trust, as the beneficiaries have no equitable interest in the trust. Most discretionary trusts, formed in the 1990s, allow new beneficiaries to be added without a CGT or stamp duty implications. You may want to obtain legal advice on any existing trust, particularly if you have high value assets in such a trust. Trust laws will change from 1 July 2000 so that the trust pays tax each year and then distributes profits (with a tax credit) like companies do (as detailed on pages 111 to 113). Increased litigation makes all forms of asset ownership risky as Courts often 'lower the corporate veil' of trusts and companies.

6) *How can you get super asset protection?*

Super funds protect your assets from litigation up to about $940,000 per person in the 1999 tax year. However, you will not be able to access your super assets (with some limited exceptions) until you reach retirement age. Due to proposed changes in legislation from May 2000 (refer to Chapter 27) you will not want to get advice before you set up a Unit Trust and use positive leverage with a super fund. Again, I encourage you to write to your local Senator and the Assistant Treasurer and complain about this legislation as soon as possible (as detailed on page 270).

7) *What is the best way to protect your assets?*

The best way to protect your assets is to *ASK* your way into the right investments in the first place. If you combine this with doing business with ethical people, your chances of litigation are massively reduced. Another method of protection is the one where I suggested that you put all of your legal agreements in writing.

Getting the right advice, initially from competent professionals who walk their talk, can save you many thousands of dollars later. I have been through litigation with some of the biggest companies in Australia in the past. It is a nightmare. There is a saying that the only people who benefit from litigation are the lawyers who represent the parties who are litigating! Avoid litigation wherever possible. You can be right and righteous yet still lose all of your riches in the battle.

The main thing to realise is that **there are solutions**. The time to solve many problems is before they arise. Get good advice prior to embarking upon any major investment initiative. I encourage you to listen to the *Building Riches* tapes, and to arrange your affairs with professional advice.

How do You Create the Time to Build Riches?

Having learned and applied all of the ideas detailed so far in this book, you will be able to build and retain your riches. Building riches is

WHEN YOUR RICHES ARE BUILDING, HOW DO YOU KEEP THEM?

important. Remember to *ASK* yourself occasionally: *'Why am I building riches in the first place?'*

At the start of this book, I observed that we all want the same things:– health, happiness, a loving family, entertainment, friends and a sense of importance and contribution. If in becoming rich, you sacrificed your health, family, integrity and happiness, would you still do it? Fortunately you can have it all, but it takes planning and follow through. You can *ASK* yourself to riches in all areas of your life.

What does is take to be rich in all of the important areas of life? In my opinion, the most important thing to do is to make or create the time for what is most important to you.

There is a law called the **Law of Use**. It simply says 'use it or lose it'. This applies to you, physically, mentally, spiritually, financially and in every other way. About fifteen years ago, I had a football accident which required a pin to be put in my shoulder. After this was done, I had my arm in a sling for six weeks. Without using that arm, the muscles lost their strength. When I finally was able to use my arm, I couldn't even lift it as high as my shoulder. My orthopaedic surgeon (Dr. Ronnie Sekel), who is in my opinion, the best in the country, encouraged me to use my arm as often as I could, to regain full strength. It was awkward and painful at first, but now it is stronger than the other arm and I have 100% of its use, strength and flexibility. You have probably seen people who have broken bones or had a limb in plaster go through the same recovery process. If you do not use your mental, physical or financial muscles it is just the same as having them taken away in an accident. The loss is just as great. Use what you have, or you will lose it.

If you take your lover, family, health, or friends for granted you may lose them also. It is when you are kind and generous and loving to others that they treat you the same way. People who are rude, ignorant, and greedy put all they have, at risk. Everyone can change their habits and get more of what is important to them in life.

You may well be thinking, how do you find the time for all of the important things in life? Every successful or busy person faces the same challenge. The answer comes in setting priorities about what is most important to you and committing the time to do that activity. If you place enough importance on something, it will get done. People often ask me how I keep so healthy and have such a great relationship with my wife, while I am so busy in business and with community work. The answer lies in what time I spend on what is important to me. If you want to know how important something is to someone, just observe where they spend their time. People who are healthy, invest their time and energy in health. People who are financially rich invest time and money in their education (*Knowledge*) about riches and then do something about it (*Strategies* and *Actions*). The same is true for all other areas of your life.

If you treat your spouse unkindly and don't show them love and attention, the chances are you will lose them. If you spend all your time making money and don't stay healthy, you may die prematurely and not enjoy your riches. Life is about balance. Setting priorities and achieving a sense of importance and joy in life, is important. I will share with you a few tips in achieving a rich life:

1) *How much is your time worth?*

Most people think that their time at work is worth a certain value. If you earn $40,000 a year and work forty hours a week for fifty weeks of the year, then your time is supposedly worth $40,000 ÷ 50 ÷ 40 = $20 an hour. Most people never realise that if they worked another twenty hours a week, getting a degree or specialised *Knowledge* in their career, that one day they may earn say $60,000 (or more) a year for the same hours worked. Now, your employer may not pay you $30 an hour, but later someone else will.

From the neck down you can do physical labour and make $40,000 a year. Using your brains, your income has no limits. People like Warren Buffet, Kerry Packer or Rupert Murdoch can earn over $1,000,000,000 a year. Rupert Murdoch made $15 billion in 1999 alone.

I have a friend who earns over $100,000 a year. When I have stayed at his home, I have observed him meticulously iron his own shirts in the mornings. At breakfast, with his wife and himself, I asked him what he thought his time was worth. He calculated it at $50 an hour. I asked him how much it would cost him to get someone to iron his shirts. He said $15 an hour. That means every hour he spends ironing his shirts, he loses $35 an hour! This principle may be more important than it first appears.

It is not the extra one hour you put in at work that makes the difference. It is the regular time you spend in *Strategizing* how to be more effective that matters. Then, single mindedly sticking to the most important things, will get the urgent priorities done. This is what makes people valuable managers and leaders. Getting the important things done well, and on time, eventually makes you a more valuable

WHEN YOUR RICHES ARE BUILDING, HOW DO YOU KEEP THEM?

employee. This is how people can earn over one million dollars a year. They get others to help them get the important done ~ even if they work eighty hours a week, fifty weeks a year. Their effective worth is $1,000,000 \div 50 \div 80 = \$250$ per hour.

Sometimes, paying people to do the things you don't like doing, frees you to do the things you should do. Employing others to: iron your clothes, mow your lawn, clean your car, clean your home, etc., etc., can sometimes earn you $50 an hour and cost you $15 an hour. Eventually you will earn a lot more. It is the hours spent planning your career and your riches, that give you a much higher reward. Yet most people don't regularly invest their time in *Strategically* planning their investments or their careers. Allocate time to get rich;

2) *How much is your family time worth?*

Many people become successful in their careers and don't allocate time for their families. They may get a high income, yet end up divorced (more than once if they don't learn the lesson) and lose half of their wealth in messy court proceedings. What is worse, after the lawyers fees are finished, there may be even less to go around. Worse still is the inability to see their children and this trauma to their children can leave huge emotional scars that money can't heal.

You don't pay the price for a happy marriage, you enjoy the benefits of a happy marriage. You can't put a monetary value on the love of a spouse or your children. Nor can you cost the pain or anguish of seeing a child turn to drugs or a spouse leave you for someone who gives them more affection than you do. Make the time for the ones you love.

My wife Tanya and our, nearly eighteen year old, son eat together whenever we are home and go out to dinner once a week. We don't need to spend much money to talk and to appreciate one another. It is the few seconds it takes to say how important, attractive, loving or well mannered your family members are, that really count. How many times a day do you acknowledge your family members? In our home, Tanya and I hug, kiss and appreciate one another at least twenty times a day. Our relationship has more fire than many who have been together for less than a year. Don't take things for granted. Be affectionate. Be sincere and be loving. My grandparents were married for seventy years and were more affectionate and loving in their nineties than some young people I meet, who have been married for a year or two. The more you invest in your loved ones, the more they will reciprocate. Become a giver;

3) **How much is your health worth?**

Many people insure their bodies against death or disability. If someone paid you one million dollars but you could never walk or make love again, would you take it? If you were given one million dollars but could never see or hear again, would you still consider yourself rich?

These may be extreme examples but I know people who are overweight and have ulcers, who worry too much. I know others with cancer or heart problems that are linked to their attitudes and habits. Many of these problems could be easily solved by more balance, attention and care being given to their own well being. My father died in front of his parents, about thirty years before he should have died. He was overweight and overstressed. I had shown him, fifteen years before, how to lose twenty kilograms and enjoy life more by doing some Tai Chi exercises and changing his diet. He didn't allocate the time to make these changes and paid the ultimate price. After he is gone, I can't teach him this lesson again. Fortunately, I was there at his death bed to ask his forgiveness and forgive him so he could die in peace. I want to live in peace and die in laughter having been all used up from *Action* and service!

One thing I like to do is combine activities. Regularly I read and use a walking machine or an exercise bike. Other times I will walk with my wife and talk. You should get your heart beat up for twenty minutes at a time (after fifteen minutes of warm up), at lease three times a week. Even when you are working hardest, your regular exercise will save you time each week, by making you more efficient.

Vitamins and a good diet pay dividends. Most people I know get sick about ten times more than I do. Part of the reasons for my health is that I not only take vitamins everyday, I also go to an Australian practitioner of Chinese medicine and a Chinese herbalist, and see others to help keep me well. With acupuncture, Chinese herbs, exercise, vitamins, and Tai Chi, maybe I am lucky to be so healthy. I work twice as many hours a week as most people I know, and am richer, healthier and happier than they are. I achieve all of this by investing in my health. You can do it too. Start from where you are. *ASK* your way to greater health;

WHEN YOUR RICHES ARE BUILDING, HOW DO YOU KEEP THEM?

4) How much time do you take to have fun?

Where do you get the most passion and joy from life? For many people it can be exercise, laughter, sex, sport, or dancing. These activities give you what is called 'flow'. Flow is like a charge of energy. When you are in a state of flow, your senses are heightened and you are more alive. Often you can enjoy many things that give you flow, without spending much money on them. Invest your time and increase your life-force energy, by regularly increasing the flow in your life.

5) How do you find the time for all of the good things?

Many people waste a lot of time in front of the TV or in a bar or just doing things that they don't like doing. Once you start your riches building, you may let others help you become more successful by doing the things you don't need to do.

Do the important things for you first. If there is time left over to sit in front of the TV, then do it. TV's are cheap to buy, maybe only a few hundred dollars, yet expensive to own. It is said, the average person watches several hours of TV a day. If they sold the TV and spent that time reading, getting healthy and loving one another then each of them would be healthier, happier and richer. TV (particularly the ABC and SBS), has many fine programs. If you must watch it, plan in advance what you will watch and then turn it off. Spend the rest of the time you would have wasted, talking with your family or reading a book or getting fit. The difference will make you rich in many ways;

6) How much time do you take to be quiet?

Meditation comes in many forms. You can sit in a park, on a beach or in your room. Just letting your mind be absent of thought (it takes a bit of practice) can recharge your creativity and body more than almost anything else. The ideas that come to you in those times of quiet can also make you rich. This is a big topic with enormous benefits. Give it a go. Even though I am very busy, I still make time to meditate daily.

Ghandi defeated the British Empire in India practising passive resistance. He meditated for twenty four hours in a row one day a week. The ideas that came to him (*Strategies*) allowed him to defeat the greatest nation on earth, (at that time) using his *Action* for his people. You can harness the same power in fifteen minutes a day a couple of days a week. I do Tai Chi for fifteen minutes each morning even when I have only have time for a few hours, or no sleep. The energy and ideas I get doing this gives me more energy than I often get from three or more hours sleep;

7) *How much time do you spend making a better world?*

Almost everyone without brain damage wants the world to be better for themselves and their families. Few do much about it. The little acts of kindness that you give other people are like pebbles dropped in a pond. The recipients often smile and pass a kindness to another and your circle of influence expands. Unfortunately, greedy, selfish people spread bad feelings the same way.

By practising little acts of daily kindness you continue to make the world better. Write these examples (however tiny) in your *Riches Journal* and look over your accomplishments often. In Chapter 33, I will encourage you to find a mission for yourself in life. This is a big step for many people. Once you have a reason to do things, your energy and personal effectiveness will increase dramatically. Take the time to *ASK* yourself why you are here. It may be some of the most productive time you have ever invested in your life;

8) *How much do you invest in yourself?*

Be kind to yourself. You are the only constant in your life.

One of America's wisest men was Benjamin Franklin. He once said:

> *'Empty the coins from your purse into your mind*
> *and your mind will fill your purse with coins.'*
> ~ **Benjamin Franklin.**

Many billionaires that I have read about, invested in their education, well into their seventies and beyond. You can practice the same principle.

Over the years I have observed many successful business people, from heads of public companies to sales people, earning hundreds of thousands of dollars a year. Almost always, the top people read books like this one, listen to tapes, attend seminars and invest in their own education. The people who remain poor say they'll do it when they get rich or don't think it is worth it. I have seen many people rise from

WHEN YOUR RICHES ARE BUILDING, HOW DO YOU KEEP THEM?

poverty to riches (including myself) by investing in their own education. Self education is what makes rich people rich.

Every time you read a book or listen to an audio tape, commit to taking *Action* on at least one idea. If you do this, then you will be taking more new initiatives in a month, than others do in a decade. Invest in yourself. Apply what you learn.

Take at least one idea from this book. Commit to apply it. Set a time to do what you set out to do. Get one or two of your most motivated friends to remind you of your commitment. Write it on three pieces of paper then stick one on your bathroom mirror, one above your bed and one in your office and remind yourself of your commitment at least ten times a day. Your *Action* levels will rise and you will get more done on this goal, in a short while, than many of your peers will in months or years.

Invest in yourself for the rest of your life. Every year I invest tens of thousands of dollars in my education. Many speakers or authors I read, have only a fraction of my experience. Yet, I am always able to find at least one thing that I can apply. You can do the same. Be a lifelong student. Unfortunately, far too many people think they know it all. The person who founded the Macdonald's hamburger chain, aged in his mid-fifties, often said:

> *'When you are green, you are growing.*
> *When you are grown, you rot.'*
> ~ **Ray Kroc.**

Always be learning, growing and investing in your education. Keep learning and yearning and you will keep earning.

It is now time to learn ...

Chapter 32

ARE THERE MORE SECRETS TO BUILDING RICHES?

'There are two things that are needed these days: first, for rich men to find out how poor men live; and second, for poor men to know how rich men work.'
~ **Edwin Atkinson.**

Having read this far, you now have a tremendous amount of *Knowledge* and many *Strategies* for building riches. This *Knowledge* and these *Strategies*, give you the ability to direct your thinking and feeling towards finding the solutions for yourself. Your experience and wisdom will continue to grow for the rest of your life. Enjoy this process and keep adding to your *Knowledge* and *Strategies*.

You may also feel compelled to use your emotions to generate *Action* that produces the results in your life. This feeling or urgency is the catalyst of change. Your emotions are the devices for your pleasure or pain in life. Having learned how to program your mind, to instruct your body to get motivated to take *Action*, I now want to caution you about doing so in such an emotional state.

As previously mentioned, when you are emotionally charged, there is a flood of energy into your system. Others can see a noticeable change in you. You run the risk of going off in a fit of passion and taking *Action* in a way that you might regret tomorrow. *Action* is necessary and desirable but it should be tempered by your *Strategies* and *Knowledge*. This will prevent you from being taken advantage of.

I encourage you to defer taking *Action* until you have cooled down and re-tested your *Knowledge* and *Strategies*. This will help you to develop greater wisdom. From a position of wisdom you will begin to generate even better *Strategies* and the capacity for stronger and more decisive *Action*, at the most appropriate time.

It can be easy to get a little confused with the concept until you become skilled at it. It is just like any other skill. The first time you drove a manual car, did you drive it perfectly? I doubt it. If you were like most people, you were probably a menace on the roads until you had driven a few blocks (or more)! On a more serious note, it is important not to be taken advantage of when you make a major decision. If your decision involves something as critical as your financial security, it is a time for caution.

There are many highly polished sales people who make a living by their wits and cunning. Many of these people encourage and evoke emotional intensity in their clients, and then sell them a product that delivers only part of what the client needs. When the client cools down, it is usually too late to escape ~ the damage is done.

People sometimes ask me why I care if others are sold a poorly performing investment? The answer to this question is linked to my concern for the victims of manipulators. As I mentioned earlier, financial pressures lead to more divorces and family breakdowns than any other cause. In a highly emotional state, people are more likely to let themselves be taken advantage of. The reason why these manipulators keep getting away with it, is caught up in some loopholes in the legal system and is too complex to allocate space in this book to detail. Legally, there is a term, **caveat emptor** meaning buyer beware. It is the buyer's responsibility to avoid being talked into a poor performing investment at the wrong time, or with the wrong mortgage securing all of his assets. I feel so strongly for the children, the marriages and the future trust of these buyers that it warrants another reminder to be cautious.

Fortunately, there is a solution. *Knowledge* protects you from risk as well as fear and also from being manipulated. Specialised *Knowledge* will warn you when someone is trying to sell you an investment that is not worthy of your hard-earned money. The better your preparation, the better your performance. World class performers, be they musicians, actors, sportsmen, entrepreneurs, salespersons or great parents, have learned and practised their skills before they achieved their greatest successes. Greg Norman has spent thousands of hours perfecting his golf in a way that has allowed him to come from behind, and win golf tournaments. Many other Australian champions including Wayne Gardiner, and Michael

ARE THERE MORE SECRETS TO BUILDING RICHES?

Doohen in motor cycle racing, and Kieran Perkins in swimming, have also perfected the art of preparation. Keiran Perkins used this skill to win himself the gold medal, in the 1,500 metres freestyle, in the 1996 Olympics, in Atlanta. The more *Knowledge* and *Strategies* you develop, before you invest large amounts of money, the better for you. There are plenty of books and courses you can learn from. I have read hundreds of books and attended over a hundred courses. Many of them have been less than ordinary! From each of them, I have been able to learn at least one new thing. Combining all of this information with the enormous amount of experience I have generated over the last twenty years, has allowed me to build riches for my family, my clients and contribute to charity. Keep investing in your education. Learn more and you will earn more. Temper your *Action* with experience. Learn from people who walk their talk.

It is time to learn more secrets to assist you to build riches faster and in a way where you retain the riches you build.

At the time of writing this book, it is the end of the twentieth century. The Asian financial crisis has begun, but is far from being resolved. Australia and America are spending more than they earn as countries. Share prices and property prices are at record highs. It is a time for caution. The economy will get worse before it gets better. The economic cycle will take its course. If you want to race out now and invest your hard-earned money, wait, because there are a few more secrets that I will share with you.

What Other Secrets do You Need to Apply Before You Take Action?

You can apply certain techniques that will improve the quality of your *Actions*. Some of these secrets have been partly discussed in this book and others are variations or new concepts that will assist you in building riches. These secrets include:

1) How do you learn from your experiences?

Do you remember the three chairs in Chapter 30 labelled *Knowledge*, *Strategy* and *Action*? That technique is capable of generating motivation and emotion. You can also develop wisdom by introducing another element that allows you to learn from your experiences.

HOW TO BUILD RICHES

Earlier in this book, I noted the aphorism that: *'the second million is easier to make than the first'*. What is presupposed here, is the fact that having made one million dollars you have the *Knowledge* and *Strategies* needed to make the second million. You also learned how to take *Action* to acquire the first million. Also, compounding makes it much easier to expand your riches as they grow. So how do you make smarter decisions in order to get the first million dollars? One technique I have developed is what I call the **observer** position.

Using the same exercise as in Chapter 30, place a fourth chair at your table. When you sit in this chair, you act as an observer and you are able to learn what happens in the other three chairs. Combining the Observer position with your *Action, Strategy* and *Knowledge* chairs (or positions) makes it easy to learn from your experiences.

Every time you go to the *Knowledge* position, you can generate questions to *ASK* yourself to build riches. If you want to invest in shares you may be in this position and *ASK* questions that use the *Knowledge* you have learned in previous chapters, such as:

- *What type of industries are likely to go up or down in value under predicted economic conditions?*

- *What companies within these industries are likely to perform best?*

- *Is now a good time to buy shares in these companies?*

*ASK*ing questions will encourage your mind to seek answers. As you learn how to answer these types of questions, your *Knowledge* grows. This base of *Knowledge*, you will continue to add to for the rest of your life. You will also be able to generate better questions that will make you even richer as you answer them. When you move to the Observer position you can learn from the questions you just *ASK*ed in the *Knowledge* position. When in the Observer position, imagine looking at yourself, still sitting in the *Knowledge* position *ASK*ing questions. From the Observer position, you can also imagine looking at yourself in the *Strategy* and *Action* positions. You can observe how each of the other three independent positions relate to one another.

Have you ever noticed how easy it is to solve a personal problem for someone else? Yet, when you have a problem, you are often so caught up in it that you can't easily find a solution. From the Observer position it is easy to solve problems. It is particularly useful when dealing with the *Action* position because of the emotion and motivation that is generated there. Like any new skill (e.g. driving a manual car) this takes practice until you get good at it. Practising this exercise will allow you to take better *Action* and to learn from the *Actions* you do take. This exercise allows you to calmly observe the process you go through, *ASK*ing yourself to riches. It will reward you and it will generate wisdom if you use it;

2) *What if you are told you will miss the deal of a lifetime?*

Although I covered this in an earlier chapter, it warrants repeating. I have looked at thousands of deals and make many millions of dollars net profit on an annual basis. Of the hundreds of deals I look at a year, I am often given the oldest sales line in the book ~ that if I don't move quickly, I will miss the deal. It is used far more often than is actually true. Sometimes it may be accurate. If the investment is a great price then maybe you have to be able to make a quick decision.

My preference is to let deals go, rather than be pressured into buying before I have been through my ASK formula. If I have a detailed *Knowledge* and the transaction works perfectly with my *Strategy*, only then will I consider buying. If it does not work, then I will let it go. Many times, I have gone back and bought investments after the supposed deadline on deciding had passed. Don't let the salesperson pressure you into an investment you may regret later. There will always be another investment. Once you get good at the observer technique mentioned above, and your *ASK* model is in place, you can decide quickly on investments. Until then, practice caution. Don't be bullied or tricked into parting with your hard-earned money until you are confident enough to take *Action*;

3) *Should you seek professional advice before you take Action?*

You would be amazed at the number of people who have *ASK*ed me for advice after they have entered into a contract, to buy a particular investment.

Many times a good adviser can show you how to save many thousands of dollars in taxes or other benefits, by getting the advice before you contract to buy that investment. You may need advice on which name (or entity) to buy the investment in, or how to structure your offer or on the many other questions you wish to *ASK*. My recommendation is, to organise your chosen specialist consultants (accountants, lawyers, sharebrokers, and others) <u>before</u> you take *Action* and sign any contract. Your initial, tax-deductible, consultant's fee is a small investment to make, compared with a potentially large cost of many thousands of dollars if you buy the wrong investment.

Gain specialist *Knowledge* to design winning *Strategies* <u>before</u> you take *Action* to build greater riches. This will be enhanced if you have the specialist advice you need <u>before you take Action</u>;

4) *How can you reduce risk when borrowing money?*

If you are entering into an Investment loan, you can reduce risk by buying the asset which will secure the investment loan (usually real estate or shares) at the right time in the business cycle. Chapter 9 described the economic cycle. Formulate your own opinion on where we are in the Econic cycle, and then *ASK* your professional advisers when the best time to buy is. You will then be better able to back your judgement next time.

If you are *ASK*ing this quality of question, then you are well on your way to reducing risk. Buying <u>before</u> the market jumps in value, which lowers your loan to value rates, and risk. I cover this in more detail in my *Building Riches* audio tapes. Eventually you have to trust your own judgement. If you do this, then your *Knowledge* and ability to make better decisions next time, increases. You also are well on your way to using the Riches Spiral to build greater riches;

5) *Should you borrow money if you are concerned about losing your job?*

Your capacity to earn income is one of the key criteria that the banks look at when lending you money. You also want the security of knowing you have an income to help support any borrowings and to generate tax refunds.

If your job is insecure, you may be best advised to defer borrowing any extra money until <u>after</u> you secure another job, or work harder (or smarter) at your existing job to make yourself so valuable that your employer will not want you to leave! Do this before you borrow large sums of money;

6) *Should you worry about investments after you make them?*

Over the years, I have studied the lives of many millionaires and

ARE THERE MORE SECRETS TO BUILDING RICHES?

billionaires. Learning from other successful people accelerates your abilities, if you apply the *Strategies* that the super-rich have already proven to be effective. If you find a Strategy that works, make it your own.

John Paul Getty, a self made billionaire, used to say that his secret to building wealth in transactions, was to do all of his analysis on a particular transaction and do all his worrying before he entered into the transaction. Once he had committed to a particular transaction, he would then concentrate all of his attention on getting the result that he wanted, and avoiding obstacles on the way to achieving his greater wealth. One thing that pays dividends, or gives you greater than average profits, is your ability to do your research before you make an investment. I have personally applied this lesson of J. P. Getty's, years after his death. It works just as well today as it did in the 1980's when he was alive;

7) *Should you be careful who you share your goals with?*

Away-from goals are goals that are phrased in a way that you want to avoid something. An example of an away-from goal is wanting to quit smoking because you do not want to suffer from ill health. Share your away-from goals with everybody. They will remind you if you go back on your goal. This will give you the stimulus to quit the things you want to give up.

Share your success goals only with people who have their own written goals and are committed to assisting you in achieving yours. Sometimes, people who love you may discourage you, for no other reason than that they do not have goals themselves. People who may discourage you and rob you of your riches come in many forms: they could be a loving mother, father, brother, sister, friend, or neighbour. They could also be a consultant, a journalist, a friend or even a bank manager. If you have absorbed all of the information in this book so far, then you know more in financial terms than the majority of the so called 'experts' in those areas. Treat this as the beginning and continue your advancement and *Knowledge* by attending seminars, reading books and taking the best of the best of these materials and using it in your life. Whenever somebody tells you that you should not make a certain investment, take one big step back and look at the person from head to toe and ask yourself; 'is this person already rich?'; 'Are they happy, healthy, confident and dynamic role models to whom I should listen?'; and 'Are they practising what they preach and making excellent money from their investments?' If the answer to any of these questions is no, then be courteous, but do not be influenced by them.

8) Should you associate with negative or cynical people?

You have probably heard that a cynic is a romantic who has lost hope. As I mentioned earlier, cynics may have a more accurate understanding of human nature in general than do wide-eyed gullible optimists, however, the optimists generally live longer, have healthier lives and better interpersonal relationships.

Earlier in this book I referred to Doctor David McClelland, of Harvard University. It is worth repeating this point because it is so critical to your success. His research concluded that you could give someone the finest motivation and skills training in the world, but let them associate with negative go-nowhere people and these highly trained people would be destined to fail. Years ago I thought I could make negative people positive. Fortunately, I gave up trying to convert people who were happy being negative. The negative person will usually make the positive person less positive.

Associate with winners and you will become a winner. Birds of a feather flock together.

What then are some of the pitfalls that you should avoid if you want to build riches faster?

What are Other Considerations You Need to Look At?

These come in many forms. You have probably heard the statement from a great US football coach: 'the best defence is a strong offence'. If you are spending your time focusing on *ASK*ing your way to riches, you are spending your time going in the right direction. There are however, certain things to consider:

1) Should you get insurance when you start investing?

Nobody can accurately predict the future. If you take good care of your body, then you greatly increase your chances of being able to manage your affairs.

As mentioned earlier in this book, Income Protection Insurance is tax-deductible and is the one insurance that best covers illness or accident. It is particularly cost-effective if you are in an office or

ARE THERE MORE SECRETS TO BUILDING RICHES?

low-risk category. It costs nothing to *ASK* a reputable insurance broker for a quote. This is one insurance that I use myself even though I have exceptional health.

Malicious Tenant Damage Insurance was covered earlier and is a good insurance if you have investment real estate.

If you have significant borrowings, life-insurance can give you the peace of mind that your loved ones will be looked after and your loans repaid, if you die unexpectedly. If you take out this policy in your supperannuation fund, your tax paid, before paying the premium is only 15%. This is a big saving on the top marginal rate of 48.5%;

2) *Should you be careful of conflicts of interest?*

Conflicts of interest happen when one party is representing several unrelated parties at the same time. For example, if your accountant suggests you buy a certain investment, you should ask your accountant if he will be paid any commission from the seller of that investment, if you buy it. It is illegal for a professional to charge you and receive a commission, if they do not disclose this fact. Be careful. It does happen. Some accountants receive payments of $5,000 or more from certain promoters of property developments. Some may lie to you. The vast majority of accountants are highly ethical. Use your ASK formula on any investment and do not buy any investment that does not fulfil your investment criteria, even if someone else advises it. It is your money. You make the final decision;

3) *Should you be careful to guard against greed?*

I know successful people who are very happy to deal with greedy people. Some greedy people have no problem lying, cheating and doing whatever it takes to seal a transaction and make a commission. My experience shows that greedy people are very predictable and that eventually you will be effected (and maybe infected) by their greed. Even if you attempt to turn a blind eye on their greed, it will eventually effect you. It is a personal choice. My preference is to avoid excessively greedy people because if they will lie to or cheat others, why would they not lie to or cheat you?;

4) *How do you build trust with people?*

My advice is, give people small tasks and observe how they handle them. If they always find reasons to blame someone else, or justify if they didn't do what they promised, then be wary. The person themselves is probably a good person. They just have developed a bad habit. If this pattern continues, you can rest assured that when things get tough, and you are in the middle of a big transaction, the same people will still be making up excuses as to why they can't deliver on their promises. I have had friends who let me down numerous times. I refuse to do business with them now for this very reason. Better a little caution than a big regret;

5) *How do you heal the greed in yourself?*

If you sense yourself becoming greedy in a particular transaction, it is cause for concern. You may be getting talked into an investment that is too good to be true. From my experiences, they usually are. You can make great profits from a great transaction, but it usually takes a lot of work to find these and realise them. Be cautious if you sense your own greed getting the better of you. Some of the toughest investors I know will not expect to get all of the profit out of a particular transaction. If they are buying shares or property at the bottom of a market and want to sell and make a profit, they will generally sell before it reaches the absolute peak. They will aim for the vast majority of the profit only. They know that if they are too greedy, they might wait just too long and the market may move against them. They know if this happens, they may lose a lot more than the little bit of profit they gained when they sold to a buyer who didn't *ASK* the right way. *Knowledge* protects you against risk. Let the other person win a little too. They will more willingly transact with you again and you can still get rich being ethical, wise and prudent.

This chapter has given you some extra tips on getting rich sooner. You will always find more. Chances are that you will keep learning until your last day of life. Part of the great joy of life is the ability to contribute. If you find a particular idea that worked wonderfully well and are generous enough to want others to get rich and build a better Australia, share your idea with others. One way, if you like, is to write to me at the address noted at the back this book. I will give you credit for your idea and put your name in print, if you are agreeable.

5

Conclusion

Chapter 33

WHAT HAPPENS WHEN YOU DO BUILD RICHES AND USE THEM WISELY?

> *'Sow a thought and reap an act;*
> *sow an act and reap a habit;*
> *sow an habit and reap a character;*
> *sow a character and reap a destiny.'*
> ~ **Ralph Waldo Emerson.**

There are tremendous benefits when you build riches. You will have much greater peace of mind and a feeling of security knowing you have the riches to handle problems or opportunities that arise. There are many benefits, including the ability to travel and see the world, wear the best clothes and eat at the finest restaurants. The options are only limited by your capacity to think of more ideas for using your riches to bring pleasure to both yourself and other people.

Riches provide more than just financial and tangible benefits. During the process of building your riches there is also the opportunity for you to benefit in other ways.

Who Will You Become When You Are Rich?

There are several journalists who go out of their way to produce unfavourable articles and books, about people who are rich. It seems that many people would rather read about a scandal or an offence that a rich person was involved in, than hear of the character building lessons they learned along the way to making their fortune or riches. In reading about great men and women, you can find clues about the types of people they became on their paths to fame and fortune. History is full of ordinary people who became rich, or great. It is often said and I agree that: **'there are no extraordinary people, just ordinary people with an extraordinary desire'**.

How strong is your desire? As your desire becomes stronger, you are more likely to take strategic *Action* that increases your *Knowledge* and skills to take even greater *Action*. Your Riches Spiral (from Chapter 30) will be activated and your self-esteem and personal power will increase. These intangible benefits happen increasingly from the time you take control of your life and start building greater riches. They are less easy to quantify than the financial assets you acquire.

I've never heard of anyone, on their death bed, wishing they had spent more time at work. If anything, they usually wish they had taken a few more risks. The common theme of people, at the end of their lives is their desire to have been more loving, generous, and wise with the people they cared for and met during their lives. Don't wait till you are old, or it will be too late. You can happily achieve instead of having to wait until you achieve to be happy. The difference is huge. Once you decide to be rich, you are well on your way to achieving your goal. You are a winner. Only winners read books like this. Decide to be more than just rich in financial terms. You can also choose to be rich every day in health, happiness, love, kindness and many other emotions or values. As you acquire financial riches while being consistent with your most important values, you become a different person.

A friend of mine writes Hollywood movie scripts as well as Australian movies. I *ASK*ed him why the media portrayed up to 90% of business people as crooks. He said other writers did this, because many people in the public eye were an easy target. It is illegal to attack racial groups, but not business people. In reality, most business owners are honest, hard-working taxpayers, like you and me. For every rich crook I have met in the last twenty years, I know twenty or more rich men and women who have great relationships with their family, friends, staff, clients, and who make a difference in Australia.

Australia needs heroes. Heroes inspire other people to achieve. They provide a beacon of light that radiates hope for others to follow. Unfortunately, far too many Australians build up a company from nothing, to a valuable business and then sell it to a foreign company. Many of our fine old Australian companies are no longer owned by Australians. (You

WHAT HAPPENS WHEN YOU DO BUILD RICHES AND USE THEM WISELY?

can find out more by phoning the AusBuy Guide on (02) 9898 0309). When this happens, one person retires rich and the profits go overseas. A few foreign shareholders may also make money. We need to encourage our fellow Australians to want more than just the money that the sale of their business offers. When Australians want to own a successful business that employs Australians and expands overseas, then the business owner can benefit in many ways. They can have ownership of assets that produce an income that makes them rich, while employing Australians and living as a role model of possibility for others. Buy Australian products, build a profitable business or career and inspire your family, friends, and acquaintances. If you do this, you too can happily achieve.

One of the greatest benefits of building riches that I enjoy, is the ability to be a great role model for young Australians. Although I have a very busy schedule and often work over seventy hours a week, I still make the time to speak with young Australians without payment. It is a delight to see young people like our son Scott (aged 18), his friends and the hundreds whom I speak with, get excited about their success. If more parents of our young people developed the *Knowledge*, *Strategies* and *Action* to inspire their own children, we would create an even greater Australia. Unfortunately, too many people are caught up making a living, rather than building riches.

There are financially rich people whose craving for money alone, has them sacrificing many things that others think are more important than their fortunes. For these people, their end justifies their means. In other words, the means they have used are evident in the end result! Many of these people end up divorced many times, their children cannot function in the world, their health is in a shambles or they are despised by their families, staff, and/or community. Fortunately these people are in a minority. Most of my millionaire friends do not want to attract the attention of the media. Most rich people are happy to have financial riches, great health and loving family relationships.

Some people wonder if there is more to life than building riches and their families. Once you start thinking of more than your family, you begin to enter the exciting world of deciding upon your mission.

What is Your Mission?

A mission is more than just a set of goals. When a person has a mission, they are filled with energy and a zest for life. History remembers people with a mission, whether it is Fred Hollows giving his time and money to give sight to the underprivileged in Africa and Australia or Mozart whose music inspires millions well after his death. Mozart used to say 'I am constantly searching for two notes who love each other'. People on a mission have seemingly endless enthusiasm and excitement about life. They make things happen.

Do you know what your mission is? I believe every person is unique and has the ability to be happy and successful in at least one area of endeavour. The tragedy of our education system is that we do not encourage our young to choose to be excellent. Peer pressure and parental factors keep most people from deciding upon a mission for themselves.

How do you find out what your mission is? If you *ASK* the right questions your mind and body will get excited and tell you what your mission is. You have to trust yourself with the answer. I encourage you to write the answers, to the following questions, in the back of this book, in the *'Personal Riches Journal'* (pages 371 to 378).

You can begin to generate your own questions as well as *ASK*ing yourself:

1) What career will give me the greatest satisfaction?

2) If I received $10 million tax free tomorrow, what would I do with your money?

3) If I only had 180 days to live, in perfect health, and I could do anything, what would I do?

4) If I knew I was absolutely guaranteed success, what career or project(s) would I select?

5) What is so important to me that I would fight or even die for it?

When you begin to get a sense of a mission for your life, everything has more meaning. If you know where you will spend your money if you have a fortune, or where you will spend your time if it is limited, you get a sense of what you should be doing now. Spending your time working at a career that gives you the greatest pleasure in life gives your life meaning.

I was enjoying forming companies and building beautiful investment homes for people to live in as well as living a full rewarding life with a

WHAT HAPPENS WHEN YOU DO BUILD RICHES AND USE THEM WISELY?

---

gorgeous wife and a handsome son. In *ASK*ing and answering the above questions, I was able to find what gives me the greatest pleasure in life. I am passionate about learning and sharing how to overcome adversities in life, and to achieve greater levels of success. The more I study success, apply this *Knowledge* in *Strategies* that work when I take *Action*, the more excited I become. When I teach these ideas to others, then I generate incredible excitement and joy in my life. This is what has driven me to take time away from just making my clients and myself rich, to write this book and run the *Building Riches* workshops from which we produced my audio tapes.

Since I started researching this book, I know I could have generated over one million dollars in profits, by using the time just making money. Using the principles in this book (and the other books that I intend to publish shortly), I have built, and will continue to build even more riches for myself and those who invest with my companies. Taking the time to research this material however, has made it possible for me to share these ideas with you, in a way that offers the opportunity for you to enrich your life. It is hard to measure the excitement that I feel when I see and hear from people who have used my book or tapes to change their lives and become richer, more confident and more influential. This gives me a pleasure that money can't buy. The interesting thing is, that as I pursue the *Knowledge* and *Strategies* to help others, I apply them to become even richer myself. It is as though I have taken two steps backwards, (in not just making more money) then take, twenty steps forward in applying these principles, with massive *Action*, that will make me richer in years to come. Combining this with the joy I get from writing and speaking makes my life even richer.

My mission is to live my life as a role model of possibility for others, so that they may achieve more with their lives. It is difficult at times. My loving wife, son and business associates give me great support however as our success grows we are able to help even more people. Part of the proceeds from your investment in this book, and from our tapes and all of my business dealings, are given to charity. It allows us to help people most in need of success *Strategies* in our society. Through helping these people to succeed, we indirectly produce a healthier Australian economy so that all Australians benefit. Learning how to expand my mission to help hundreds of thousands of people in the coming years, is a part of my larger mission in life. Will there be a day in your life when you decide to achieve something great for yourself and others? Why not make that day today?

How Can You Make an Impact and Change the World?

Throughout this book, I have proposed that we all want the same things in life ~ health, wealth, happiness and financial riches so we can achieve our desires and help others we care about. My maternal grandmother has been working on our family tree for many years and has traced our family history back hundreds of years. In looking at the available information on my relatives, I thought of a fascinating question to *ASK*. If your relatives (or others) in five hundred years from now (in the 26th century) were to read your Riches Journal(s), what would they find out about you?

If you live each day thinking of the consequences your *Actions* may have on people for the next 500 years, how will you choose to live today? What will be the values you will live by? What noble goals will you pursue? What mission will you decide upon? What type of role model will you be for your family and friends? How will the riches you build help your fellow humans (and other living creatures on earth) in coming centuries? Will you take *Actions* in your life that will help others who are not even born yet?

When you dream noble dreams and then pursue these dreams *ASK*ing for *Knowledge*, *Strategies*, and *Actions*, your life changes. You become more involved in the process and you begin to become a role model for others. The more you invest in people and companies who are playing for more than just profits, the greater will be your impact on the world. Do you remember the example showing companies with a moral focus outperforming the sharemarket by over ten times? As you continue to develop more *Knowledge*, better *Strategies* and take more *Action* in accordance with your mission, then you are less likely to be affected by fear or greed. Playing win/win builds better customer and staff loyalty, which escalates your long-term viability and profit. All of my investments, and companies contribute to charities to assist in building a better future for others. Are you going to start to enjoy and program yourself for greater riches and abundance, by helping other people?

You can Build the Riches You Desire and Make the Impact You Want!

It is often said that you do not truly know something until you teach that principle or skill to another person. You now have the *Knowledge* you

WHAT HAPPENS WHEN YOU DO BUILD RICHES AND USE THEM WISELY?

---

need to build riches. Share your *Knowledge* with people who also want to be rich and who will play WIN/WIN. Support and encourage them to build riches also. When you do this, you begin to change the world. History reveals that the people who achieve riches in any form of endeavour, Mozart, Greg Norman, Einstein or Mother Theresa, all inspired others. Great people begin like everyone else and one day decide that their mission is to inspire others. Within you, are dreams of greatness, which can produce a spark that you can fan into a mighty fire through your *Actions*.

Once you take *Action* on the principles contained in this book, you will cement your imagination into goals, values, and a mission. This alone puts you in the top one percent of our population. This book may just be the beginning of your quest for more *Action*, *Strategies* and *Knowledge*. There are many fine authors and teachers and I encourage you to continue to learn and grow. Some of us are older than twenty or thirty, or want to accumulate even greater riches. In our *Building Riches* audio tapes I show people how to accelerate the growth of their riches, and how to build that into a compelling plan for their lives. Over the decades I have learned much by investing many hundreds of thousands of dollars in my *Knowledge*. Continue learning and your investments will continue earning for the whole of your life.

As you apply the *Knowledge* in this book, you will come across various challenges and, possibly, experience adversity. By *ASK*ing better questions you will develop your character through persistence and courage, every time you overcome each challenge. In the process, your goals, values, and mission will become as much a part of you as your heart. When you reach this level, you will probably be one in a thousand or more. Not only will you then build riches, you will also be transforming the world into the 21st century. I salute you and hope you join other, like-minded people on the journey towards your riches. Build riches as well as being a loving, healthy, inspiring individual.

Thank you for allowing me to share some of my life experiences with you, in a way that I truly desire will encourage you to build a richer life. Even though we may not have met in person, I believe our spirits or hearts are aligned, in that we both are actively seeking and taking *Action* to improve our lives. You've invested your valuable time in reading this book and allowed me to pursue my mission. Please take *Action* on the *Strategies* and *Knowledge* in this book.

The chances are good that we may meet at a seminar or charity event or even at an airport. Please introduce yourself or write a note and share your successes with me in some way. A part of the responsibility and joy of success, is sharing with others. Until that day, remind yourself that you are unique and that you <u>do</u> possess the desire to build a rich life and to inspire others. Pursue your dreams and inspire others by your examples. May God reward and bless your efforts and may you learn to appreciate yourself more every day.

Appendices

APPENDIX 1:

STATEMENT OF INCOME & EXPENDITURE

Date   /   /

Expenditure (average monthly)   **Income (average monthly)**

Consumer Expenses   *Personal Income*

Expenditure		Income	
Tax Income earner 1		Income earner 1	
Tax Income earner 2		Income earner 2	
Personal loans		Regular overtime	
Credit cards		Bonuses, etc	
Rent/ Board		Other Income	
Power, phone, etc		Superannuation	
Motor vehicle(s)			
Food and Living			
Entertaining			
Alcohol/ Tobacco			
Medical expenses			
Children's Education			
Children's Other			
Insurance			
Travel & Holidays			
Donations/ Tithing			
Educational			
Other Expenses			

Security Expenses

Housing loan	
House rates etc	
Repairs, etc.	

SUB TOTAL *(1)*   SUB TOTAL *(2)*

APPENDIX 1 (Continued):

STATEMENT OF INCOME & EXPENDITURE

Date / /

Expenditure (average monthly)   **Income (average monthly)**

Investment Expenses   ### Investment Income

Interest Expense		Interest Income	
Real Estate Expenses		Rent Received	
Share Tax Credits		Dividends before	
Education, etc.		franking credits	
Investment Taxes		Capital Profits	
Capital Gains Taxes		Taxation Refunds	
Other Expenses		Other Income	

Business Expenses   ### Business Income

Interest Expense		Income After Wages	
Self Education		Other Income	
Business Taxes			
Other Expenses			

Add: Sub total from previous page *(1)*   Add: Sub total from previous page *(2)*

Total Expenditure *(3)*   **Total Income** *(4)*

Total Expenditure *(3)*

Available Income

APPENDIX 2:

PETER & ANNE WISE'S FIRST INVESTMENT PROPERTY CASH FLOW

	1st Year	2nd Year	3rd Year	4th Year	5th Year	6th Year	7th Year	8th Year	9th Year	10th Year	TOTAL
Peter's Income (after super.)	$40,700	$42,328	$44,021	$45,782	$47,613	$49,518	$51,498	$53,558	$55,701	$57,929	$488,649
Tax before property	*$9,200*	*$9,713*	*$10,247*	*$10,801*	*$11,378*	*$11,978*	*$12,782*	*$13,678*	*$14,610*	*$15,579*	*$119,966*
Add: Rent	$15,300	$15,912	$16,548	$17,210	$17,899	$18,615	$19,359	$20,134	$20,939	$21,777	$183,693
Total Income with rent	$56,000	$58,240	$60,570	$62,992	$65,512	$68,133	$70,858	$73,692	$76,640	$79,705	$672,342
Less: Tax deductions											
Interest	($18,850)	($18,850)	($18,850)	($18,850)	($18,850)	($18,850)	($18,850)	($18,850)	($18,850)	($18,850)	($188,500)
Cash Expenses (26% of Rent)	($4,000)	($4,137)	($4,303)	($4,475)	($4,654)	($4,840)	($5,033)	($5,235)	($5,444)	($5,662)	($47,782)
Depr'n on Fixtures	($6,475)	($3,088)	($3,088)	($3,088)	($3,088)	($3,088)	($3,088)	($1,747)	$0	$0	($26,750)
Depr'n on Construction	($1,850)	($1,850)	($1,850)	($1,850)	($1,850)	($1,850)	($1,850)	($1,850)	($1,850)	($1,850)	($18,500)
Borrowing Costs	($520)	($520)	($520)	($520)	($520)						
Total Deductions	($31,695)	($28,445)	($28,611)	($28,783)	($28,962)	($28,628)	($28,821)	($27,682)	($26,144)	($26,362)	($284,132)
New Taxable Income	$24,305	$29,795	$31,959	$34,210	$36,550	$39,505	$42,036	$46,010	$50,496	$53,344	$388,210
Tax AFTER property	*$4,036*	*$5,765*	*$6,447*	*$7,156*	*$7,893*	*$8,824*	*$9,621*	*$10,873*	*$12,346*	*$13,584*	*$86,547*
TAX REFUND (Old-New Tax)	*$5,164*	*$3,948*	*$3,800*	*$3,645*	*$3,485*	*$3,154*	*$3,160*	*$2,805*	*$2,264*	*$1,995*	*$33,419*
Less Pre-Tax Cash Flow	($7,550)	($7,075)	($6,604)	($6,114)	($5,605)	($5,075)	($4,524)	($3,951)	($3,355)	($2,735)	($52,589)
After-tax Profit/ (cost)	($2,386)	($3,127)	($2,805)	($2,469)	($2,120)	($1,921)	($1,364)	($1,146)	($1,091)	($741)	($19,170)
WEEKLY COST	($45.89)	($60.14)	($53.93)	($47.48)	($40.77)	($36.94)	($26.22)	($22.05)	($20.98)	($14.24)	**($36.86)**

APPENDIX 3:

CONSUMER PRICE INDEX USED IN THE CALCULATION OF CAPITAL GAINS TAX

Capital Gains Tax is reduced by the inflationary effect on the sold assets, if the asset is owned for in excess of one year for sales before 22 September 1999.

To calculate the inflation reduction on Capital Gains Tax ("C.G.T."), the following Consumer Price Index ("C.P.I") (average of all groups) figures apply since the introduction of C.G.T on 19th September 1985:

CPI index	March	June	September	December
1985	N/A	N/A	71.3	72.7
1986	74.4	75.6	77.6	79.8
1987	81.4	82.6	84.0	85.5
1988	87.0	88.5	90.2	92.0
1989	92.9	95.2	97.4	99.2
1990	100.9	102.5	103.3	106.0
1991	105.8	106.0	106.6	107.6
1992	107.6	107.3	107.4	107.9
1993	108.9	109.3	109.8	110.0
1994	110.4	111.2	111.9	112.8
1995	114.7	116.2	117.6	118.5
1996	119.0	119.8	120.1	120.3
1997	120.5	120.2	119.7	120.0
1998	120.3	121.0	121.3	121.9
1999	121.8	122.3	123.4	N/A

APPENDIX 4:

THE PROCEDURE FOR CALCULATING THE NET CAPITAL GAINS TAX PAYABLE BY A TAXPAYER

Step 1: Calculate the Indexation Factor for the asset(s) sold:

Step 2: Calculate the Indexed Cost Base:
Multiply the cost of the asset and purchase costs, by the Indexation Factor (from step 1).

Step 3: Calculate each Capital Gain:
Deduct the Indexed Cost Base (step 2) from the sales price after deducting selling expenses.

Step 4: Calculate the Net Capital Gain:
Add all capital gains and then deduct any capital losses accrued from previous years.

Step 5: Show the Taxpayer's other taxable income.

Step 6: Calculate the tax payable on the Taxpayer's other income.

Step 7: Capital Gain (from above).

Step 8: Add the Taxpayer's other taxable income to the Capital Gain. (Step 5 plus Step 7).

Step 9: New Tax on the Taxpayer's other taxable income plus the Capital Gain. (Tax on Step 8).

Step 10: Calculate the CGT payable. (Step 9 less Step 6).

APPENDICES

APPENDIX 5:

COMPARISON OF THE NEW CAPITAL GAINS TAX SYSTEM WITH THE INDEXING SYSTEM FOR THE PERIOD IT WAS IN FORCE

ASSUMPTIONS	
Property Purchase Price Less: Fixtures that are depreciated (not included for CGT Indexing) Oct. 85	$200,000
Purchase Costs (Stamp Duty, Legals)	$8,000
CPI Index when property bought 30 Sept 1985	72.7
Property Sale Value assumed in late 2000	$850,000
Sale Costs future (Real Estate Agents, Legals, etc)	$25,000
CPI Index when Frozen 30 Sept 1999	123.4

Steps 1 & 2: Calculate the Indexation Factor and the Indexed Cost Base

for the asset's) sold:	Old CGT Index System	New CGT No Index
Property Cost $200,000 × 123.4 / 72.7 =	$339,477	$200,000
Purchase Costs $8,000 × 123.4 / 72.7 =	$13,579	$8,000
Indexed Cost Base/ Cost	$353,056	$208,000

	Old CGT Index System	New CGT No Index
Steps 3 & 4: Calculate the Net Capital Gain:		
Selling Price	$850,000	$850,000
Less: Selling Costs	($25,000)	($25,000)
Less: Indexed Cost Base	($353,056)	($208,000)
Capital Gain	$471,944	$617,000
Step 5: Taxpayer's other taxable income.	$40,000	$40,000
Step 6: Tax payable on the Taxpayer's other income.	$9,180	$9,180
Step 7: Capital Gain (from above).	$471,944	
50% Capital Gain (from above).		$308,500
Step 8: Add the Taxpayer's other taxable income to Capital Gain. (Step 5 plus Step 7).	$511,944	$348,500
Step 9: New Tax on Taxpayer's other taxable income plus Capital Gain.	$235,673	$156,403
Step 10: Calculate the Capital Gains Tax Payable: (Step 9 less Step 6).	**$226,493**	**$147,223**

APPENDIX 6:

EXAMPLE CALCULATING THE NET CAPITAL GAINS TAX PAYABLE BY A TAXPAYER USING THE NEW CGT SYSTEM

ASSUMPTIONS	
Property Purchase Price Less: Fixtures that are depreciated	$222,250
Purchase Costs (Stamp Duty, Legals)	$8,000
Renovations (Feb. 2018)	$25,000
Property Sale Value	$3,600,000
Sale Costs future (Real Estate Agents, Legals, etc) in year 2036	$90,000

Step 1:	Calculate the Net Capital Gain:	**In-Retirement**
	Selling Price	$3,600,000
	Less: Selling Costs	($90,000)
	Less: Property Purchase Price (less fittings)	($222,250)
	Less: Purchase Costs	($8,000)
	Less: Renovations	($25,000)
	Capital Gain	$3,254,750
		In-Retirement
Step 2:	Show the Taxpayer's other taxable income.	$30,000
Step 3:	Show the tax payable on the Taxpayer's other income.	$5,930
Step 4:	50% of Capital Gain (from above).	$1,627,375
Step 5:	Add the Taxpayer's other taxable income to 50% of Capital Gain.	$1,657,375
Step 6:	New Tax on Taxpayer's other taxable income plus 50% of Capital Gain.	$791,207
Step 7:	Capital Gains Tax Payable: (Step 6 less Step 3).	**$785,277**

CASH AVAILABLE AFTER SALE

Selling Price	$3,600,000
Less: Selling Costs	($90,000)
Less: Loan on Property & Renovations	($285,000)
Less: Capital Gains Tax Payable:	($785,277)
CASH AVAILABLE AFTER SALE	**$2,439,723**

About the Bruce Davis Companies

The Bruce Davis companies comprise of a dedicated group of men and women, who are committed to ethically building riches in every investment that they make, while striving for excellence in all their endeavours.

The extraordinary success that we continue to achieve, is a direct consequence of our determined focus to be leaders in our respective areas of enterprise. We provide the following services:

- **Real Estate Investment:** We specialise in assisting you to build greater riches through real estate. Phone or write for more details;

- **Real Estate Development:** We are experts in joint venturing real estate developments with client investments ranging from $50,000 to millions of dollars. We can also assist you to develop your land;

- **Building Riches:** *ASK* us about our latest products or courses designed to transform your beliefs, certainty and strategies about how to build riches in your life much faster;

- **Consulting Services:** Individual and corporate consultation by Bruce Davis is available on a variety of subjects, which will facilitate for you, extraordinary changes and lasting results.

If you are interested in any of these services and would like Bruce to contact you, please MAIL or FAX us at:

>Bruce Davis
>Signature Apartments Pty Ltd
>P.O. Box 620
>Newtown NSW 2042
>
>Phone: 1800 67 22 30
>Fax: 02 9516 4655
>
>Internet: buildingriches.com.au
>Email: info@buildingriches.com.au

Keep ASKing!
Keep Learning!
Keep Building Riches!

Mail or fax this coupon today to build greater riches:

☐ Please keep me informed about any new books, tapes or courses that you provide that can help me become richer.

☐ Please contact me about investment opportunities that I may wish to consider building riches in.

☐ I want to meet for a consultation with Bruce on my personal affairs.

☐ I am already well on my way to building riches and am interested in larger investments to accelerate the compounding of my riches.

Mr / Mrs / Ms: _____ Surname: _____
Address: _____
_____ Postcode: _____
Telephone: (H) _____ (B) _____
(M) _____
Email: _____

MAIL or FAX this coupon to:
    Bruce Davis
    Signature Books Pty Ltd Phone: 1800 67 22 30
    P.O. Box 620 Fax: 02 9516 4655
    Newtown NSW 2042 Internet: buildingriches.com.au
                                  Email: info@buildingriches.com.au

(So as not to damage your book, this page may be photocopied)

Order Form

Congratulations! You now know how to *ASK* your way to *Building Riches* for yourself and your loved ones. Why not share this knowledge and give someone else the opportunity to *ASK* their way to riches?

To order more copies of *How to Build Riches* for your family and friends (or staff), simply complete the order form below and we will post or courier them to you. Why not surprise someone by having *How to Build Riches* sent to them as a gift?
Please send: me/my friend:
_____ autographed copies of *How to Build Riches* @ $29.00 each including postage and handling (in Australia). (Or six copies in Australia for $120:00). If you nominate a work address we can often courier your copies within 48 hours. $39:00 Australian for NZ orders.

I enclose Cheque ❒ Money Order ❒ for $_____
(payable to: Signature Books Pty Ltd)
or Debit my Bank Card ❒ Master Card ❒ Visa Card ❒ for $ _____
Cardholder's Name (on card): _____

No. |_|_|_|_| |_|_|_|_| |_|_|_|_| |_|_|_|_| Exp____/____

Card Holder's Signature _____

Please print your details below and post or fax or phone your order to us:

    Signature Books Pty Ltd   Phone: 1800 67 22 30
    P.O. Box 620   Fax: 02 9516 4655
    Newtown NSW 2042   Internet: buildingriches.com.au
                                      Email: info@buildingriches.com.au

Mr/Mrs/Ms: _____ Surname: _____
Address: _____
_____ Postcode: _____
For dispatch the above address is at: Work / Home
Telephone: (H) _____ (B) _____
Telephone: (M) _____

(So as not to damage your book, this page may be photocopied)

Order Form

Building Riches Audio Program utilises advanced training techniques in the application of **Action, Strategies and Knowledge** to create even greater personal and financial wealth.

A Personal Note from Bruce Davis

Dear Fellow Australian,
*This program will give you the strategies and principles to build greater financial riches. I **personally** guarantee that if, by the end of the audio tape program, you are not convinced that what you have learned has the potential to return you a profit on your investment, tell me, and I'll refund your $439 investment in full (inclusive of GST). Complete the Order Form below.*
Warm Regards

Bruce S. Davis

I enclose Cheque ☐ Money Order ☐ for $439.00
(payable to: Signature Books Pty Ltd)
or Debit my Bank Card ☐ Master Card ☐ Visa Card ☐ for $439.00
Cardholder's Name (on card): _____

No. |__|__|__|__| |__|__|__|__| |__|__|__|__| |__|__|__|__| Exp____/____

Card Holder's Signature _____

Please print your details below and post or fax or phone your order to us:

       Signature Books Pty Ltd   Phone: 1800 67 22 30
       P.O. Box 620   Fax: 02 9516 4655
       Newtown NSW 2042   Internet: buildingriches.com.au
          Email: info@buildingriches.com.au

Mr/Mrs/Ms: _____ Surname: _____
Address: _____
_____ Postcode: _____
For dispatch the above address is at: Work / Home
Telephone: (H) _____ (B) _____
Telephone: (M) _____

(So as not to damage your book, this page may be photocopied)

Personal Riches Journal

HOW TO BUILD RICHES

PERSONAL RICHES JOURNAL

HOW TO BUILD RICHES

PERSONAL RICHES JOURNAL

HOW TO BUILD RICHES

PERSONAL RICHES JOURNAL

HOW TO BUILD RICHES

PERSONAL RICHES JOURNAL

HOW TO BUILD RICHES

Index

INDEX

action benefits 318–319
action muscles 311
adding value 157, 287
adversity into value 305–306
ASK your way to Riches 10
Appointor 280
assets
   business assets 63
   consumer assets 63
   investment assets 63
attention 286, 288
Australia today 20
Australian Bureau of Statistics (ABS) 98, 233
Australian Securities and Investment Commission (ASIC) 109, 204
Australian Stock Exchange (ASX) *see* shares
Australian Taxation Office (ATO) 232
Average Weekly Ordinary Times Earnings (AWOTE) 210
Away-from goals 341
Baby Boomer Crisis 29–30
Baby Boomers 29
bank managers 293, 294
BAT formula 286
beliefs 294–298
Bonaparte, Napoleon 285
Buffet, Warren 51, 96, 107–108, 118, 123
build trust 343
buy low 286
capital gain *see* Tax
   gains tax *see* Tax
capital loss *see* Tax
capital profit 110, 127, 144

Cash Payments Journal 58–60
caveat emptor 336
census 34
Certified Practising Accountant (CPA) 114
Chartered Accountant 114
comfort zone 301–303, 317
companies 280, 324–325
comparing shares and real estate 219–224
compound interest *see* Interest
conflict of interest 343
consumer price index (CPI) 98
debt 64–69
   bad debt 65
   good debt 65
deflation 102
deposit gap 68
depreciation 165–167
discretionary (family trust) 280, 325
diversified portfolio 267
economic cycle 103
   boom 105
   downturn 105
   gloom 106
   monetary policy 105
   Reserve Bank of Australia 105
   upturn 107
education 42
e-motion 301
family time 329
FEAR (False Evidence Appearing Real) 11
   overcoming fear 197–200, 302–303
fight or flight syndrome
financial inertia 301
four steps to build riches 7

fund manager, choosing 255
Getty, John Paul 200, 341
goals, sharing 341
Goods and Services Tax *see* Tax
government housing dilemma 179
Great Australian Dream, 63
greed 343–344
health value 329
hidden agenda 288
home loan
  before-tax cost savings 79
  line of credit 73
  paid off in half the time 71
  principal & interest home loan 72
home ownership 25–27
impact the world 352–353
income 21–23
income position at age sixty-five 37
inflation 92–94, 98, 100–102
information age 42–45
insurance 173, 199, 200, 342
intention 286, 294
interest
  after-tax and inflation 101
    compound interest 88
  inflation and interest rates 98
  Rule of 72 90–93
  Simple Interest 88
invest in yourself 332
Law of Use 327
learn from past 317
liabilities *see* loans
limiting emotions, using 314
loans
  business loans 65, 81–85
  consumer loans 64
  interest only loans 176

investment loans 65
security loans 64
tax deductible 175, 182
longevity 24–25
major reasons why people don't set goals 10
managed funds
  asset management fee 252
  benefits of a listed trust 204
  Capital Guaranteed 202, 203
  Enhanced Cash 202
  entry fee 252
  Equity Trust 202
  exit fee 252
  fees 252, 254, 266
  fund manager 252
  Income Trust 202
  Industrial Equity Trust 202
  master fund 254
  Mortgage Funds 202
  Multi Sector Trusts 203
  Overseas Equity Trust 202
  Property Securities Trust 202
  Property Trusts 201, 267
  Regional Fund 203
  Resources Equity Trust 202
  switching 254
  switching fee 204, 254
  Unlisted Property Trust 202
master fear 307–310
mission 348–353
monetary policy 105
motivation 304
Murdoch, Rupert 328
negative beliefs replaced 297–298
negative leverage 191
observer 338
obstacles overcome 299
overseas debt 27–28

INDEX

Packer, Kerry 107, 328
partnership 292, 324
Personal Riches Journal 61, 236, 371–380
positive leverage 190
protecting assets 324–326
quiet time 331
rate of return on investments 263
react 311
real estate
  Building Inspection Services 158
  buying like a professional 157–159
  cash flow 184–185, Appendix 2
  conveyancing 182
  conveyancing kit 187
  deposit gap 68
  diminishing value method of depreciation 165
  fixtures and fittings 165
  inflows and outflows 163
  loan to value ratio (LVR) 174
  managing agent 163, 291–292
  median priced properties 148
  mortgage insurance 173
  negative gearing 180, 188–189
  negative leverage 190
  non cash deductions 183–184
  pre-tax cash flow 183
  positive leverage 190
  prime cost method of depreciation 165–166
  quantity surveyor 159, 166
  real estate compared 152–154
  rental income 146
  settlement agent 182
Reserve Bank of Australia 105
respond 311
retirement in Australia 31–38
retirement income growth 273
richer person 320
Riches Journal 61
Riches Spiral 309–310
Right Spiral 309–310
security assets 63
Security Dealer's Licence 109
seven steps to a richer life 217–218 236–240
share and property comparisons, biased 225
shares
  All Ordinaries Index 121
  Australian Stock Exchange 109, 124
  bear market 125
  brokerage fees 114
  bull market 125
  Convertible Preference Shares 123
  debt to equity ratio (D/E) 120
  discount brokerage firms 114
  dividend imputation 111
  dividend reinvestment scheme 132
  dividend yield 120
  dividends 110, 111, 120
  earnings per share (EPS) 119
  Efficient Market Theory 118
  franked dividends 112
  franking credit 112
  Fundamental Analysis 117
  Main Board 110
  margin calls 136
  margin loans 135

net tangible assets (NTA) 120
partly franked dividends 112
price earnings ratio (P/E) 119
prospectus 204
protected equity loans 140
public companies 132
Second Board 110
sharebrokers 109, 114–115
stocks 109, 114
Stock Exchange, Australia (ASX) 109, 124
Stock Exchange Automated Trading System (SEATS) 109
Technical Analysis 122
unfranked dividends 111
volatility 127
Spending Plan 58–60
stagflation 99
Statement of Assets and Liabilities 61–62, 236, Appendix 1
Statement of Income & Expenditure 57, 356–357
superannuation
  annuity 208, 275
  complying funds 208
  compulsory superannuation 124
  contributions 210
  freedom of choice 209
  roll over 209
  surcharge 211
  Superannuation Guarantee Charge (SGC) 52, 281, 257
Syndicates 292
tax
  capital gain 110, 127, 144
  capital gains tax (CGT) 81–82, 114, 123, 229–234, Appendices 3, 4, 5 and 6
    active assets 81–82
    nominal gain 82, 230
  capital loss 111, 127
  Goods and Services Tax (GST) 46, 53–56, 79, 146, 163–164, 180
    input tax 79, 144
  income tax 53–54
  marginal taxation rate 53
  Medicare levy 53
  small business 140
  rates 54
  tax records 293
testamentary trust 280, 324
Trusts 325
time value 328
timing 287
unemployment 39–41
unit trust 270, 325, 326
Values 304–305
wealth after death 279
Winners Spiral 309–310